The BIG BOOK of DESIGN IDEAS 3

The BIG BOOK of DESIGN IDEAS 3

edited by

David E. Carter
Suzanna MW Stephens

COLLINS DESIGN
An Imprint of HarperCollinsPublishers

HarperCollins books may be purchased for educational, business, or sales promotional use.
For information, please write: Special Markets Department, HarperCollins*Publishers*,
10 East 53rd Street, New York, NY 10022.

First Edition

First published in 2008 by:
Collins Design
An Imprint of HarperCollins*Publishers*
10 East 53rd Street
New York, NY 10022
Tel: (212) 207-7000
Fax: (212) 207-7654
collinsdesign@harpercollins.com
www.harpercollins.com

Distributed throughout the world by:
HarperCollins*Publishers*
10 East 53rd Street
New York, NY 10022
Fax: (212) 207-7654

Book design by:

Designs on You!

Suzanna & Anthony Stephens

Library of Congress Control Number: 2007942860

ISBN: 978-0-06-137480-7

Produced by Crescent Hill Books, Louisville, KY.

Printed in China by Everbest Printing Company.

First Printing, 2008

TABLE OF CONTENTS

FOREWORD

Psst. Hey there…YOU.

You have this book in your hand, maybe in a bookstore, deciding whether to buy it or not.

Take my word for it. **Buy**.

If that one word isn't enough, let me tell you **why** you should buy this book.

This is the third book of its kind. The first one, *The Big Book of Design Ideas*, became one of the best-selling graphics books. Ever.

Each piece in this book was chosen for its ability to inspire others to get great ideas. You may see a logo with a certain technique used, and you are inspired for the direct mail piece you're working on. Or you may see a layout for a letterhead set that gives you an idea for a brochure layout.

You get the idea.

This is a book that you can turn to whenever you're stuck for an idea. And, ***shazam***! You are inspired by the work shown here.

That's why you should buy this book.

As a designer, one of the greatest pleasures I derive from working on *The Big Book* collections is seeing so much new and innovative design used in so many different venues. We receive work from every state in America and many other countries as well. The goal of some of it is to be seen coast-to-coast. Some has been created for an international market. Some was much more specifically designed—maybe just for a wedding party. The size of the audience won't have a negative effect on the process and product born of the creative professional!

There's great inspiration in being exposed to great work. Look through *The Big Book of Design Ideas 3* and be inspired.

martini grasshoper
olate
tini
PRIVATT
invitación
4o. aniversario
privattmartini
07.septiembre.05
rigurosa invitación
GÖTLAND VODKA

creative firm
EUPHORIANET
Monterrey, Mexico
creative people
Mabel Morales, Carmen Rodríguez
client
Club Privatt

intensity.
Razor-sharp timing and a laser-like focus. An intense passion for making the right move at the right time. These are hallmarks of a market leader. At K&L Gates, we can help hone your competitive edge to take advantage of limitless opportunities ahead.
K&L | GATES
www.klgates.com
Kirkpatrick & Lockhart Preston Gates Ellis LLP 1400 LAWYERS ON THREE CONTINENTS

creative firm
RIGHT HAT, LLC
Boston, Massachusetts
creative people
Charlyne Fabi, Elonide Semmes
client
K&L Gates

creative firm
GRAPHIC ADVANCE
Palisades Park, New Jersey
creative people
Aviad Stark
client
Weckerle Cosmetics

weckerlecosmetics
200 WEST 57TH STREET, SUITE 604, NEW YORK, NY 10019 / WWW.WECKERLE.COM

creative firm
2FRESH
Istanbul, Turkey
creative people
2FRESH
client
Snickers

creative firm
LOOK DESIGN
San Carlos, California
creative people
Betsy Todd
client
KLA-Tencor

1
YOU'VE PERFECTED YOUR WINE.
g-3enterprises.com

2
YOU WANT THE PERFECT PACKAGE.
g-3enterprises.com

G3
HAYES
RANCH
PINOT GRIGIO
LET G3 DELIVER IT.
LABELS • CLOSURES
LOGISTICS • BOTTLE DECORATING
G3 Enterprises offers you more products and services
to get your wine primed for market.
g-3enterprises.com
QUALITY • VALUE • SERVICE
G3
ENTERPRISES
(800) 321-8747

creative firm
NEVER BORING DESIGN ASSOCIATES, INC.
Modesto, California
creative people
Julie Orona
client
G3

creative firm
TLC DESIGN
Churchville, Virginia
creative people
Trudy L. Cole
client
Bob Driver, Musician

Bob Driver
guitarist
ceremonies
& receptions
434-2318
ensemble also available

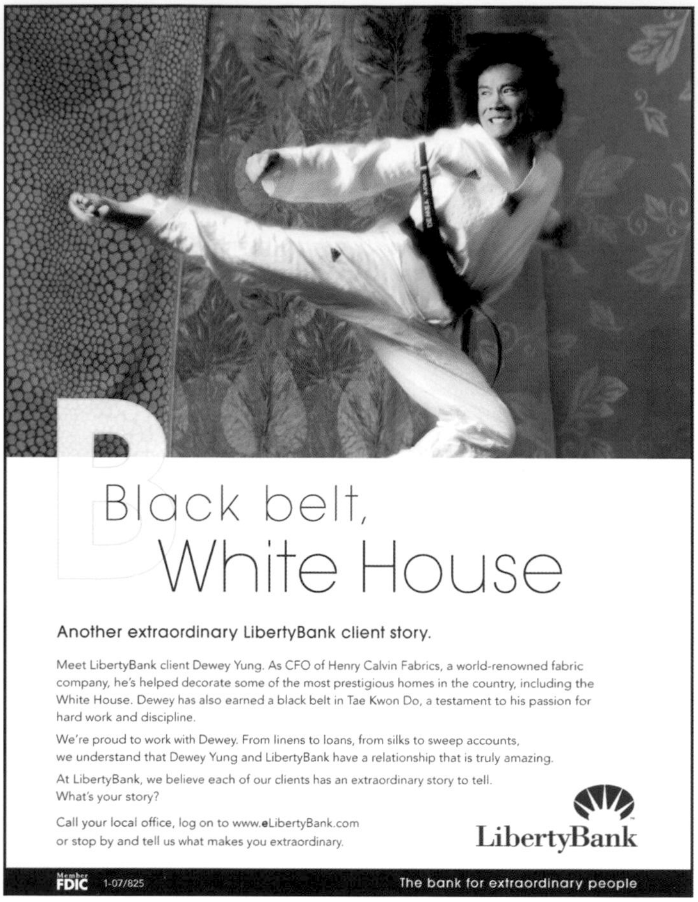
Black belt,
White House
Another extraordinary LibertyBank client story.
Meet LibertyBank client Dewey Yung. As CFO of Henry Calvin Fabrics, a world-renowned fabric company, he's helped decorate some of the most prestigious homes in the country, including the White House. Dewey has also earned a black belt in Tae Kwon Do, a testament to his passion for hard work and discipline.
We're proud to work with Dewey. From linens to loans, from silks to sweep accounts, we understand that Dewey Yung and LibertyBank have a relationship that is truly amazing.
At LibertyBank, we believe each of our clients has an extraordinary story to tell. What's your story?
Call your local office, log on to www.eLibertyBank.com or stop by and tell us what makes you extraordinary.
LibertyBank
Member FDIC
1-07/825
The bank for extraordinary people

creative firm
FUNK/LEVIS & ASSOCIATES
Eugene, Oregon
creative people
Lada Korol
client
LibertyBank

creative firm
AYSE ÇELEM DESIGN
Istanbul, Turkey
creative people
Ayse Çelem, Cengiz Zorlu
client
Sporx Sports Portal

Türkiye'nin en büyük spor sitesi
sporx
www.sporx.com

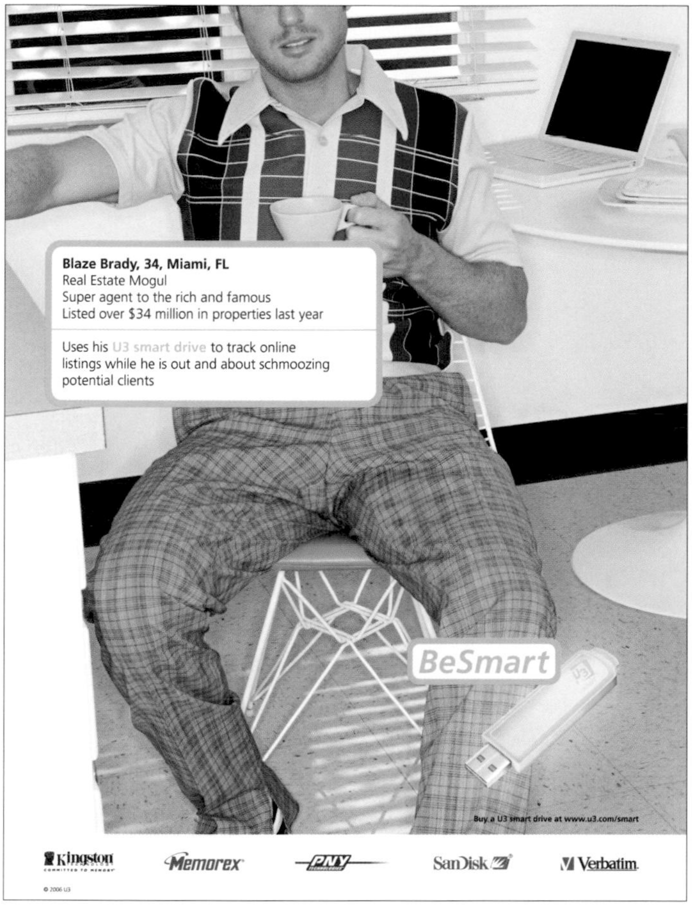

creative firm
LOOK DESIGN
San Carlos, California
creative people
Andrew Henderson
client
U3

creative firm
RIGHT HAT, LLC
Boston, Massachusetts
creative people
Charlyne Fabi, Elonide Semmes
client
Foley Hoag LLP

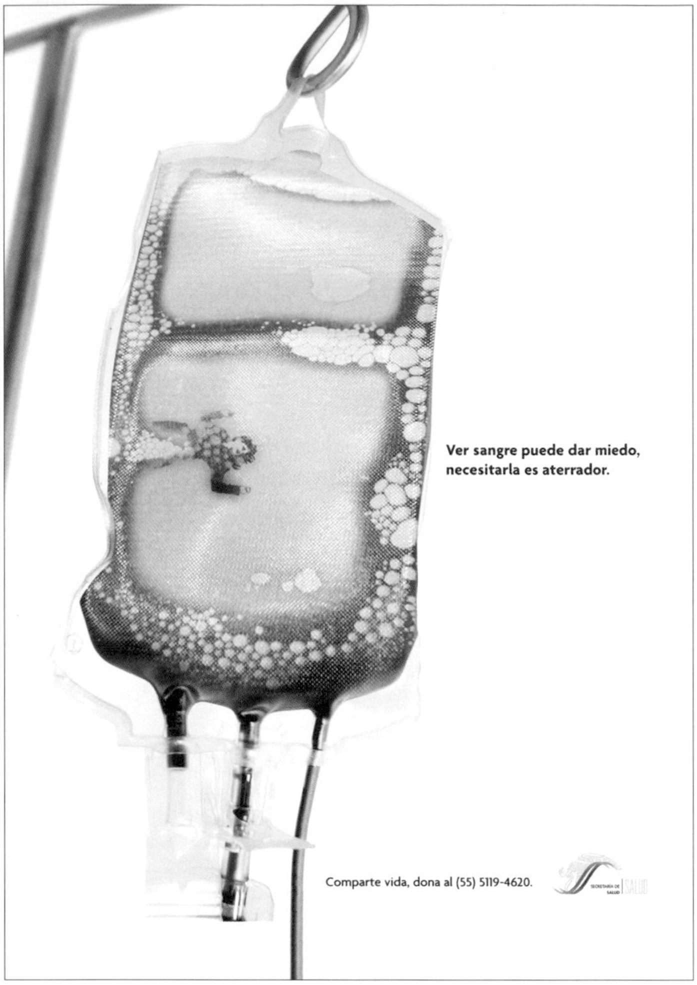

creative firm
021 COMUNICACIONES
Mexico City, Mexico
creative people
Vladimir Nabor, Erick Guerrero
client
Secretaría de Salud

creative firm
GRAPHIC ADVANCE
Palisades Park, New Jersey
creative people
Aviad Stark
client
MyHome

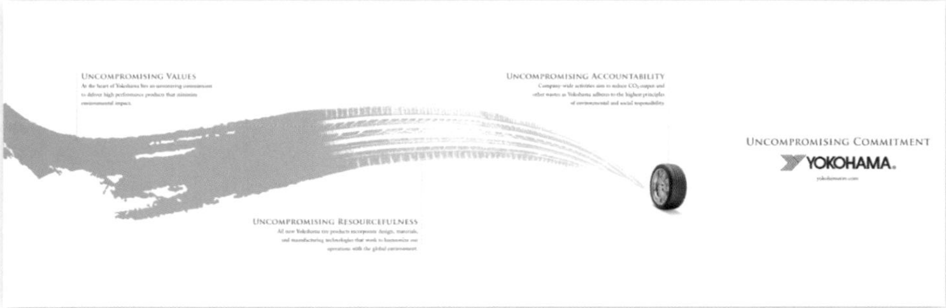

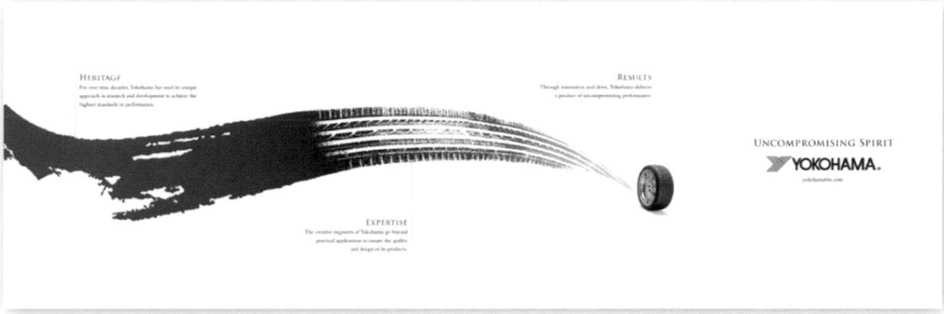

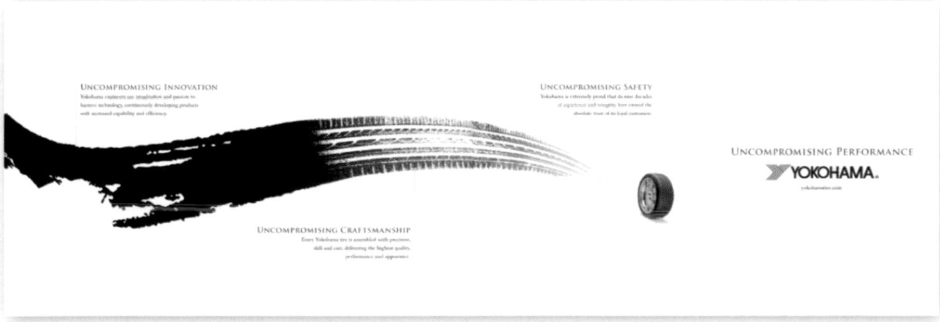

creative firm
EVENSON DESIGN GROUP
Culver City, California
creative people
Mark Sojka
client
Yokohama Tires

creative firm
2FRESH
Istanbul, Turkey
creative people
2FRESH
client
Hillside SU Hotel

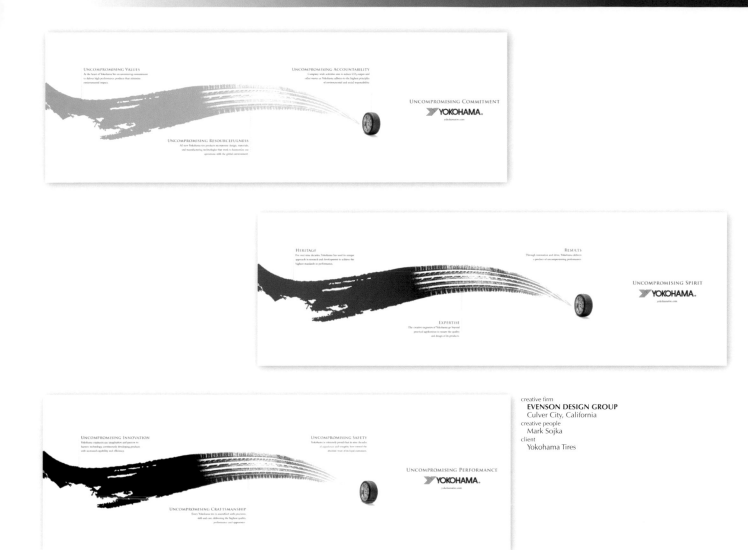

creative firm
THE IMAGINATION COMPANY
Bethel, Vermont
creative people
Kristen Smith, Jim Giberti, Greg Crawford
client
Olympic Regional Development Authority

creative firm
NEVER BORING DESIGN ASSOCIATES, INC.
Modesto, California
creative people
Jill/Shawna
client
Dehart Plumbing, Heating & Air

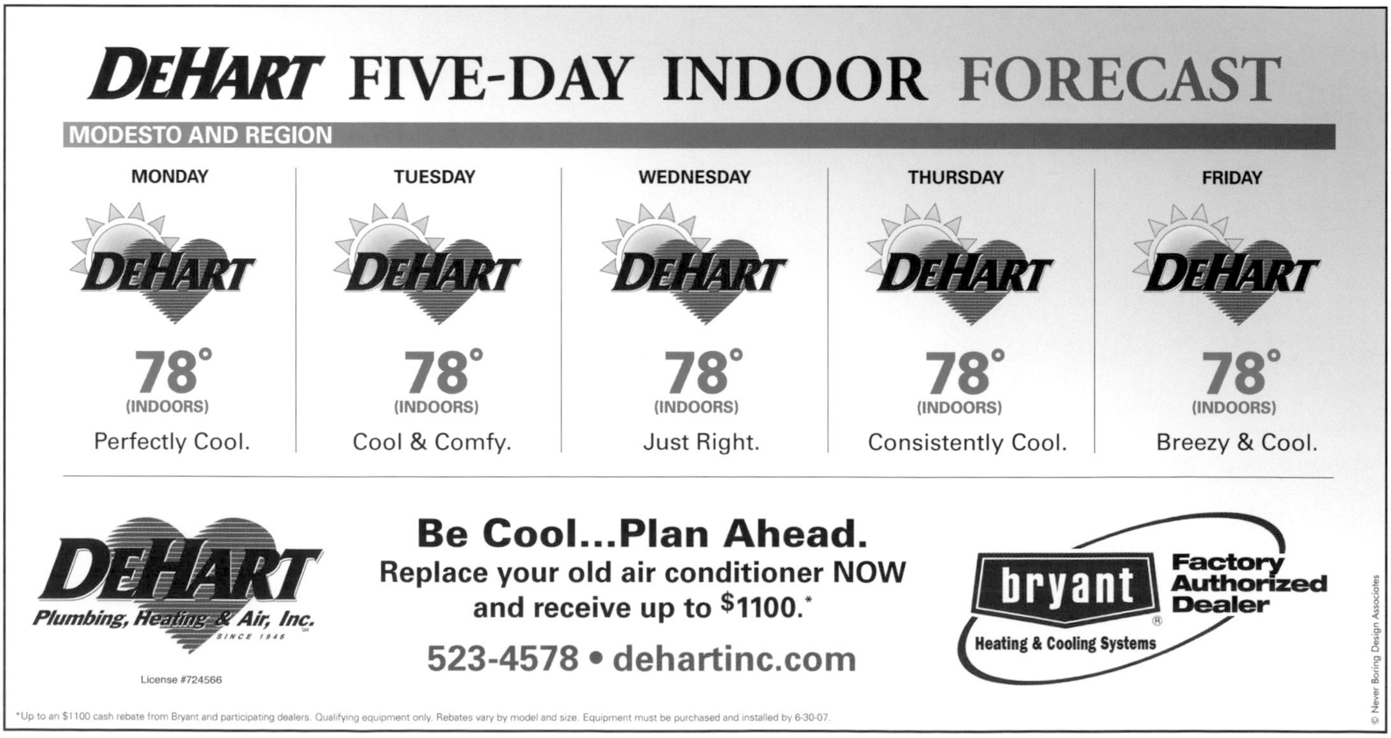

creative firm
LEKASMILLER DESIGN
Walnut Creek, California
creative people
Lana Ip
client
Cork Supply USA

REDEFINING QUALITY
MICHAEL
ZIN
Emphasize Embellishment
Embellish it as you like. Embossing, stamping, precision perfect printing. Elegant intricate detail or sophisticated simplicity, almost anything you can imagine Rivercap can realize for you. Not only is our product beautiful, our service is impeccable. Rivercap. Our premium tin capsule is the ultimate finishing touch to your premium bottle of wine. Period.
RIVERCAP USA
A DIVISION OF CORK SUPPLY USA
537-F Stone Road, Benicia, CA 94510 • Phone 707.747.3630 • Fax 707.746.7471

creative firm
RIGHT HAT, LLC
Boston, Massachusetts
creative people
Charlyne Fabi, Elonide Semmes
client
Berman & Simmons

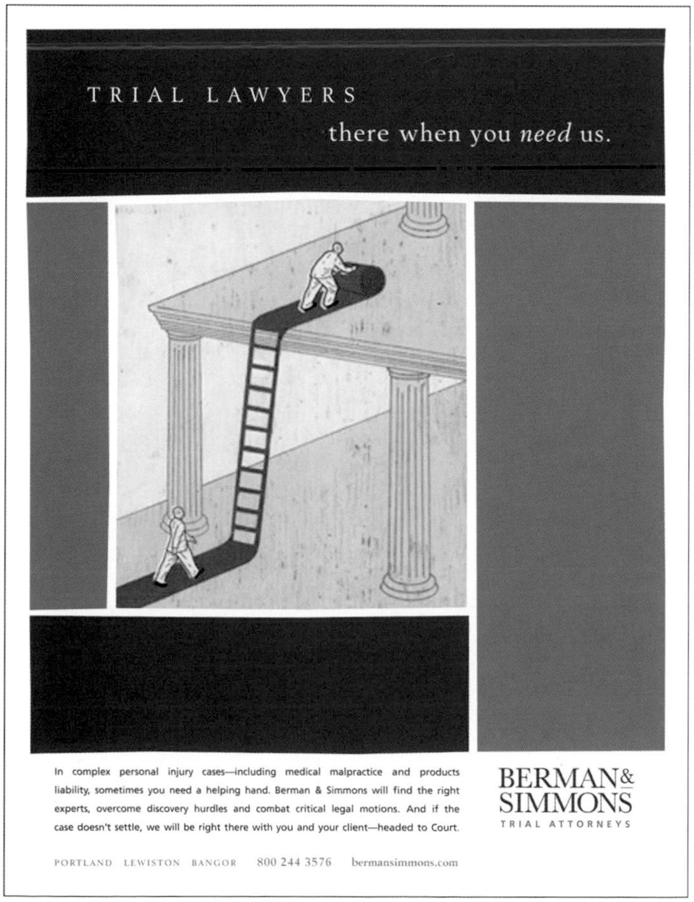
TRIAL LAWYERS
there when you *need* us.
In complex personal injury cases—including medical malpractice and products liability, sometimes you need a helping hand. Berman & Simmons will find the right experts, overcome discovery hurdles and combat critical legal motions. And if the case doesn't settle, we will be right there with you and your client—headed to Court.
BERMAN & SIMMONS
TRIAL ATTORNEYS
PORTLAND LEWISTON BANGOR 800 244 3576 bermansimmons.com

IT'S DUMB TO BE DUMB
Smart people are heading to booth 622 to win a FREE U3 smart drive and a chance at $1,000. Much more than data storage.
BeSmart
Buy a U3 smart drive at www.U3.com
Kingston
PNY
SanDisk
Verbatim

creative firm
LOOK DESIGN
San Carlos, California
creative people
Andrew Henderson
client
U3

creative firm
THE COLLEGE OF SAINT ROSE, OFFICE OF PUBLIC RELATIONS & MARKETING
Albany, New York
creative people
Mark Hamilton, Chris Parody
client
The College of Saint Rose

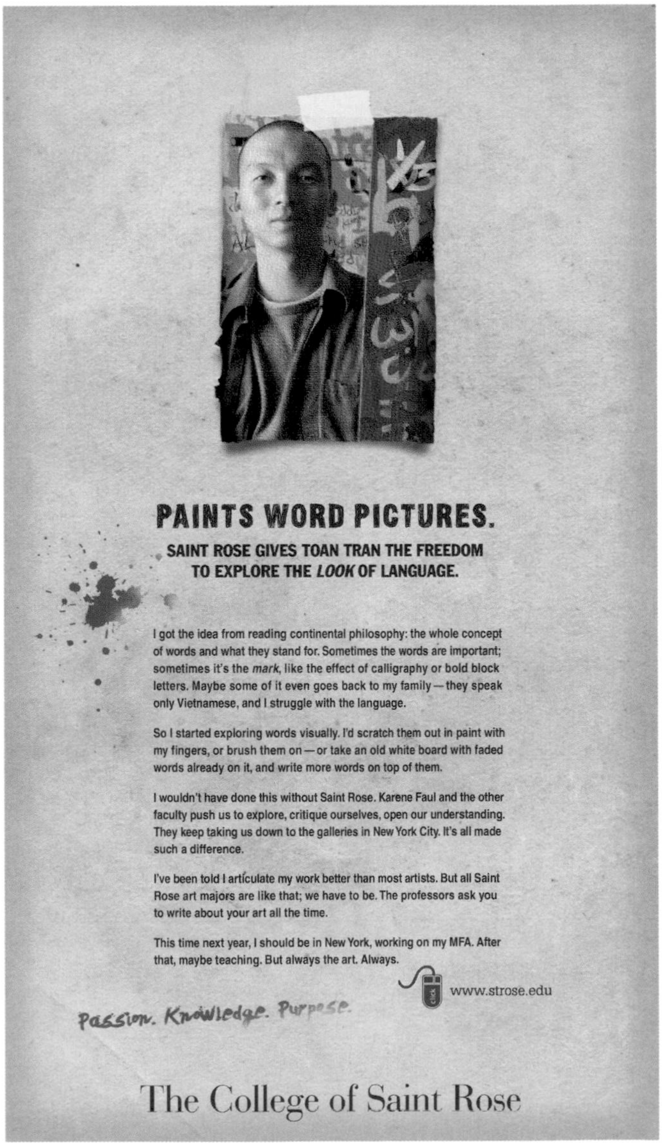
PAINTS WORD PICTURES.
SAINT ROSE GIVES TOAN TRAN THE FREEDOM TO EXPLORE THE LOOK OF LANGUAGE.
I got the idea from reading continental philosophy: the whole concept of words and what they stand for. Sometimes the words are important; sometimes it's the mark, like the effect of calligraphy or bold block letters. Maybe some of it even goes back to my family—they speak only Vietnamese, and I struggle with the language.
So I started exploring words visually. I'd scratch them out in paint with my fingers, or brush them on—or take an old white board with faded words already on it, and write more words on top of them.
I wouldn't have done this without Saint Rose. Karene Faul and the other faculty push us to explore, critique ourselves, open our understanding. They keep taking us down to the galleries in New York City. It's all made such a difference.
I've been told I articulate my work better than most artists. But all Saint Rose art majors are like that; we have to be. The professors ask you to write about your art all the time.
This time next year, I should be in New York, working on my MFA. After that, maybe teaching. But always the art. Always.
www.strose.edu
Passion. Knowledge. Purpose.
The College of Saint Rose

creative firm
LOOK DESIGN
San Carlos, California
creative people
Betsy Todd
client
KLA-Tencor

creative firm
RIGHT HAT, LLC
Boston, Massachusetts
creative people
Charlyne Fabi, Elonide Semmes
client
Winston & Strawn LLP

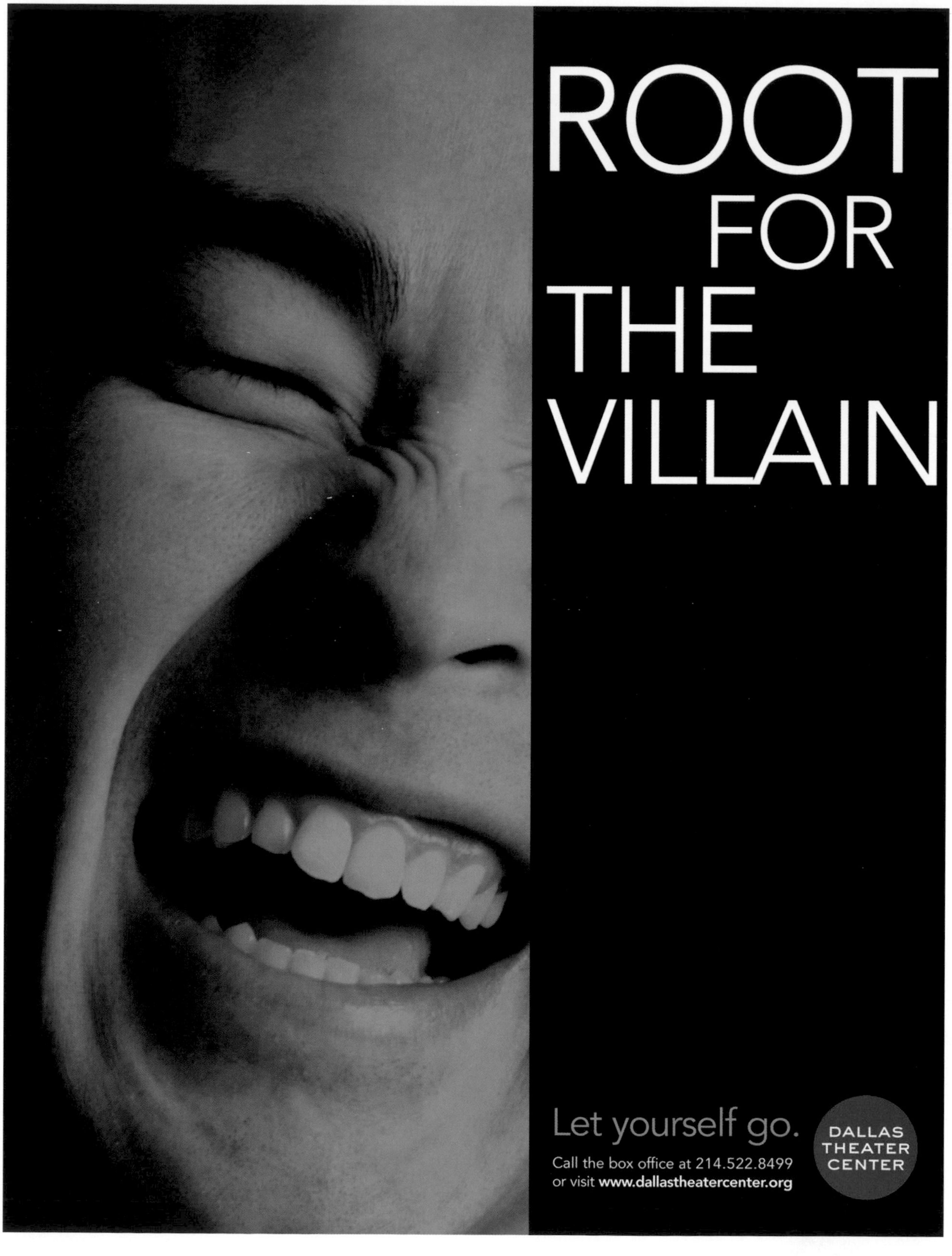
ROOT
FOR
THE
VILLAIN
Let yourself go.
Call the box office at 214.522.8499
or visit www.dallastheatercenter.org
DALLAS
THEATER
CENTER

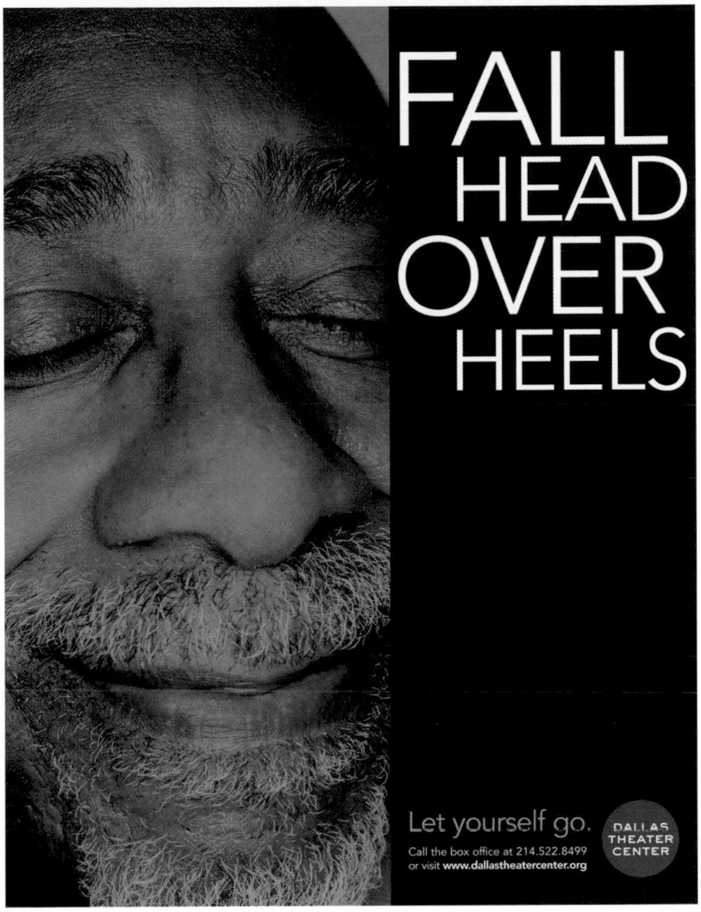

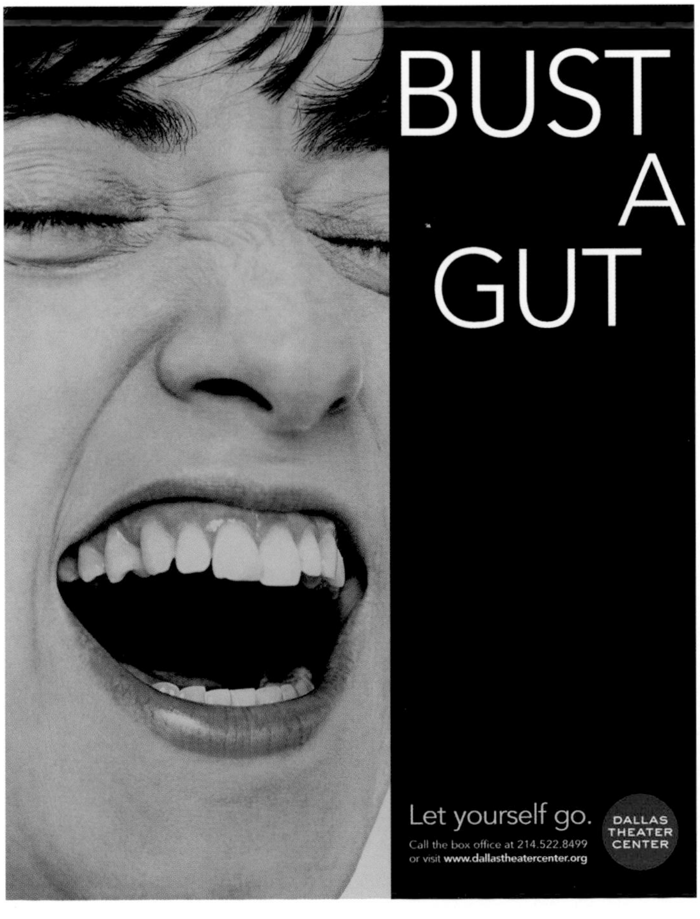

creative firm
RIGHT HAT, LLC/CONTENT PILOT
Boston, Massachusetts
creative people
Charlyne Fabi
client
Dallas Theater Center

La grandeza de México sobresale.
Alejandro González Iñárritu, mexicano galardonado
como el mejor director de cine del festival de Cannes 2006.
Café Punta del Cielo
El Gran Café de México.

La grandeza de México sobresale.
Octavio Paz, mexicano Premio Nobel de Literatura 1990.
Café Punta del Cielo
El Gran Café de México.

creative firm
021 COMUNICACIONES
Mexico City, Mexico
creative people
Dahian Rau, Álvaro Fong
client
Café Punta del Cielo

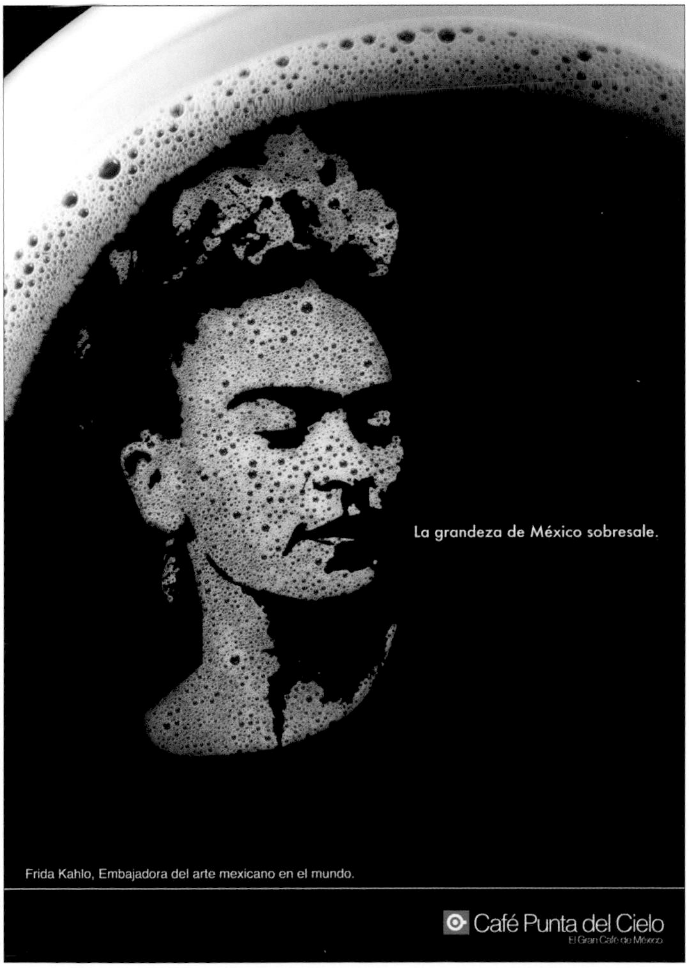
La grandeza de México sobresale.
Frida Kahlo, Embajadora del arte mexicano en el mundo.
Café Punta del Cielo

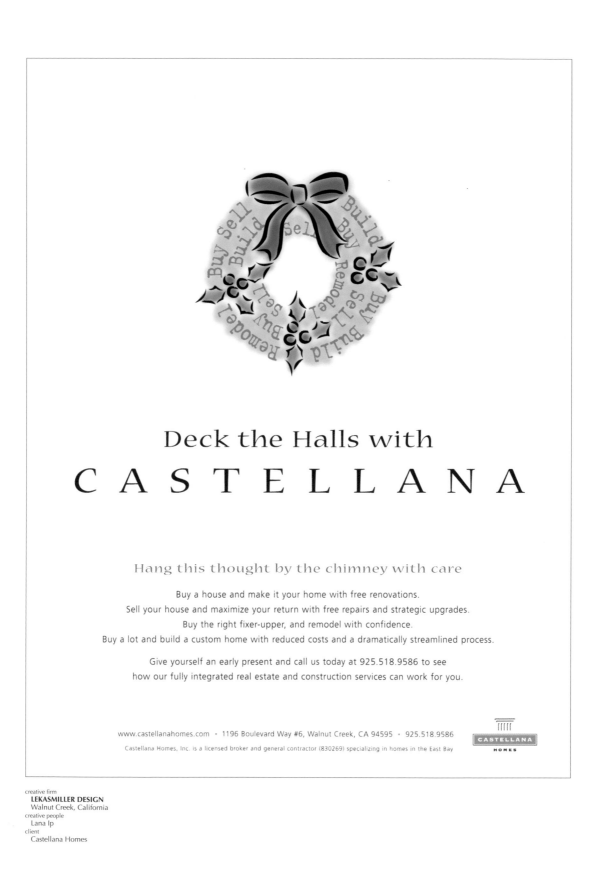

Deck the Halls with

CASTELLANA

Hang this thought by the chimney with care

Buy a house and make it your home with free renovations.
Sell your house and maximize your return with free repairs and strategic upgrades.
Buy the right fixer-upper, and remodel with confidence.
Buy a lot and build a custom home with reduced costs and a dramatically streamlined process.

Give yourself an early present and call us today at 925.518.9586 to see
how our fully integrated real estate and construction services can work for you.

www.castellanahomes.com • 1196 Boulevard Way #6, Walnut Creek, CA 94595 • 925.518.9586

Castellana Homes, Inc. is a licensed broker and general contractor (830269) specializing in homes in the East Bay

CASTELLANA HOMES

creative firm
LEKASMILLER DESIGN
Walnut Creek, California
creative people
Lana Ip
client
Castellana Homes

C A S T E L L A N A
Get Going on that Dream Home
Our fully integrated real estate and
construction services will make it a reality
Buy a house and make it your home with free renovations.
Sell your house and maximize your return with free repairs and strategic upgrades.
Buy the right fixer-upper, and remodel with confidence.
Buy a lot and build a custom home with reduced costs and a dramatically streamlined process.
Don't hit the snooze alarm on this one!
Call us today at 925.518.9586 to see what we can do for you.
www.castellanahomes.com · 1196 Boulevard Way #6, Walnut Creek, CA 94595 · 925.518.9586
Castellana Homes, Inc. is a licensed broker and general contractor (830269) specializing in homes in the East Bay
CASTELLANA
HOMES

C A S T E L L A N A
A Really Groovy Idea
Contemplate This
Buy a house and make it your home with free renovations.
Sell your house and maximize your return with free repairs and strategic upgrades.
Buy the right fixer-upper, and remodel with confidence.
Buy a lot and build a custom home with reduced costs and a dramatically streamlined process.
Call us today at 925.518.9586 to see how our fully integrated real estate and
construction services can work for you.
www.castellanahomes.com · 1196 Boulevard Way #6, Walnut Creek, CA 94595 · 925.518.9586
Castellana Homes, Inc. is a licensed broker and general contractor (830269) specializing in homes in the East Bay
CASTELLANA
HOMES

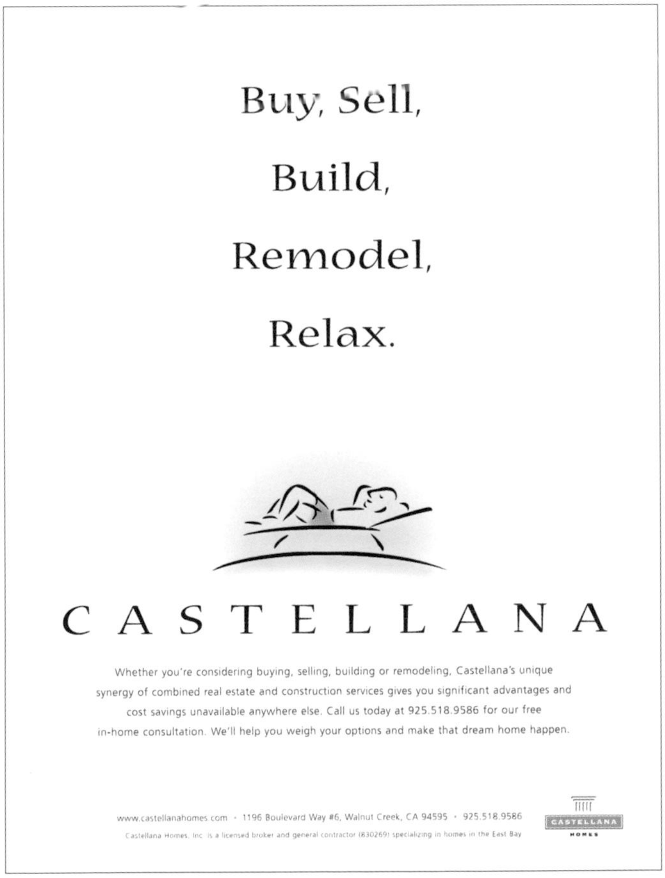
Buy, Sell,
Build,
Remodel,
Relax.
C A S T E L L A N A
Whether you're considering buying, selling, building or remodeling, Castellana's unique
synergy of combined real estate and construction services gives you significant advantages and
cost savings unavailable anywhere else. Call us today at 925.518.9586 for our free
in-home consultation. We'll help you weigh your options and make that dream home happen.
www.castellanahomes.com · 1196 Boulevard Way #6, Walnut Creek, CA 94595 · 925.518.9586
Castellana Homes, Inc. is a licensed broker and general contractor (830269) specializing in homes in the East Bay
CASTELLANA
HOMES

C A S T E L L A N A
Real Estate Solutions Up the Yang
Bring Nirvana Home
Buy a house and make it your home with free renovations.
Sell your house and maximize your return with free repairs and strategic upgrades.
Buy the right fixer-upper, and remodel with confidence.
Buy a lot and build a custom home with reduced costs and a dramatically streamlined process.
Call us today at 925.518.9586 to see how our fully integrated real estate and
construction services can work for you.
www.castellanahomes.com · 1196 Boulevard Way #6, Walnut Creek, CA 94595 · 925.518.9586
Castellana Homes, Inc. is a licensed broker and general contractor (830269) specializing in homes in the East Bay
CASTELLANA
HOMES

creative firm
021 COMUNICACIONES
Mexico City, Mexico
creative people
Rodolfo Vargas, Álvaro Fong, Jesús Moreno, Héctor González
client
American Express

creative firm
TOM FOWLER, INC.
Norwalk, Connecticut
creative people
Elizabeth P. Ball, Phillip Doherty
client
The Connecticut Grand Opera & Orchestra

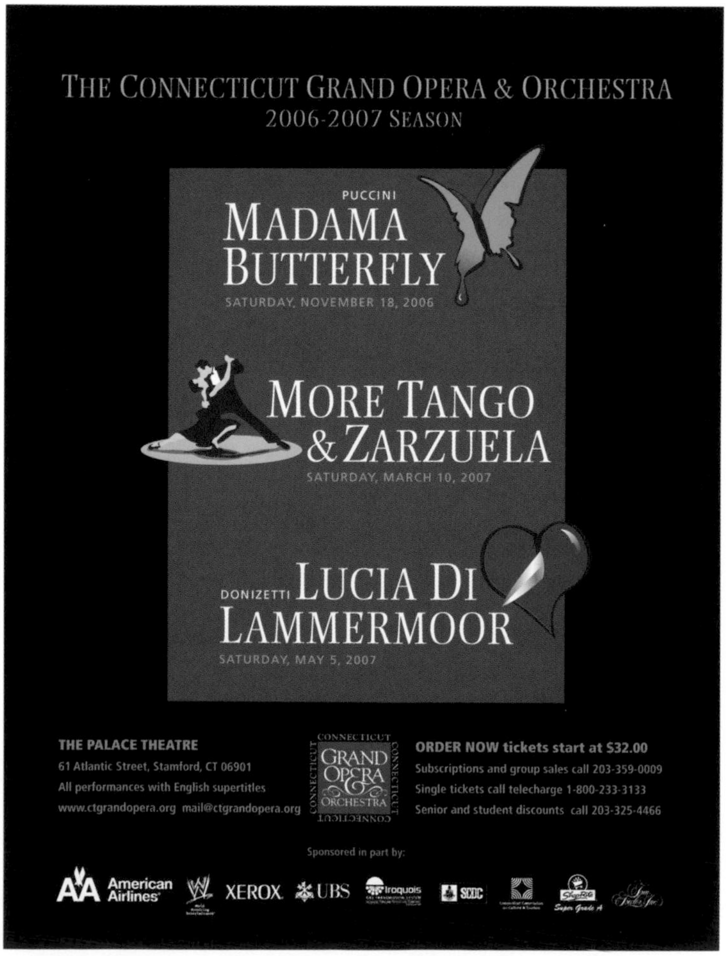

creative firm
LOOK DESIGN
San Carlos, California
creative people
Betsy Todd
client
KLA-Tencor

creative firm
RIGHT HAT, LLC
Boston, Massachusetts
creative people
Charlyne Fabi, Elonide Semmes
client
Berman & Simmons

creative firm
NEVER BORING DESIGN ASSOCIATES, INC.
Modesto, California
creative people
Julie Orona
client
Curtis & Arata

creative firm
021 COMUNICACIONES
Mexico City, Mexico
creative people
Ivan Pedraza, Javier Torres, Mauricio Gutiérrez, Ivan Pedraza, Arno Avilés
client
Mail Boxes Etc.

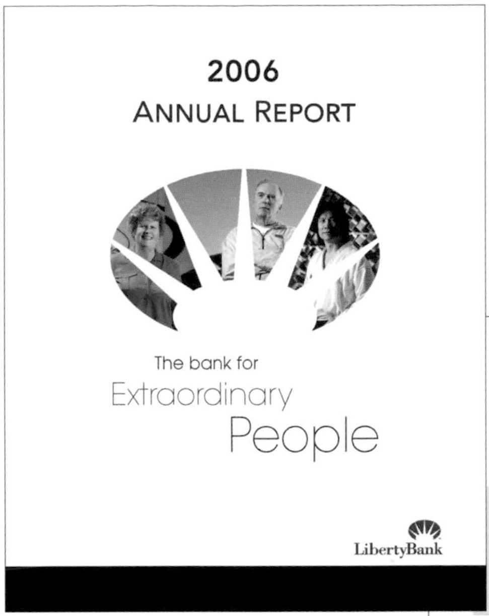

creative firm
FUNK/LEVIS & ASSOCIATES
Eugene, Oregon
creative people
Claudia Villegas, Lada Korol
client
LibertyBank

creative firm
GRAPHICAT LIMITED
Hong Kong, China
creative people
Colin Tillyer
client
Asia Satellite Telecommunications Holdings Limited

creative firm
BERRY DESIGN, INC.
Alpharetta, Georgia
creative people
Bob Berry, Chip Waller, Julie Acquesta
client
Dunkin' Brands

creative firm
DEVER DESIGNS
Laurel, Maryland
creative people
Byron Holly, Jeffrey L. Dever
client
National Fish and Wildlife Foundation

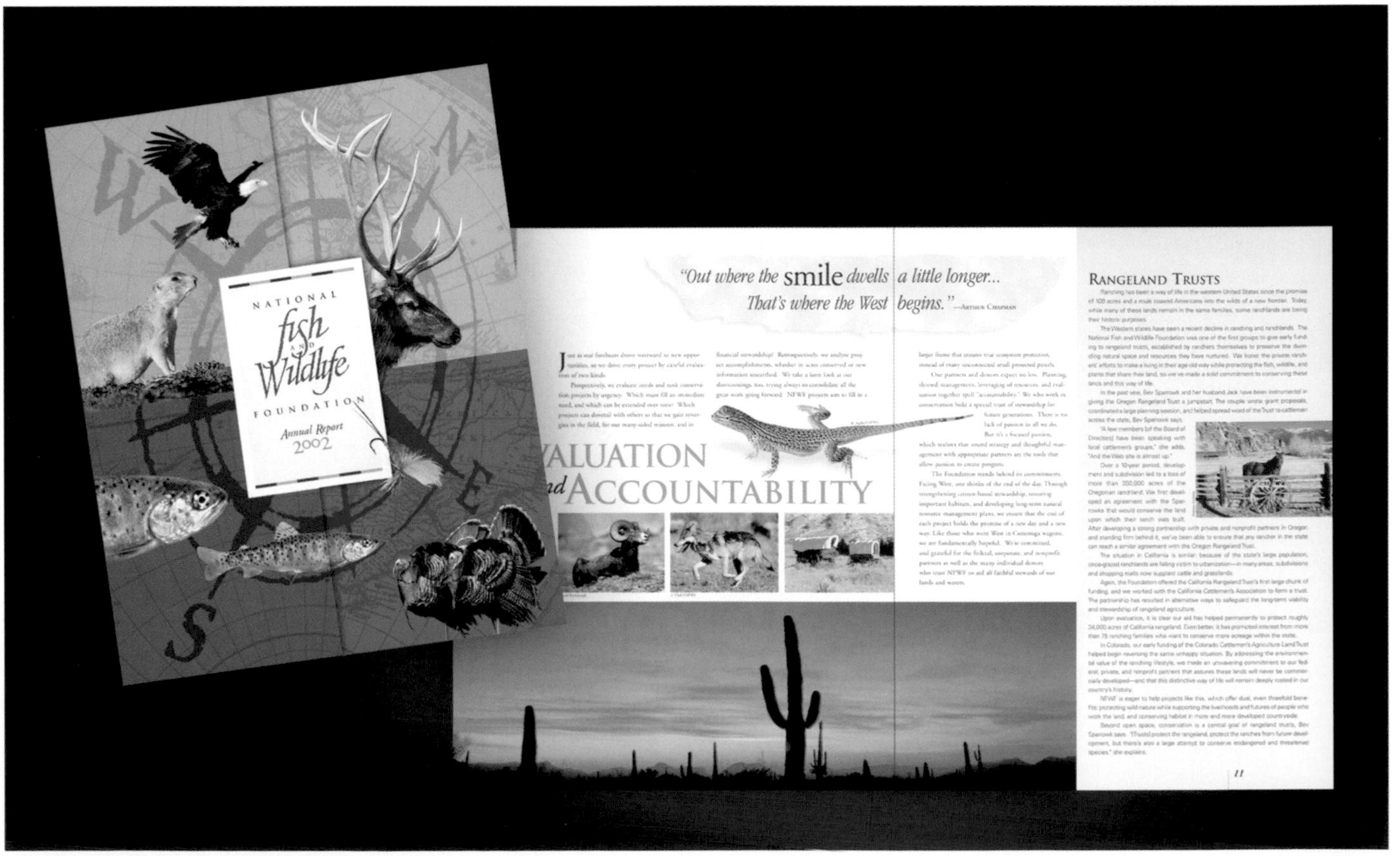

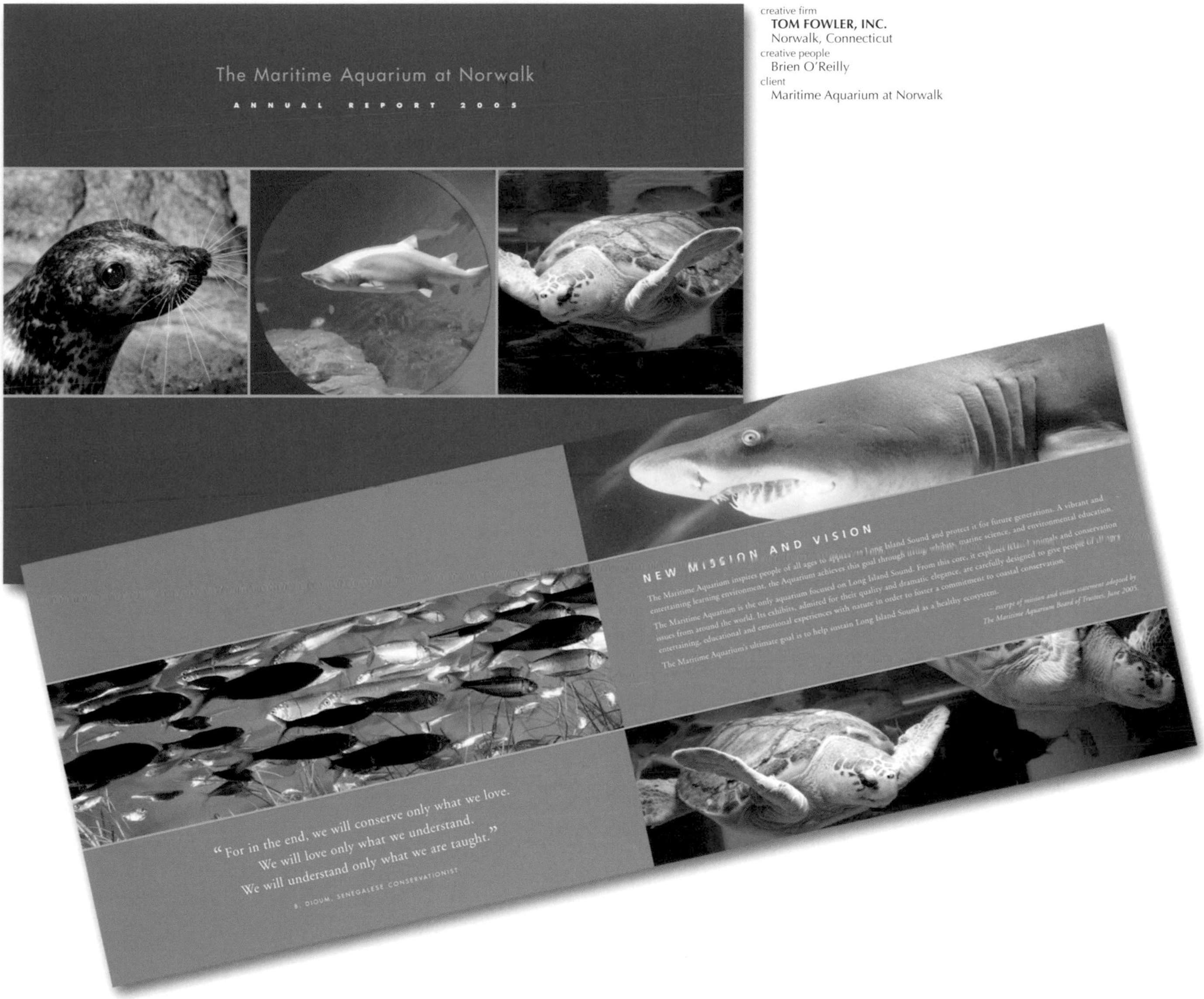
The Maritime Aquarium at Norwalk
ANNUAL REPORT 2005
NEW MISSION AND VISION
"For in the end, we will conserve only what we love.
We will love only what we understand.
We will understand only what we are taught."
B. DIOUM, SENEGALESE CONSERVATIONIST

creative firm
TOM FOWLER, INC.
Norwalk, Connecticut
creative people
Brien O'Reilly
client
Maritime Aquarium at Norwalk

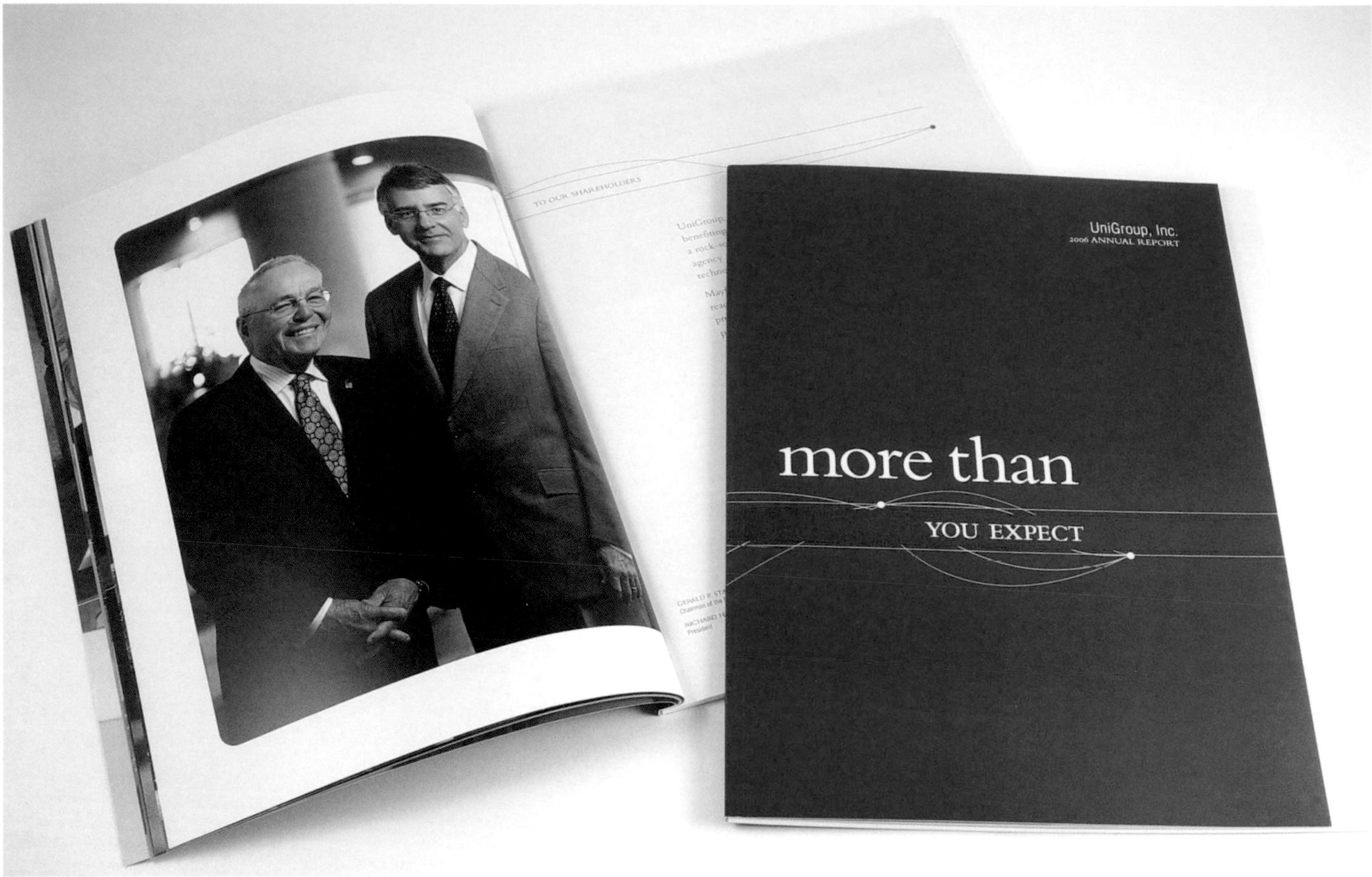

creative firm
STAN GELLMAN GRAPHIC DESIGN
St. Louis, Missouri
creative people
Jill Frantti, Teresa Thompson
client
UniGroup, Inc. 2006

creative firm
Q
Wiesbaden, Germany
creative people
Matthias Frey, Laurenz Nielbock, Christoph Dahinten
client
Nassauische Sparkasse

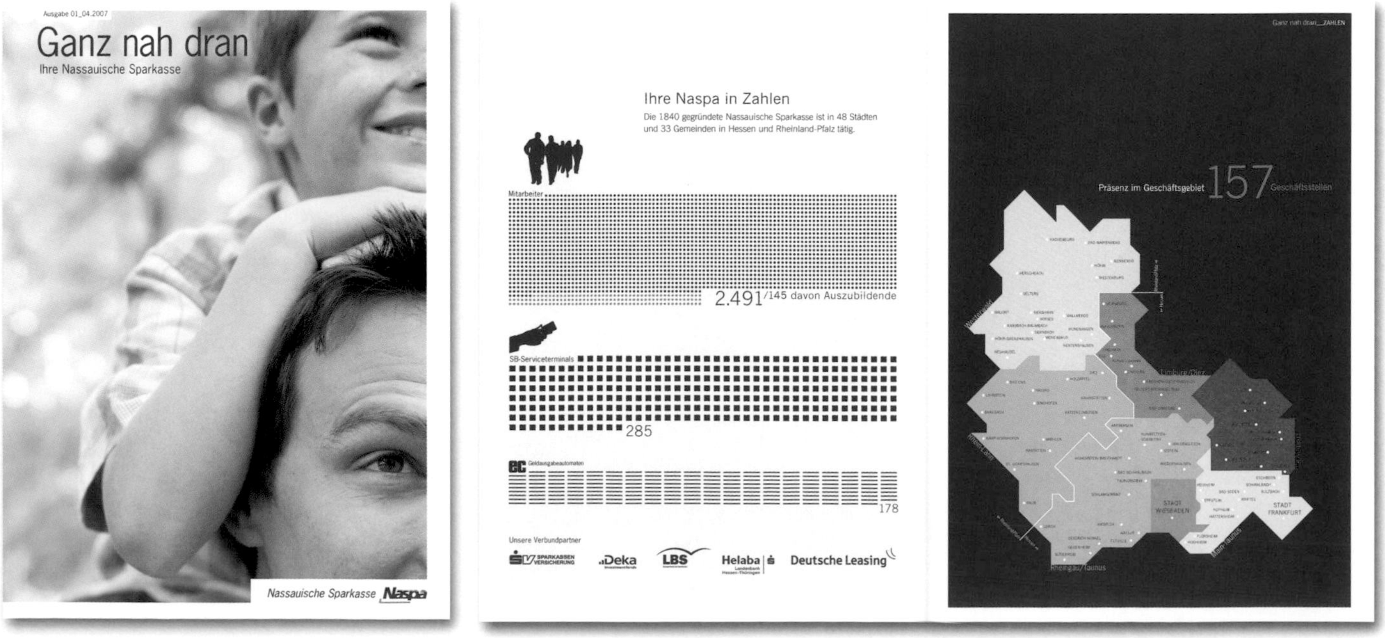

National Cherry Blossom Festival
annual review 2006

creative firm
PENSARÉ DESIGN GROUP
Washington, D.C.
creative people
Lauren Emeritz
client
National Cherry Blossom Festival

creative firm
LEKASMILLER DESIGN
Walnut Creek, California
creative people
Lana Ip
client
John Muir Health Foundation

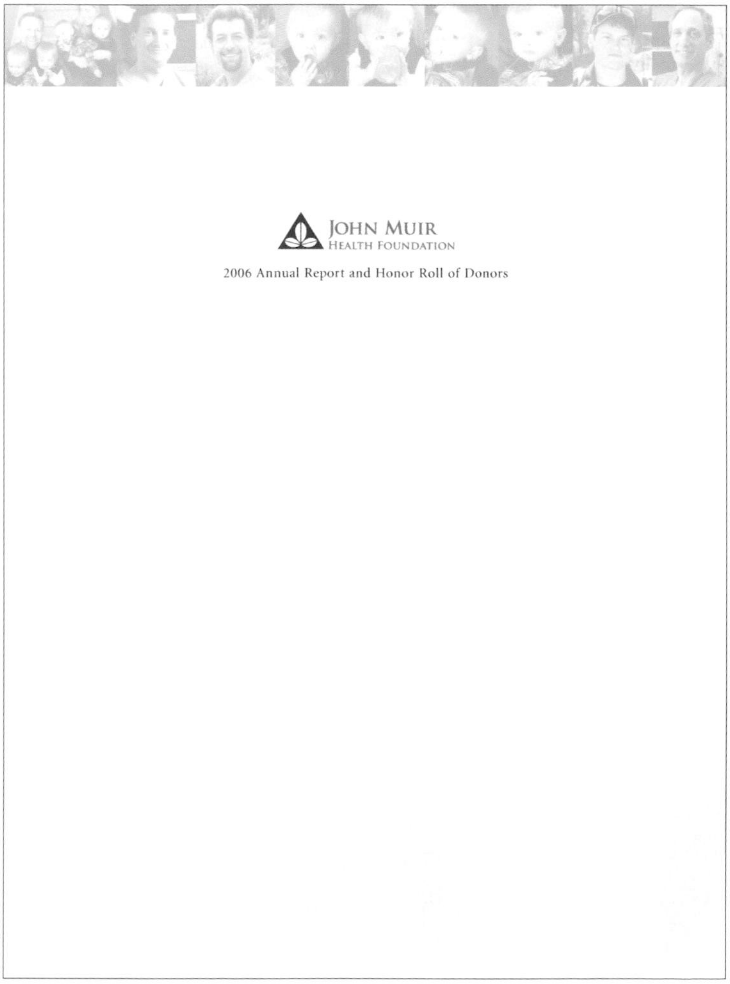
John Muir
Health Foundation
2006 Annual Report and Honor Roll of Donors

creative firm
Q
Wiesbaden, Germany
creative people
Matthias Frey, Thilo von Debschitz
client
Nummer gegen Kummer

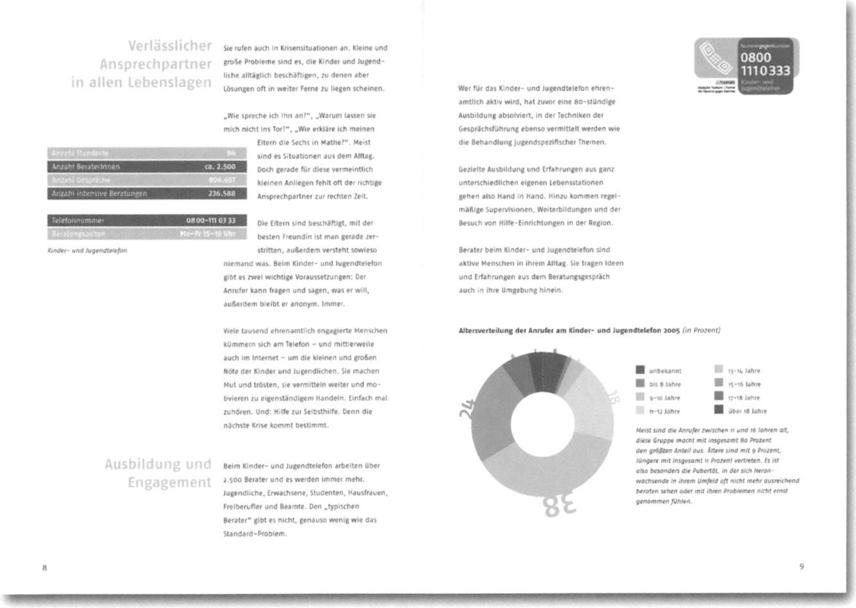

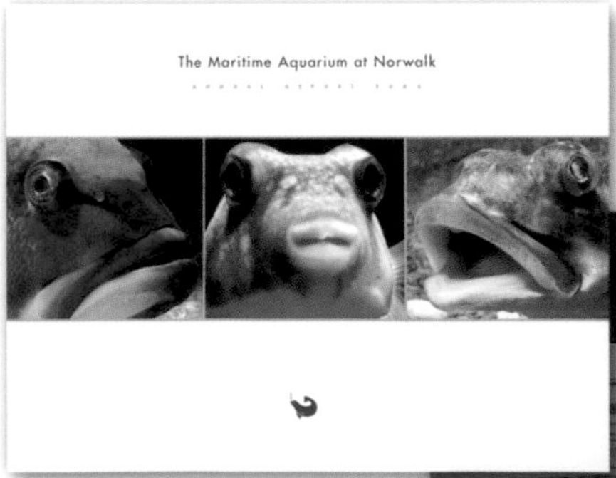

creative firm
TOM FOWLER, INC.
Norwalk, Connecticut
creative people
Brien O'Reilly
client
Maritime Aquarium at Norwalk

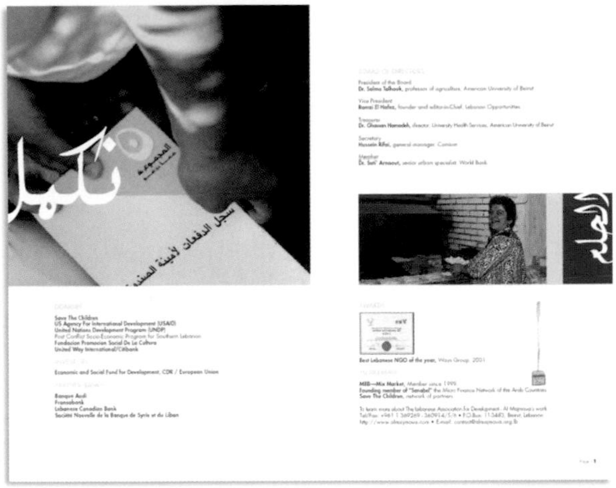

creative firm
GO GRAPHIC
Beirut, Lebanon
creative people
Maria Assi, Morava Zgheib
client
Al Majmoua

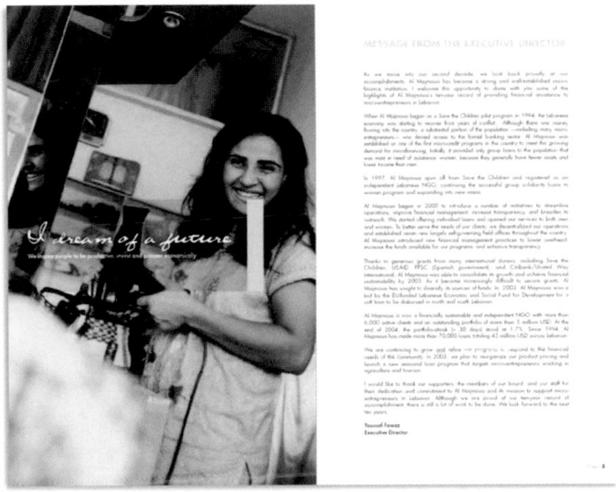

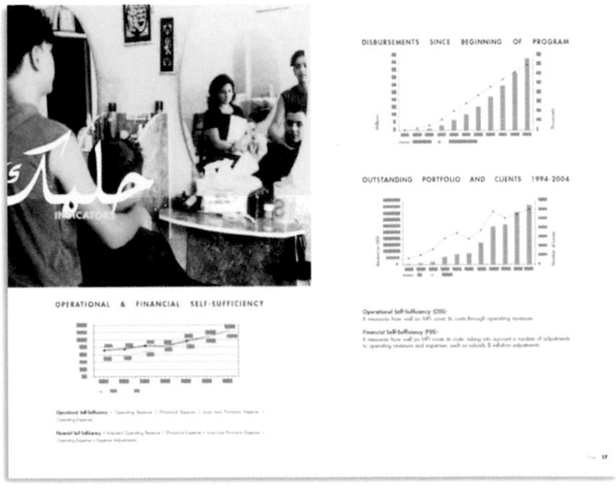

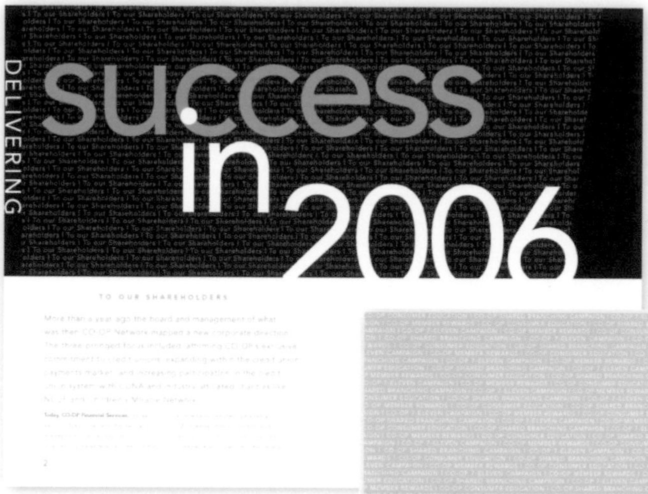

creative firm
EVENSON DESIGN GROUP
Culver City, California
creative people
Dallas Duncan
client
CO-OP Financial Services

creative firm
GRAPHICAT LIMITED
Hong Kong, China
creative people
Colin Tillyer
client
ASM Pacific Technology Limited

creative firm
DEVER DESIGNS
Laurel, Maryland
creative people
Kim Pollock
client
National Fish and Wildlife Foundation

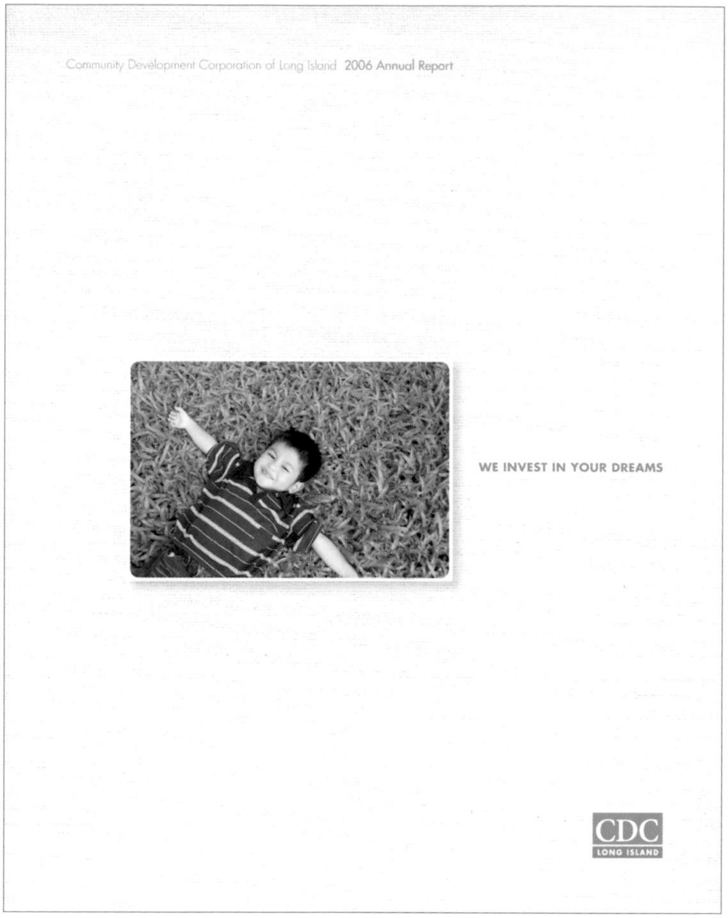
Community Development Corporation of Long Island 2006 Annual Report
WE INVEST IN YOUR DREAMS
CDC
LONG ISLAND

creative firm
ZERO GRAVITY DESIGN GROUP
Smithtown, New York
creative people
Zero Gravity Design Group
client
CDC of Long Island

"Here I am... a full-fledged homeowner. It is one of the most gratifying and serene feelings you'll ever know."
– Antoinette

Achieving the HomeOwnership Dream

MEETING THE CHALLENGES OF A CHANGING HOUSING MARKET

The average home sales price has reached over $500,000, a price that is more than 5 1/2 times the median annual income for a family of four. How does a working Long Island family manage to purchase a home in this market? A growing number of families, spanning a wide range of incomes, face this difficult question. CDC offers critical assistance specially tailored for our clients' individual needs. CDC's NeighborWorks HomeOwnership Centers assist clients by designing a household budget, providing credit counseling, and shopping for the best available mortgage financing products. In addition, many clients qualify for leveraging options for attaining homeownership. Take for example, the Smith family. They recently purchased a home with the appraised value of $345,000 for a subsidized price of $240,500 in Freeport. CDC's services, programs and partnerships were instrumental in bringing this project to fruition and helped to fulfill the Smith Family's dream of owning their first home (see insert). Grant funds listed include provisions for home energy conservation and safety measures.

How does a family with a household income of $58,000 afford a $373,000 home?

Down Payment: $13,350	$3,350 homebuyer's own savings $5,000 from Northrop Grumman's employee homeownership program $5,000 from Long Island Employer Assisted Housing Program
Bethpage Federal Credit Union Mortgage: $287,720	Paid monthly for 30 years
CDC Tandem Mortgage: $71,930	Paid monthly for 30 years

CDC made homeownership affordable for the Williams Family of Shirley.

BUILDING COMMUNITY PARTNERSHIPS THAT RESPOND TO CHANGING NEEDS

CDC of Long Island supports forward-directed community change. Collaborating with the Town of Southold, CDC will construct the first subdivision to be developed under Southold's Affordable Housing District zone. During the spring of 2007, our Cottages at Mattituck development will provide twenty-two families with affordable homes to purchase. These two-bedroom homes are priced at levels affordable to families with incomes below 80% and 100% of Long Island's median income, and at less than half the median sales price on Long Island today. This unique and cutting-edge approach will assure that the homes will remain affordable in perpetuity. CDC would not be able to accomplish this development without the cooperation of several key partners. Suffolk County provided funds for land acquisition, through their workforce housing acquisition program, and purchase price subsidies under the Suffolk County HOME Program. The State of New York Affordable Housing Corporation is providing additional subsidies. Finally, the private banking community is providing permanent mortgage financing that suits the needs of these first-time home buyers. CDC's Board of Directors has played a crucial role as well – their commitment to invest CDC's own resources into the development is a key to its success.

CDC-sponsored rental housing for Long Island seniors.

CDC of Long Island also initiates small-scale change, one home at a time. Our weatherization and housing rehabilitation programs serve 800 households annually. In partnership with the Town of Brookhaven and Suffolk County, CDC is continuing a collaborative effort through which the Town and County transfers abandoned properties to CDC. CDC uses its own funds to rehabilitate these properties, which are then rented and eventually sold at an affordable price to first time home buyers.

CDC of Long Island supports families' financial needs. During 2006, CDC established a not-for-profit mortgage brokerage operation in conjunction with our private banking industry partners. Through this new line of business, homebuyers receive competitive mortgage finance products that include brokered loans for banking partners and portfolio products. CDC offers some of these options through Neighborhood Housing Services of America, which serves as a secondary market for CDC, as a NeighborWorks organization.

6 7

A REWARDING HISTORY

The past decade has been one of great growth for CDC of Long Island. During this period, our staff has more than doubled in size, and we have strengthened our ability to address our mission of helping Long Islanders gain access to "The American Dream." Today, CDC's Board of Directors moves forward with vision and creativity to meet the ever-changing challenges that inhibit our constituents from seeking and fulfilling their dreams. With that aim in mind, we are proud to announce Marianne Garvin, as President of the Corporation.

Wilbur Klatsky
CDC Chief Executive Officer

James Coughlan
CDC Chair; Principal and Co-Founder, TRITEC Real Estate Co., Inc.

A PROMISING FUTURE

After 14 years with CDC of Long Island, it is with great excitement, that I take the reins as President of this remarkable organization. A national vanguard, CDC directly confronts every significant community development challenge that besets our suburban community. Our board, management and staff promote our core values as they explore creative and innovative solutions to ensure that our clients obtain their dreams.

As detailed within this report, CDC took another leap forward this year. Responding to our constituents' genuine needs, CDC established new specialized financial and educational services and brought new partners to the table to better serve the needs of Long Island communities.

To our partners – we value your efforts on CDC's behalf. Your guidance and assistance allows CDC to address some of the most pervasive needs of Long Islanders. Thank you for your steadfast support.

Marianne Garvin
CDC President

"I am very grateful to CDC of Long Island. With this assistance you are helping keep my dreams alive."
– Kimberly

How We Invest in Your Dreams

CDC of Long Island's Board of Directors conducted a Strategic Visioning Process over the past year, which reaffirmed our Strategic Plan established at the beginning of the new millennium. Central to this Strategic Vision is CDC's core mission of building resources to help Long Island's individuals, families, and business owners to obtain their desires and aspirations, or put more succinctly: We Invest in Your Dreams.

CDC's Suffolk office, located in Centereach

For many of the families who are touched by our activities, the dream takes the shape of owning their first home. This dream is increasingly elusive due to the high housing costs on Long Island, however, as a NeighborWorks HomeOwnership Center, CDC offers a variety of solutions to our clients to make these dreams come true.

For others, the dream is to own and operate their own business, to sustain their home and family through a job where they retain control, and perhaps provide employment to others. CDC's small business lending and business technical assistance programs help Long Islanders to accomplish this specific dream.

With the opportunity to purchase a retiring competitor's business, the Knapp Family turned to CDC for a loan. Their expanded Bohemia-based business, Design Works Crafts, Inc., is now more successful than ever before.

For many on fixed incomes, including seniors, who may have paid off their mortgages, the rising costs of utilities makes it difficult for them to retain their home. CDC helps them to retain their dream by providing energy conservation installations and other home improvement measures that increase the home's affordability.

For thousands of renters throughout Long Island, affording rental housing is their dream. With fair market rents ranging from $1,200 – $1,800, these residents have difficulty making the ends meet. For over 3,300 CDC clients who receive housing choice voucher assistance, CDC helps them come one step closer to achieving their dream of sustainability.

CDC of Long Island is a chartered member of NeighborWorks, a nationwide network of more than 240 trained and certied community development organizations at work in more than 4,000 communities across America. Working in partnership with others, NeighborWorks organizations are leaders in revitalizing communities and creating affordable housing opportunities for low-and moderate-income families. As a chartered member of NeighborWorks, CDC of Long Island is certified to meet a high standard of fiscal integrity and service performance to assist local residents in developing leadership, improving their neighborhoods, and securing decent, affordable housing. These core values are embraced with renewed energy and creativity as evidenced by CDC's recent activities, strategic vision, and this year's successes highlighted in this report.

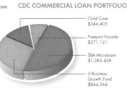

CDC COMMERCIAL LOAN PORTFOLIO

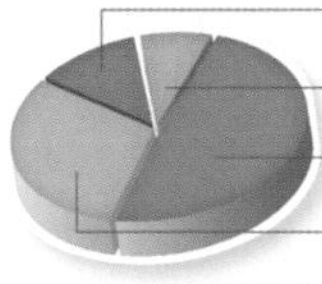

Child Care $344,405
Freeport Façade $271,121
SBA Microloans $1,383,428
LI Business Growth Fund $864,564

August 2006 $2.8 million

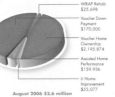

CDC RESIDENTIAL LOAN PORTFOLIO

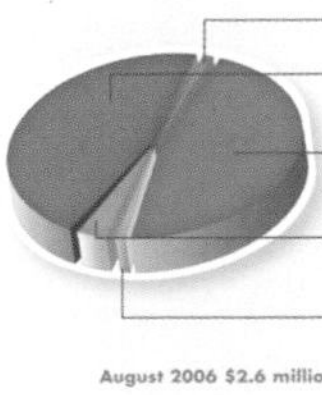

WRAP Rehab $25,698
Voucher Down Payment $170,000
Voucher Home Ownership $2,195,874
Assisted Home Performance $159,936
LI Home Improvement $55,077

August 2006 $2.6 million

4 5

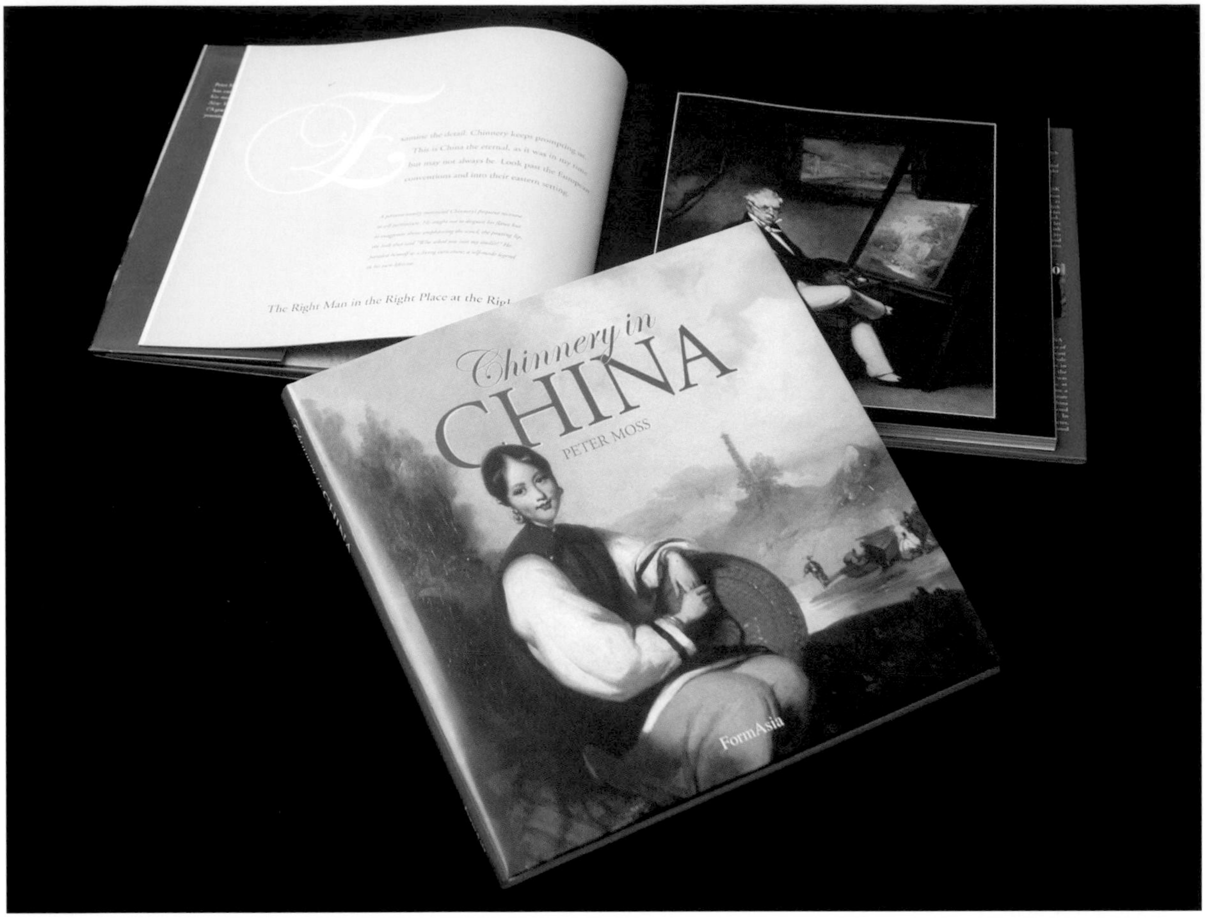

creative firm
GRAPHICAT LIMITED
Hong Kong, China
creative people
Colin Tillyer
client
FormAsia Limited

creative firm
SAYLES GRAPHIC DESIGN
Des Moines, Iowa
creative people
John Sayles
client
American Graphic Design Awards: Design Annual III

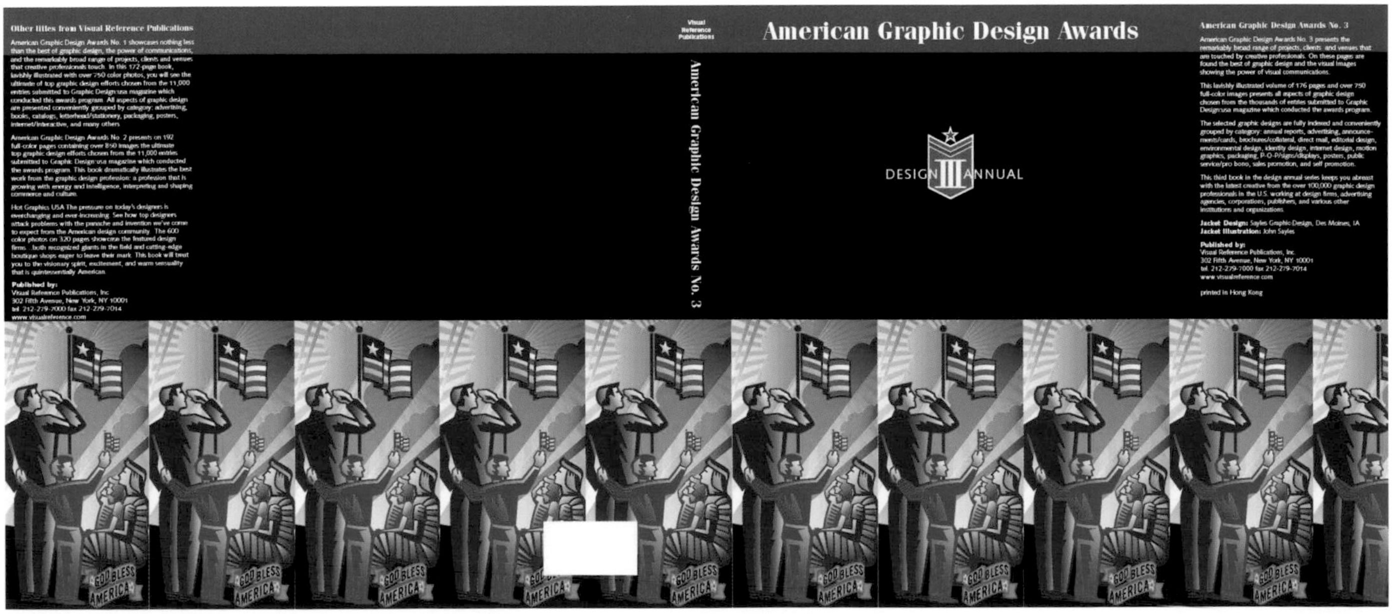

creative firm
EVENSON DESIGN GROUP
Culver City, California
creative people
John Krause
client
Andrews McMeel Publishing

creative firm
TANGRAM STRATEGIC DESIGN
Novara, Italy
creative people
Enrico Sempi, Annika Schorstein
client
ETI

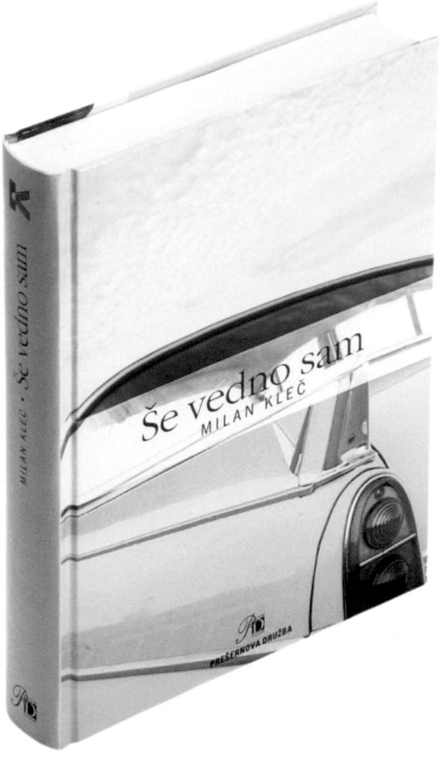

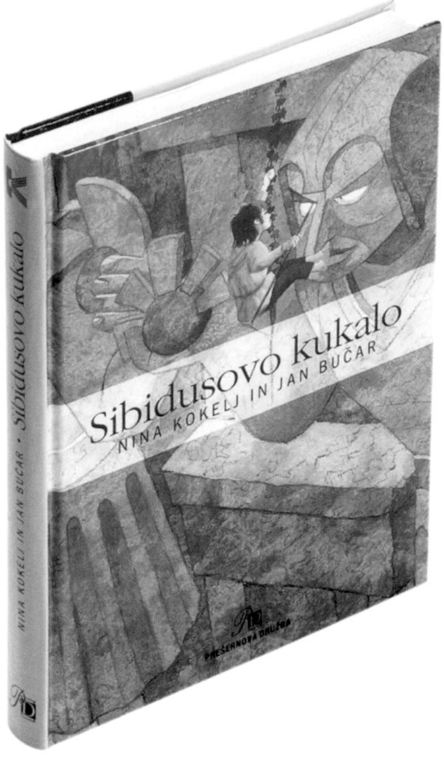

creative firm
KROG
Ljubljana, Slovenia
creative people
Edi Berk
client
Prešernova družba

creative firm
314CREATIVE
Duluth, Georgia
creative people
Shawn Jenks
client
DayDreamer Books

creative firm
JENN DAVID DESIGN
Irvine, California
creative people
Jenn David Connolly
client
Agog Creative

creative firm
MELISSA FLICKER
Rancho Cucamonga, California
creative people
Melissa Flicker
client
California State University, Fullerton
Department of Natural Sciences and Mathematics

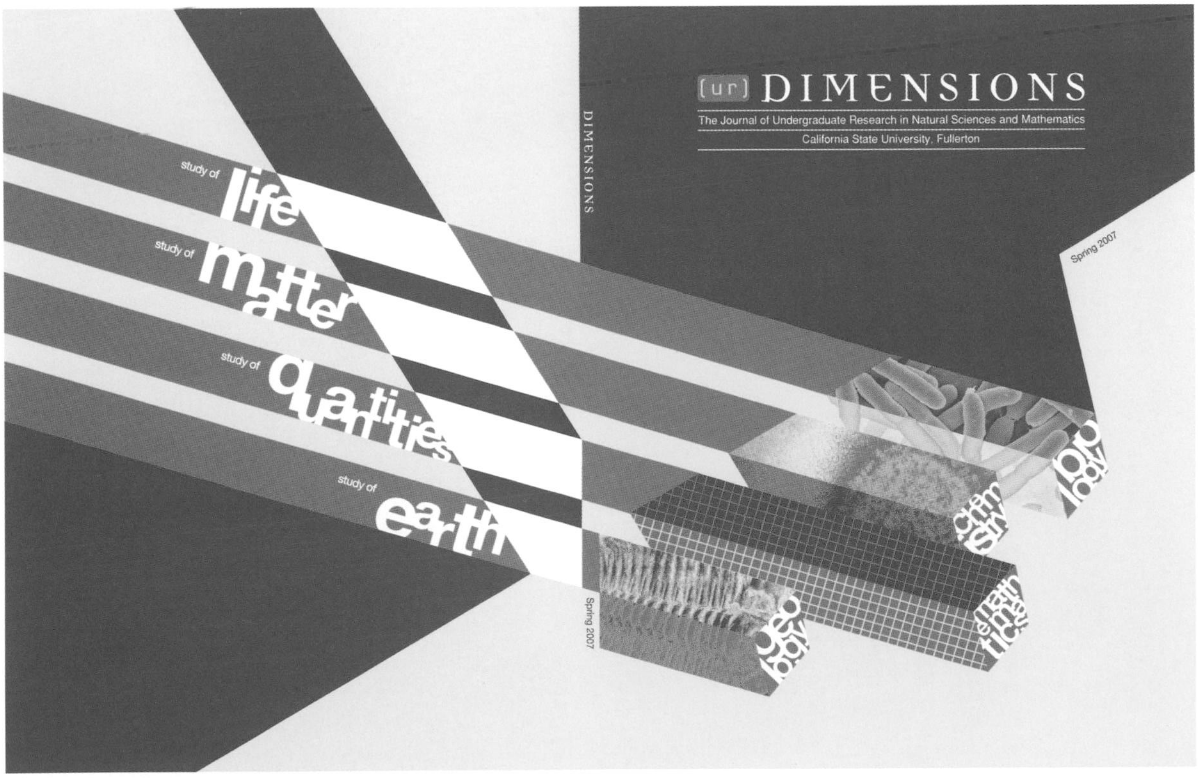

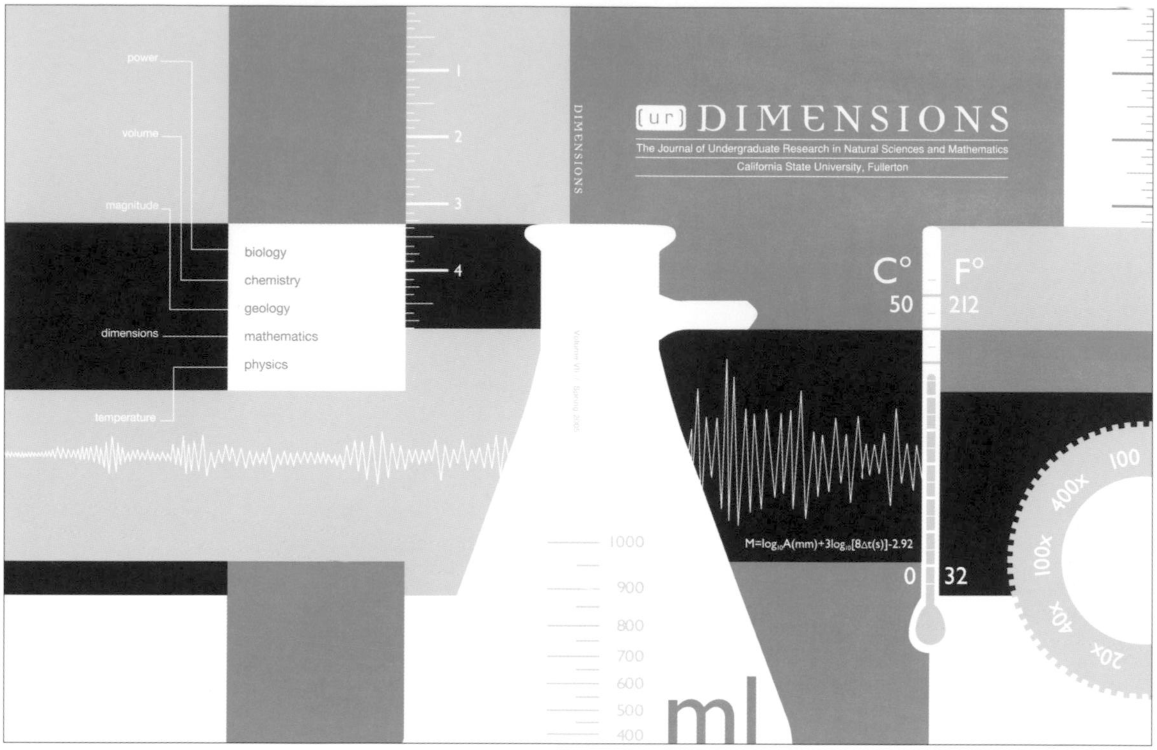

creative firm
MELISSA FLICKER
Rancho Cucamonga, California
creative people
Melissa Flicker
client
California State University, Fullerton
Department of Natural Sciences and Mathematics

creative firm
KROG
Ljubljana, Slovenia
creative people
Edi Berk
client
Univerzitetna knjižnica Maribor

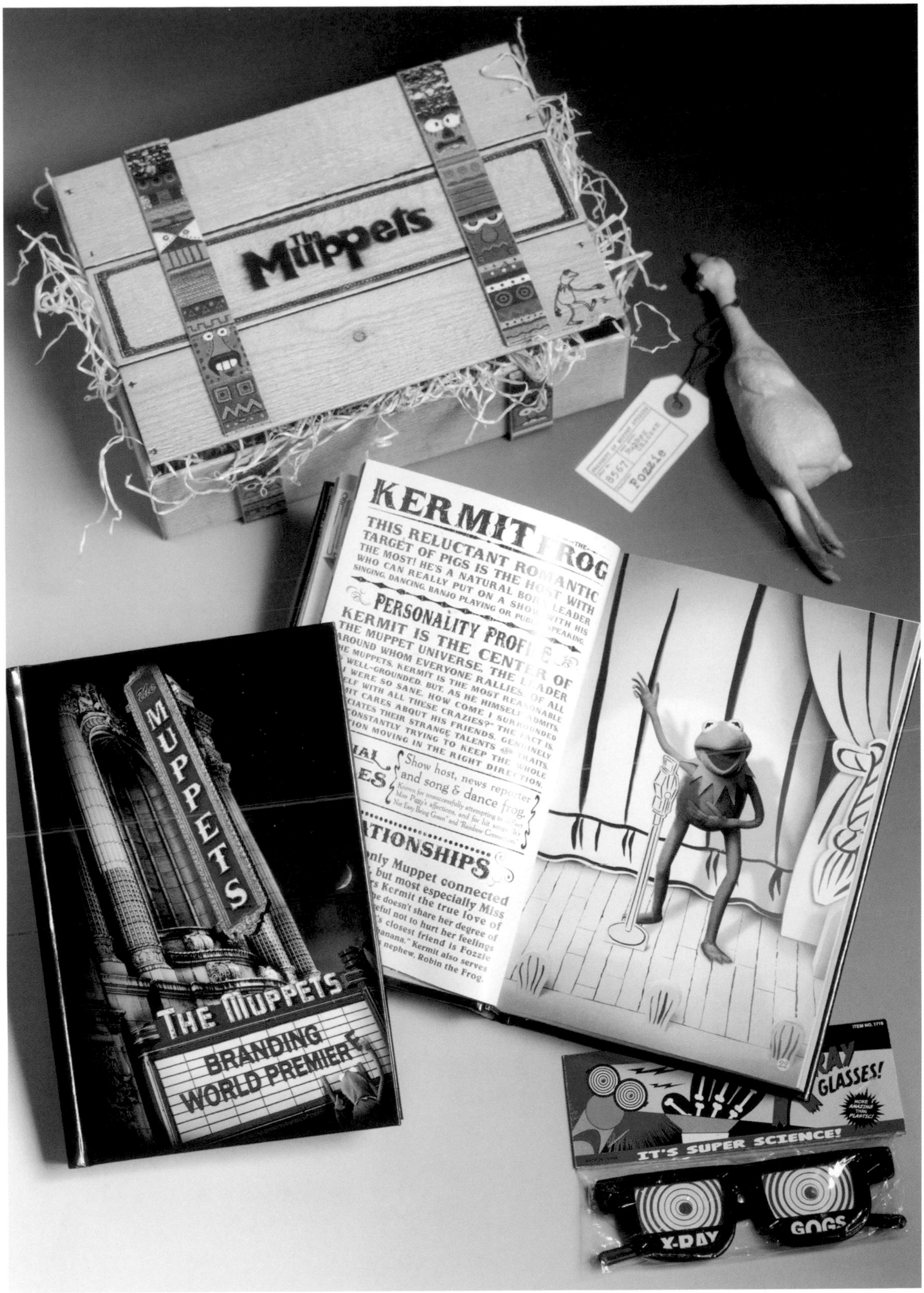

creative firm
30SIXTY ADVERTISING+DESIGN, INC.
Los Angeles, California
creative people
Henry Vizcarra, David Fuscellaro, Lee Barett, Suzana Lakatos, Yujin Ono, Bruce Ventanilla
client
Disney Consumer Products

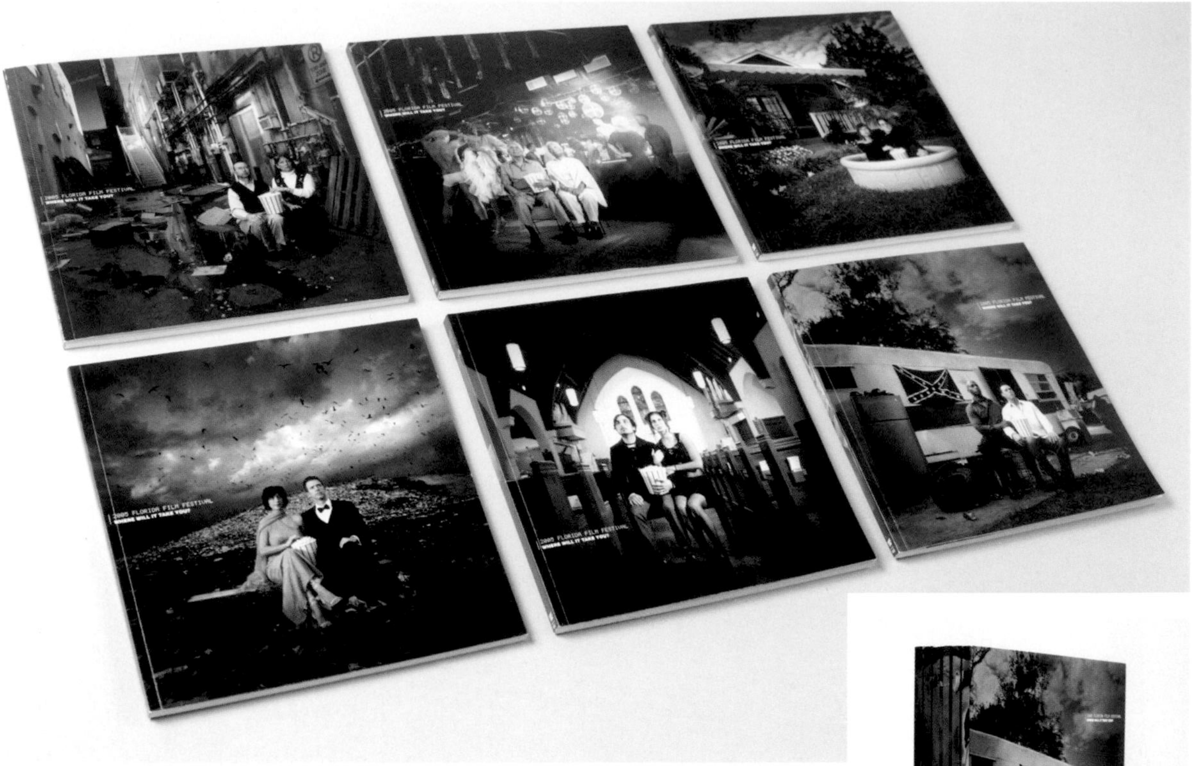

creative firm
FRY HAMMOND BARR
Orlando, Florida
creative people
Tim Fisher, Sean Brunson, Lara Mann
client
Florida Film Festival

eative firm
KROG
Ljubljana, Slovenia
creative people
Edi Berk
client
Pravna fakulteta, Ljubljana

creative firm
CHRIS CORNEAL
East Lansing, Michigan
creative people
Chris Corneal
client
Mark A. Largent

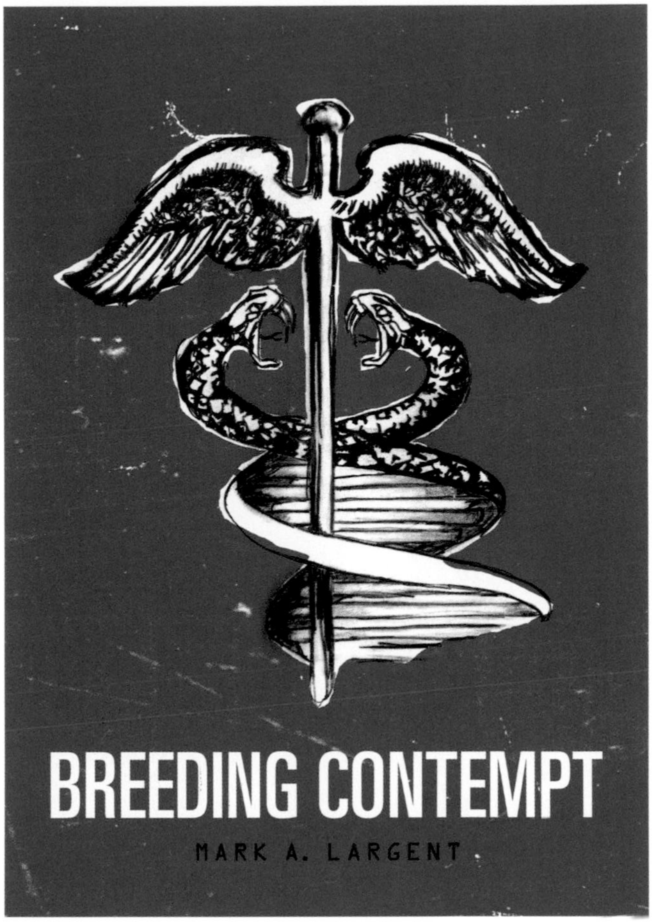

creative firm
MELISSA FLICKER
Rancho Cucamonga, California
creative people
Melissa Flicker
client
California State University, Fullerton
Department of Natural Sciences and Mathematics

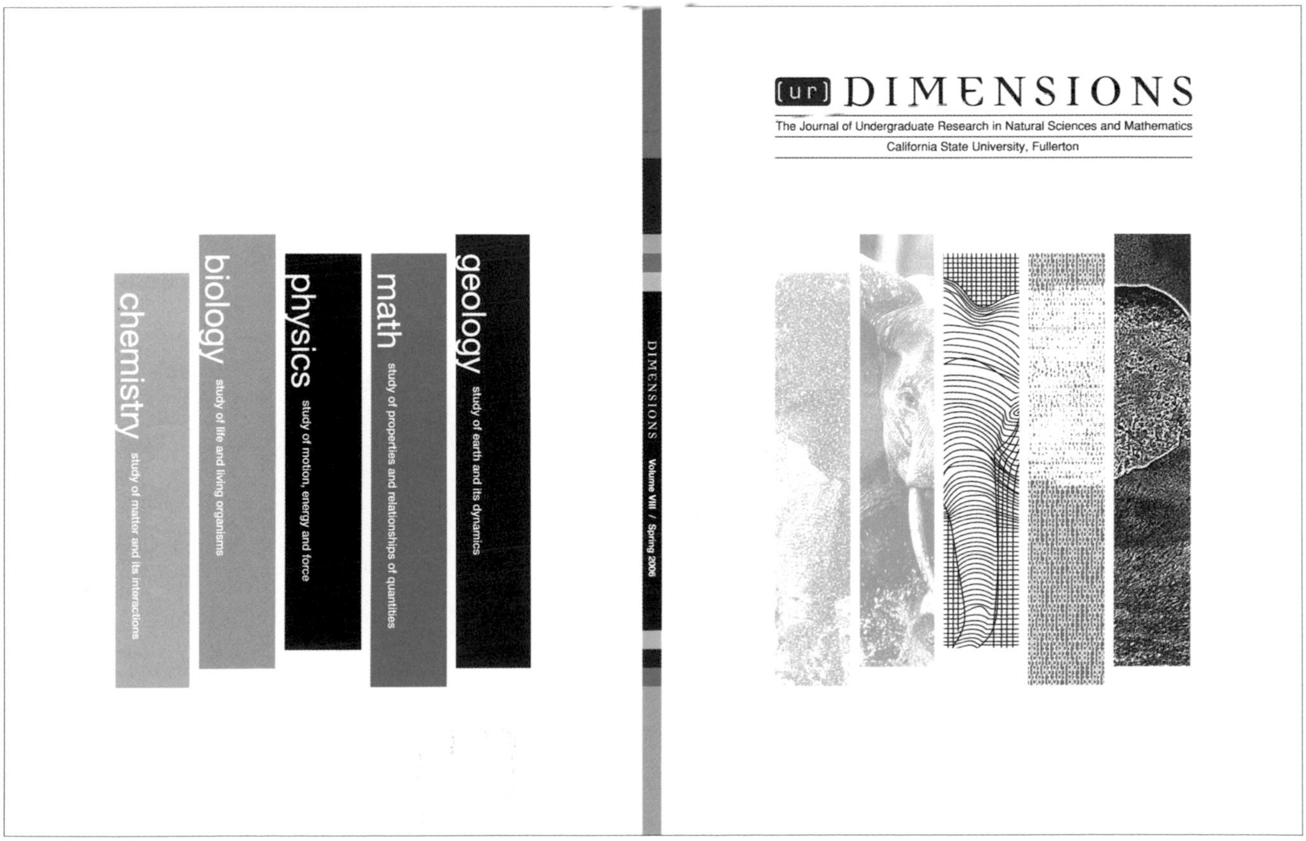

creative firm
KROG
Ljubljana, Slovenia
creative people
Edi Berk, Dragan Arrigler
client
KROG

creative firm
GO GRAPHIC
Beirut, Lebanon
creative people
Maria Assi, Rasha Jeaid
client
Caritas Migrants Center

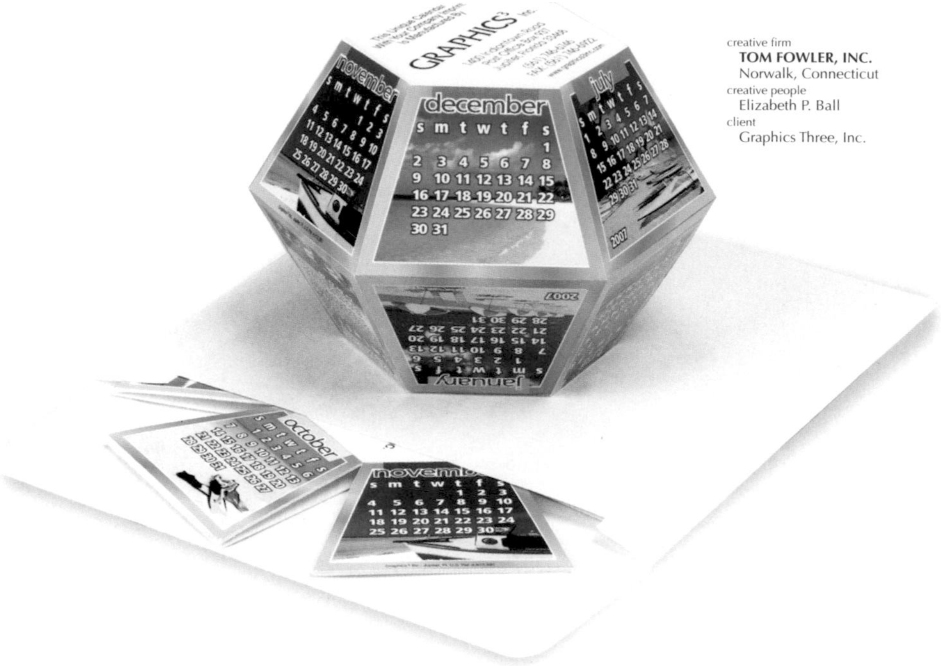

creative firm
TOM FOWLER, INC.
Norwalk, Connecticut
creative people
Elizabeth P. Ball
client
Graphics Three, Inc.

creative firm
KENNETH DISEÑO
Uruapan, Mexico
creative people
Kenneth Treviño
client
Calendario Michoacan

A TOY STORY 07
January 2007
01
A TOY STORY 07

creative firm
RIORDON DESIGN
Oakville, Canada
creative people
Shirley Riordon, Alan Krpan, Ric Riordon
client
Riordon Design

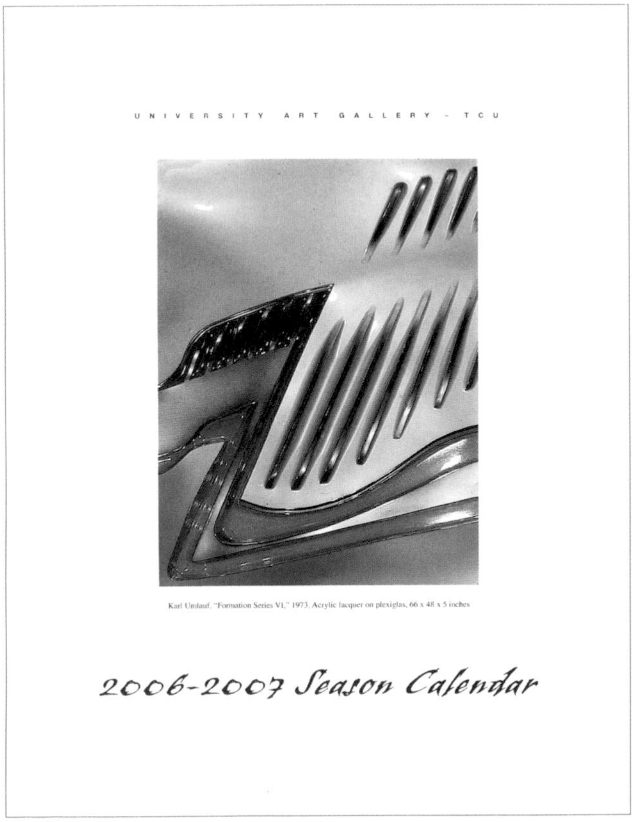
UNIVERSITY ART GALLERY - TCU
Karl Umlauf, "Formation Series VI," 1973, Acrylic lacquer on plexiglas, 66 x 48 x 5 inches
2006-2007 Season Calendar

creative firm
PAT SLOAN DESIGN
Fort Worth, Texas
creative people
Pat Sloan
client
University Art Gallery—TCU

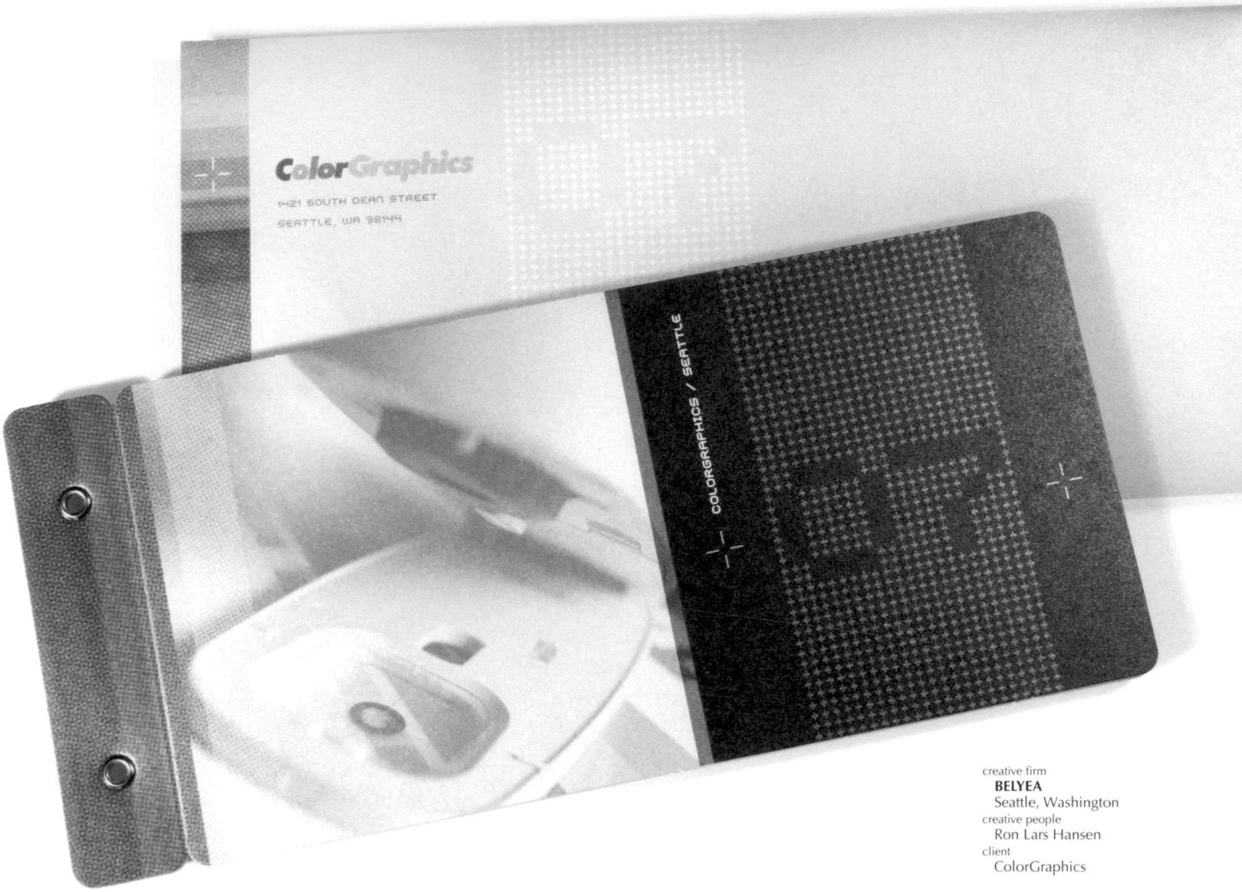

creative firm
BELYEA
Seattle, Washington
creative people
Ron Lars Hansen
client
ColorGraphics

Juli 07/07
Kopenhagen
Malmö
Öresundverbindung / Kopenhagen–Malmö

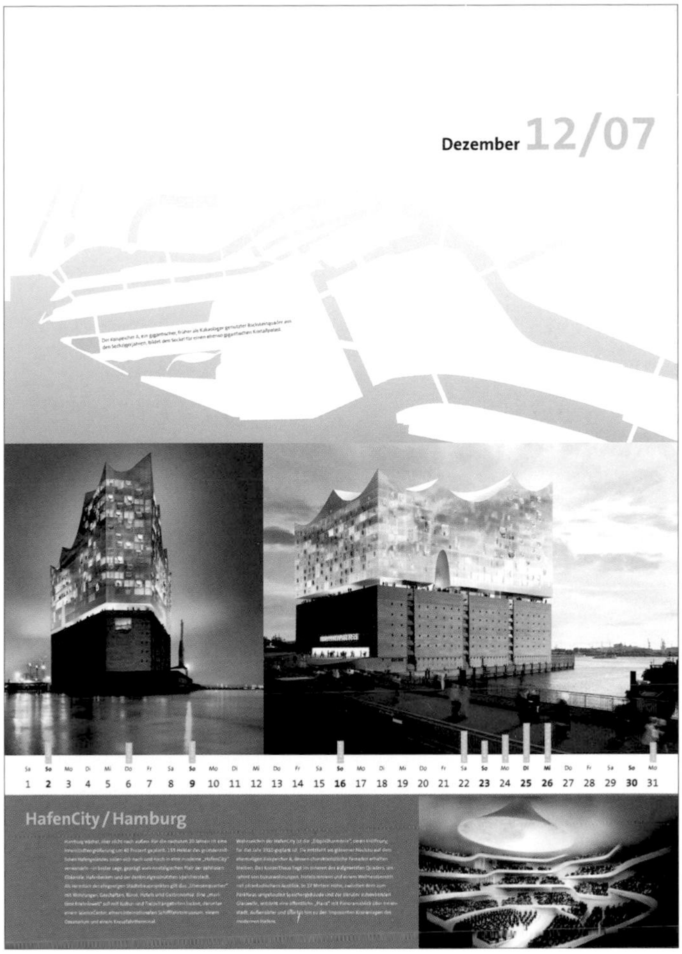
Dezember 12/07
HafenCity / Hamburg

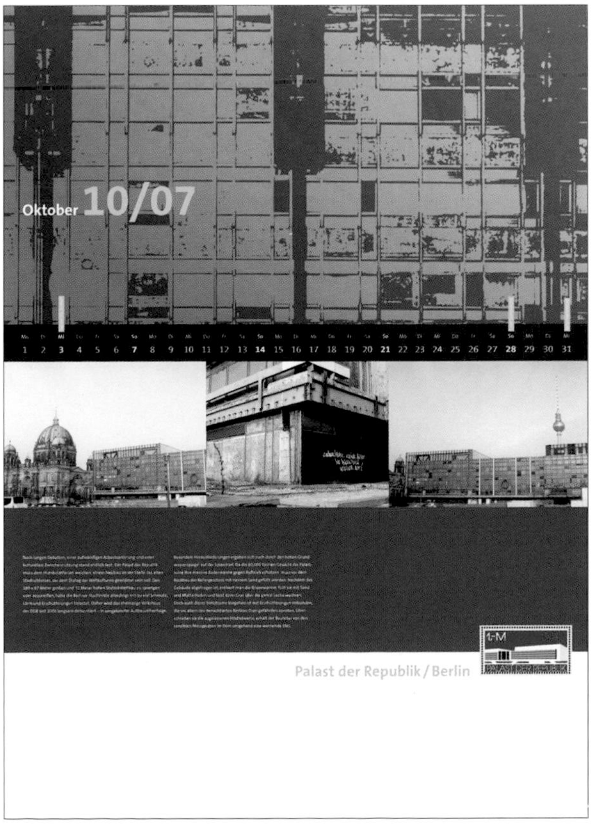
Oktober 10/07
Palast der Republik / Berlin

creative firm
Q
Wiesbaden, Germany
creative people
Matthlas Frey
client
SOKA-BAU

JANUAR/JANUARY 2006

Če v prosincu ni snega, ga mali traven da. Narava vse leto spreminja svojo podobo in pogoje za življenje. Vendar je človek v preteklostih pogosto veliko bolj skladno živel z naravo in se tudi z najrazličnejšimi izumi, orodji in napravami prilagajal izjemnim vremenskim, podnebnim in še kakšnim razmeram. V zimskem času si je nadel krplje, ki so mu omogočale gibanje po zasneženi pokrajini. **Should January be free of snow, April is likely to bring it though.** Nature keeps changing its image and thus living conditions throughout the year. However, in the past people knew how to live in harmony with nature much better, managing to adapt to extreme weather and other conditions by various inventions, tools and devices. During winters, people used snowshoes, which enabled them to walk around in the snowy countryside.

2	3	4	5	6
9	10	11	12	13
16	17	18	19	20
23/30	24/31	25	26	27

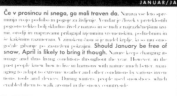

creative firm
KROG
Ljubljana, Slovenia
creative people
Edi Berk, Boris Gaberšcik
client
Kmecki glas, Ljubljana

JUNIJ/JUNE 2006

Junija toliko dežuje, da zadnji korenini zadostuje. Košnje sodijo med značilna poletna opravila. Danes imamo za to delo sodobna orodja in traktorske priključke. Ročna košnja, ki se je začela kmalu po jutranjem svitu, ni več domena krepkih rok s kosami, ki so morale biti primerno naostrene. Ročni brusni kamen ali osla je bilo orodje za pasom vsakega kosca, shranjeno v lesenem ali roženem oselniku. **June brings rain from the sky, so no root is left dry.** Haymaking is a typical summer activity. Today, there are modern tools and tractor trailers available. Manual mowing, which begins soon after dawn, is no longer reserved to strong hands with sickles, which had to be adequately honed. The manual whetstone, or hone, was a tool kept behind the belt of each mower, stored in a scythestone container made of wood or horn.

			1	2	3	4
5	6	7	8	9	10	11
12	13	14	15	16	17	18
19	20	21	22	23	24	25
26	27	28	29	30		

Lane contributes to a robust local economy by helping meet our community's need for a deep pool of skilled labor. Our professional and technical programs prepare students for careers in the fastest-growing job sectors. Additionally, our Apprenticeship program allows students to learn highly skilled occupations in eight trades through on-the-job training and related instruction. And Lane's English as a Second Language program further strengthens the workplace by providing English language training for students from more than 40 nations.
إنجليزي
Inglés
английский
tiếng Anh
영어
英語
LCC
skilled
labor

creative firm
FUNK/LEVIS & ASSOCIATES
Eugene, Oregon
creative people
Lada Korol, Chris Berner
client
Lane Community College

Lane Community College

SEPTEMBER 2006

SUNDAY	MONDAY	TUESDAY	WEDNESDAY	THURSDAY	FRIDAY	SATURDAY
					1	2
3	4 Labor Day holiday	5	6	7 Fall term registration begins	8	9
10	11	12	13	14	15	16
17	18	19 Fall all-staff gathering, college closed	20	21	22	23
24	25 Fall term classes begin	26	27	28	29	30

OCTOBER 2006

SUNDAY	MONDAY	TUESDAY	WEDNESDAY	THURSDAY	FRIDAY	SATURDAY
1	2	3	4	5	6	7
8	9	10	11	12	13	14
15	16	17	18	19	20	21
22	23	24	25	26	27	28
29	30	31				

NOVEMBER 2006

SUNDAY	MONDAY	TUESDAY	WEDNESDAY	THURSDAY	FRIDAY	SATURDAY
			1	2	3	4
5	6	7	8	9	10 Veterans Day holiday observed	11
12	13	14	15	16	17	18
19	20	21	22	23 Nov 23 - 26 Thanksgiving holiday	24	25
26	27	28	29	30		

DECEMBER 2006

SUNDAY	MONDAY	TUESDAY	WEDNESDAY	THURSDAY	FRIDAY	SATURDAY
There's still time to make a year-end donation to the Lane Community College Foundation. Your gift makes change happen in a student's life. Call the Foundation at (541) 463-5226.					1	2
3	4	5	6 Winter term registration begins	7	8	9
10	11	12	13	14	15	16
17	18	19	20	21	22	23
24 / 31	25	26	27	28	29	30

www.lanecc.edu (541) 463-3000

creative firm
HORNALL ANDERSON DESIGN
Seattle, Washington
creative people
Jack Anderson, Kathy Saito,
Peter Anderson, Ed Lee, Chris Freed
client
CitationShares

creative firm
CREATIVESOURCE/THE COCA-COLA COMPANY
Atlanta, Georgia
creative people
Dawn Shelton
client
Coca-Cola Supply Chain Operations

07
international fair
performance
The 2007 Lunar New Year Unity Parade & International Fair is delighted to bring to you a culturally diverse presentation featuring musicians, dancers and performers from local schools and throughout the community. This year, the stage performances will be presented at Quinlan Commons at Memorial Park.
International Night 2007 International Night seeks to promote community unity through celebrating our diversity. The 2007 International Night was held on Saturday, February 10th, 2007 at Lynbrook High School. Students performed acts featuring the art and tradition of India, Vietnam, France, Spain, China and others. To date, the show has raised about $5,200 - all of which will be donated to Action Against Hunger. Action Against Hunger is an international relief and development organization committed to saving the lives of malnourished children and families while seeking long-term, sustainable solutions to hunger. To learn more about Action Against Hunger, please visit www.actionagainsthunger.org.
Don't miss this extravaganza next year - make plans now to attend International Night 2008!!
4
schedule
12:00pm Music Eaton Elementary School
12:15pm Music Garden Gate Elementary School
12:30pm Chinese Dance CPAA Arts Center
12:45pm Tai Chi & Kung Fu Li's Tai Chi & Kung Fu Academy
1:00pm Indian Dance Kupur Folk Dance Academy
1:10pm Violin Solo James Xuan Studio
1:20pm Wushu Ben's Shaolin Kung Fu Studio
1:40pm Children's Dance CPAA Arts Center
1:50pm Variety Show FCSN
2:00pm Indian Dance Expressions
2:15pm Martial Arts U.S. Kung Fu Studio
2:30pm Music Regnart Elementary School
2:45pm Chinese Dance Yao Yong Dance
3:00pm Gu-Zheng Ensemble Chiffon Fu Gu-Zheng Ensemble
3:10pm Indian Dance Uma Chinthalapati
3:20pm Hip Hop Bing Bing Hip Hop
3:30pm Chen's Tai Chi YMCA
3:45pm Indian Dance Megha Shetty

creative firm
ANGRYPORCUPINE*DESIGN
Park City, Utah
creative people
Cheryl Roder-Quill
client
Lunar New Year Unity Parade 07

lunar new year unity parade 07
Lunar New Year Unity Parade

creative firm
BETH SINGER DESIGN LLC
Arlington, Virginia
creative people
Scott Getchonis, Deborah Eckbreth
client
American Israel Public Affairs Committee (AIPAC)

Israel's Search for Peace
KEY EXCERPTS FROM THE HAMAS CHARTER
Key Points
BOLD STEPS: ISRAEL'S DECADES-LONG SEARCH FOR PEACE
AIPAC
2007
BRIEFING BOOK
AIPAC

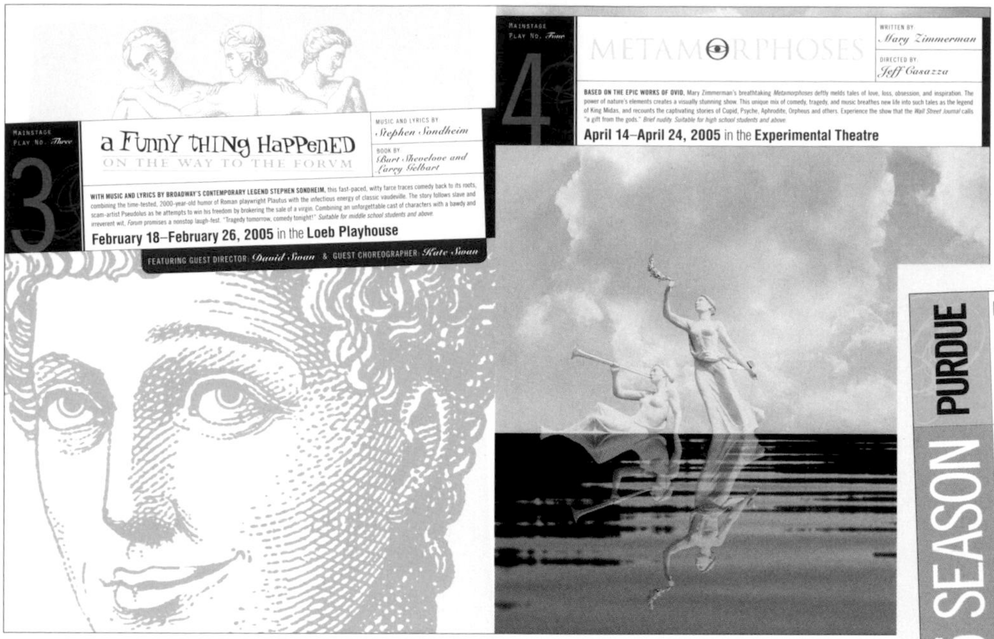

creative firm
DAVIS DESIGN PARTNERS
Holland, Ohio
creative people
Matt Davis, Karen Davis
client
Purdue Theatre, Purdue University

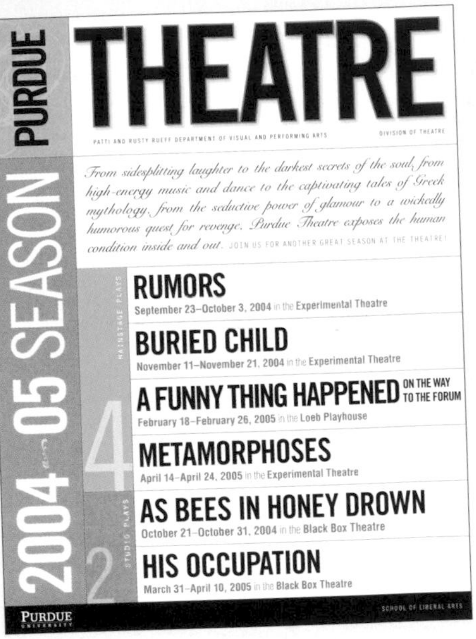

creative firm
TOM FOWLER, INC.
Norwalk, Connecticut
creative people
Brien O'Reilly
client
Xerox

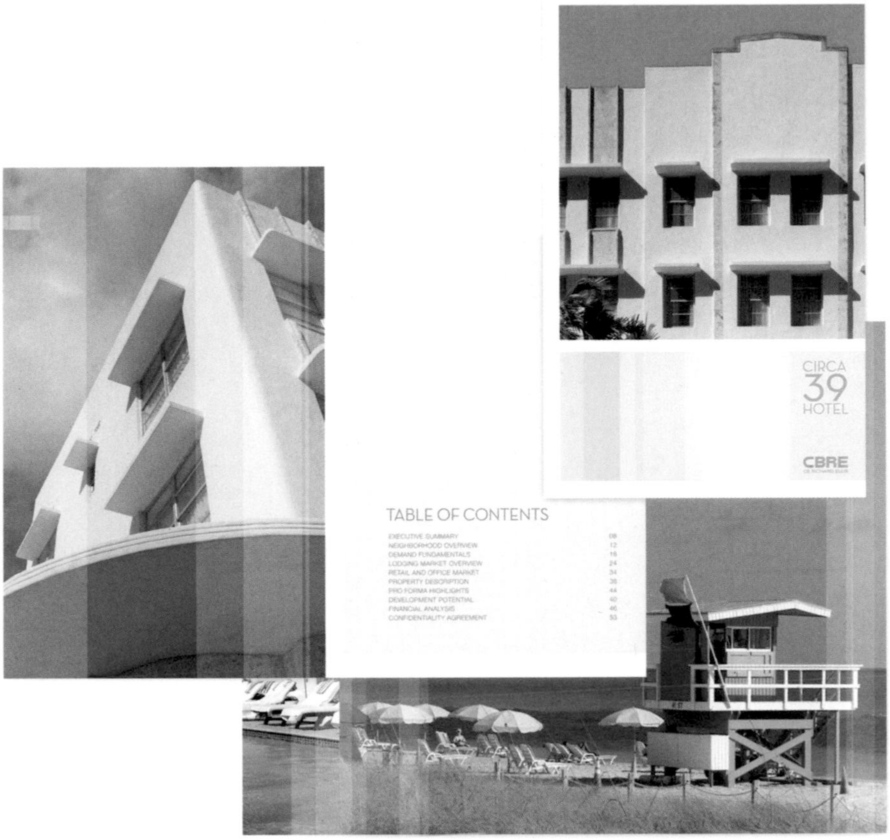

creative firm
3RD EDGE COMMUNICATIONS
Jersey City, New Jersey
creative people
Frankie Gonzalez, Nick Schmitz
client
CB Richard Ellis

creative firm
HORNALL ANDERSON DESIGN
Seattle, Washington
creative people
Jack Anderson, Andrew Wicklund, Belinda Bowling, Peter Anderson, Ensi Mofasser, Peg Johnson, Cindy Chin, Beckon Wyld, Andi Pihl, Javas Lehn, Kathleen Gibson
client
Majestic America Line

Welcome
to the ultimate ride.
Whether you ride professionally or for pleasure, choosing a surface for your arena is an important decision. Attwood Equestrian Surfaces offers a full range of arena surface products, as well as the experience and knowledge to guide you through the process.
The next step in footing.
Attwood Equestrian Surfaces' premier arena footings are all-weather, dust-free and require no watering. Our footing provides a consistent, stable surface with viscoelastic rebound that greatly reduces concussion. Our surfaces are specifically designed and formulated for horse safety and injury reduction.
Water the grass, not the sand.
Attwood Equestrian Surfaces never require watering! And a dust-free arena means a healthier environment — for both you and your horse.

Your provider for premier arena surfaces,
design and construction.
EQUESTRIAN
SURFACES

creative firm
ZERO GRAVITY DESIGN GROUP
Smithtown, New York
creative people
Zero Gravity Design Group
client
Attwood Equestrian Surfaces

Our history.
Attwood Equestrian Surfaces has been building quality riding arenas for over fifteen years. We are innovators of equine surfaces and Equation® is the original dust-free footing. Our background in chemistry, construction, and manufacturing enables us to research and create carefully balanced products that perform consistently in any climate.
We understand the needs of each discipline. Our clients range from nationally recognized competitors to the private discerning rider. We know it's essential to provide meticulously engineered surfaces that benefit the horse and the rider. Using advances in technology and our continuous innovation, we remain at the forefront of footing development.

Our products.
Attwood Equestrian Surfaces is the original manufacturer of polymer-coated footing in the USA. Our footings are engineered from meticulously selected sand, blended with micro poly-fibers and coated with a viscoelastic polymer.
All of our polymer-coated footings are:
• Dust-free
• Need no watering
• Non-tacky
• Low-maintenance
• Consistent
• Tuned for different disciplines
• Manufactured From premium raw materials
• Appropriate for indoor and outdoor applications
• Reduced concussion with viscoelastic rebound
• Freeze-resistant and stable over a wide temperature range
Equation™
The original dust-free footing was developed over 15 years ago and early installations remain dust-free today. Today's Equation incorporates the latest advances in footing technology. Equation is installed to a depth of 4 inches over a carefully graded compacted base.
Terra 2000™
This superb product is the result of Attwood Equestrian Surfaces' continuous investment in research and development. Terra 2000 incorporates premium materials which enhance viscoelastic rebound and minimize concussion.
Pinnacle™
This ultimate riding surface combines the latest in technology and our 15 years of footing experience. Pinnacle is engineered with additional premium materials to bring you the optimum in shear strength, minimal concussion and maximum viscoelastic rebound. Pinnacle is laser graded to a uniform depth of five inches over a carefully graded compacted base.
Ameritrack™
This complete race track system is specifically designed and formulated for horse safety and injury reduction. Ameritrack is engineered with a free-draining base and all-weather cushion. It incorporates a vertical drainage system which eliminates movement of the cushion to the rail and results in a consistent, no bias track. The characteristics of the surface are minimal kick-back, low concussion and optimal viscoelastic rebound.
Minimal harrowing is needed to maintain consistency and track appearance. With Ameritrack, watering for dust control, leveling and re-establishing the grade of the slope are not required.
Our low maintenance footings require only periodic dragging to keep them in excellent condition.
About the surfaces.
Our products are formulated from meticulously selected sand, viscoelastic polymer, and microfibers. Our dust-free footing system does not require watering and, when used indoors, will not freeze. In outdoor applications the water-repellent nature of the polymer ensures fast drainage. It won't "mix" with water so the arena can be used even after heavy rainfall, unlike conventional footings which can become sloppy and muddy with excess moisture.
In comparison to traditional arenas, maintenance is significantly reduced. To maintain the arena involves only light harrowing and manure removal.

creative firm
TOM FOWLER, INC.
Norwalk, Connecticut
creative people
Brien O'Reilly
client
Toys R Us

creative firm
WESTGROUP CREATIVE
New York, New York
creative people
Chip Tolaney
client
New Dance Group

creative firm
HORNALL ANDERSON DESIGN
Seattle, Washington
creative people
John Anicker, Andrew Wicklund, Leo Raymundo, Holly Craven
client
Schnitzer Northwest

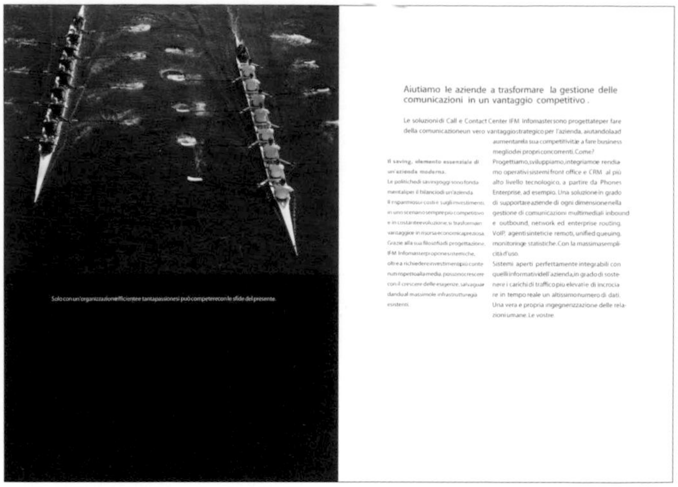

creative firm
TANGRAM STRATEGIC DESIGN
Novara, Italy
creative people
Enrico Sempi, Antonella Trevisan
client
IFM Infomaster

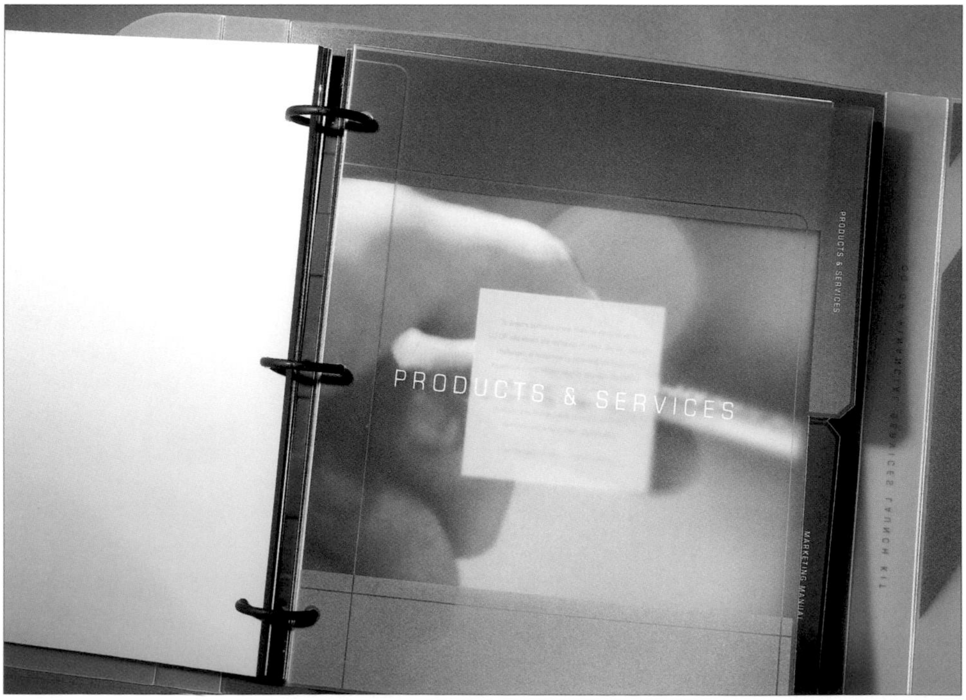

creative firm
EVENSON DESIGN GROUP
Culver City, California
creative people
Mark Sojka
client
CO-OP Financial Services

creative firm
ANNE LEHMAN DESIGN
Cranberry Township, Pennsylvania
creative people
Anne Lehman
client
In-Vision Studio

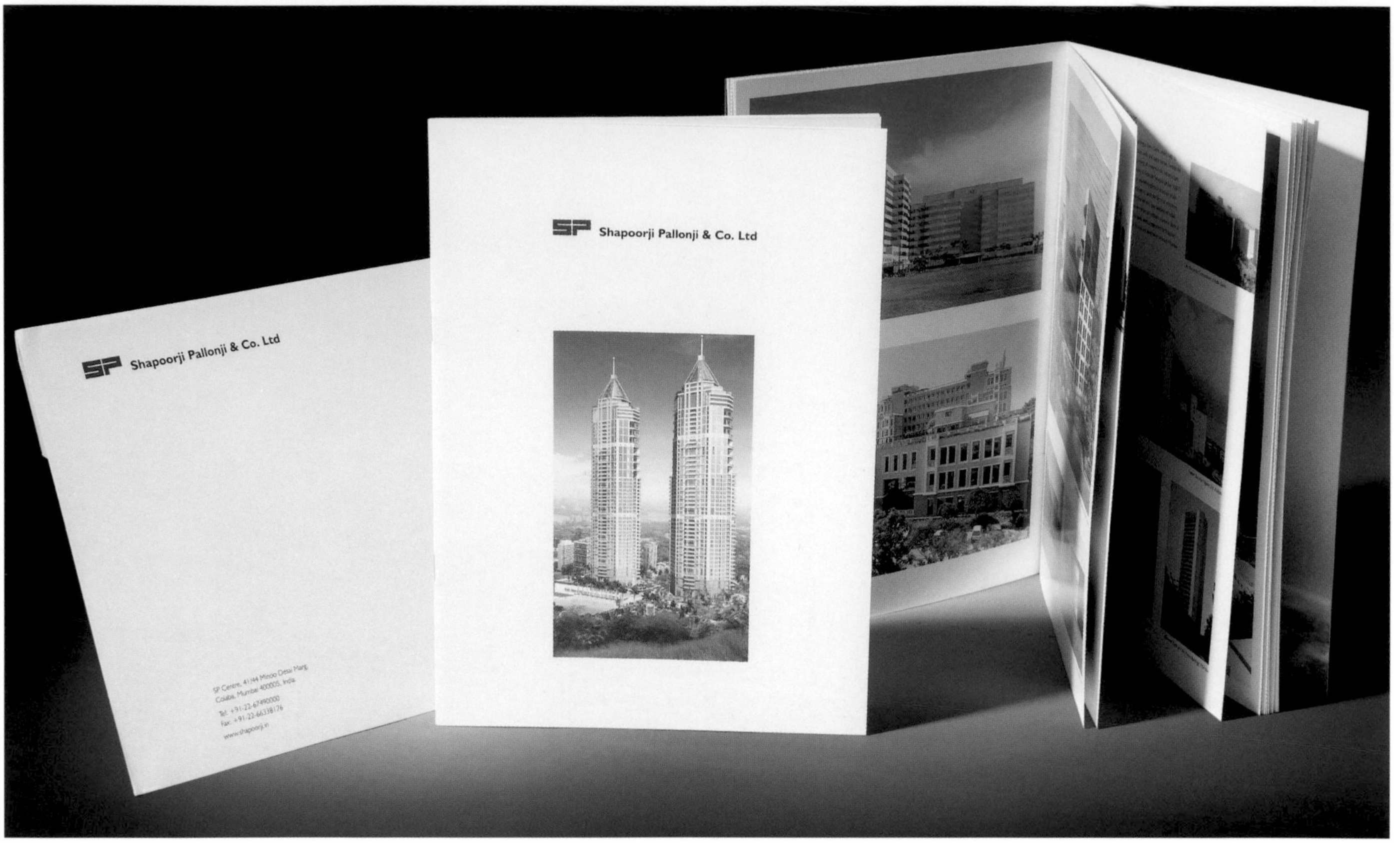

creative firm
DOIT ADVERTISING
Mumbai, India
creative people
Tushar Chikodikar, Rajesh Mewada, Nilesh Parab
client
Shapoorji Pallonji & Co., Ltd.

creative firm
HORNALL ANDERSON DESIGN
Seattle, Washington
creative people
John Anicker, Andrew Wicklund, Leo Raymundo, Yuri Shvets
client
Schnitzer Northwest

creative firm
BELYEA
Seattle, Washington
creative people
Ron Lars Hansen
client
Weyerhaeuser

creative firm
WESTGROUP CREATIVE
New York, New York
creative people
Chip Tolaney
client
Fred Johnson

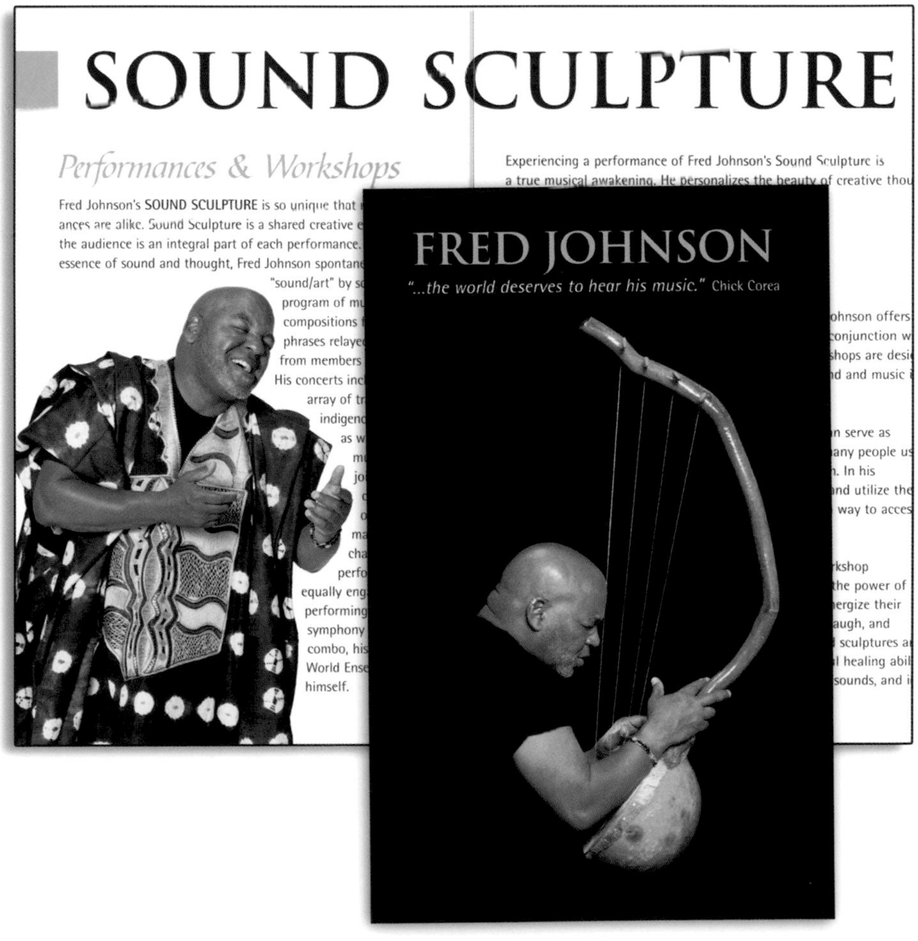

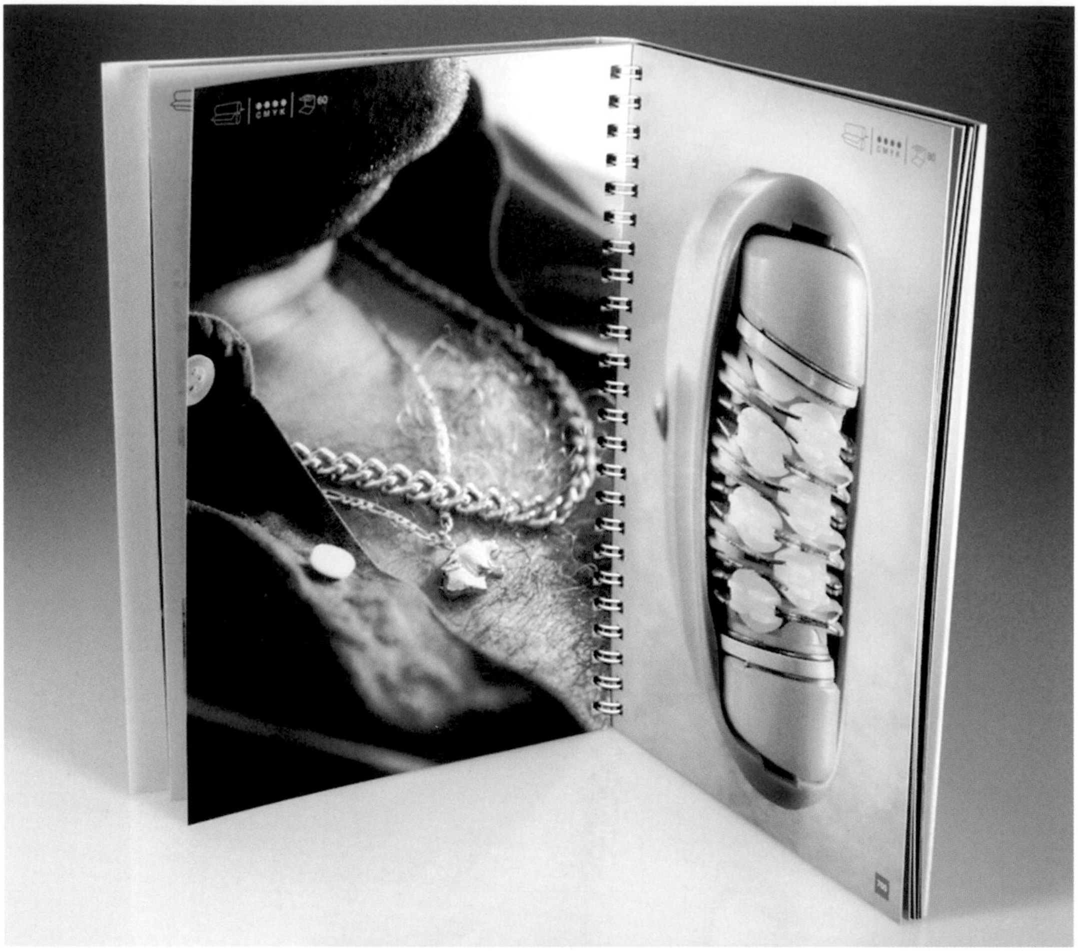

creative firm
Q
Wiesbaden, Germany
creative people
Matthias Frey, Laurenz Nielbock
client
m-real Zanders

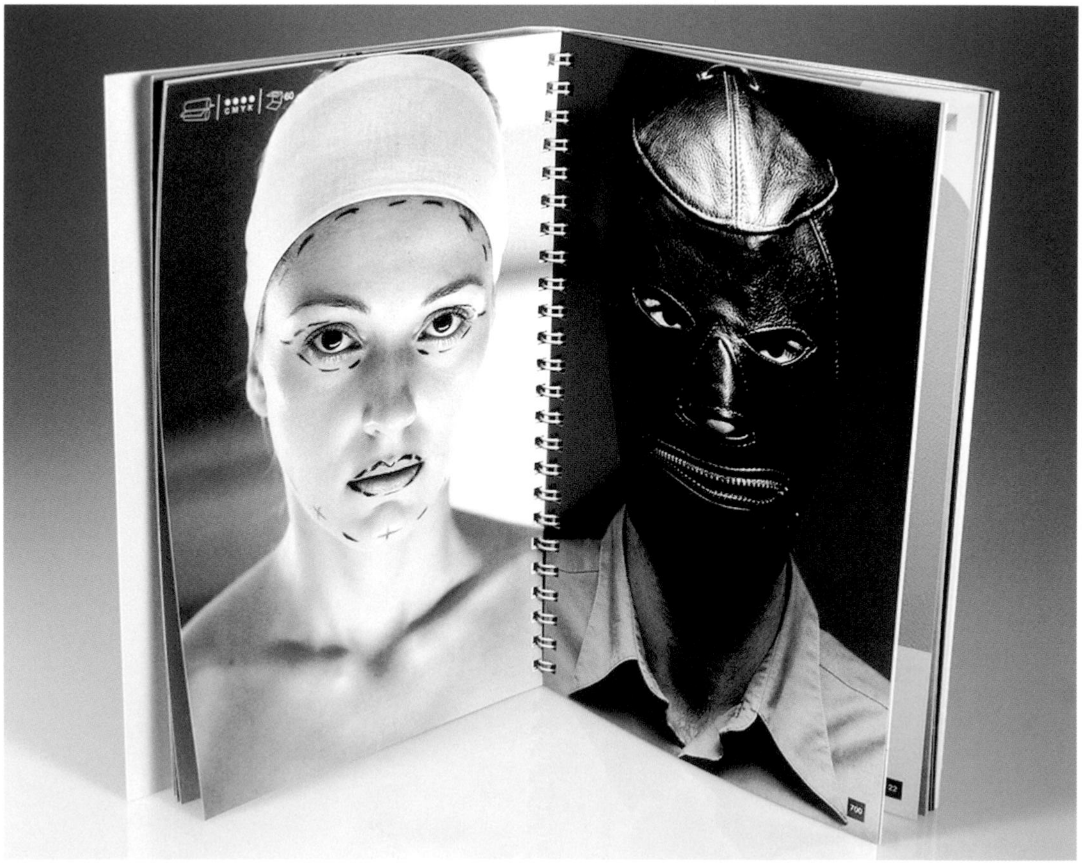

creative firm
Q
Wiesbaden, Germany
creative people
Matthias Frey
client
Anja Gockel London

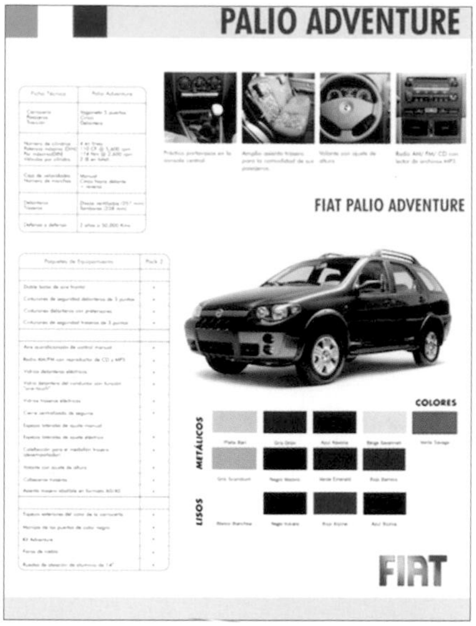

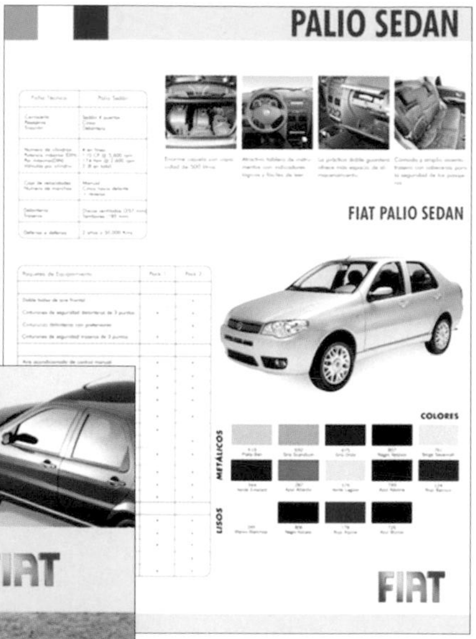

creative firm
EUPHORIANET
Monterrey, Mexico
creative people
Mabel Morales, Laura Pérez
client
Fiat Mexico

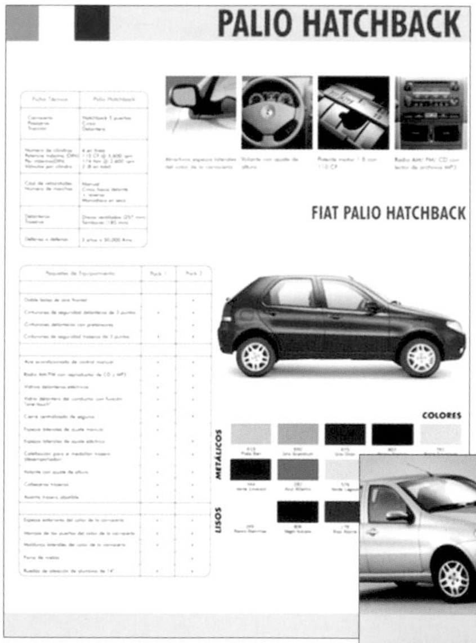

creative firm
BRAIN MAGNET
St. Louis Park, Minnesota
creative people
David Maloney
client
M. Lavine Design Workshop

creative firm
EVENSON DESIGN GROUP
Culver City, California
creative people
Melanie Usas
client
Yokohama Tires

creative firm
DOIT ADVERTISING
Mumbai, India
creative people
Tushar Chikodikar, Nilesh Parab
client
Hindustan Construction Co. Ltd.

creative firm
DAVIS DESIGN PARTNERS
Holland, Ohio
creative people
Matt Davis, Karen Davis
client
University School (US)

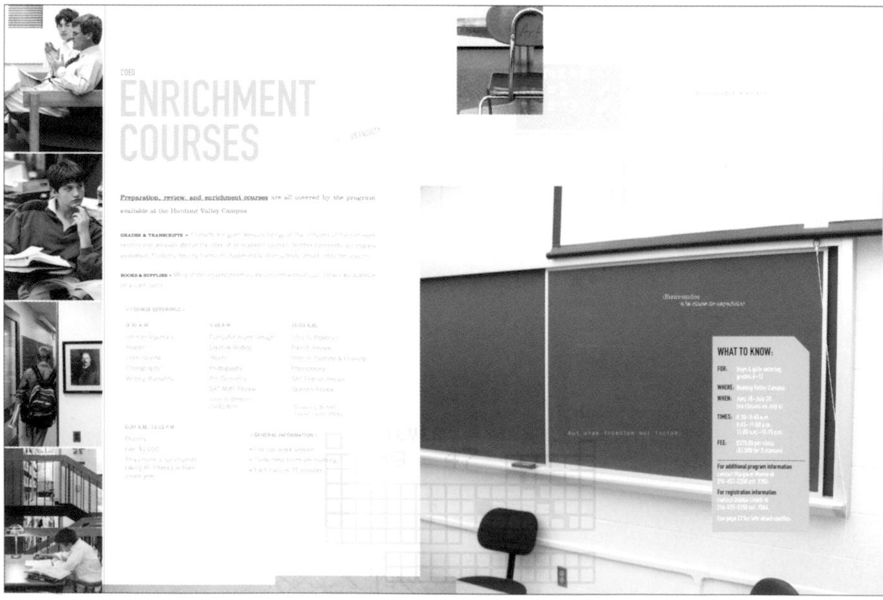

creative firm
WESTGROUP CREATIVE
New York, New York
creative people
Chip Tolaney
client
Mahwish & Chaimera

creative firm
CREATIVE/THE COCA-COLA COMPANY
Atlanta, Georgia
creative people
Dawn Shelton
client
Coca-Cola North America Supply Chain

creative firm
DOIT ADVERTISING
Mumbai, India
creative people
Nilesh Parab
client
Business Link Automation Ltd.

creative firm
FRANKE+FIORELLA
Minneapolis, Minnesota
creative people
Craig Franke, Leslie McDougall, Shawn Nielsen
client
Rock-Tenn Paperboard

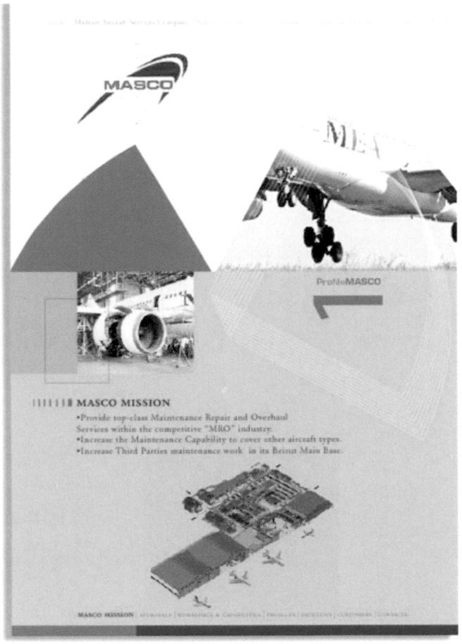

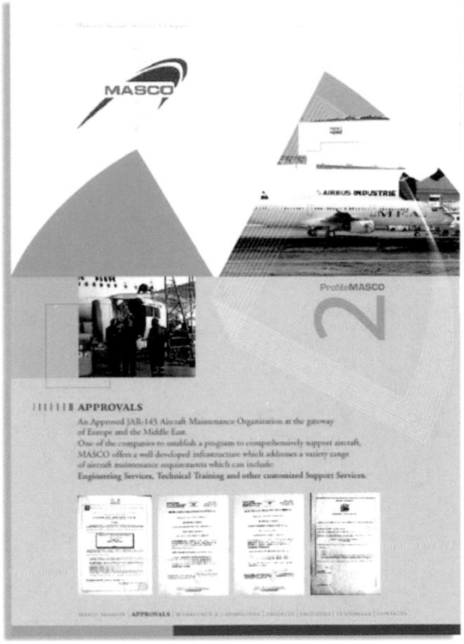

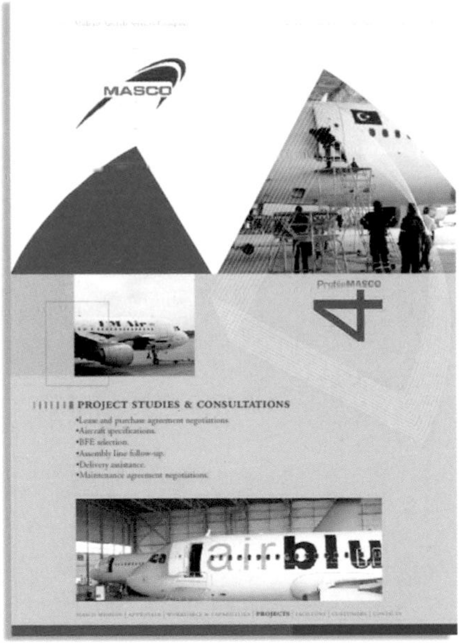

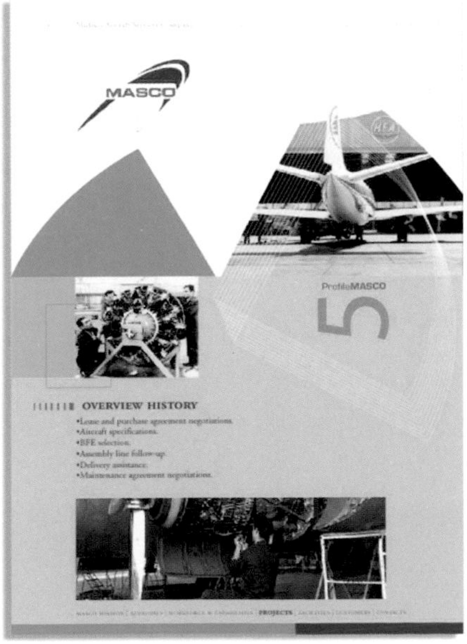

creative firm
GO GRAPHIC
Beirut, Lebanon
creative people
Maria Assi, Mina Abdul Hussein
client
MASCO, Middle East Airlines

PRESERVE
the PAST
PROVIDE
for the FUTURE

PLANNED GIFT:
Bequest
LIFE INCOME ARRANGEMENTS:
Charitable Gift Annuity
Charitable Remainder Trust
Beneficiary Designations
Life Insurance
Charitable Lead Trust
Retained Life Estate
Tower Living Legacy Endowment
BEQUEST
A Bequest is a statement in your will or revocable living trust, which passes a portion, or all of your estate to a charitable organization.
Typically, charitable bequests come from accumulated assets rather than from current income, allowing most donors to make far larger charitable gifts through their will or revocable living trust, than by making an outright gift during their lifetime.
Bequests are revocable during your lifetime, thus providing a hedge against unforeseen events.
You can give a specified dollar amount, specific assets, retirement account assets, a residuary bequest in which US receives all or a percentage of the remainder of your estate, or a contingent bequest in which US becomes the beneficiary only if the named beneficiary is unable to accept the bequest.
Henry W. Hoover '29 left a bequest, which will allow US to continue to educate boys in the tradition of responsibility, loyalty and consideration to be tomorrow's leaders.

creative firm
DAVIS DESIGN PARTNERS
Holland, Ohio
creative people
Matt Davis, Karen Davis
client
University School (US)

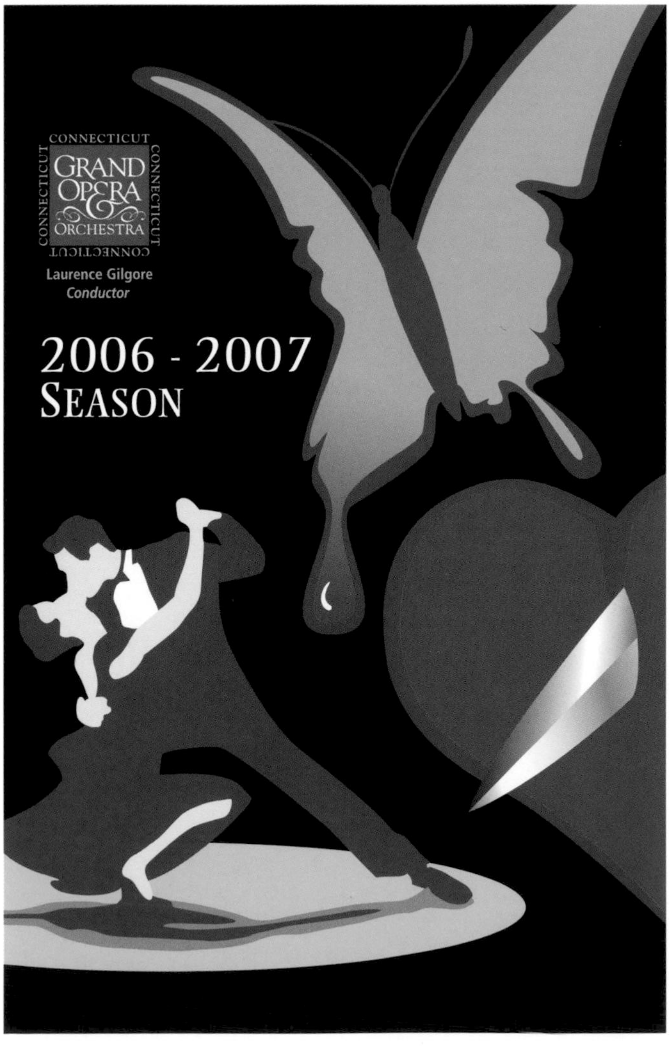
CONNECTICUT
GRAND OPERA & ORCHESTRA
Laurence Gilgore
Conductor
2006 - 2007
SEASON

creative firm
TOM FOWLER, INC.
Norwalk, Connecticut
creative people
Elizabeth P. Ball, Phillip Doherty
client
The Connecticut Grand Opera & Orchestra

GIS. Geographic Information System.
ifm
INFOMASTER
Localizzare le risorse a propria disposizione è diventato facile.
Gestione reti tecnologiche delle Utility
1
Fleet Management
2
Geo CRM
Geo Call Center
4
Sportello Turistico
5

creative firm
TANGRAM STRATEGIC DESIGN
Novara, Italy
creative people
Enrico Sempi, Antonella Trevisan, Andrea Sempi
client
IFM Infomaster

share
get
get
learn
learn
T · ·Mobile·
Introducing the
T-Mobile Brand Portal
Aa
Learn it. Get it. Share it.

creative firm
HORNALL ANDERSON DESIGN
Seattle, Washington
creative people
Mark Popich, Jon Graeff, Rachel Lancaster, Peg Johnson, Danial Crookston
client
T-Mobile

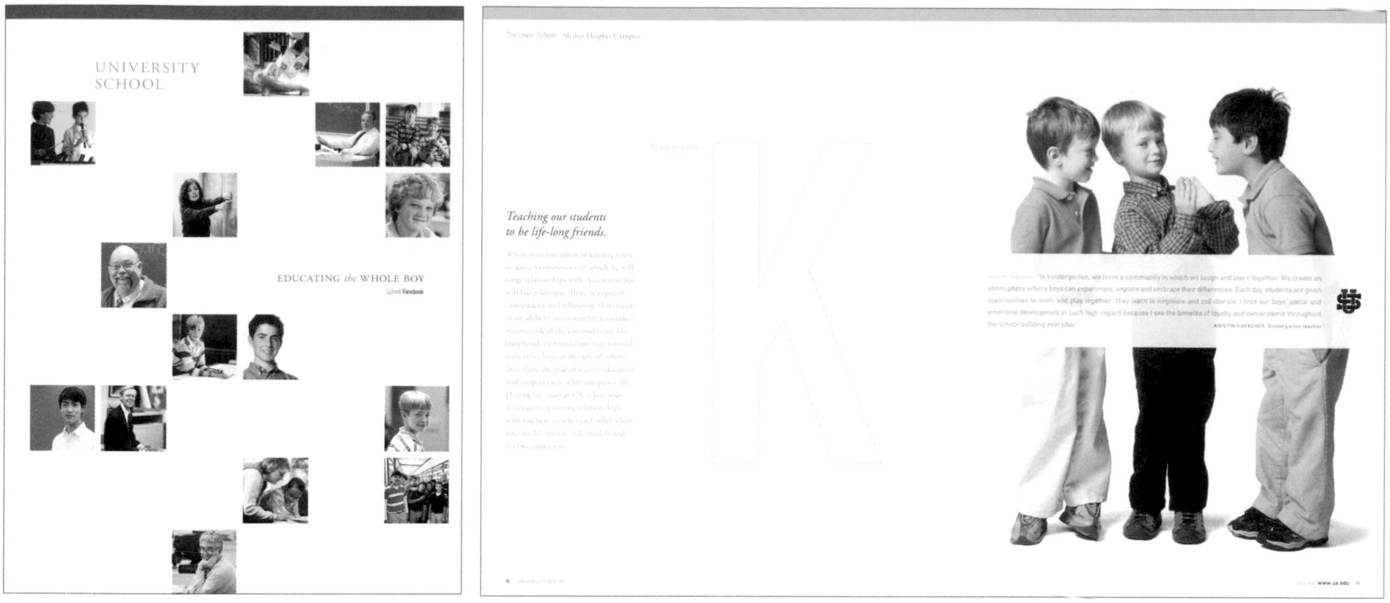

creative firm
DAVIS DESIGN PARTNERS
Holland, Ohio
creative people
Matt Davis, Karen Davis
client
University School (US)

creative firm
HORNALL ANDERSON DESIGN
Seattle, Washington
creative people
Jack Anderson, Michael Connors,
Leo Raymundo, Ensi Mofasser
client
Jobster

creative firm
GO GRAPHIC
Beirut, Lebanon
creative people
Maria Assi
client
InterContinental Phoenicia

creative firm
FRANKE+FIORELLA
Minneapolis, Minnesota
creative people
Craig Franke, Todd Monge
client
3M Human Resources

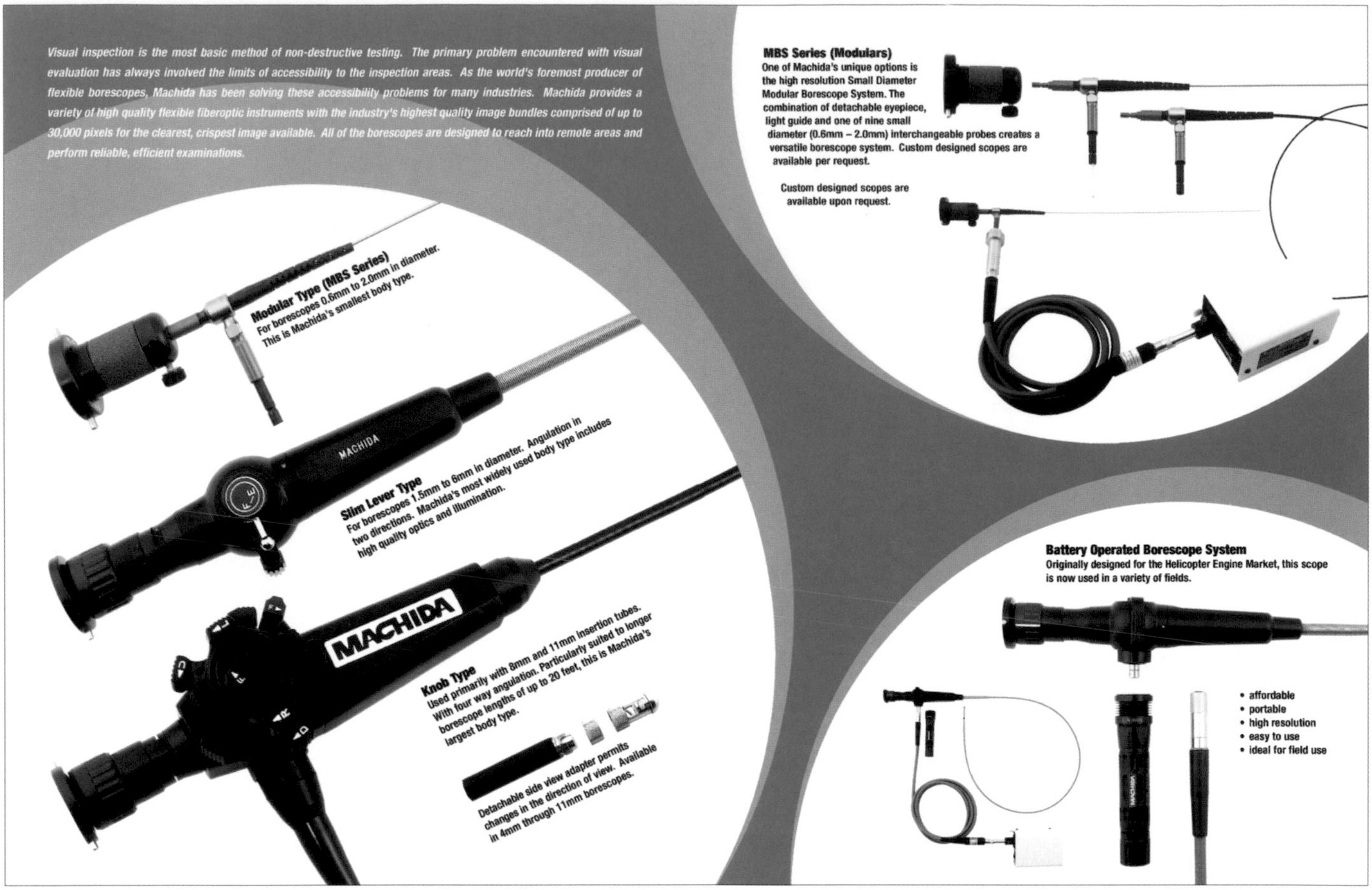
Visual inspection is the most basic method of non-destructive testing. The primary problem encountered with visual evaluation has always involved the limits of accessibility to the inspection areas. As the world's foremost producer of flexible borescopes, Machida has been solving these accessibility problems for many industries. Machida provides a variety of high quality flexible fiberoptic instruments with the industry's highest quality image bundles comprised of up to 30,000 pixels for the clearest, crispest image available. All of the borescopes are designed to reach into remote areas and perform reliable, efficient examinations.
Modular Type (MBS Series)
For borescopes 0.6mm to 2.0mm in diameter. This is Machida's smallest body type.
MACHIDA
Slim Lever Type
For borescopes 1.5mm to 6mm in diameter. Angulation in two directions. Machida's most widely used body type includes high quality optics and illumination.
MACHIDA
Knob Type
Used primarily with 8mm and 11mm insertion tubes. With four way angulation. Particularly suited to longer borescope lengths of up to 20 feet, this is Machida's largest body type.
Detachable side view adapter permits changes in the direction of view. Available in 4mm through 11mm borescopes.
MBS Series (Modulars)
One of Machida's unique options is the high resolution Small Diameter Modular Borescope System. The combination of detachable eyepiece, light guide and one of nine small diameter (0.6mm – 2.0mm) interchangeable probes creates a versatile borescope system. Custom designed scopes are available per request.
Custom designed scopes are available upon request.
Battery Operated Borescope System
Originally designed for the Helicopter Engine Market, this scope is now used in a variety of fields.
• affordable
• portable
• high resolution
• easy to use
• ideal for field use

creative firm
GRAPHIC ADVANCE
Palisades Park, New Jersey
creative people
Aviad Stark
client
Machida Borescopes

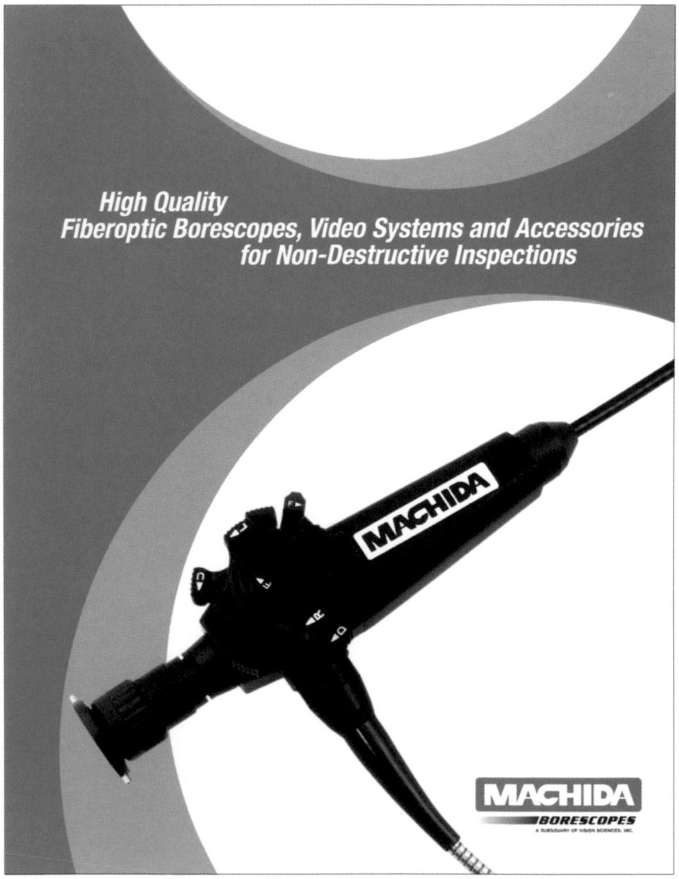
High Quality
Fiberoptic Borescopes, Video Systems and Accessories
for Non-Destructive Inspections
MACHIDA
MACHIDA
BORESCOPES

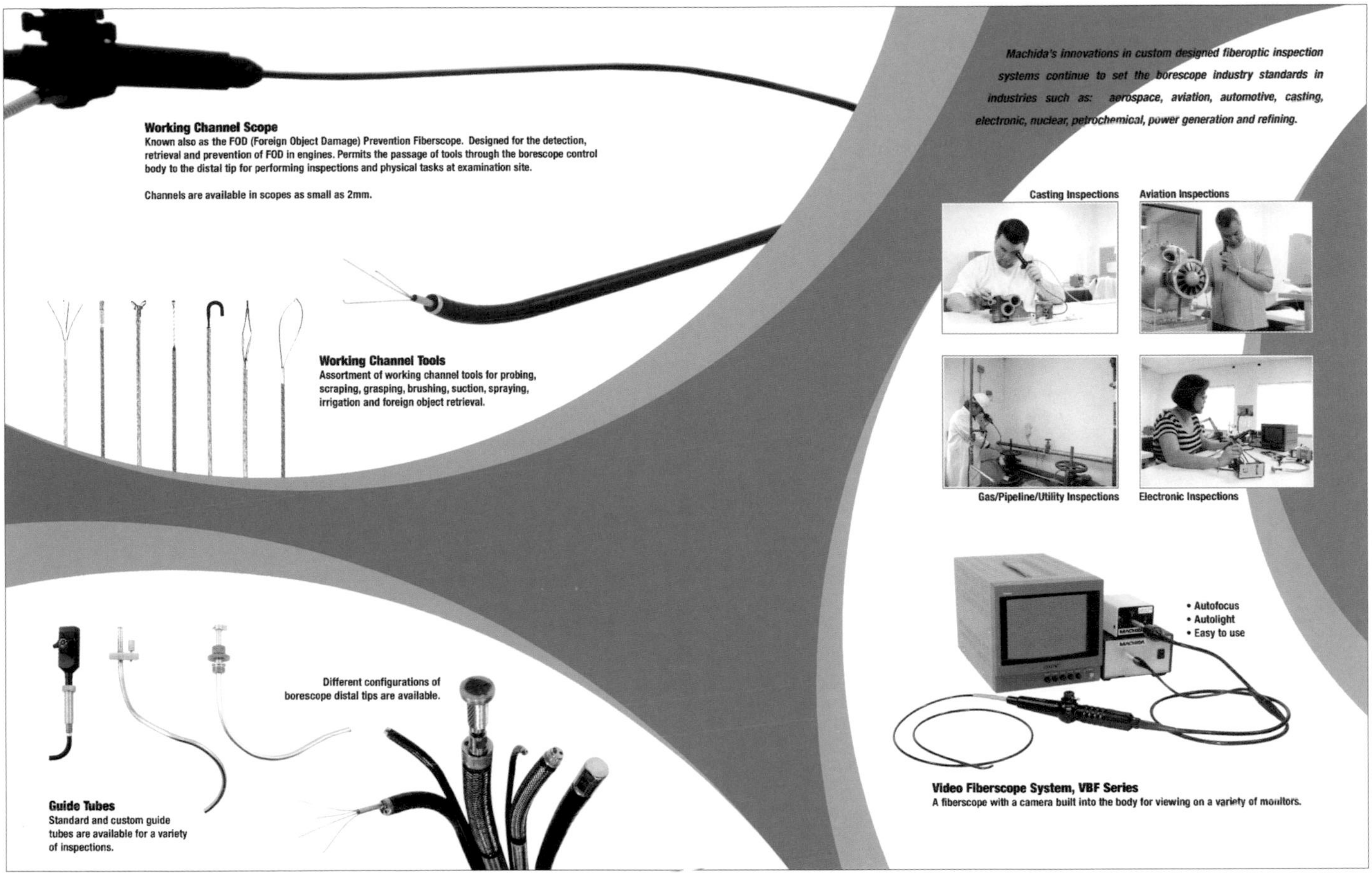

Machida's innovations in custom designed fiberoptic inspection systems continue to set the borescope industry standards in industries such as: aerospace, aviation, automotive, casting, electronic, nuclear, petrochemical, power generation and refining.

Working Channel Scope
Known also as the FOD (Foreign Object Damage) Prevention Fiberscope. Designed for the detection, retrieval and prevention of FOD in engines. Permits the passage of tools through the borescope control body to the distal tip for performing inspections and physical tasks at examination site.

Channels are available in scopes as small as 2mm.

Working Channel Tools
Assortment of working channel tools for probing, scraping, grasping, brushing, suction, spraying, irrigation and foreign object retrieval.

Casting Inspections

Aviation Inspections

Gas/Pipeline/Utility Inspections

Electronic Inspections

Different configurations of borescope distal tips are available.

Guide Tubes
Standard and custom guide tubes are available for a variety of inspections.

- Autofocus
- Autolight
- Easy to use

Video Fiberscope System, VBF Series
A fiberscope with a camera built into the body for viewing on a variety of monitors.

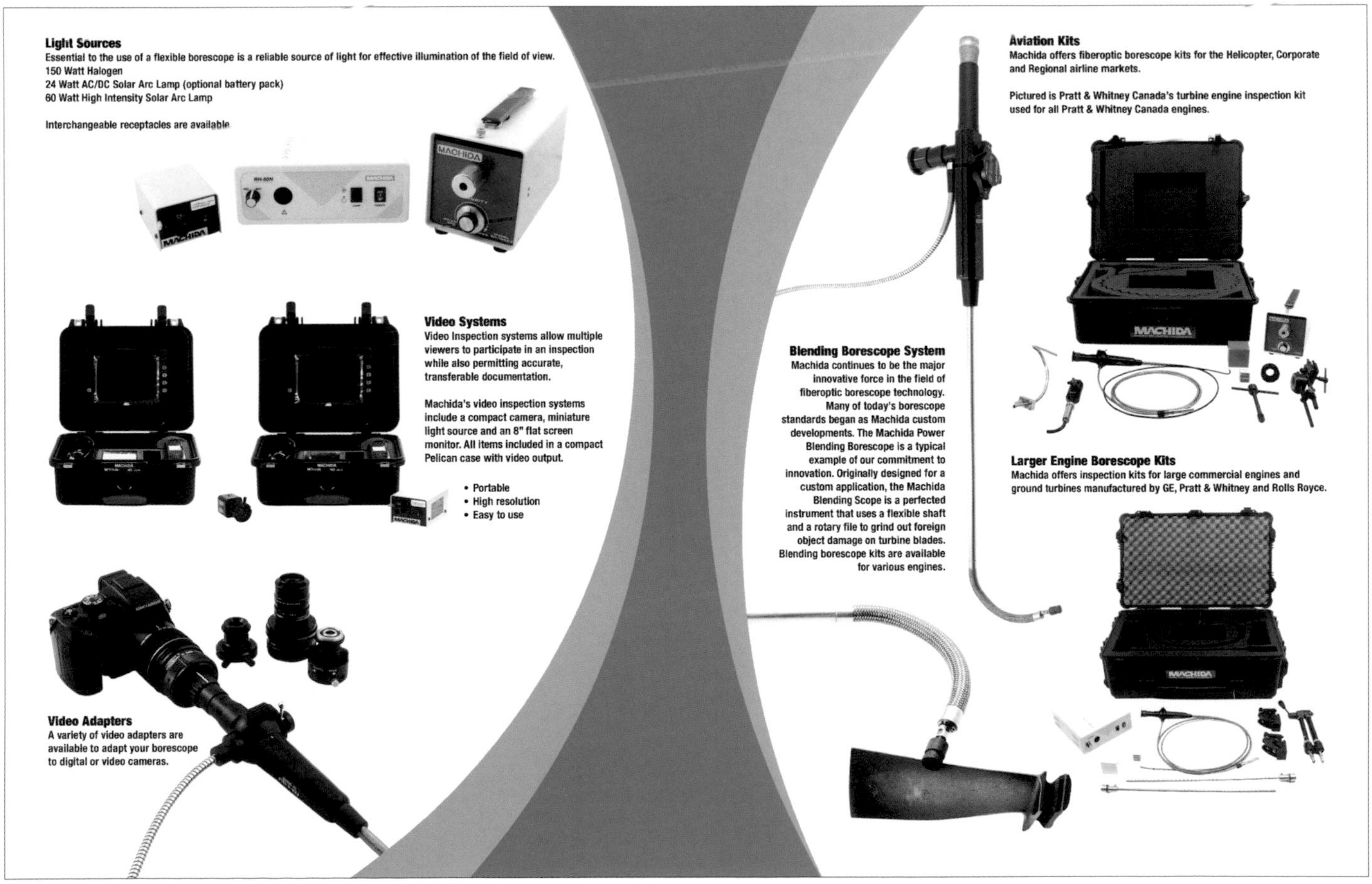

Light Sources
Essential to the use of a flexible borescope is a reliable source of light for effective illumination of the field of view.
150 Watt Halogen
24 Watt AC/DC Solar Arc Lamp (optional battery pack)
60 Watt High Intensity Solar Arc Lamp

Interchangeable receptacles are available.

Video Systems
Video Inspection systems allow multiple viewers to participate in an inspection while also permitting accurate, transferable documentation.

Machida's video inspection systems include a compact camera, miniature light source and an 8" flat screen monitor. All items included in a compact Pelican case with video output.

- Portable
- High resolution
- Easy to use

Video Adapters
A variety of video adapters are available to adapt your borescope to digital or video cameras.

Blending Borescope System
Machida continues to be the major innovative force in the field of fiberoptic borescope technology. Many of today's borescope standards began as Machida custom developments. The Machida Power Blending Borescope is a typical example of our commitment to innovation. Originally designed for a custom application, the Machida Blending Scope is a perfected instrument that uses a flexible shaft and a rotary file to grind out foreign object damage on turbine blades. Blending borescope kits are available for various engines.

Aviation Kits
Machida offers fiberoptic borescope kits for the Helicopter, Corporate and Regional airline markets.

Pictured is Pratt & Whitney Canada's turbine engine inspection kit used for all Pratt & Whitney Canada engines.

Larger Engine Borescope Kits
Machida offers inspection kits for large commercial engines and ground turbines manufactured by GE, Pratt & Whitney and Rolls Royce.

creative firm
SAYLES GRAPHIC DESIGN
Des Moines, Iowa
creative people
John Sayles
client
P.E.O. Sisterhood

creative firm
MAMORDESIGN
Tehran, Iran
creative people
Maliheh Ghajargar
client
Veresk2

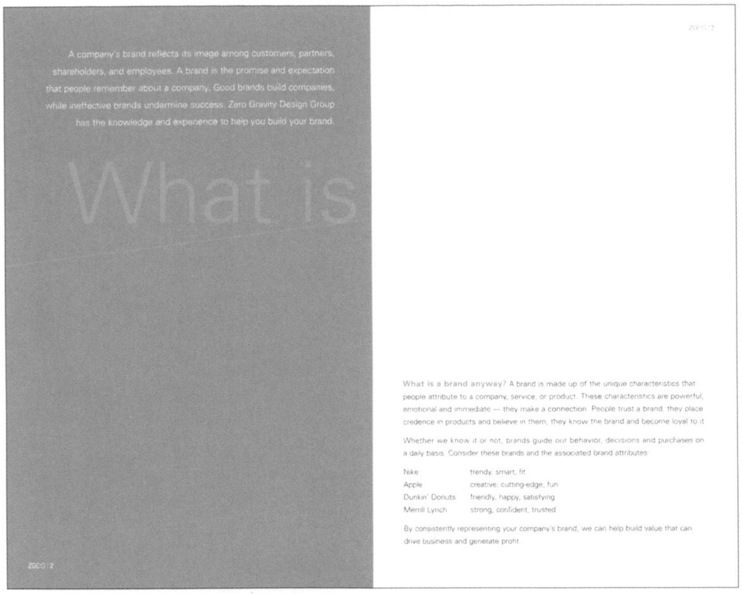

creative firm
ZERO GRAVITY DESIGN GROUP
Smithtown, New York
creative people
Zero Gravity Design Group
client
Zero Gravity Design Group

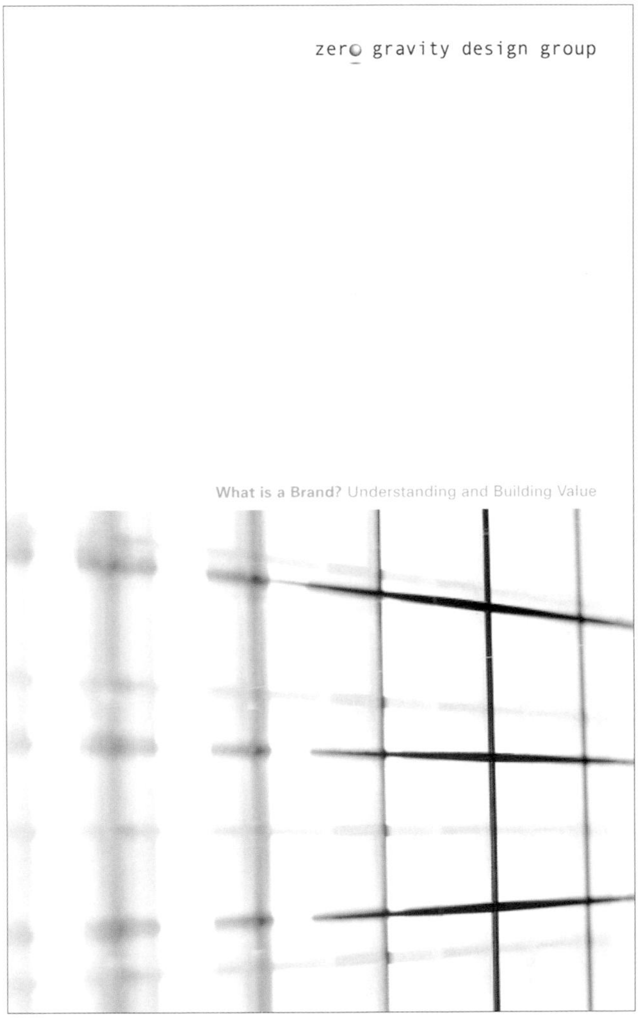

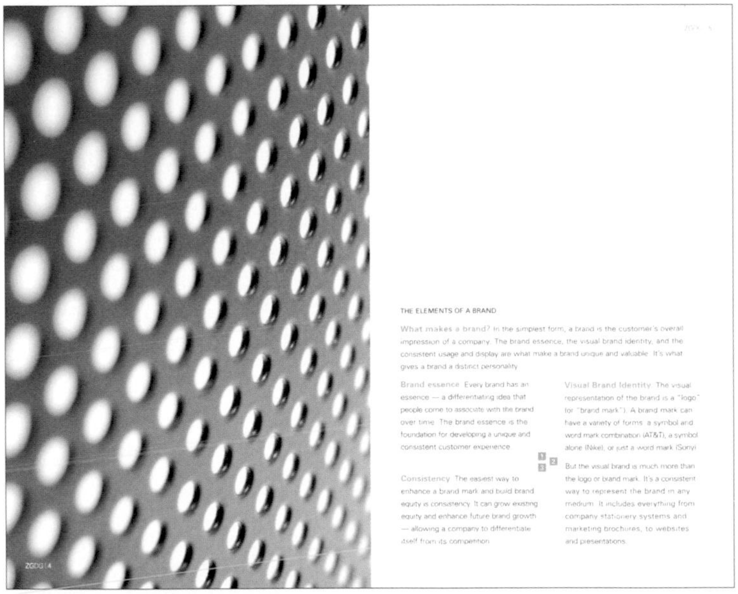

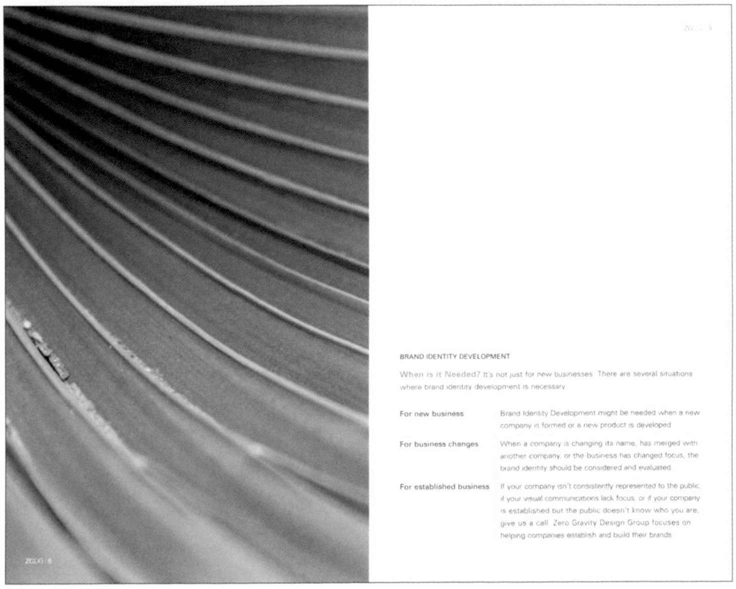

creative firm
HORNALL ANDERSON DESIGN
Seattle, Washington
creative people
Jack Anderson, James Tee, Andrew Wicklund, Elmer dela Cruz, Holly Craven, Jay Hilburn, Hayden Schoen, Belinda Bowling, Yuri Shvets, Michael Connors, Larry Anderson, Chris Freed, Erin McFarlan
client
Weyerhaeuser Corporation

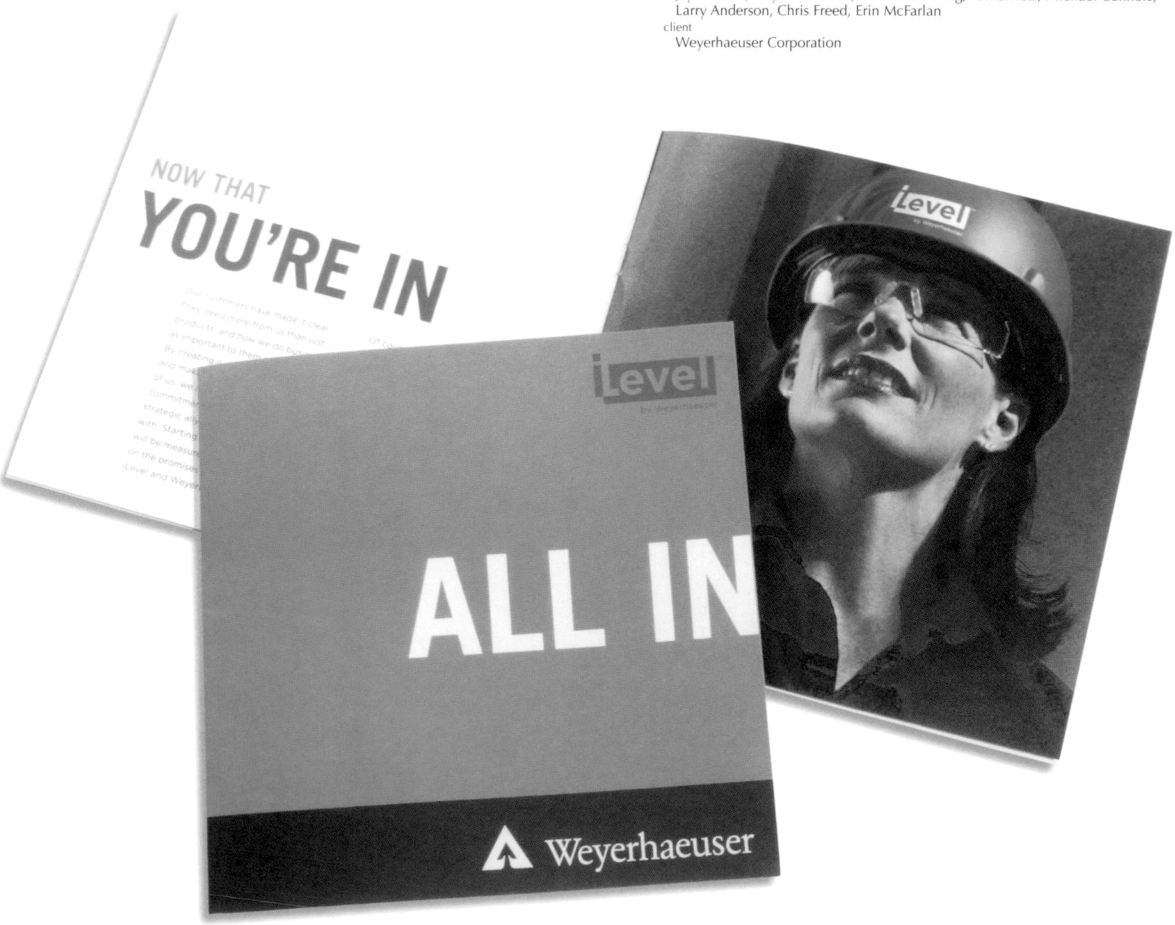

iLevel
by Weyerhaeuser
DEMANDED BY CUSTOMERS. DELIVERED BY
WEYERHAEUSER
ONE NEW
PROMISE
STARTING TODAY
WE ARE
Weyerhaeuser

USE YOUR
TOOLS
STARTING
NOW
Weyerhaeuser

WELCOME
TO MERRILL GARDENS
MERRILL GARDENS
A one of a kind retirement community
A ONE OF A KIND RETIREMENT COMMUNITY
WELCOME TO MERRILL GARDENS, A ONE OF A KIND RETIREMENT COMMUNITY. IT'S A PLACE WHERE YOU ARE ABSOLUTELY FREE TO BE YOURSELF. YOU CAN ENJOY ALL THE PLEASURES OF INDEPENDENT LIVING, OR THE QUIET COMFORTS OF ASSISTED LIVING CARE. AT MERRILL GARDENS, THE DOOR IS ALWAYS OPEN FOR CREATING A LIFESTYLE THAT'S RICH, REWARDING AND ONE OF A KIND. JUST LIKE YOU.
THE FAMILY THAT OWNS AND OPERATES MERRILL GARDENS HAS BEEN IN BUSINESS FOR MORE THAN 100 YEARS. WE ARE ABSOLUTELY DEDICATED TO PROVIDING A QUALITY LIVING ENVIRONMENT THAT'S MINDFUL OF YOUR SECURITY AND RESPECTFUL OF YOUR NEEDS.
ONLY at MERRILL GARDENS
ANYTIME DINING
ACTIVE LIVING
CONNECTIONS
PERSONALIZED CARE
60-DAY GUARANTEE
The Merrill Gardens Guarantee

creative firm
HIGGINS DESIGN
Shoreline, Washington
creative people
Jane Higgins, Sam Day
client
Merrill Gardens

creative firm
Q
Wiesbaden, Germany
creative people
Matthias Frey, Laurenz Nielbock
client
m-real Zanders

old ways of life
grand exhibition opening > 22. nov > historic museum of mankind > berlin
exhibition catalog

creative firm
HELENA SEO DESIGN
Sunnyvale, California
creative people
Helena Seo
client
Ineke, LLC

creative firm
IF MARKETING
Chicago, Illinois
creative people
Tracy Drumm
client
IF Marketing

creative firm
THE IMAGINATION COMPANY
Bethel, Vermont
creative people
Kristen Smith, Jim Giberti, John Turner
client
Rock of Ages Corporation

creative firm
STAN GELLMAN GRAPHIC DESIGN, INC.
St. Louis, Missouri
creative people
Jill Frantti, Barry Tilson
client
Eureka College

creative firm
GRAPHIC ADVANCE
Palisades Park, New Jersey
creative people
Aviad Stark
client
MyHome

VV
VSTOPANJEVRAČANJE
Ne VSTOPANJE
ampak
vračanje
Prof. dr. Janez Bogataj
Filozofska fakulteta
Predsednik Strokovne komisije OZS
Letošnja, že 15. razstava domačih in umetnostnih obrti v Slovenj Gradcu in Ljubljani sovpada s pomembnim dogodkom v življenju sodobne in samostojne Republike Slovenije, t.j. z vstopom v Evropsko unijo. Torej v druščino držav, med katerimi ni več admistrativnih meja, ostajajo pa razlike v kulturah in življenjskih slogih posameznih območij in regij.

15
2004
DOMAČIH IN UMETNOSTNIH OBRTI
Slovenj Gradec
16.4.–2.5.2004
10.–30.5.2004
Ljubljana

creative firm
KROG
Ljubljana, Slovenia
creative people
Edi Berk, Boris Gaberšcik
client
Obrna zbornica Slovenije, Ljubljana

KK
KRASKAMEN
KAMEN
Kraški.
ponos in
zanos
Miroslav Klun
Župan Občine Sežana
Predsednik Obrtne zbornice Slovenije
Kras je zaradi svojih značilnosti krasna posebnost. In na te značilnosti smo Kraševci prav ljubosumno ponosni, zato je tudi naša zaljubljenost v kamen in njegove krasote nekaj čisto posebnega. Je več kot le značilnost - je tradicija, je ljubezen, je kultura in je definitivno umetnost.

creative firm
TANGRAM STRATEGIC DESIGN
Novara, Italy
creative people
Enrico Sempi, Anna Grimaldi, Annika Schorstein
client
Prénatal

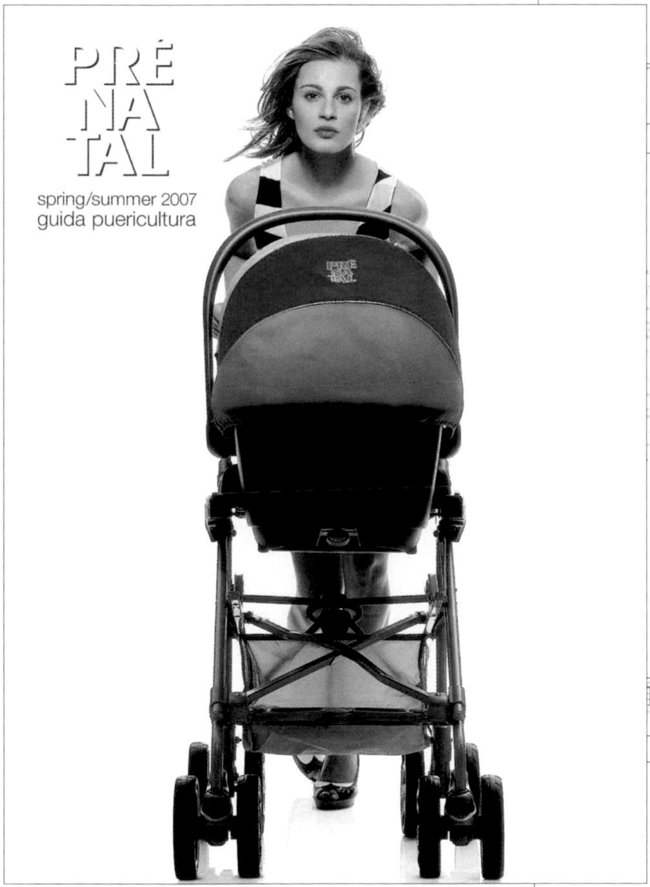

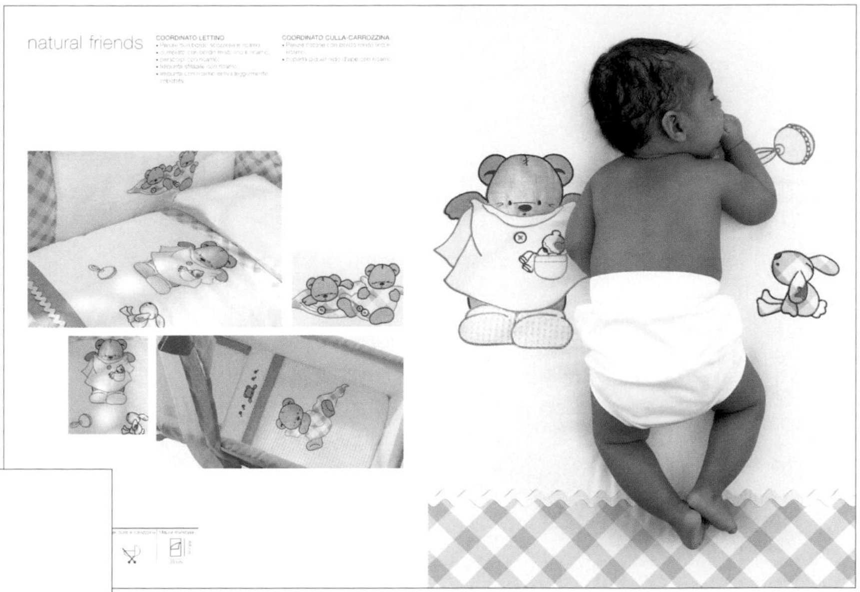

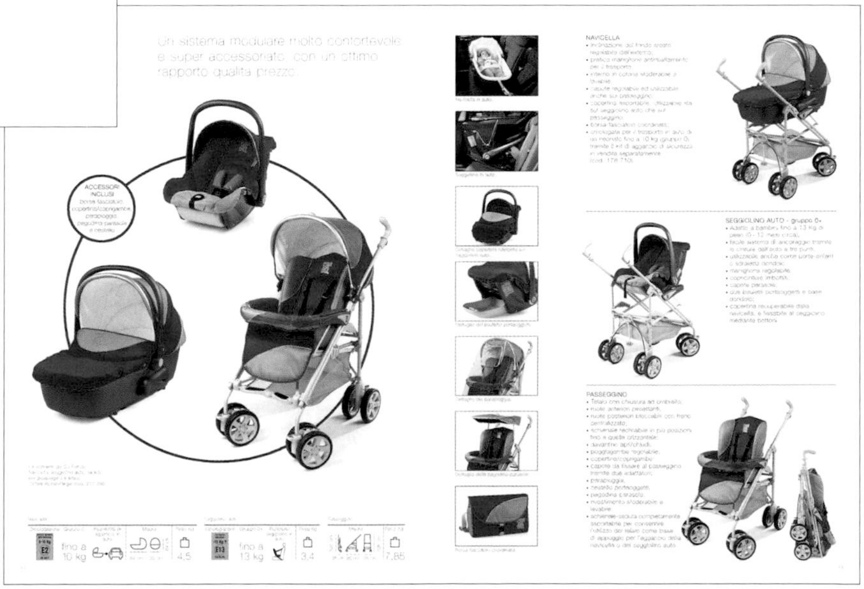

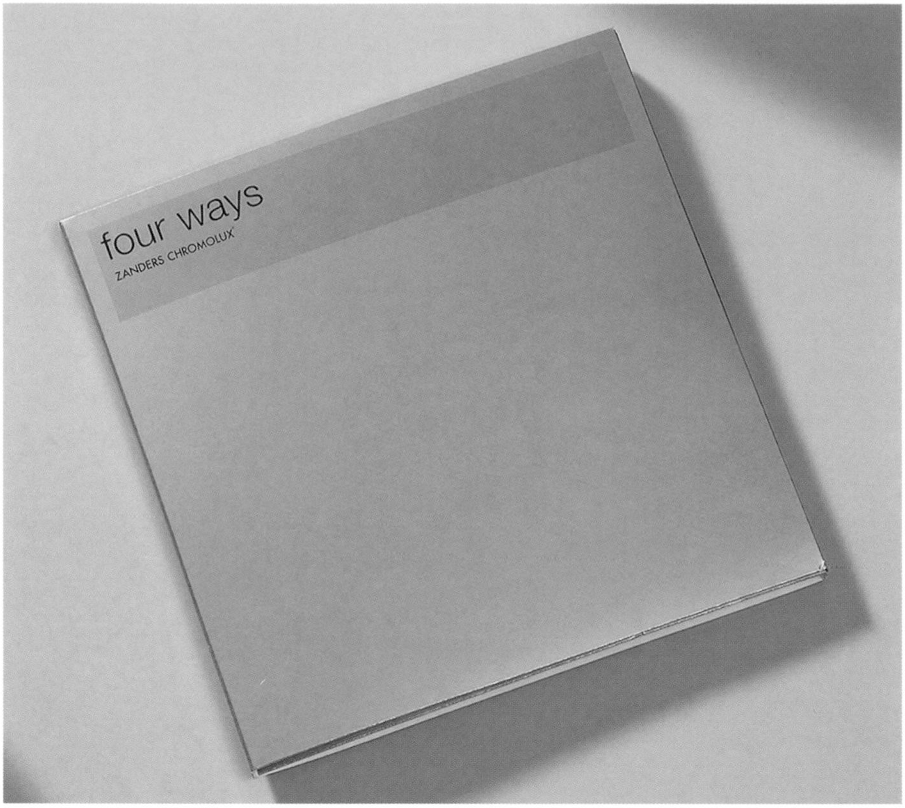

creative firm
Q
Wiesbaden, Germany
creative people
Matthias Frey, Ute Dersch, Laurenz Nielbock
client
m-real Zanders

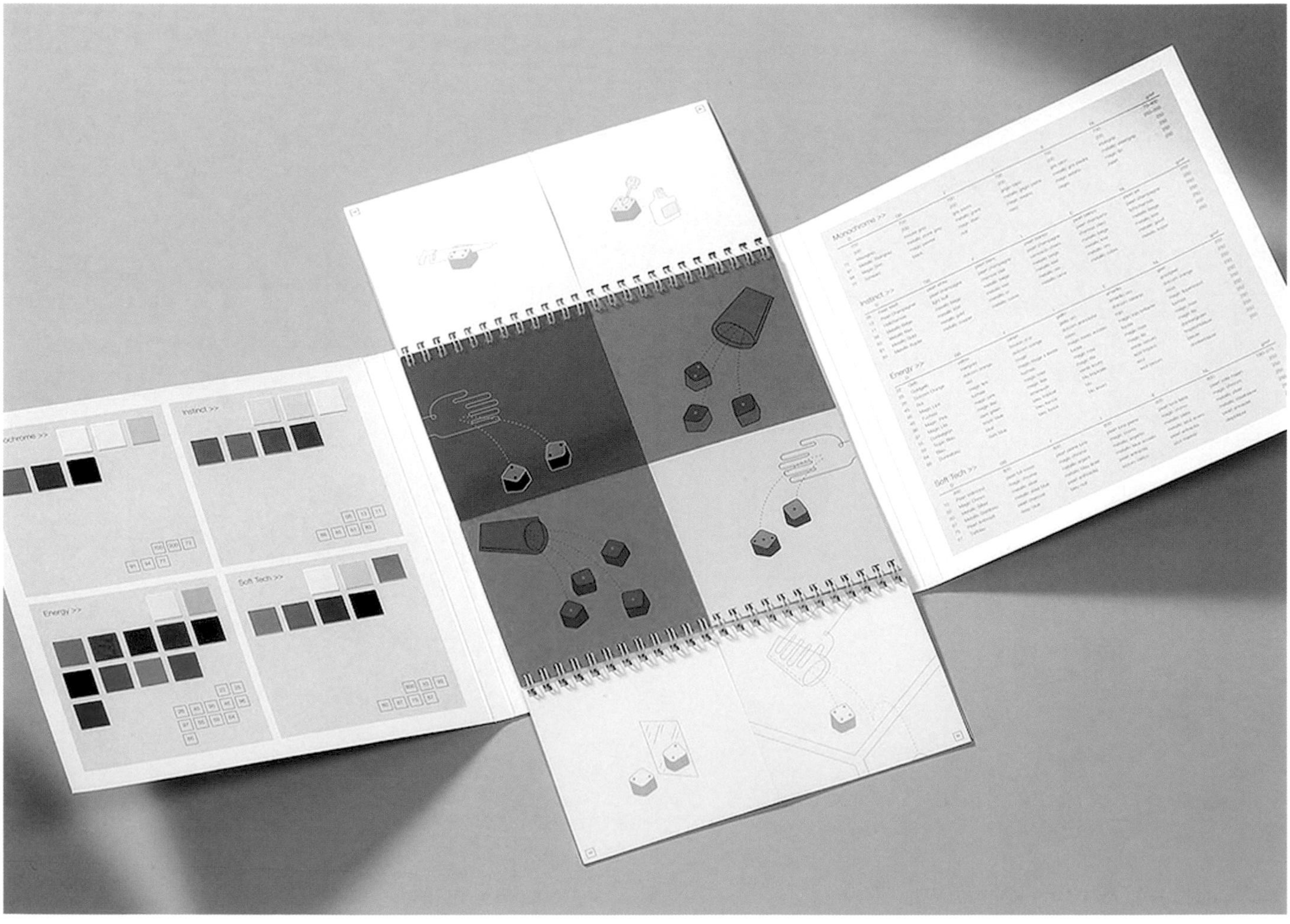

www . nk-Group . com
Novin Khak Delijan Company (NK-D) is a subsidiary of Novin Khak Group, established in 2003 in the field of mining activities and development. Located in Markazi province, Delijan district, the compant consist of two mines: Mozvash Clay and Mozvash Barite, situated in the 35 Km proximity of Delijan city.
NK-D's outlook is to expand into the International markets with large reserves available to the company and the expertise, experience and professionalism of the team within the company structure.
Tehran
Saveh
Ghom
Arak
Delijan
Kashan
Esfahan
DELIJAN
Address : Unit 17, No. 51, Shaghayegh St . Valiasr Sq ., Tehran, Iran
Tel : +98-21-66 48 56 20,1 Fax : +98-21-66 96 65 10
e-mail : Info @ nk-Group . com

creative firm
MAMORDESIGN
Tehran, Iran
creative people
Maliheh Ghajargar
client
Delijan-NK group

INTEGRATED
CORPORATE RELATIONS

creative firm
Q
Wiesbaden, Germany
creative people
Katja Wittrowski, Thilo von Debschitz
client
ICR Integrated Corporate Relations

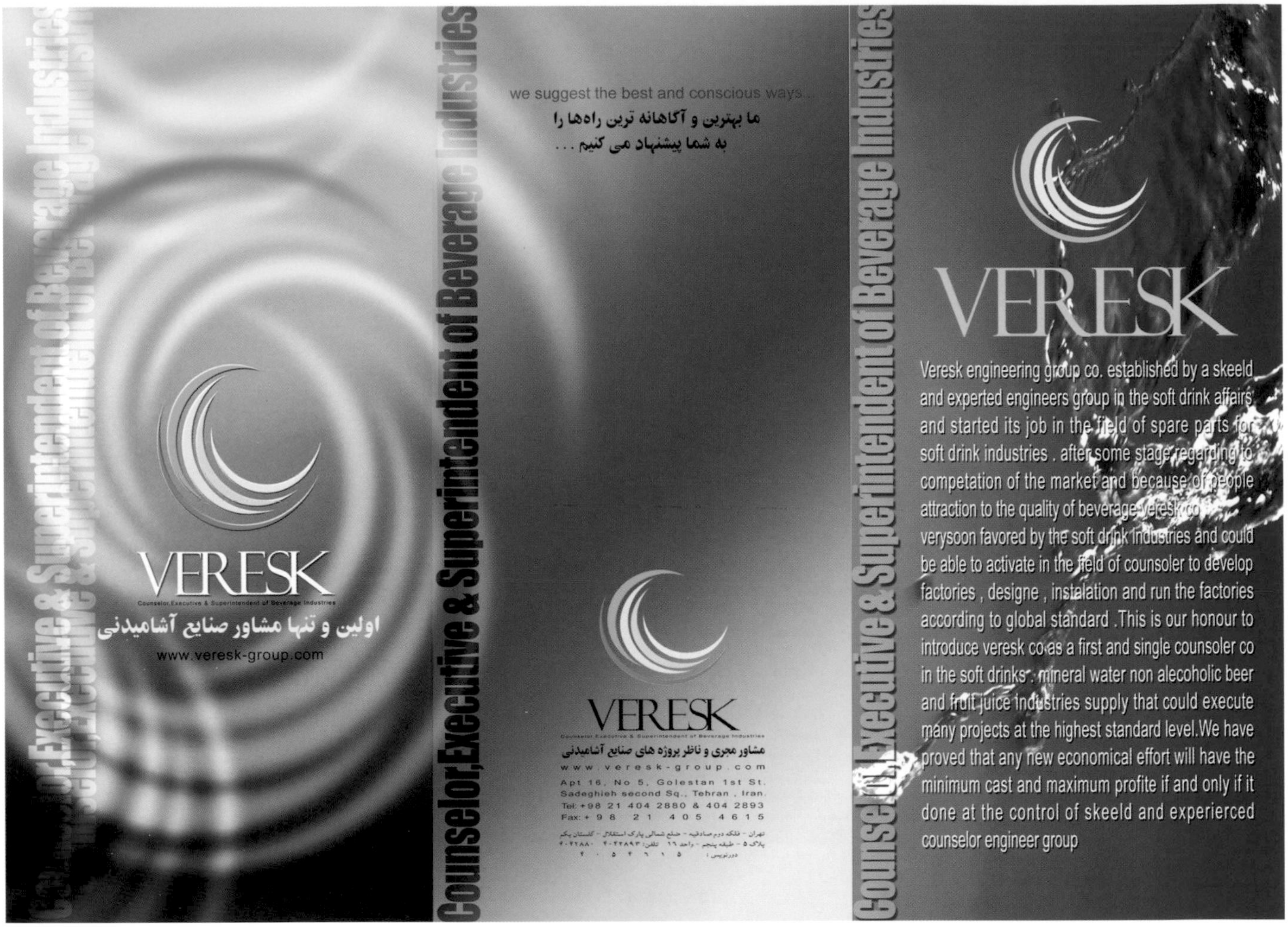
Counselor,Executive & Superintendent of Beverage Industries
VERESK
Counselor Executive & Superintendent of Beverage Industries
اولین و تنها مشاور صنایع آشامیدنی
www.veresk-group.com
we suggest the best and conscious ways...
ما بهترین و آگاهانه ترین راه‌ها را
به شما پیشنهاد می کنیم . . .
Counselor,Executive & Superintendent of Beverage Industries
VERESK
Counselor Executive & Superintendent of Beverage Industries
مشاور مجری و ناظر پروژه های صنایع آشامیدنی
www.veresk-group.com
Apt 16, No 5, Golestan 1st St.
Sadeghieh second Sq., Tehran, Iran.
Tel: +98 21 404 2880 & 404 2893
Fax: + 98 21 405 4615
Counselor,Executive & Superintendent of Beverage Industries
VERESK
Veresk engineering group co. established by a skeeld and experted engineers group in the soft drink affairs and started its job in the field of spare parts for soft drink industries . after some stage regarding to competation of the market and because of people attraction to the quality of beverage veresk co verysoon favored by the soft drink industries and could be able to activate in the field of counsoler to develop factories , designe , instalation and run the factories according to global standard .This is our honour to introduce veresk co as a first and single counsoler co in the soft drinks , mineral water non alecoholic beer and fruit juice industries supply that could execute many projects at the highest standard level.We have proved that any new economical effort will have the minimum cast and maximum profite if and only if it done at the control of skeeld and experierced counselor engineer group

creative firm
MAMORDESIGN
Tehran, Iran
creative people
Maliheh Ghajargar
client
Veresk

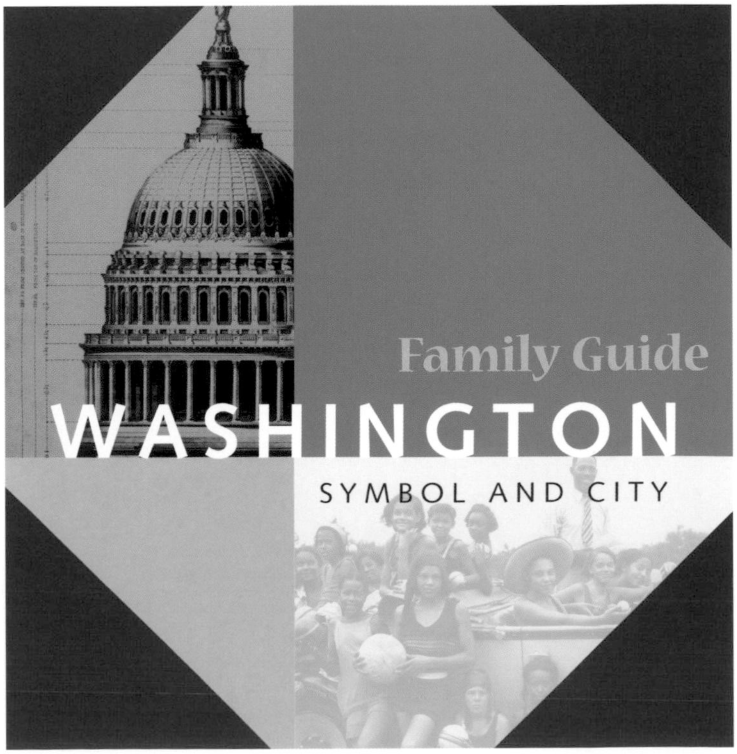
Family Guide
WASHINGTON
SYMBOL AND CITY

creative firm
PENSARÉ DESIGN GROUP
Washington, D.C.
creative people
Amy E. Billingham
client
National Building Museum

creative firm
Q
Wiesbaden, Germany
creative people
Matthias Frey, Laurenz Nielbock
client
m-real Zanders

creative firm
KROG
Ljubljana, Slovenia
creative people
Edi Berk, Dragan Arrigler
client
Vodovod-Kanalizacija, Ljubljana

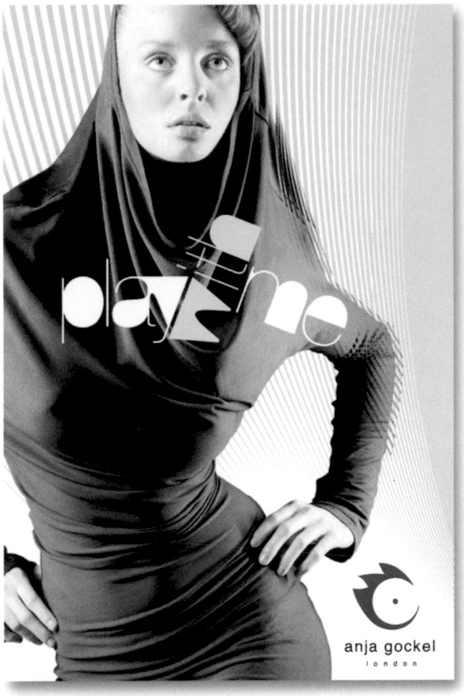
anja gockel
london

10
09

creative firm
Q
Wiesbaden, Germany
creative people
Matthias Frey
client
Anja Gockel London

LUNAR
NEW 06
YEAR
UNITY
PARADE
1
e Lunar New Year Unity Parade is to bring our
spectrum of cultures together while celebrating the
producing this event, we encourage people from all
rk together as a team to showcase our diverse
y program. We encourage people of all ethnicities,
nds to participate in this fun event and make it an
stival for the future.
Lunar New Year Unity Parade
2006 LNYUP Parade : International Fair Schedule
10:00am Pre-parade face painting (Jollyman Park)
Brought to you by Homestead High National Art Honor Society
10:30am Opening Ceremony : Parade begins (Jollyman Park)
11:30am International Fair (Cultural & Food Booths) begins (Memorial Park)
12:30pm Parade ends : International Fair Stage Performances begin (Amphitheater at Memorial Park)
4:00pm International Fair (Cultural & Food Booths) ends
5:00pm International Fair Stage Performances end
2006 LNYUP PARADE LINE UP & VIPS
(Sports Anchor of KPIX / Channel 5) is the 2006 Lunar New Year Unity Parade Master of Ceremonies. In 2000, 2001 and 2002, Rick was voted favorite local TV news anchor and "media person of the year" by the Northern California Arthritis Foundation and by readers of the Oakland Tribune and the Alameda Times Star. You can find Rick at the Announcing Stand at Redeemer Lutheran Church.
is the Grand Marshal of the 2006 Lunar New Year Unity Parade. Don is Chairman of Cupertino National Bank and a member of the Rotary Club of Cupertino (Don serves as Chair of the New Models for Rotary task force). He has served as Club President and is currently District 5170 Annual Giving Chair. Don is also active with the Boy Scouts of America, Chamber of Commerce and California Banker's Association.
9
ch 25, 2006 from 7:00 to 9:30pm at
Cupertino, Lynbrook and Monta Vista
ational Night 2006, a fundraiser
s clean sustainable water in Africa.
ONAL NIGHT
0 for adults and $7.00
tact Jon Kaplan at
Pump Aid, please
has resulted in
nternational
ing money for
's diversity.

creative firm
ANGRYPORCUPINE*DESIGN
Park City, Utah
creative people
Cheryl Roder-Quill
client
Lunar New Year Unity Parade 06

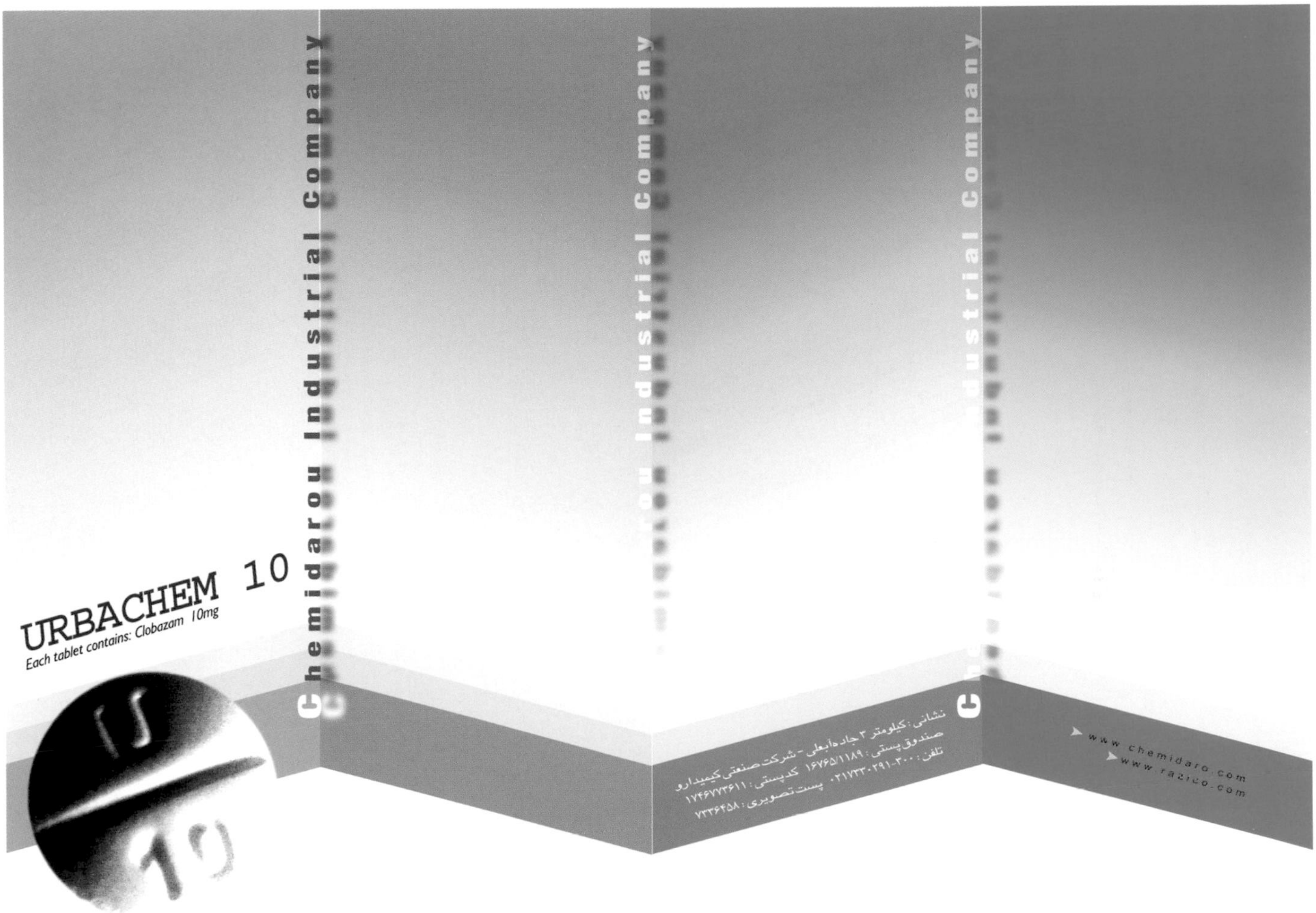

creative firm
MAMORDESIGN
Tehran, Iran
creative people
Maliheh Ghajargar
clients
Urbachem-Chemidarou Pharma

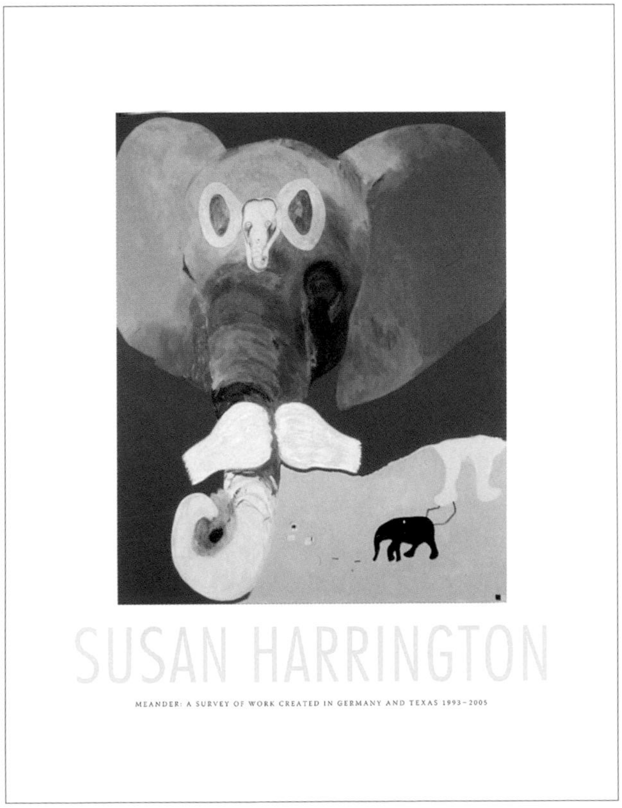
SUSAN HARRINGTON
MEANDER: A SURVEY OF WORK CREATED IN GERMANY AND TEXAS 1993–2005

creative firm
PAT SLOAN DESIGN
Fort Worth, Texas
creative people
Pat Sloan
clients
Susan Harrington,
University Art Gallery—TCU

creative firm
DEB NEUFELL DESIGN
Waltham, Massachusetts
creative people
Deb Neufell
client
Deb Neufell Design

2007
Mt. Auburn Cemetery
Visitor Guide
580 Mount Auburn Street | Cambridge, MA 02138
© 2007 Deb Neufell

creative firm
ROMAN DESIGN
Golden, Colorado
creative people
Lisa Romanowski
client
Radian Guaranty, Inc.

Understanding and choosing the right mortgage products for your financial situation.
RADIAN
Radian. For the last 40 years, the mortgage insurance (MI) industry has served an important purpose: helping consumers with limited savings achieve homeownership. However, until the advent of MI, lenders required a cash down payment of 20%–a hardship for many, an impossibility for many more.
Radian is committed to developing new products and services that help both lenders and borrowers achieve their financial objectives.

creative firm
SAYLES GRAPHIC DESIGN
Des Moines, Iowa
creative people
John Sayles
client
Art Fights Back

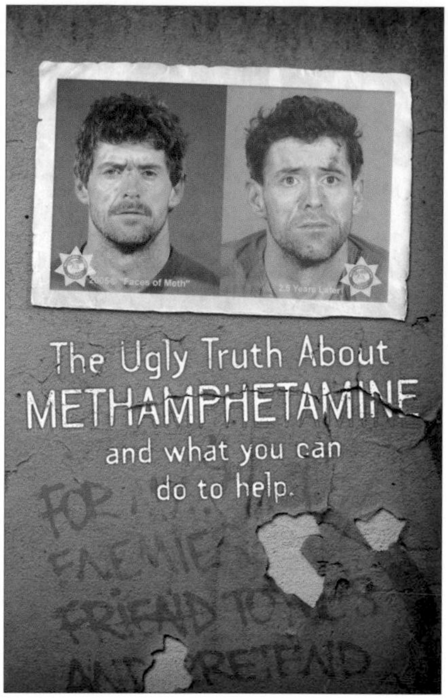
2005© "Faces of Meth"
2.5 Years Later
The Ugly Truth About
METHAMPHETAMINE
and what you can
do to help.

2005© "Faces of Meth"
2.5 Years Later
Don't risk it...
Know the law.
Making, selling, and using methamphetamine is illegal in every state
Stay informed.
In 2004, meth use sent more people to the hospital emergency room than any other 'club' drug
Get the facts.
Meth is made from dangerous chemicals that are flammable, corrosive, and toxic. These chemicals can cause fires and explosions, and release toxic vapors that damage the environment and the health of meth makers and the people around them.
Know the risks using meth can cause:
• A severe "crash" after the first intense effects wear off
• Irreversible damage to blood vessels in your brain
RESOURCES
The Partnership for a Drug-Free America
Information for this brochure was provided by The Partnership for a Drug-Free America, 2006. Used with permission.
For more information about methamphetamine, visit www.drugfree.org.
Additional Information can be found at:
www.methresources.gov
www.nometh.org

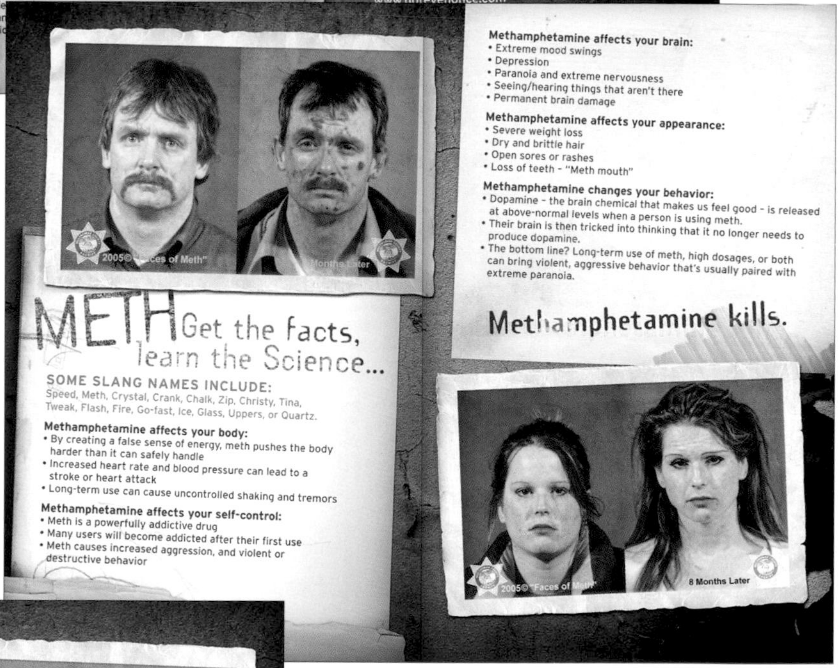
2005© "Faces of Meth"
METH Get the facts, learn the Science...
SOME SLANG NAMES INCLUDE:
Speed, Meth, Crystal, Crank, Chalk, Zip, Christy, Tina, Tweak, Flash, Fire, Go-fast, Ice, Glass, Uppers, or Quartz.
Methamphetamine affects your body:
• By creating a false sense of energy, meth pushes the body harder than it can safely handle
• Increased heart rate and blood pressure can lead to a stroke or heart attack
• Long-term use can cause uncontrolled shaking and tremors
Methamphetamine affects your self-control:
• Meth is a powerfully addictive drug
• Many users will become addicted after their first use
• Meth causes increased aggression, and violent or destructive behavior
Methamphetamine affects your brain:
• Extreme mood swings
• Depression
• Paranoia and extreme nervousness
• Seeing/hearing things that aren't there
• Permanent brain damage
Methamphetamine affects your appearance:
• Severe weight loss
• Dry and brittle hair
• Open sores or rashes
• Loss of teeth - "Meth mouth"
Methamphetamine changes your behavior:
• Dopamine - the brain chemical that makes us feel good - is released at above-normal levels when a person is using meth.
• Their brain is then tricked into thinking that it no longer needs to produce dopamine.
• The bottom line? Long-term use of meth, high dosages, or both can bring violent, aggressive behavior that's usually paired with extreme paranoia.
Methamphetamine kills.
2005© "Faces of Meth"
8 Months Later

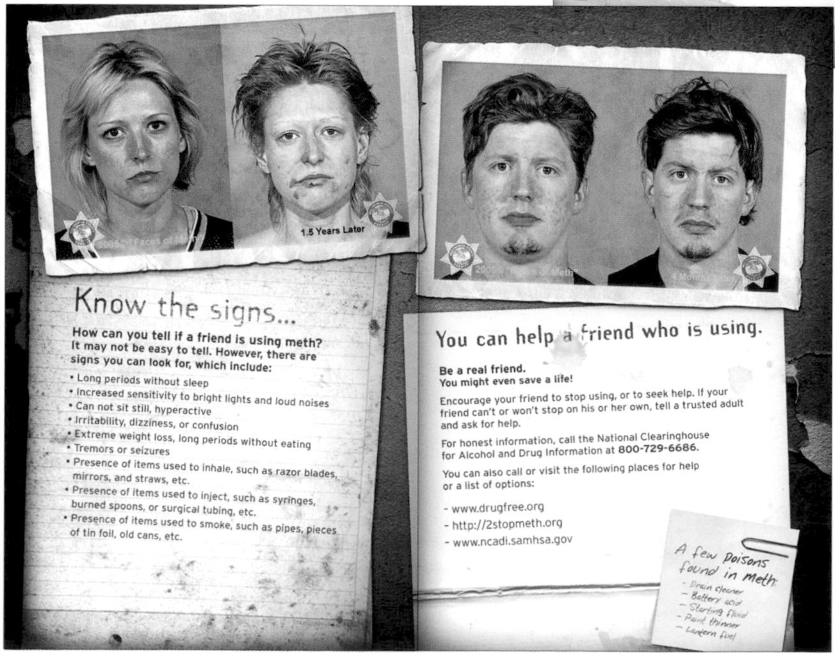
1.5 Years Later
Know the signs...
How can you tell if a friend is using meth? It may not be easy to tell. However, there are signs you can look for, which include:
• Long periods without sleep
• Increased sensitivity to bright lights and loud noises
• Can not sit still, hyperactive
• Irritability, dizziness, or confusion
• Extreme weight loss, long periods without eating
• Tremors or seizures
• Presence of items used to inhale, such as razor blades, mirrors, and straws, etc.
• Presence of items used to inject, such as syringes, burned spoons, or surgical tubing, etc.
• Presence of items used to smoke, such as pipes, pieces of tin foil, old cans, etc.
You can help a friend who is using.
Be a real friend.
You might even save a life!
Encourage your friend to stop using, or to seek help. If your friend can't or won't stop on his or her own, tell a trusted adult and ask for help.
For honest information, call the National Clearinghouse for Alcohol and Drug Information at 800-729-6686.
You can also call or visit the following places for help or a list of options:
- www.drugfree.org
- http://2stopmeth.org
- www.ncadi.samhsa.gov
A few poisons found in meth:
- Drain cleaner
- Battery acid
- Starting fluid
- Paint thinner
- Lantern fuel

creative firm
RED CIRCLE AGENCY
St. Louis Park, Minnesota
creative people
David Maloney
client
Mille Lacs Band of Ojibwe

the food
The unique menu features Progressive American cuisine using cutting edge technique and new varieties of American desserts. The award-winning wine list features sophisticated boutique wines from around the world. Bluestem strives to constantly evolve with new menu transitions, change of seasons, and a passion for outstanding ingredients.
b
RESTAURANT

creative firm
INDICIA DESIGN, INC.
Kansas City, Missouri
creative people
Ryan Glendening
client
BlueStem Restaurant

creative firm
ON THE EDGE DESIGN, INC.
Newport Beach, California
creative people
Nicole Geiger-Brown
client
Cambridge

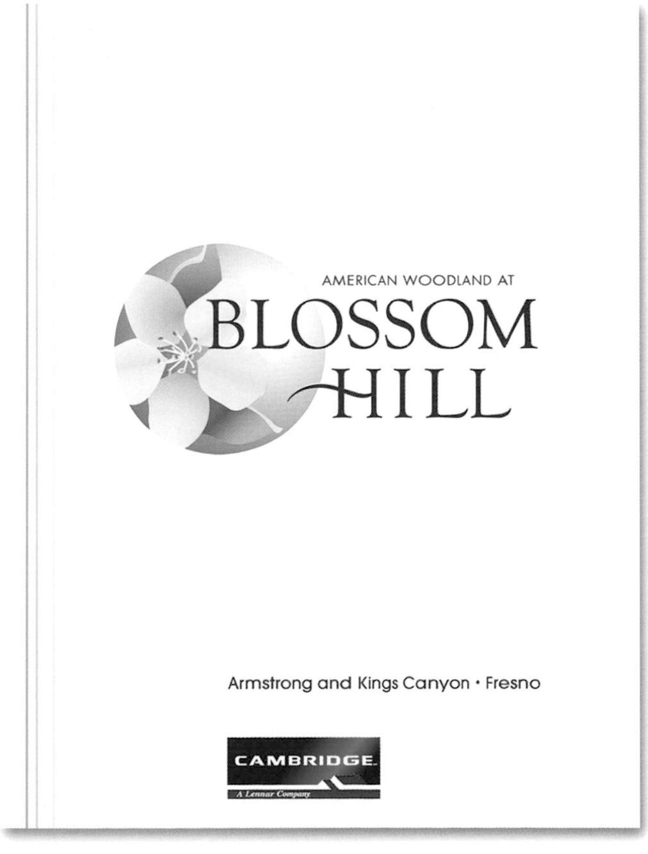
AMERICAN WOODLAND AT
BLOSSOM
HILL
Armstrong and Kings Canyon • Fresno
CAMBRIDGE
A Lennar Company

creative firm
ON THE EDGE DESIGN, INC.
Newport Beach, California
creative people
Nicole Geiger-Brown
client
Cambridge

creative firm
LOOK DESIGN
San Carlos, California
creative people
Monika Kegel
client
Lahlouh

creative firm
EUPHORIANET
Monterrey, Mexico
creative people
Mabel Morales, Laura Pérez
client
Fiat Mexico

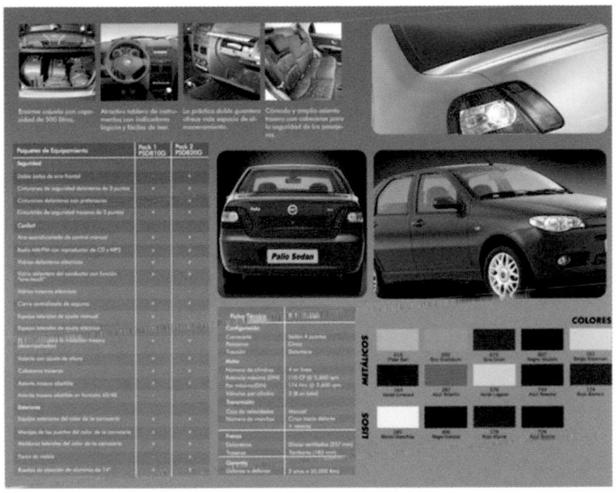

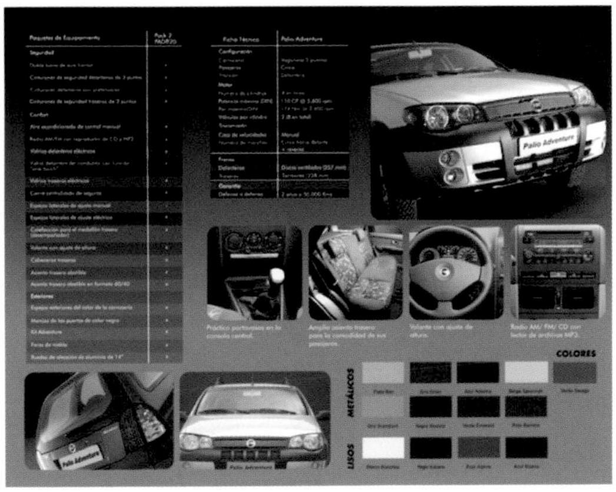

creative firm
HORNALL ANDERSON DESIGN
Seattle, Washington
creative people
Jack Anderson, Kathy Saito,
Hayden Schoen, Elmer dela Cruz, Chris Freed
client
CitationShares

creative firm
Q
Wiesbaden, Germany
creative people
Matthias Frey, Ute Dersch,
Laurenz Nielbock
client
Rheingau Musik Festival

creative firm
LEKASMILLER DESIGN
Walnut Creek, California
creative people
Lana Ip
client
GSE Construction

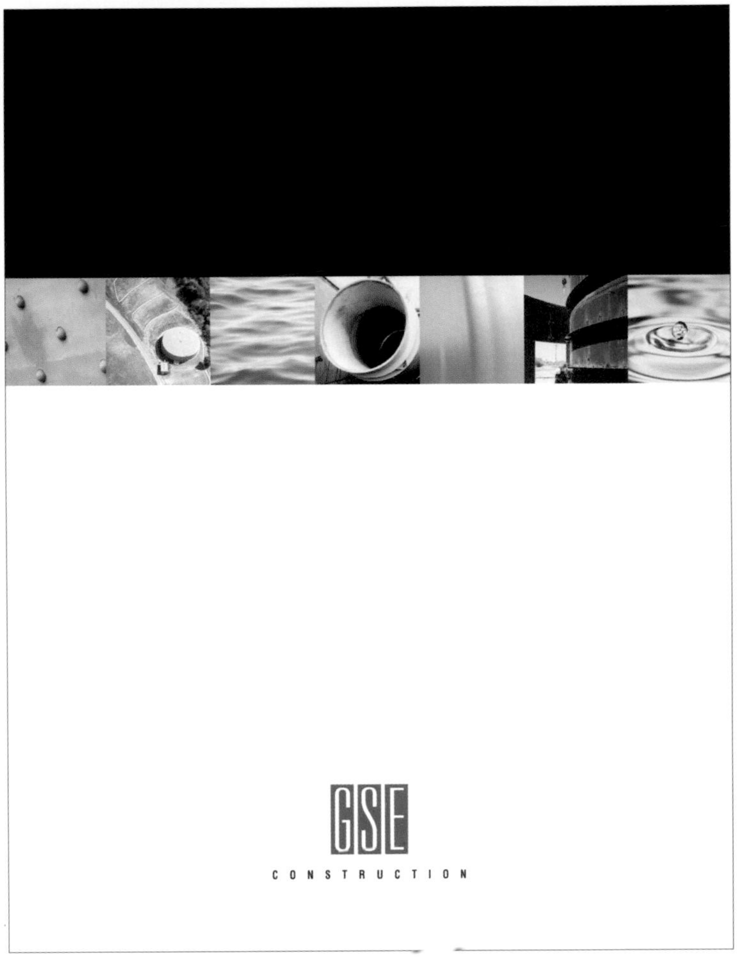
GSE
CONSTRUCTION

creative firm
ZERO GRAVITY DESIGN GROUP
Smithtown, New York
creative people
Zero Gravity Design Group
client
Big Apple Visual Group

BIG APPLE
VISUAL GROUP
Fresh ideas.
Fresh thinking.
New York • Dubai • Hong Kong

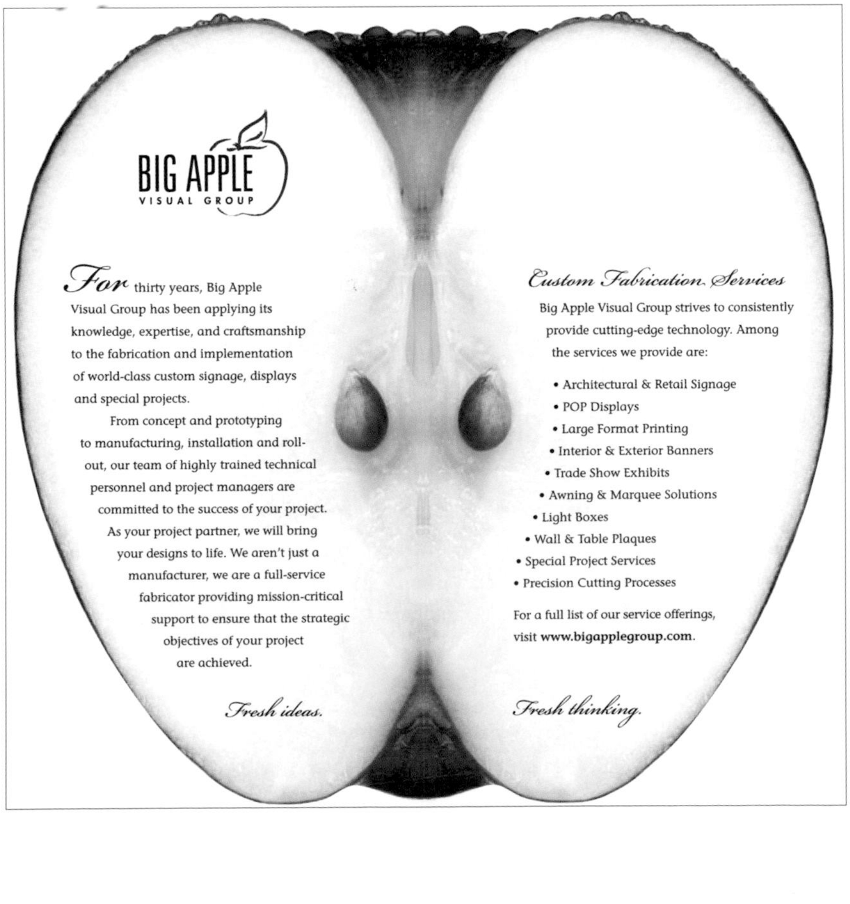
BIG APPLE
VISUAL GROUP
For thirty years, Big Apple Visual Group has been applying its knowledge, expertise, and craftsmanship to the fabrication and implementation of world-class custom signage, displays and special projects.
From concept and prototyping to manufacturing, installation and roll-out, our team of highly trained technical personnel and project managers are committed to the success of your project. As your project partner, we will bring your designs to life. We aren't just a manufacturer, we are a full-service fabricator providing mission-critical support to ensure that the strategic objectives of your project are achieved.
Fresh ideas.
Custom Fabrication Services
Big Apple Visual Group strives to consistently provide cutting-edge technology. Among the services we provide are:
• Architectural & Retail Signage
• POP Displays
• Large Format Printing
• Interior & Exterior Banners
• Trade Show Exhibits
• Awning & Marquee Solutions
• Light Boxes
• Wall & Table Plaques
• Special Project Services
• Precision Cutting Processes
For a full list of our service offerings, visit www.bigapplegroup.com.
Fresh thinking.

creative firm
TANGRAM STRATEGIC DESIGN
Novara, Italy
creative people
Alberto Baccari, Anna Grimaldi, Andrea Sempi
client
Davide Cenci

22.1 Motor jacket
Weathered leather
$ 1300
22.2 Bermuda shorts
Elasticized cotton
$ 395
22.3 Three button jacket
Linen hopsack
$ 950
22.4 V neck polo
Linen and cotton
$ 215
22.5 Skinny leg trouser
Tropical wool
$ 325
Cabo de São Vicente, north view
MOTO GUZZI

6.1 Denim suit
Washed cotton
$ 1300
6.2 Pure cotton pocket square
$ 30
6.3 Contrasting collar shirt
French cuffs
$ 185
Pure silk
$ 95
6.5 Silk cufflinks
$ 160
6.6 Canvas mailman bag
$ 315

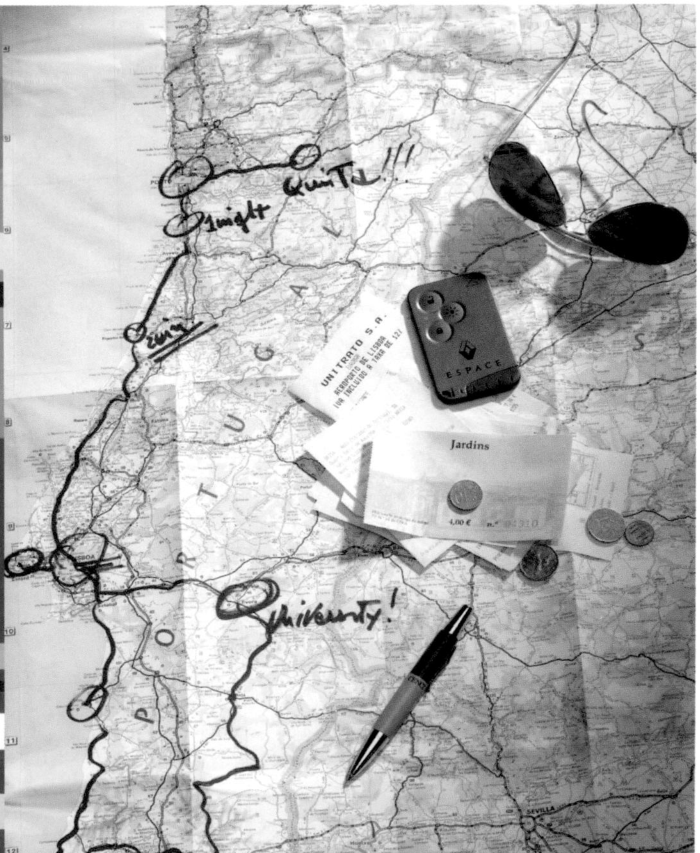
ESPACE
Jardins
SEVILLA

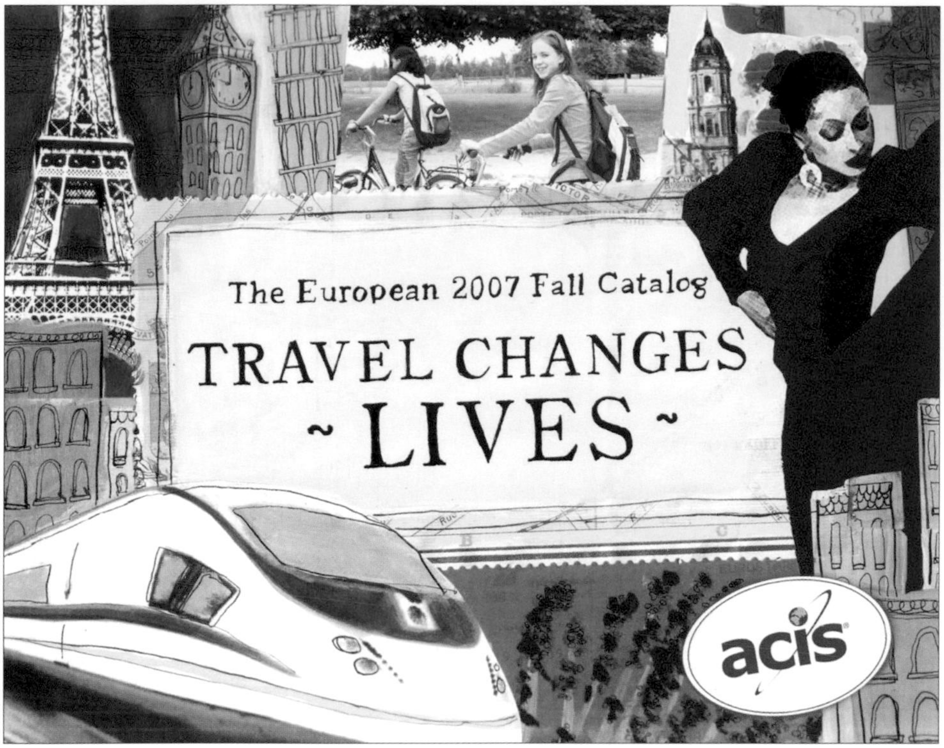

creative firm
RIGHT HAT, LLC
Boston, Massachusetts
creative people
Charlyne Fabi, Char Wong, Elonide Semmes
client
ACIS

creative firm
DEVER DESIGNS
Laurel, Maryland
creative people
Chris Komisar, Jeffrey L. Dever
client
National Geographic

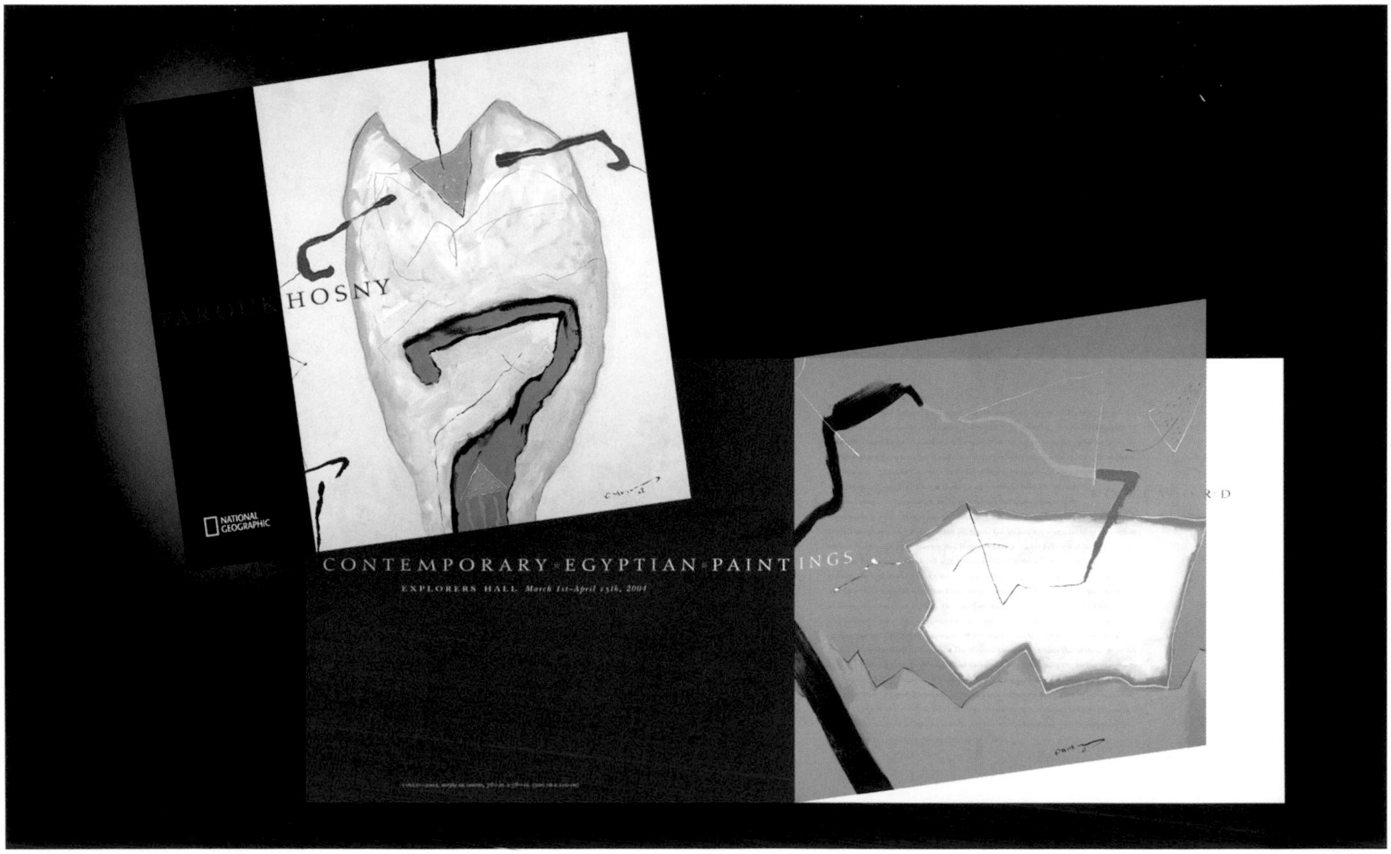

GE's programs create many opportunities for students at Aiken High School.
Various programs include:
• Tutoring & coaching for the Ohio Graduation Test
• Mentoring for education and careers in mathematics, science, engineering and college acceptance programs
Education is the power to think clearly, the power to act well in the world's work, and the power to APPRECIATE LIFE
-Brigham Young
Aiken University High School
5641 Belmont Ave.
Cincinnati, OH 45224
513/363-6800
Programs Sponsored by
GE
Academic Advantage
AIKEN UNIVERSITY HIGH SCHOOL
College Bound
3(m+5)=21

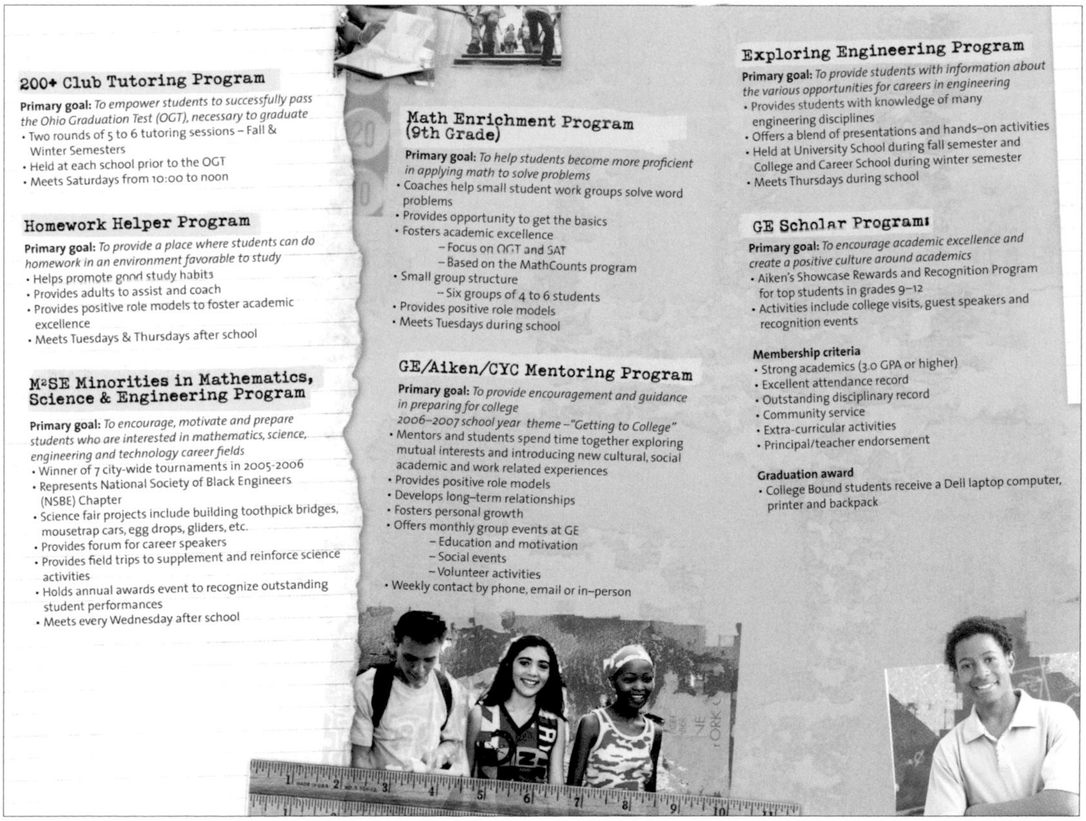
200+ Club Tutoring Program
Primary goal: To empower students to successfully pass the Ohio Graduation Test (OGT), necessary to graduate
• Two rounds of 5 to 6 tutoring sessions – Fall & Winter Semesters
• Held at each school prior to the OGT
• Meets Saturdays from 10:00 to noon
Homework Helper Program
Primary goal: To provide a place where students can do homework in an environment favorable to study
• Helps promote good study habits
• Provides adults to assist and coach
• Provides positive role models to foster academic excellence
• Meets Tuesdays & Thursdays after school
M²SE Minorities in Mathematics, Science & Engineering Program
Primary goal: To encourage, motivate and prepare students who are interested in mathematics, science, engineering and technology career fields
• Winner of 7 city-wide tournaments in 2005-2006
• Represents National Society of Black Engineers (NSBE) Chapter
• Science fair projects include building toothpick bridges, mousetrap cars, egg drops, gliders, etc.
• Provides forum for career speakers
• Provides field trips to supplement and reinforce science activities
• Holds annual awards event to recognize outstanding student performances
• Meets every Wednesday after school
Math Enrichment Program (9th Grade)
Primary goal: To help students become more proficient in applying math to solve problems
• Coaches help small student work groups solve word problems
• Provides opportunity to get the basics
• Fosters academic excellence
– Focus on OGT and SAT
– Based on the MathCounts program
• Small group structure
– Six groups of 4 to 6 students
• Provides positive role models
• Meets Tuesdays during school
GE/Aiken/CYC Mentoring Program
Primary goal: To provide encouragement and guidance in preparing for college
2006–2007 school year theme – "Getting to College"
• Mentors and students spend time together exploring mutual interests and introducing new cultural, social academic and work related experiences
• Provides positive role models
• Develops long-term relationships
• Fosters personal growth
• Offers monthly group events at GE
– Education and motivation
– Social events
– Volunteer activities
• Weekly contact by phone, email or in-person
Exploring Engineering Program
Primary goal: To provide students with information about the various opportunities for careers in engineering
• Provides students with knowledge of many engineering disciplines
• Offers a blend of presentations and hands-on activities
• Held at University School during fall semester and College and Career School during winter semester
• Meets Thursdays during school
GE Scholar Program:
Primary goal: To encourage academic excellence and create a positive culture around academics
• Aiken's Showcase Rewards and Recognition Program for top students in grades 9–12
• Activities include college visits, guest speakers and recognition events
Membership criteria
• Strong academics (3.0 GPA or higher)
• Excellent attendance record
• Outstanding disciplinary record
• Community service
• Extra-curricular activities
• Principal/teacher endorsement
Graduation award
• College Bound students receive a Dell laptop computer, printer and backpack

creative firm
FIVE VISUAL COMMUNICATION & DESIGN
Mason, Ohio
creative people
Laura Broermann, Rondi Tschopp
client
GE Aviation

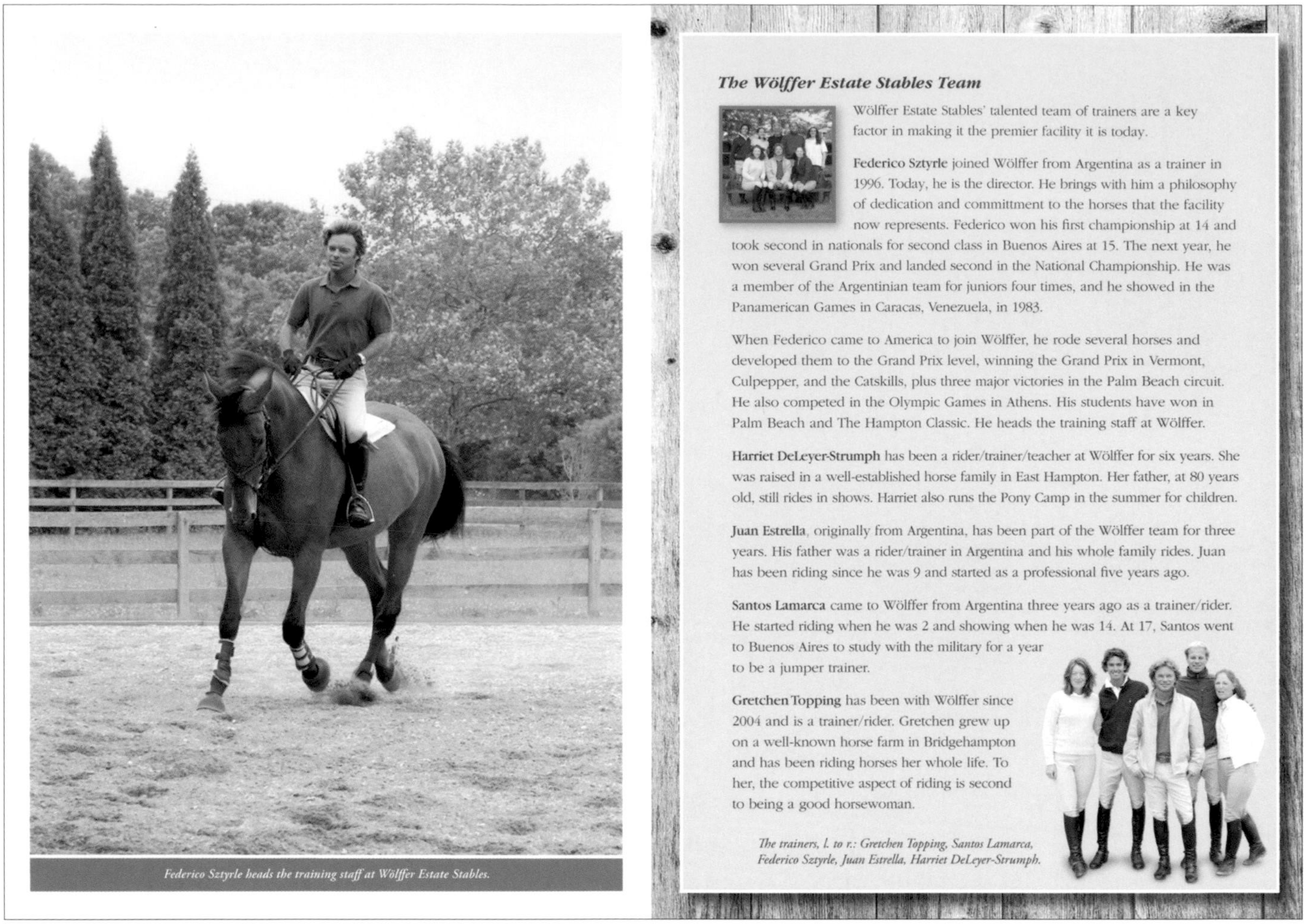

Federico Sztyrle heads the training staff at Wölffer Estate Stables.

The Wölffer Estate Stables Team

Wölffer Estate Stables' talented team of trainers are a key factor in making it the premier facility it is today.

Federico Sztyrle joined Wölffer from Argentina as a trainer in 1996. Today, he is the director. He brings with him a philosophy of dedication and committment to the horses that the facility now represents. Federico won his first championship at 14 and took second in nationals for second class in Buenos Aires at 15. The next year, he won several Grand Prix and landed second in the National Championship. He was a member of the Argentinian team for juniors four times, and he showed in the Panamerican Games in Caracas, Venezuela, in 1983.

When Federico came to America to join Wölffer, he rode several horses and developed them to the Grand Prix level, winning the Grand Prix in Vermont, Culpepper, and the Catskills, plus three major victories in the Palm Beach circuit. He also competed in the Olympic Games in Athens. His students have won in Palm Beach and The Hampton Classic. He heads the training staff at Wölffer.

Harriet DeLeyer-Strumph has been a rider/trainer/teacher at Wölffer for six years. She was raised in a well-established horse family in East Hampton. Her father, at 80 years old, still rides in shows. Harriet also runs the Pony Camp in the summer for children.

Juan Estrella, originally from Argentina, has been part of the Wölffer team for three years. His father was a rider/trainer in Argentina and his whole family rides. Juan has been riding since he was 9 and started as a professional five years ago.

Santos Lamarca came to Wölffer from Argentina three years ago as a trainer/rider. He started riding when he was 2 and showing when he was 14. At 17, Santos went to Buenos Aires to study with the military for a year to be a jumper trainer.

Gretchen Topping has been with Wölffer since 2004 and is a trainer/rider. Gretchen grew up on a well-known horse farm in Bridgehampton and has been riding horses her whole life. To her, the competitive aspect of riding is second to being a good horsewoman.

The trainers, l. to r.: Gretchen Topping, Santos Lamarca, Federico Sztyrle, Juan Estrella, Harriet DeLeyer-Strumph.

Where a passion for riding
meets a history of excellence.
Wölffer Estate
Stables

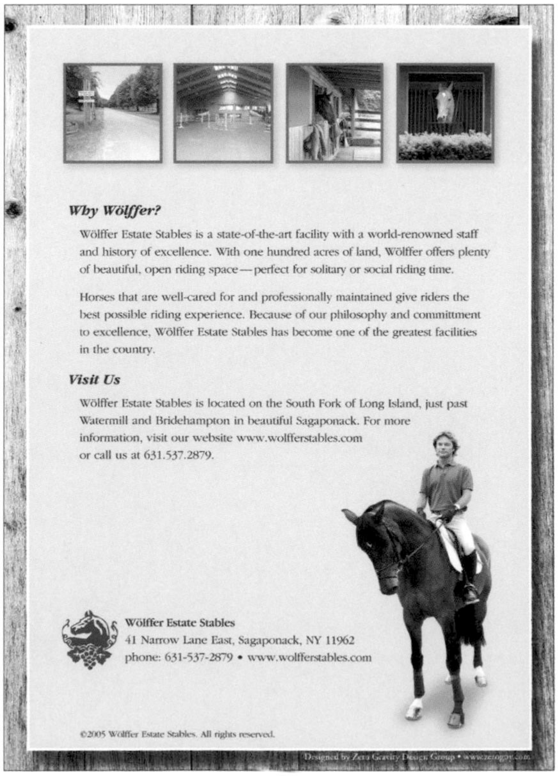

Why Wölffer?

Wölffer Estate Stables is a state-of-the-art facility with a world-renowned staff and history of excellence. With one hundred acres of land, Wölffer offers plenty of beautiful, open riding space—perfect for solitary or social riding time.

Horses that are well-cared for and professionally maintained give riders the best possible riding experience. Because of our philosophy and committment to excellence, Wölffer Estate Stables has become one of the greatest facilities in the country.

Visit Us

Wölffer Estate Stables is located on the South Fork of Long Island, just past Watermill and Bridehampton in beautiful Sagaponack. For more information, visit our website www.wolfferstables.com or call us at 631.537.2879.

Wölffer Estate Stables
41 Narrow Lane East, Sagaponack, NY 11962
phone: 631-537-2879 • www.wolfferstables.com

©2005 Wölffer Estate Stables. All rights reserved.

creative firm
ZERO GRAVITY DESIGN GROUP
Smithtown, New York
creative people
Zero Gravity Design Group
client
Wölffer Estate Stables

The horses are the top priority at Wölffer Estate Stables.

A Rich History

From the moment you enter the grounds, the magnificence of Wölffer Estate Stables is evident. It is a place of tranquility and beauty, a haven for horses and riders alike with a marble fountain and cobblestone courtyard. What began with the acquisition of 14 acres of potato farms in 1979 has grown into one hundred acres of first-class horse facilities.

When Christian Wölffer first bought the property, all that stood was a small farmhouse and some barns. Soon after, Christian built a six-stall horse barn for his daughters, Joanna and Georgina, who learned to ride before they could walk. Christian acquired more land and further expanded the barns. After petitioning the Town of Southampton for a law to allow the building of an indoor riding ring, Christian seized the opportunity to grow his facility. Wölffer Estate Stables has since become one of the premier riding facilities for hunters, jumpers, and dressage.

Today the stables have more than 80 stalls, thirty individual paddocks, four state-of-the-art riding rings, a totally resurfaced Olympic-size dressage ring, and a Grand Prix field with natural and traditional jumps.

Our Philosophy

The horses are the top priority at Wölffer Estate Stables. Our experienced staff understands the needs of the horses and are committed to their well-being. We strive to provide the highest quality facilities. From the Grand Prix field with natural obstacles to the functionally laid-out barns and courtyard, everything has been designed with the horses in mind. From working with specialized vets to heat lamps for the horses' backs during the cold season, we go above and beyond traditional care and maintenance.

Our trainers are gifted professionals who have a passion for what they do. Being experienced competitors themselves, they can train riders and horses at any level. Their knowledge and talents are an integral part of the instructional experience.

We bring horses over from Argentina and Europe to train and develop them for competition. Developing riders and horses to their fullest potential is a common goal at Wölffer Estate Stables. Providing exceptional care for our horses is our mission and our passion.

Facilities and Services

Wölffer Estate Stables sits on over one hundred lush acres and employs an experienced staff with a passion for excellence. The farm offers direct access to miles of natural trails, and our top-notch facilities include over 80 stalls with 39 individual paddocks. The large, indoor riding ring can accommodate up to eight students and features an elevated viewing room.

Outside, several well-equipped riding rings including a totally resurfaced Olympic-size dressage ring and a Grand Prix field, feature rubber mulch-padded floors and a variety of natural and traditional jumps. A covered hard walker is available for exercising the horses during inclement weather.

Boarding: We offer full boarding with tack-up service for both year-round and summer boarders. Our hand-crafted, climate-controlled tack rooms are also available.

Lessons: Whether your equine interests are recreational or competitive, our trainers will design a program best suited to your individual needs. Lessons are given in dressage and show jumping from the novice to the advanced level. Choose from half-hour or one-hour sessions in private, semi-private, or group settings.

We offer lessons for every level of rider. Our ponies make it easy for children to learn. Beginning riders learn not only to ride but how to groom and tack their horse. For experienced riders, horses are also available to rent or lease.

Horses for Sale: We continually purchase young horses from Argentina and Europe to train and develop them for competition. Trained by German-born, Olympic rider Sören von Rönne, we develop our horses to their greatest potential. Only the best are brought to the U.S. and are put up for sale. Visit our website for a list of current horses available for purchase.

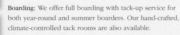

Christian Wölffer, with granddaughter Katalina

Christian Wölffer, proprietor, started with a few acres of potato farm and a single barn.

300 orthopedic surgeons are on 125 different planes landing at JFK. They are expected at the Waldorf Astoria by 7pm for the meeting kickoff.

creative firm
GRAPHIC ADVANCE
Palisades Park, New Jersey
creative people
Aviad Stark
client
UrbanRide

UrbanRide
UrbanRide simply delivers consistent, exceptional service event after event, month after month, year after year
UrbanRide was founded with the simple goal of serving the transportation needs of Professional Meeting & Event Planners. Our philosophy has always been clear – provide an overwhelming level of service to the professional meeting planner. From the initial planning stages through the execution stage to the final billing, our "Serve the Meeting Planner" attitude drives everything we do.
Over the years, UrbanRide has grown into the leading provider of meeting & event transportation solutions. We work in close partnerships with meeting and event planners and do not serve retail customers. By limiting our focus, we are able to provide planners with an unparalleled level of support and execution. Seasoned meeting and event planners have come to rely on UrbanRide so they are free to focus on areas of core competency. From a 1,500 person sales meeting in Las Vegas to a 20 person Board meeting in Palm Springs to a 1,000 event dinner series – UrbanRide will provide the right solution. We are the Special Event Specialist.
"Their service comes in for high praise. They are the best in the business, bar none." – Patrice, CMP
400 top sales representatives from 20 countries are about to land at Charles De Gaulle. They are expected at the conference commencement celebration in time for the champagne toast.
The Special Event Specialist
Worldwide

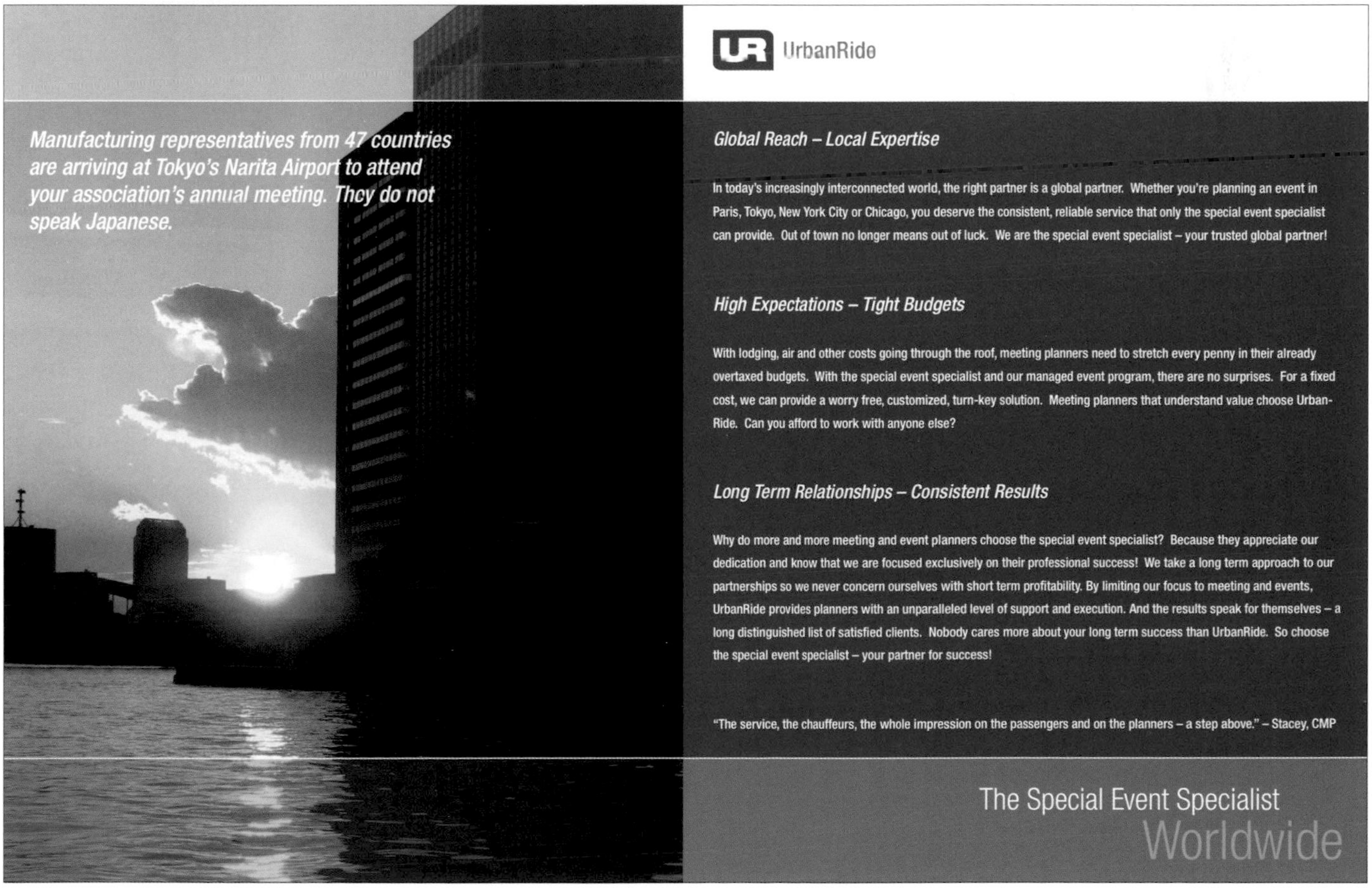

UrbanRide
Manufacturing representatives from 47 countries are arriving at Tokyo's Narita Airport to attend your association's annual meeting. They do not speak Japanese.
Global Reach – Local Expertise
In today's increasingly interconnected world, the right partner is a global partner. Whether you're planning an event in Paris, Tokyo, New York City or Chicago, you deserve the consistent, reliable service that only the special event specialist can provide. Out of town no longer means out of luck. We are the special event specialist – your trusted global partner!
High Expectations – Tight Budgets
With lodging, air and other costs going through the roof, meeting planners need to stretch every penny in their already overtaxed budgets. With the special event specialist and our managed event program, there are no surprises. For a fixed cost, we can provide a worry free, customized, turn-key solution. Meeting planners that understand value choose UrbanRide. Can you afford to work with anyone else?
Long Term Relationships – Consistent Results
Why do more and more meeting and event planners choose the special event specialist? Because they appreciate our dedication and know that we are focused exclusively on their professional success! We take a long term approach to our partnerships so we never concern ourselves with short term profitability. By limiting our focus to meeting and events, UrbanRide provides planners with an unparalleled level of support and execution. And the results speak for themselves – a long distinguished list of satisfied clients. Nobody cares more about your long term success than UrbanRide. So choose the special event specialist – your partner for success!
"The service, the chauffeurs, the whole impression on the passengers and on the planners – a step above." – Stacey, CMP
The Special Event Specialist
Worldwide

creative firm
CREATIVESOURCE/THE COCA-COLA COMPANY
Atlanta, Georgia
creative people
Adebayo Adedoyin, Dawn Shelton,
Iconologic, Leo Burnet
client
Coca-Cola Global Talent Management

creative firm
FIVE VISUAL COMMUNICATION & DESIGN
Mason, Ohio
creative people
Rondi Tschopp
client
West Chester Chamber Alliance

creative firm
SABINGRAFIK, INC.
Carlsbad, California
creative people
Tracy Sabin
client
Sabingrafik, Inc.

creative firm
GRAPHIC ADVANCE
Palisades Park, New Jersey
creative people
Aviad Stark
client
Saash

creative firm
A3 DESIGN
Charlotte, North Carolina
creative people
Alan Altman, Amanda Altman
client
Wetlands Estate

creative firm
30SIXTY ADVERTISING+DESIGN, INC.
Los Angeles, California
creative people
Henry Vizcarra, David Fuscellaro, Lee Barrett, Yujin Ono
client
King's Seafood Company

creative firm
SAYLES GRAPHIC DESIGN
Des Moines, Iowa
creative people
John Sayles
client
Des Moines Playhouse

creative firm
MAYHEM STUDIOS
Los Angeles, California
creative people
Calvin Lee
client
Calvin Lee Design

creative firm
BRAIN MAGNET
St. Louis Park, Minnesota
creative people
David Maloney, Matthew Benka
client
Brain Magnet

creative firm
INDICIA DESIGN
Kansas City, Missouri
creative people
Peter Heffner, Ryan Glendening
client
DJSite.com

creative firm
GRAPHIC ADVANCE
Palisades Park, New Jersey
creative people
Aviad Stark
client
Sword Diagnostics

creative firm
ZEIST DESIGN LLC
Sausalito, California
creative people
Oscar V. Mulder, Richard Scheve, Jacques Rossouw
client
CKE Restaurants La Salsa

creative firm
KROG
Ljubljana, Slovenia
creative people
Edi Berk
client
Pravna fakulteta, Ljubljana

creative firm
ART270, INC.
Jenkintown, Pennsylvania
creative people
Carl Mill, Jamie Head, Jessa Pion
client
Forman Signs

creative firm
AYSE ÇELEM DESIGN
Istanbul, Turkey
creative people
Ayse Çelem
client
Seymel Vintage Clothing Store

creative firm
EUPHORIANET
Monterrey, Mexico
creative people
Mabel Morales, Meissa Basañez
client
Opto

creative firm
HORNALL ANDERSON DESIGN
Seattle, Washington
creative people
Jack Anderson, Yuri Shvets
client
EIE

creative firm
SAYLES GRAPHIC DESIGN
Des Moines, Iowa
creative people
John Sayles
client
The Killjoys

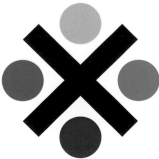

creative firm
KROG
Ljubljana, Slovenia
creative people
Edi Berk
client
Pravna fakulteta, Ljubljana

creative firm
021 COMUNICACIONES
Mexico City, Mexico
creative people
Héctor González
client
American Express

Enlázate
El orgullo de ser AMEX

creative firm
BETH SINGER DESIGN LLC
Arlington, Virginia
creative people
Suheun Yu
client
Singing Cat Productions

SINGING CAT PRODUCTIONS
Documentary Film & Media

creative firm
KENNETH DISEÑO
Uruapan, Mexico
creative people
Kenneth Treviño
client
20 Years Class of 86
UAG Graphic Design

20 1986 2006
AÑOS
DISEÑO GRÁFICO

creative firm
ZERO GRAVITY DESIGN GROUP
Smithtown, New York
creative people
Zero Gravity Design Group
client
Crescent Beach Productions

CRESCENT BEACH
PRODUCTIONS

creative firm
KIKU OBATA & COMPANY
St. Louis, Missouri
creative people
Troy Guzman, Teresa Norton-Young
client
Great Rivers Greenway

Great Rivers Greenway

creative firm
GRAPHIC ADVANCE
Palisades Park, New Jersey
creative people
Aviad Stark
client
Nurel Events

Nurel EVENTS

creative firm
TRUEFACES CREATION SDN BHD
Subang Jaya, Malaysia
creative people
True FACES Creative Team
client
BeanSproutz

creative firm
VELOCITY DESIGN WORKS
Winnipeg, Canada
creative people
Lasha Orzechowski
client
Prairie Orchard Farms

creative firm
ATLANTIS VISUAL GRAPHICS
Saratoga Springs, New York
creative people
Phil Rogers
client
Mind's Eye Illustration

creative firm
ESTUDIO IMAGINA
Mexico City, Mexico
creative people
Edgardo Reza
client
Eurobistrot/Miguel Bautista

creative firm
CDI STUDIOS
Las Vegas, Nevada
creative people
Brian Felgar
client
Frio

creative firm
INDICIA DESIGN
Kansas City, Missouri
creative people
Ryan Glendening
client
Spinnaker Web

creative firm
KROG
Slovenia, Ljubljana
creative people
Edi Berk
client
Restaurant Glažuta

creative firm
LOOK DESIGN
San Carlos, California
creative people
Pam Matsuda
client
Amoura

creative firm
ZEIST DESIGN LLC
Sausalito, California
creative people
Oscar V. Mulder, Richard Scheve,
Toby Sudduth
client
CKE Restaurants Red Burrito

creative firm
HORNALL ANDERSON DESIGN
Seattle, Washington
creative people
John Anicker, Andrew Wicklund,
Leo Raymundo, Yuri Shvets
client
Schnitzer Northwest

creative firm
GRAPHIC ADVANCE
Palisades Park, New Jersey
creative people
Aviad Stark
client
Ben Hur

creative firm
ANASTASIA DESIGN
Dedham, Massachusetts
creative people
Emily Titcomb
client
Phuket Restaurant

creative firm
PENSARÉ DESIGN GROUP
Washington, D.C.
creative people
Amy E. Billingham
client
Pensaré Design Group

creative firm
MISENHEIMER CREATIVE, INC.
Alpharetta, Georgia
creative people
Mark Misenheimer
client
Johns Creek Playhouse

creative firm
NEVER BORING DESIGN ASSOCIATES, INC.
Modesto, California
client
Never Boring Design Associates, Inc.

creative firm
FUNK/LEVIS & ASSOCIATES
Eugene, Oregon
creative people
Chris Berner
client
Oregon Association of Nurseries

creative firm
TRUEFACES CREATION SDN BHD
Subang Jaya, Malaysia
creative people
True FACES Creative Team
client
Dragon Palace

creative firm
BETH SINGER DESIGN LLC
Arlington, Virginia
creative people
Chris Hoch, Sucha Snidvongs
client
Cable in the Classroom

creative firm
CROUCH & NAEGELI
Carlsbad, California
creative people
Jim Crouch, Tracy Sabin
client
University of San Diego

creative firm
HORNALL ANDERSON DESIGN
Seattle, Washington
creative people
Jack Anderson, Andrew Wicklund, Larry Anderson, Peter Anderson, Ensi Mofasser, Belinda Bowling, Kathleen Gibson, Steve Rentschler
client
Majestic America Line

creative firm
TLC DESIGN
Churchville, Virginia
creative people
Trudy L. Cole
client
TLC Design

creative firm
314CREATIVE
Duluth, Georgia
creative people
Shawn Jenks
client
Pacific Food and Beverage

creative firm
STEPHEN LONGO DESIGN ASSOCIATES
West Orange, New Jersey
creative people
Stephen Longo
client
Art Directors Club of NJ

creative firm
EVENSON DESIGN GROUP
Culver City, California
creative people
Mark Sojka
client
MogoMedia

creative firm
GRAPHIC ADVANCE
Palisades Park, New Jersey
creative people
Aviad Stark
client
GNR Equities

creative firm
ROMAN DESIGN
Golden, Colorado
creative people
Lisa Romanowski
client
Routt County Department of Human Services

creative firm
CRAMERSWEENEY
Mount Laurel, New Jersey
creative people
Dave Girgenti
client
Contemporary Healthcare LLC

creative firm
MFDI
Selinsgrove, Pennsylvania
creative people
Mark Fertig
client
Midd-West School District

creative firm
314CREATIVE
Duluth, Georgia
creative people
Shawn Jenks
client
Redmond Duckworth

creative firm
ZEIST DESIGN LLC
Sausalito, California
creative people
Oscar V. Mulder, Richard Scheve
client
CKE Restaurants Channel Islands

creative firm
WILLIAM HOMAN DESIGN
Minneapolis, Minnesota
creative people
William Homan
client
Brightwater Fly Angler

creative firm
TLC DESIGN
Churchville, Virginia
creative people
Trudy L. Cole
client
Ridge Creek Ranch, TX

creative firm
KROG
Ljubljana, Slovenia
creative people
Edi Berk
client
Vinska družba Slovenije/
Wine Union of Slovenija

creative firm
HORNALL ANDERSON DESIGN
Seattle, Washington
creative people
Jack Anderson, Kathy Saito, Henry Yiu,
Elmer dela Cruz, Sonja Max, Hayden Schoen
client
CitationShares

creative firm
ART270, INC.
Jenkintown, Pennsylvania
creative people
Carl Mill, Jamie Head
client
Keith Mill

creative firm
MONDERER DESIGN
Cambridge, Massachusetts
creative people
Stewart Monderer, Stuart McCoy
client
Connected Software

creative firm
AYSE ÇELEM DESIGN
Istanbul, Turkey
creative people
Ayse Çelem
client
Anayapi Construction Firm

creative firm
GRAPHIC ADVANCE
Palisades Park, New Jersey
creative people
Aviad Stark
client
Mr Locks

creative firm
A3 DESIGN
Charlotte, North Carolina
creative people
Alan Altman, Amanda Altman,
Lauren Gualdoni
client
Carbonhouse

creative firm
HELENA SEO DESIGN
Sunnyvale, California
creative people
Helena Seo
client
Label Kings

creative firm
GRAPHIC ADVANCE
Palisades Park, New Jersey
creative people
Aviad Stark
client
Group Investment

creative firm
CDI STUDIOS
Las Vegas, Nevada
creative people
Tracy Casstevens,
Dan McElhattah III
client
Strip CD

creative firm
ESTUDIO IMAGINA
Mexico City, Mexico
creative people
Edgardo Reza
client
Super Fresh/Alfonso Pieza

creative firm
BRAIN MAGNET
St. Louis Park, Minnesota
creative people
David Maloney
client
Northland Connection

creative firm
KROG
Ljubljana, Slovenia
creative people
Edi Berk
client
Hotel Mons, Ljubljana

creative firm
FAI DESIGN GROUP
Irvington, New York
creative people
Robert Scully, Joshua Dillard
client
New Jersey Ironmen/Newark Area

creative firm
A3 DESIGN
Charlotte, North Carolina
creative people
Alan Altman, Amanda Altman,
Lauren Gualdoni
client
Carbonhouse

creative firm
TLC DESIGN
Churchville, Virginia
creative people
Trudy L. Cole
client
JMU School of Art & Art History

creative firm
TYPE G DESIGN
Carlsbad, California
creative people
Mike Nelson, Tracy Sabin
client
Pasta Pasta

creative firm
TRUEFACES CREATION SDN BHD
Subang Jaya, Malaysia
creative people
True FACES Creative Team
client
JF Appliances Sdn Bhd

creative firm
EVENSON DESIGN GROUP
Culver City, California
creative people
Mark Sojka, Wayne Watford
client
Dilu Entertainment & Design Inc.

creative firm
DIVERSIONS DESIGN GROUP
Frederick, Maryland
creative people
Joseph Silovich
client
Engineered Fire Protection

creative firm
KROG
Ljubljana, Slovenia
creative people
Edi Berk
client
Government's Media Office

creative firm
DEVER DESIGNS
Laurel, Maryland
creative people
Jeffrey L. Dever
client
National Association of Counties

creative firm
WESTGROUP CREATIVE
New York, New York
creative people
Chip Tolaney
client
New Dance Group

NEW DANCE GROUP

creative firm
GRAPHIC ADVANCE
Palisades Park, New Jersey
creative people
Aviad Stark
client
MyHome

MYHOME
DESIGN BUILD

creative firm
OCTAVO DESIGNS
Frederick, Maryland
creative people
Sue Hough, Mark Burrier
client
Strategic Partnerships International

Strategic Partnerships
INTERNATIONAL

creative firm
NOISE 13
San Francisco, California
creative people
Kerry Nehil, Julia Ringholtz
client
Solace Health

SOLACE HEALTH
ayurveda

creative firm
HORNALL ANDERSON DESIGN
Seattle, Washington
creative people
David Bates, Yuri Shvets
client
Redfin

REDFIN

creative firm
BRAIN MAGNET
St. Louis Park, Minnesota
creative people
David Maloney
client
St. Cloud CVB

GRANITE COUNTRY
• usa •

creative firm
A3 DESIGN
Charlotte, North Carolina
creative people
Alan Altman, Amanda Altman, Lauren Gualdoni
client
Bryant and Duffey

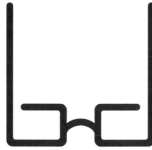

creative firm
RIGHT HAT, LLC
Boston, Massachusetts
creative people
Charlyne Fabi
client
Right Hat, LLC

creative firm
HELENA SEO DESIGN
Sunnyvale, California
creative people
Helena Seo
client
Reality Digital, Inc.

creative firm
JENN DAVID DESIGN
Irvine, California
creative people
Jenn David Connolly
client
AdtekMedia

creative firm
KENNETH DISEÑO
Uruapan, Mexico
creative people
Kenneth Treviño
client
Soluna Wines

creative firm
STEPHEN LONGO DESIGN ASSOCIATES
West Orange, New Jersey
creative people
Stephen Longo
client
Ekko Restaurant

creative firm
KIKU OBATA & COMPANY
St. Louis, Missouri
creative people
Paul Scherfling
client
Stoltz

McKINLEY
MALL

creative firm
KROG
Ljubljana, Slovenia
creative people
Edi Berk
client
Vodovod-Kanalizacija, Ljubljana

creative firm
ONE PICA, INC.
Boston, Massachusetts
creative people
Gregory Segall
client
American Innovative, LLC

AMERICAN
INNOVATIVE™
Products that make sense.™

creative firm
ATLANTIS VISUAL GRAPHICS
Saratoga Springs, New York
creative people
Phil Rogers
client
Worker Bee Productions

WORKER BEE
PRODUCTIONS

creative firm
TLC DESIGN
Churchville, Virginia
creative people
Trudy L. Cole
client
Open Door Properties, Jeff Robbie

OPEN
DOOR
properties LLC

creative firm
KROG
Ljubljana, Slovenia
creative people
Edi Berk
client
Grupa X, Ljubljana

GRUPA X
Aspice, odorare, degusta!

creative firm
SAYLES GRAPHIC DESIGN
Des Moines, Iowa
creative people
John Sayles
client
Knoxville Raceway

creative firm
TRUEFACES CREATION SDN BHD
Subang Jaya, Malaysia
creative people
True FACES Creative Team
client
HML Auto Industries Sdn Bhd

creative firm
D2DESIGNS
Houston, Texas
creative people
David Dooley
client
MTrak GPS

creative firm
STEPHEN LONGO DESIGN ASSOCIATES
West Orange, New Jersey
creative people
Stephen Longo
client
Flying Penguin Pictures

creative firm
UNIVERSITY OF CINCINNATI FOUNDATION
Cincinnati, Ohio
creative people
Melissa Lutz, Dustin Osterman
client
Blaze for Glory Music Group

creative firm
NANCY FRAME DESIGN
Durham, North Carolina
creative people
Sue Sneddon, Shallotte, NC
Holly Dickens, Chicago, IL

creative firm
MISENHEIMER CREATIVE, INC.
Alpharetta, Georgia
creative people
Mark Misenheimer
client
City of Alpharetta

creative firm
RED CIRCLE AGENCY
St. Louis Park, Minnesota
creative people
David Maloney
client
Suquamish Clearwater Casino Resort

creative firm
LAW CREATIVE
Carlsbad, California
creative people
Anne Law, Tracy Sabin
client
Corky McMillin Companies

creative firm
MISENHEIMER CREATIVE, INC.
Alpharetta, Georgia
creative people
Mark Misenheimer
client
Foundations

creative firm
EVENSON DESIGN GROUP
Culver City, California
creative people
Mark Sojka
client
Luna Roasters Gourmet Coffee & Tea

creative firm
GREENHAUS
Carlsbad, California
creative people
Craig Fuller, Tracy Sabin
client
Monroe Station

creative firm
NEVER BORING DESIGN ASSOCIATES, INC.
Modesto, California
creative people
Julie Orona
client
1 Degree

creative firm
KIKU OBATA & COMPANY
St. Louis, Missouri
creative people
Rich Nelson
client
Southeast Missourian

creative firm
MONDERER DESIGN
Cambridge, Massachusetts
creative people
Stewart Monderer, Jessica deBry
client
Belmont Media Center

creative firm
SAYLES GRAPHIC DESIGN
Des Moines, Iowa
creative people
John Sayles
client
AK O'Connors

creative firm
NANCY FRAME DESIGN
Durham, North Carolina
creative people
Becky Heavner,
Denver, Colorado

creative firm
VITRO/ROBERTSON
Carlsbad, California
creative people
Mike Brower, Paul Lambert,
Tracy Sabin
client
Giving Groves

creative firm
PENSARÉ DESIGN GROUP
Washington, D.C.
creative people
Amy E. Billingham
client
New Hampshire Network of Child Advocacy Centers

NEW HAMPSHIRE NETWORK OF
CHILD ADVOCACY CENTERS

creative firm
Q
Wiesbaden, Germany
creative people
Marcel Kummerer
client
tks solutions

tks solutions

creative firm
RIORDON DESIGN
Oakville, Canada
creative people
Dawn Charney, Ric Riordon,
Steven Noble
client
Chelster Hall

CHELSTER HALL
The Building of a Legacy

creative firm
TYPE G DESIGN
Carlsbad, California
creative people
Mike Nelson, Tracy Sabin
client
Bird Rock Entertainment

BIRD ROCK
ENTERTAINMENT

creative firm
TLC DESIGN
Churchville, Virginia
creative people
Trudy L. Cole
client
Ridge Creek Ranch, TX

Ridge Creek Ranch

creative firm
RIGHT HAT, LLC
Boston, Massachusetts
creative people
Charlyne Fabi
client
Emerging Enterprise Center

Emerging Enterprise Center

creative firm
NEVER BORING DESIGN ASSOCIATES, INC.
Modesto, California
creative people
Betty Gay
client
Boyer

boyer learning center

creative firm
ROUGHSTOCK STUDIOS
San Francisco, California
creative people
Jessica Sand
client
Vista Clara Films

CRUDE IMPACT

creative firm
VELOCITY DESIGN WORKS
Winnipeg, Canada
client
Midnight Ritual

MIDNIGHT RITUAL

creative firm
SERRANO
Carlsbad, California
creative people
Jose Serrano, Tracy Sabin
client
Deleo Clay Tile

DELEO CALIFORNIO Spanish Revival Tiles AUTHENTIC

creative firm
A3 DESIGN
Charlotte, North Carolina
creative people
Alan Altman, Amanda Altman,
Lauren Gualdoni
client
Carbonhouse

venuelements ™

creative firm
NEVER BORING DESIGN ASSOCIATES, INC.
Modesto, California
creative people
Shawn Branstetter
client
Modesto Sand & Gravel

MODESTO SAND AND GRAVEL DEMOLITION & EXCAVATION

creative firm
KENNETH DISEÑO
Uruapan, Mexico
creative people
Kenneth Treviño
client
Aqui Nomas Cantina

creative firm
ATLANTIS VISUAL GRAPHICS
Saratoga Springs, New York
creative people
Phil Rogers
client
Baby's Books

creative firm
NEVER BORING DESIGN ASSOCIATES, INC.
Modesto, California
creative people
Katrina Furton
client
Not For Nothin'

creative firm
NOISE 13
San Francisco, California
creative people
David Handlong
client
Vanilla Elephant

creative firm
OCTAVO DESIGNS
Frederick, Maryland
creative people
Seth Glass, Sue Hough
client
National Association of School Psychologists

creative firm
PINWHEEL STUDIO
Carlsbad, California
creative people
Michele Travis, Tracy Sabin
client
Shepherd's Ranch

creative firm
TLC DESIGN
Churchville, Virginia
creative people
Trudy L. Cole
client
James Madison University

creative firm
LEKASMILLER DESIGN
Walnut Creek, California
creative people
Lana Ip
client
Raymus Homes

creative firm
SPECIAL MODERN DESIGN
Los Angeles, California
creative people
Karen Barranco
client
Skeleton Crew

creative firm
GRAPHIC ADVANCE
Palisades Park, New Jersey
creative people
Aviad Stark
client
Graphic Advance

creative firm
SAYLES GRAPHIC DESIGN
Des Moines, Iowa
creative people
John Sayles
client
Grand Piano Bistro

creative firm
VITRO/ROBERTSON
Carlsbad, California
creative people
Paul Lambert, Tracy Sabin
client
Yamaha Watersports

creative firm
MISENHEIMER CREATIVE, INC.
Alpharetta, Georgia
creative people
Mark Misenheimer
client
Zeal Intl.

creative firm
A3 DESIGN
Charlotte, North Carolina
creative people
Alan Altman, Amanda Altman, Lauren Gualdoni
client
Visit Charlotte

creative firm
TLC DESIGN
Churchville, Virginia
creative people
Trudy L. Cole
client
Bob Driver

creative firm
AIRHART & CO.
St. Louis Park, Minnesota
creative people
David Maloney
client
Cornerstone Church

creative firm
CDI STUDIOS
Las Vegas, Nevada
creative people
Dan McElhattan III
client
Attitude

creative firm
TRUEFACES CREATION SDN BHD
Subang Jaya, Malaysia
creative people
TrueFACES Creative Team
client
DR

creative firm
SAYLES GRAPHIC DESIGN
Des Moines, Iowa
creative people
John Sayles
client
Des Moines Playhouse

TUESDAYS WITH MORRIE

creative firm
VELOCITY DESIGN WORKS
Winnipeg, Canada
creative people
Lasha Orzechowski, Dave Hardy
client
Carbon Interactive Software

carbon INTERACTIVE

creative firm
TLC DESIGN
Churchville, Virginia
creative people
Trudy L. Cole
client
Citizens Against Sexual Assault

Building Community one person at a time

creative firm
BETH SINGER DESIGN LLC
Arlington, Virginia
creative people
Suheun Yu
client
American Israel Public Affairs Committee (AIPAC)

AIPAC NATIONAL SUMMIT
HOUSTON, TEXAS 2006

creative firm
VELOCITY DESIGN WORKS
Winnipeg, Canada
creative people
Lasha Orzechowski
client
Quantus Software

QUANTUS

creative firm
CDI STUDIOS
Las Vegas, Nevada
creative people
Dan McElhattan III
client
MainStream

MAINSTREAM
mind body spirit

creative firm
NEVER BORING DESIGN ASSOCIATES, INC.
Modesto, California
creative people
Betty Gay
client
Joyce Mowry

jma
j. mowry and associates

creative firm
VELOCITY DESIGN WORKS
Winnipeg, Canada
creative people
Lasha Orzechowski
client
Wasabi Restaurant

Wasabi
next door

creative firm
ZERO GRAVITY DESIGN GROUP
Smithtown, New York
creative people
Zero Gravity Design Group
client
Zero Gravity Design Group

zero gravity design group

creative firm
HORIZON MARKETING COMMUNICATIONS
Carlsbad, California
creative people
George Henderson, John Rahe
client
HEP Cat Staffing

creative firm
DESIGN SOURCE
Aptos, California
creative people
Cari Class, Stacey Boscoe
client
Design Source

creative firm
GRAPHIC ADVANCE
Palisades Park, New Jersey
creative people
Aviad Stark
client
Giant Steps

creative firm
BRAIN MAGNET
St. Louis Park, Minnesota
creative people
David Maloney, Gatis Cirulis
client
Paramount Arts

creative firm
SAYLES GRAPHIC DESIGN
Des Moines, Iowa
creative people
John Sayles
client
Sexicide

creative firm
TOM FOWLER, INC.
Norwalk, Connecticut
creative people
Thomas G. Fowler
client
Maritime Aquarium at Norwalk

creative firm
WILLIAM HOMAN DESIGN
Minneapolis, Minnesota
creative people
William Homan
client
Great Waters Fly Fishing Expo

creative firm
DAVID MALONEY
St. Louis Park, Minnesota
creative people
David Maloney
client
In the Basement Productions

creative firm
VELOCITY DESIGN WORKS
Winnipeg, Canada
creative people
Lasha Orzechowski
client
Composites Innovation

creative firm
TOM FOWLER, INC.
Norwalk, Connecticut
creative people
Mary Ellen Butkus
client
Acme United Corporation

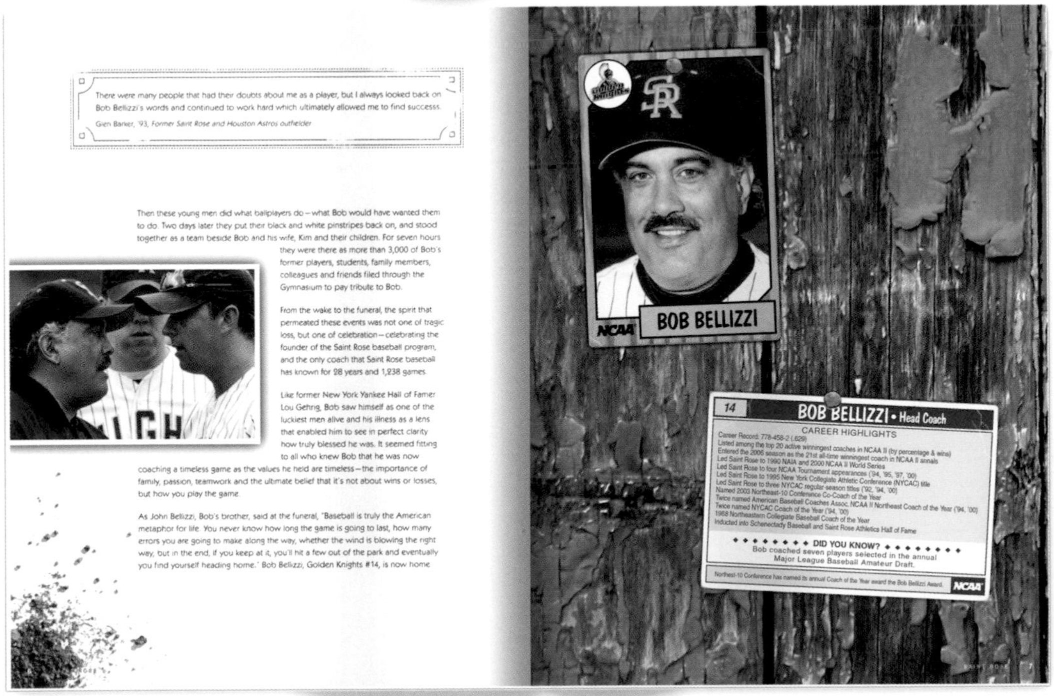

creative firm
THE COLLEGE OF SAINT ROSE,
OFFICE OF PUBLIC RELATIONS & MARKETING
Albany, New York
creative people
Mark Hamilton, Chris Parody
client
The College of Saint Rose

creative firm
STRESSDESIGN
Syracuse, New York
creative people
Christine Walker
client
LC Smith College of
Engineering and Computer Science

creative firm
DEVER DESIGNS
Laurel, Maryland
creative people
Kristin Deuel Duffy,
Jeffrey L. Dever,
Gordon Studer
client
APICS magazine

CrEaTivE concrete

Just add imagination

By Martha Camacho

Colorful, unique, stylish, chic—words not typically associated with concrete. But, as many area homeowners can attest, concrete has the power to transform. Counters, fireplaces, sinks, tables, furniture, patios, driveways—all become customized concrete treasures. All you need is a working imagination and a flexible wallet.

Concrete, when brought inside the home, can be extremely versatile. "What people like about concrete is that it is moldable," says Steve Eyler, owner of Eycon, a decorative concrete company for interior and exterior schemes in Myersville. "The texture of concrete is unique in that it has its own look." Concrete can also be stained just about any color, can take any shape, and can be embellished with glass, copper chips, or tile.

When compared to granite, marble, and other natural stones, concrete is not exceedingly expensive. In fact, concrete is about equal to natural stone when it comes to price. The major difference, says Eyler, is that concrete is a labor-intensive product, but, with natural stone, you are paying for the product. Concrete involves several steps. There's the color to consider (and with the many different color choices, concrete already surpasses natural stone), creating the unique mold, setting the mold, and applying the finishing options.

51

creative firm
DIVERSIONS DESIGN GROUP
Frederick, Maryland
creative people
Joseph Silovich,
Tom Gorsline,
Susan Jansen
client
Frederick Magazine—Creative Concrete

NAVY / MARINE CORPS / COAST GUARD / MERCHANT MARINE
SEAPOWER
HUMANS WILL FIGHT SIDE-BY-SIDE WITH
NEW ERA ROBOTS
May 2007 $4.50
NAVY LEAGUE OF THE
UNITED STATES
www.navyleague.org
INTELLIGENCE, SURVEILLANCE & RECONNAISSANCE / INTERVIEW: JAY M. COHEN

creative firm
PENSARÉ DESIGN GROUP
Washington, D.C.
creative people
Amy E. Billingham
client
Navy League of the United States

creative firm
DESIGN CENTER LTD
Ljubljana, Slovenia
creative people
Eduard Cehovin
client
Design Center Ltd

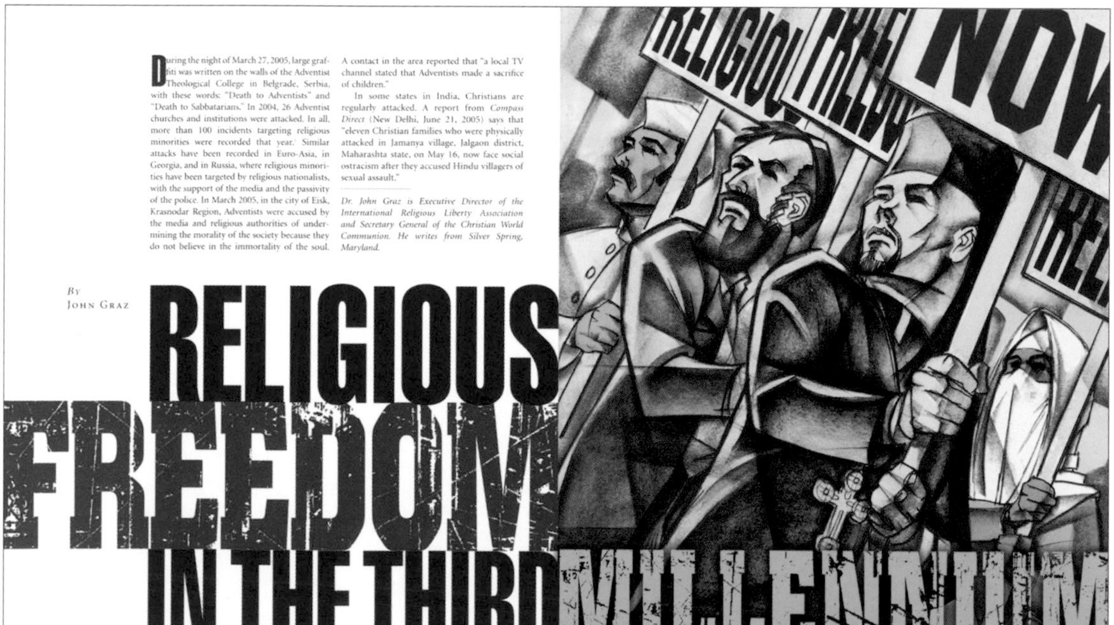

During the night of March 27, 2005, large graffiti was written on the walls of the Adventist Theological College in Belgrade, Serbia, with these words: "Death to Adventists" and "Death to Sabbatarians." In 2004, 26 Adventist churches and institutions were attacked. In all, more than 100 incidents targeting religious minorities were recorded that year.[1] Similar attacks have been recorded in Euro-Asia, in Georgia, and in Russia, where religious minorities have been targeted by religious nationalists, with the support of the media and the passivity of the police. In March 2005, in the city of Eisk, Krasnodar Region, Adventists were accused by the media and religious authorities of undermining the morality of the society because they do not believe in the immortality of the soul. A contact in the area reported that "a local TV channel stated that Adventists made a sacrifice of children."

In some states in India, Christians are regularly attacked. A report from *Compass Direct* (New Delhi, June 21, 2005) says that "eleven Christian families who were physically attacked in Jamanya village, Jalgaon district, Maharashta state, on May 16, now face social ostracism after they accused Hindu villagers of sexual assault."

Dr. John Graz is Executive Director of the International Religious Liberty Association and Secretary General of the Christian World Communion. He writes from Silver Spring, Maryland.

By
John Graz

RELIGIOUS FREEDOM IN THE THIRD MILLENNIUM

2 LIBERTY SEPTEMBER/OCTOBER 2006

ILLUSTRATION BY DAVID KLEIN

creative firm
DEVER DESIGNS
Laurel, Maryland
creative people
Jeffrey L. Dever,
David Klein
client
Liberty Magazine

cool Beans
College coeds on the quest for caffeine
As two Hood College seniors, we're always looking for new, unique places to get a much-needed caffeine buzz for the long hours we spend on papers and studying for exams. We can't even count how many times we've been to the nearby Starbucks and the other great, local coffee joints. So this time we hopped in the car and spent a long—but very fun—afternoon on a mini-road trip, finding coffeehouses outside of Frederick that are not only great places to hang out, but also serve delicious drinks and snacks.
BY BRIDGETTE HARWOOD AND ALISON WALKER
PHOTOGRAPHY BY TIMOTHY JACOBSEN
Frederick November 2005 85

creative firm
DIVERSIONS DESIGN GROUP
Frederick, Maryland
creative people
Joseph Silovich,
Tom Gorsline,
Susan Jansen
client
Frederick Magazine—Cool Beans

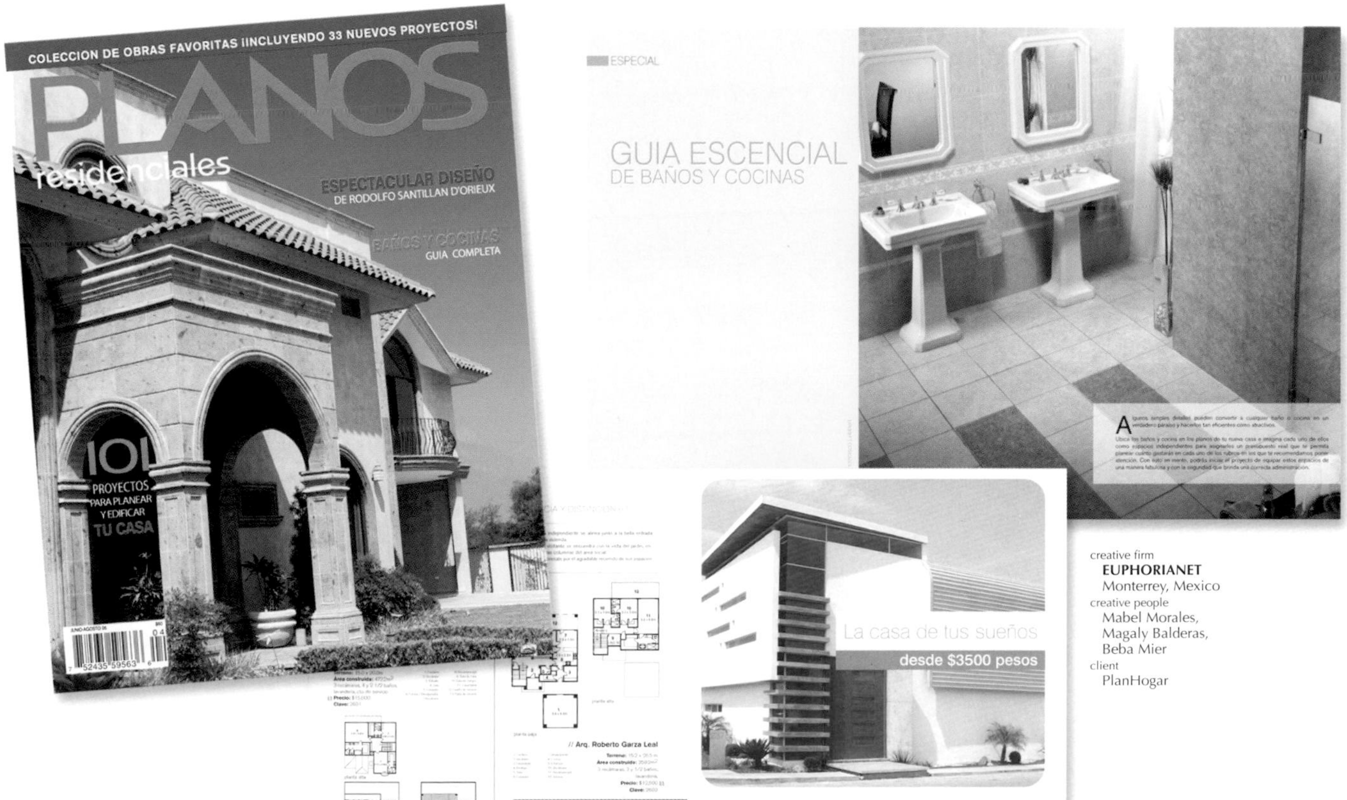
COLECCION DE OBRAS FAVORITAS ¡INCLUYENDO 33 NUEVOS PROYECTOS!
PLANOS
residenciales
ESPECTACULAR DISEÑO
DE RODOLFO SANTILLAN D'ORIEUX
BAÑOS Y COCINAS
GUIA COMPLETA
101
PROYECTOS
PARA PLANEAR
Y EDIFICAR
TU CASA
ESPECIAL
GUIA ESCENCIAL
DE BAÑOS Y COCINAS
La casa de tus sueños
desde $3500 pesos
planos constructivos
// Arq. Roberto Garza Leal

creative firm
EUPHORIANET
Monterrey, Mexico
creative people
Mabel Morales,
Magaly Balderas,
Beba Mier
client
PlanHogar

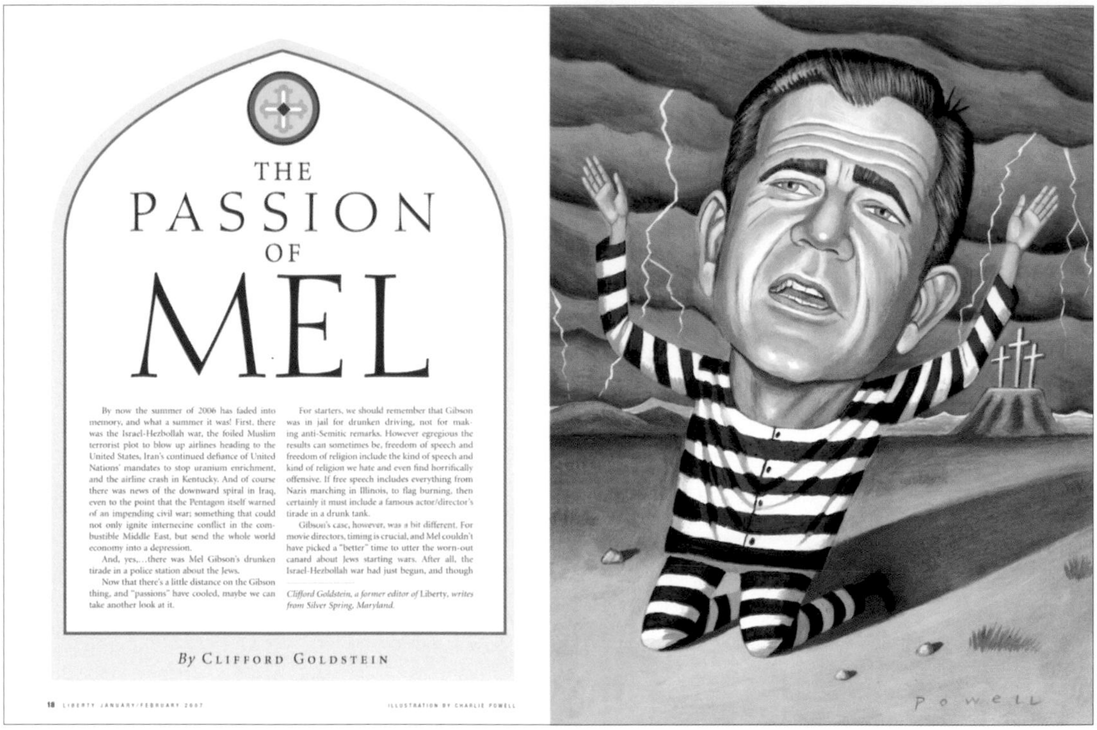

THE PASSION OF MEL

By now the summer of 2006 has faded into memory, and what a summer it was! First, there was the Israel-Hezbollah war, the foiled Muslim terrorist plot to blow up airlines heading to the United States, Iran's continued defiance of United Nations' mandates to stop uranium enrichment, and the airline crash in Kentucky. And of course there was news of the downward spiral in Iraq, even to the point that the Pentagon itself warned of an impending civil war; something that could not only ignite internecine conflict in the combustible Middle East, but send the whole world economy into a depression.

And, yes,…there was Mel Gibson's drunken tirade in a police station about the Jews.

Now that there's a little distance on the Gibson thing, and "passions" have cooled, maybe we can take another look at it.

For starters, we should remember that Gibson was in jail for drunken driving, not for making anti-Semitic remarks. However egregious the results can sometimes be, freedom of speech and freedom of religion include the kind of speech and kind of religion we hate and even find horrifically offensive. If free speech includes everything from Nazis marching in Illinois, to flag burning, then certainly it must include a famous actor/director's tirade in a drunk tank.

Gibson's case, however, was a bit different. For movie directors, timing is crucial, and Mel couldn't have picked a "better" time to utter the worn-out canard about Jews starting wars. After all, the Israel-Hezbollah war had just begun, and though

Clifford Goldstein, a former editor of Liberty, *writes from Silver Spring, Maryland.*

By CLIFFORD GOLDSTEIN

18 LIBERTY JANUARY/FEBRUARY 2007

ILLUSTRATION BY CHARLIE POWELL

creative firm
DEVER DESIGNS
Laurel, Maryland
creative people
Jeffrey L. Dever,
Charlie Powell
client
Liberty Magazine

creative firm
DOIT ADVERTISING
Mumbai, India
creative people
Tushar Chikodikar
client
Afcons Infrastructure Ltd.

creative firm
CHUTE GERDEMAN RETAIL
Columbus, Ohio
creative people
Dennis Gerdeman, Brian Shafley, Wendy Johnson, Bess Anderson, Steve Boreman, Steve Pottschmidt, Susan Siewny, Steve Johnson, George Waite
client
Mars Retail Group

(continued)
creative firm
CHUTE GERDEMAN RETAIL
Columbus, Ohio
client
Mars Retail Group

Broadway
ONE WAY

MANDALAY BAY
MANDALAY BAY
MANDALAY BAY
sidekick 3

T · · Mobile ·
OFFICIAL PARTNER
STEP INTO THE MIND OF D. WADE
T · · Mobile ·
sidekick 3

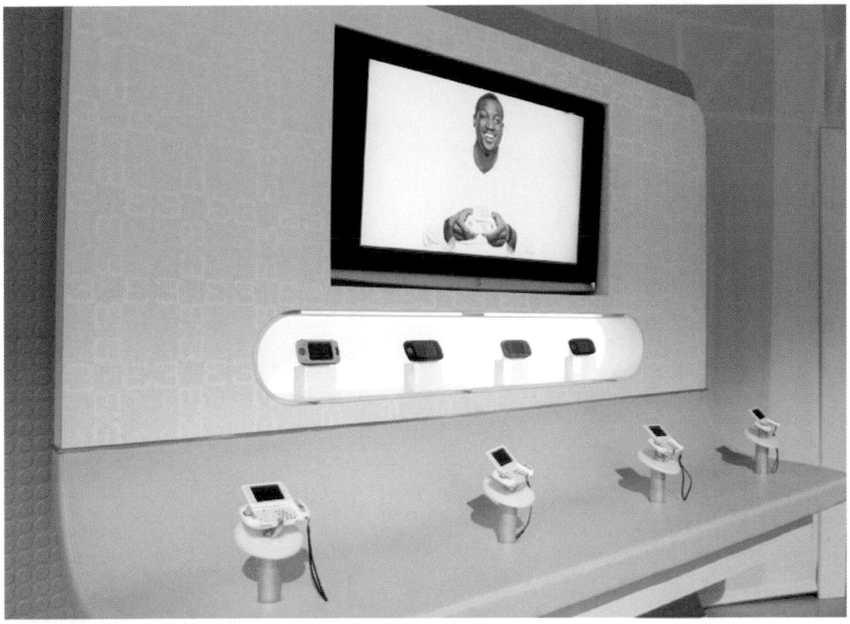

creative firm
HORNALL ANDERSON DESIGN
Seattle, Washington
creative people
James Tee, Mark Popich, Andrew Well, Jon Graeff, Ethan Keller, Javas Lehn, Kalani Gregoire, Brenna Pierce, Peg Johnson, Chris Nielson, Judy Dixon, Rachel Lancaster, Ryan Hickner, Jordan Lee, Thad Donat, Wexley School for Girls, Blank Design, Media Alchemy, Lens Films, Atmosphere, Popich Sign Inc., Nichols Printing
client
T-Mobile

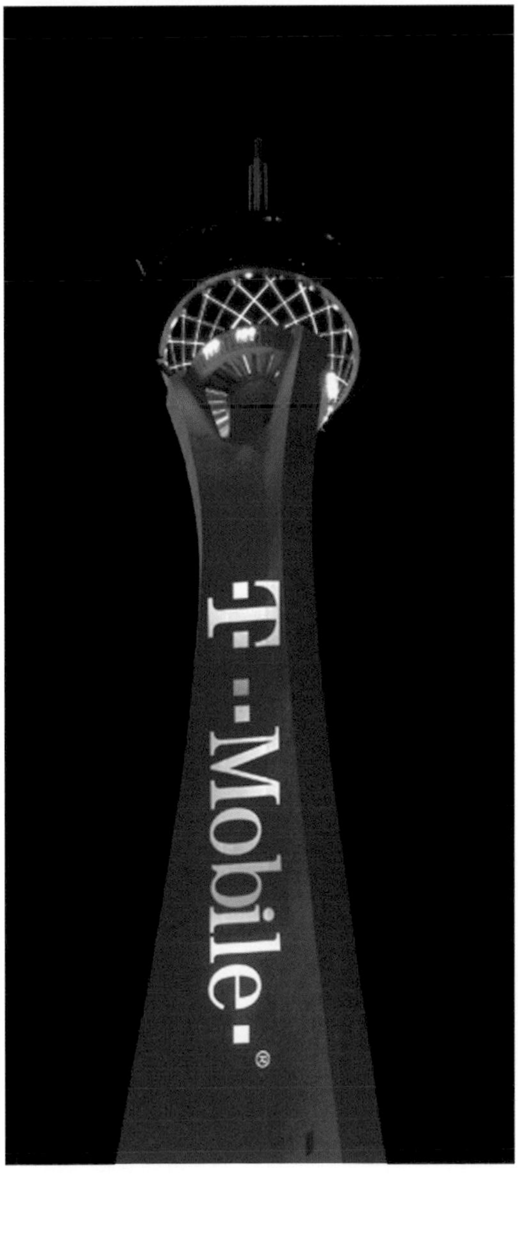

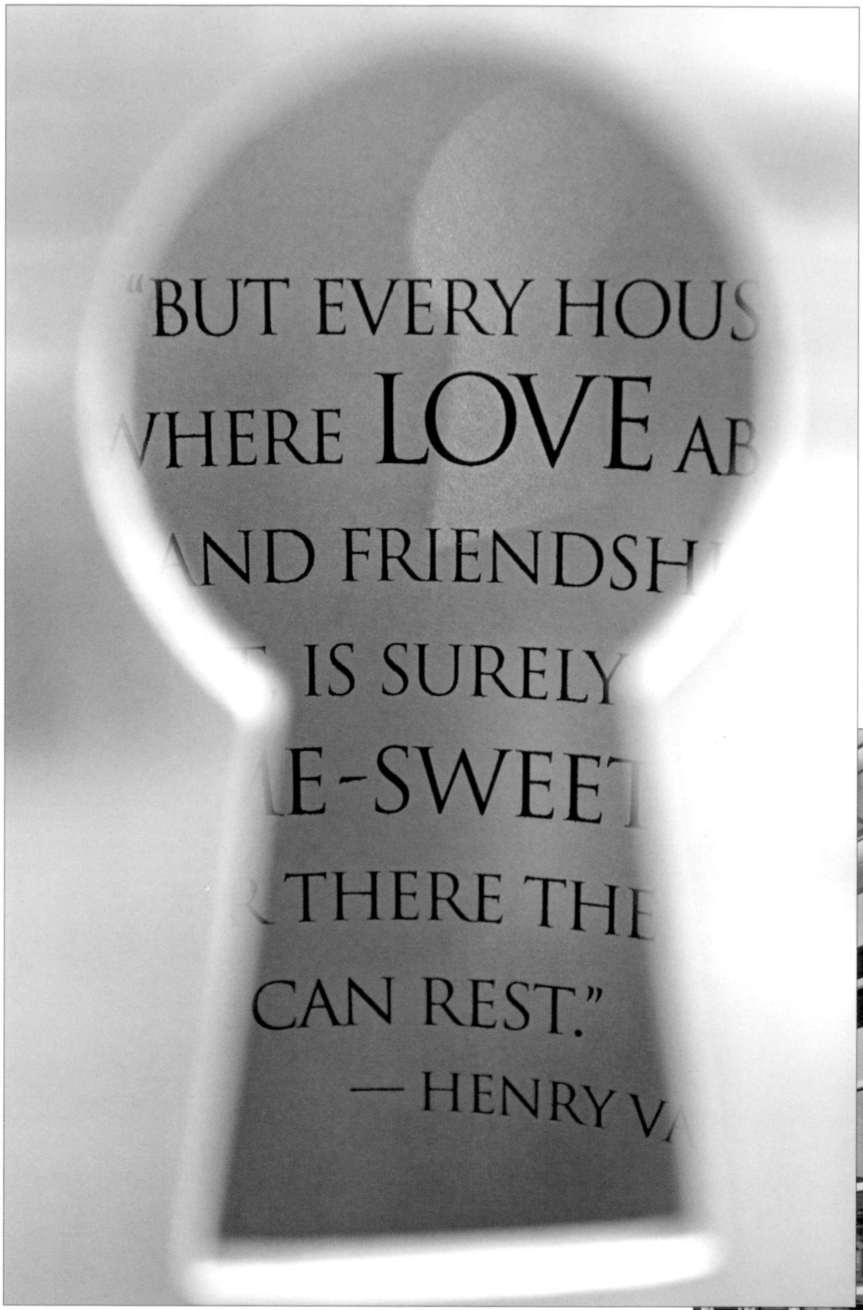
"BUT EVERY HOUS
WHERE LOVE
AND FRIENDSH
IS SURELY
THERE
CAN REST."
— HENRY

creative firm
BETH SINGER DESIGN LLC
Arlington, Virginia
creative people
Beth Singer, Howard Smith, Lolan O'Rourke
client
National Association of Realtors

"WHEREVER
WE SEE
THIS TRUTH

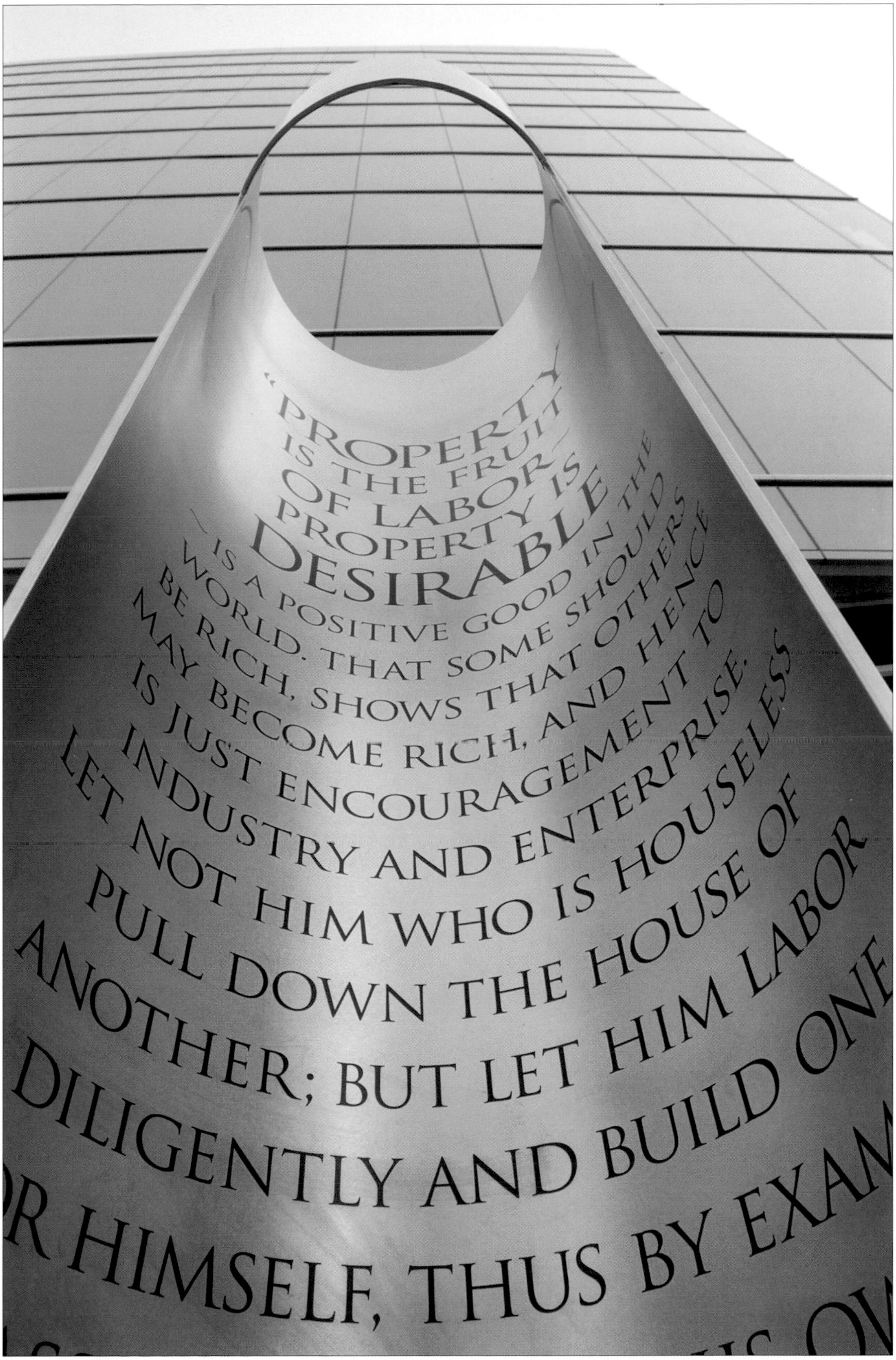
"PROPERTY
IS THE FRUIT
OF LABOR—
PROPERTY IS
DESIRABLE
IS A POSITIVE GOOD IN THE
WORLD. THAT SOME SHOULD
BE RICH, SHOWS THAT OTHERS
MAY BECOME RICH, AND HENCE
IS JUST ENCOURAGEMENT TO
INDUSTRY AND ENTERPRISE.
LET NOT HIM WHO IS HOUSELESS
PULL DOWN THE HOUSE OF
ANOTHER; BUT LET HIM LABOR
DILIGENTLY AND BUILD ONE
HIMSELF, THUS BY

CIÈLLA
11759

creative firm
KIKU OBATA & COMPANY
St. Louis, Missouri
creative people
Kiku Obata, Kevin Flynn, AIA, Russell Buchanan, Jr., Paul Scherfling, Farrah Katzer, Carole Jerome, Carla Cruz, Sarah Royal, Jon Miller
client
Bakers Footwear Group

creative firm
KIKU OBATA & COMPANY
St. Louis, Missouri
creative people
Kiku Obata, Kevin Flynn, AIA, Dennis Hyland, AIA, Denise Fuehne, Jim Redington, Mel Lim-Keylon, Allan Karchmer
client
Mills Corporation

tical
casa

Blanco

creative firm
HORNALL ANDERSON DESIGN
Seattle, Washington
creative people
Jamie Monberg, Nathan Young, Joe King, Hans Krebs, Javas Lehn, David Bates, Adrien Lo, Corey Paganucci, Ryan Hickner, Jordan Lee, Chris Monberg, Chris Freed, Kevin Roth, Halli Brunkella
client
Space Needle

creative firm
LORENC+YOO DESIGN
Roswell, Georgia
creative people
Jan Lorenc, Steve McCall, Ken Boyd, Sakchai Rangiskhorn, Susie Caldwell Norris, Janice McCall
client
Haworth Showroom

creative firm
FUNK/LEVIS & ASSOCIATES
Eugene, Oregon
creative people
Chris Berner
client
Imagine Graphics

creative firm
CHUTE GERDEMAN RETAIL
Columbus, Ohio
creative people
Dennis Gerdeman, Brian Shafley, Wendy Johnson, Steve Pottschmidt, Bess Anderson, Steve Boreman, Susan Siewny, Jon Knodell
client
Mars Retail Group

creative firm
LORENC+YOO DESIGN
Roswell, Georgia
creative people
Jan Lorenc, Steve McCall, David Park
client
Phillips Edison & Company

creative firm
SAYLES GRAPHIC DESIGN
Des Moines, Iowa
creative people
John Sayles
client
Temple for Performing Arts

creative firm
DOIT ADVERTISING
Mumbai, India
creative people
Nilesh Parab
client
Goldshield Healthcare Pvt. Ltd.

creative firm
PENSARÉ DESIGN GROUP
Washington, D.C.
creative people
Lauren Emeritz
client
Midtown Association

creative firm
HORNALL ANDERSON DESIGN
Seattle, Washington
creative people
Jack Anderson, James Tee, Andrew Wicklund, Elmer dela Cruz, Holly Craven, Jay Hilburn, Hayden Schoen, Belinda Bowling, Yuri Shvets, Michael Connors, Larry Anderson, Chris Freed, Erin McFarlan
client
Weyerhaeuser Corporation

creative firm
STRESSDESIGN
Syracuse, New York
creative people
Christine Walker
client
Syracuse University School of Education

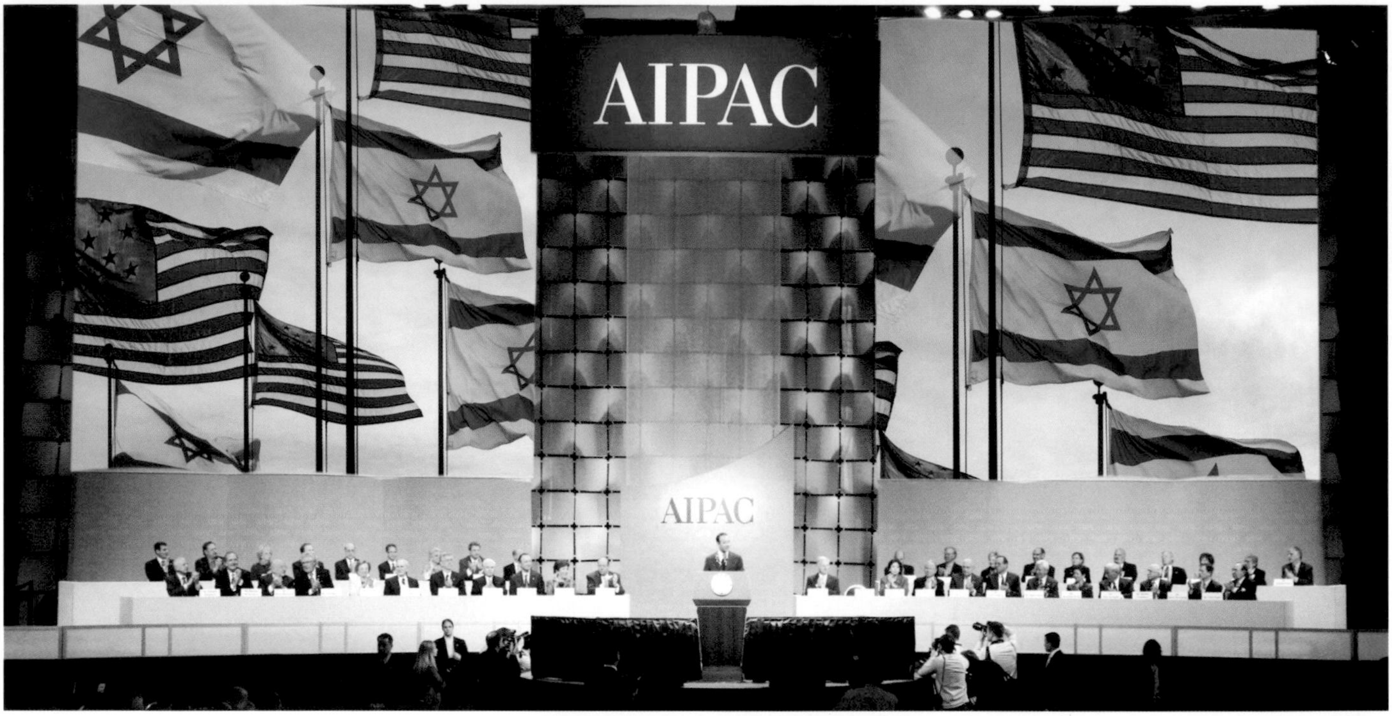

creative firm
BETH SINGER DESIGN LLC
Arlington, Virginia
creative people
Sucha Snidvongs, Suheun Yu
client
American Israel Public Affairs Committee (AIPAC)

creative firm
LORENC+YOO DESIGN
Roswell, Georgia
creative people
Jan Lorenc, Steve McCall, Chung Youl Yoo
client
Gaylord Texan Resort and Convention Center

creative firm
KIKU OBATA & COMPANY
St. Louis, Missouri
creative people
Kiku Obata, Kevin Flynn, AIA, Dennis Hyland, AIA, Jim Redington, Lisa Bollmann, Sarah Royal, Jon Miller
client
Joe Edwards

Brunswick

BOWLING

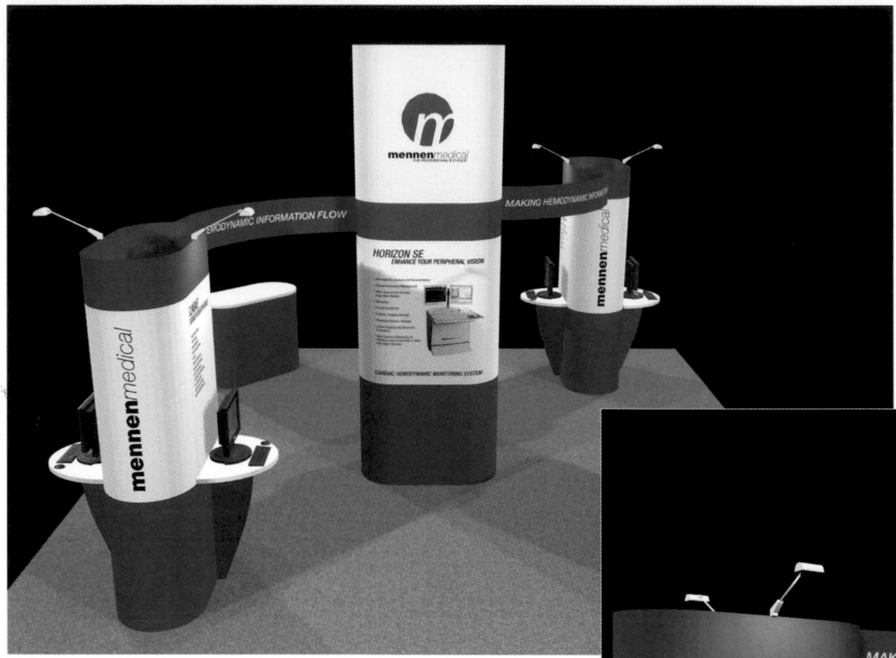

creative firm
GRAPHIC ADVANCE
Palisades Park, New Jersey
creative people
Aviad Stark
client
Mennen Medical

creative firm
LORENC+YOO DESIGN
Roswell, Georgia
creative people
Jan Lorenc
client
North Carolina State University

CUSHMAN & WAKEFIELD
CUSHMAN & WAKEFIELD
Retail Services
A|X
A/X ARMANI
EXCHANGE
CUSHMAN & WAKEFIELD

creative firm
LORENC+YOO DESIGN
Roswell, Georgia
creative people
Jan Lorenc, Jisun An, Ken Boyd
client
Cushman & Wakefield

creative firm
STEPHEN LONGO DESIGN ASSOCIATES
West Orange, New Jersey
creative people
Stephen Longo
client
Ekko Restaurant

creative firm
INDICIA DESIGN
Kansas City, Missouri
creative people
Isaiah Crabb
client
SKC Communications

creative firm
LORENC+YOO DESIGN
Roswell, Georgia
creative people
Jan Lorenc, Steve McCall, Chung Youl Yoo, David Park, Jisun An, Ken Boyd
client
Mayo Clinic Heritage Hall

HEY,
are
My
some
call
them
plain,
we
call
them
perfect

NASCAR
NASCAR
Official Chocolate of NASCAR
38
citifinancial
CLEVITE
WIX
GOODYEAR
Gillette
Commit
JESEL

creative firm
CHUTE GERDEMAN RETAIL
Columbus, Ohio
creative people
Dennis Gerdeman, Brian Shafley, Wendy Johnson, Steve Pottschmidt, Bess Anderson, Steve Boreman, Susan Siewny, Jon Knodell
client
Mars Retail Group

creative firm
KIKU OBATA & COMPANY
St. Louis, Missouri
creative people
Kiku Obata, Laura McCanna, Rich Nelson, Carole Jerome, Russell Buchanan, Jr., David Leavey, Todd Mayberry, Denise Fuehne, Jef Ebers, Sam Fentress
client
Busch Stadium

LEFT FIELD
LEFT FIELD
LEFT FIELD

AIPAC
Conference Programs

AIPAC Policy Conference 2007
Café
Registration
AIPAC Policy Conference 2007
Three of the Most Important Days
Affecting Israel's Future
AIPAC Policy Conference 2007
Registration
Coat Check
Café

creative firm
BETH SINGER DESIGN LLC
Arlington, Virginia
creative people
Howard Smith, Nate West
client
American Israel Public Affairs Committee (AIPAC)

creative firm
RIORDON DESIGN
Ontario, Canada
creative people
Dawn Charney, Ric Riordon
client
S-VOX

creative firm
STEPHEN LONGO DESIGN ASSOCIATES
West Orange, New Jersey
creative people
Stephen Longo
client
Ekko Restaurant

creative firm
OCTAVO DESIGNS
Frederick, Maryland
creative people
Sue Hough
client
The Temple, A Paul Mitchell Partner School

CARGO
We carry the complete
Cargo product line.
www.edwardcarriere.com

Bumble and bumble.
Bb.
Seaweed
SHAMPOO
Bumble and bumble.
Bb.
Seaweed
CONDITIONER
après-shampooing
We carry the complete
Bumble and bumble
product line.
www.edwardcarriere.com

creative firm
VELOCITY DESIGN WORKS
Winnipeg, Canada
client
Edward Carriere Salon

fábrica
SAN PEDRO
MUESTRA DE
MAQUINARIA TEXTIL
del
SIGLO XIX
FUNCIONANDO
URUAPAN MICHOACAN

creative firm
KENNETH DISEÑO
Uruapan, Mexico
creative people
Kenneth Treviño
client
San Pedro Textile Museum

creative firm
SIGHTLINE MARKETING
Washington, D.C.
creative people
Clay Marshall
client
TRC Companies

BREAKING NEW GROUND
Making the right investment. Every day, our clients must decide whether to fix something or build something new—and we help them evaluate their options and make the right choice. When it comes to investing your money in a new venture, you need a partner who gets the big picture and can help you plan, implement, and deliver the results you expect and need. At TRC, we not only share your goals, we also take responsibility for reaching them.
Solving your legacy issues. Businesses and government must often deal with legacy issues that can distract them from their current operational needs and future plans. Whether it's maintaining a highway or remediating an environmentally impaired site, TRC helps our clients navigate their most complex legacy issues—often resolving them once and for all, so our clients can focus on their core operations.
TRC brings an entrepreneurial spirit to every project—breaking new ground with insightful solutions to each challenge. Some of our most innovative solutions, such as our Exit Strategy® Program, have pioneered new ways of tackling business and community problems and improved the quality, efficiency, and cost of resolving them. Our team gives you the comprehensive perspective you need to ensure your projects are executed properly. When we are accountable for a project from start to finish, we are able to head off potential problems or mitigate their impact.
TRC

creative firm
MCNULTY CREATIVE
Carlsbad, California
creative people
Mary McNulty, Tracy Sabin
client
National First Credit Union

creative firm
TYP-A-LICIOUS
Columbia, Missouri
creative people
Deborah Huelsbergen
client
Deborah Huelsbergen
"Annie's Stars"

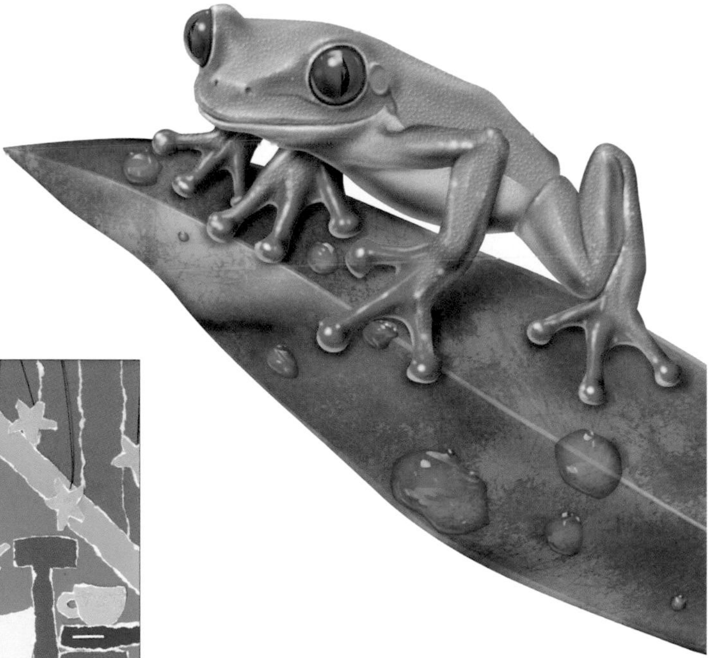

creative firm
SERRANO
Carlsbad, California
creative people
Jose Serrano, Tracy Sabin
client
Costa Rican Properties

creative firm
VELOCITY DESIGN WORKS
Winnipeg, Canada
creative people
Lasha Orzechowski, Eric Peters
client
Child Find Manitoba

creative firm
TYP-A-LICIOUS
Columbia, Missouri
creative people
Deborah Huelsbergen
client
Missouri Department of Ag
and Lincoln University

creative firm
GO GRAPHIC
Beirut, Lebanon
creative people
Maria Assi, Yasmina Baz
client
Sahtein Restaurant

creative firm
VELOCITY DESIGN WORKS
Winnipeg, Canada
creative people
Lasha Orzechowski,
Charlene Kasdorf
client
Edward Carriere Salon

creative firm
RONI HICKS & ASSOCIATES
Carlsbad, California
creative people
Tracy Sabin, Stephen Sharp
client
4S Ranch

creative firm
SERRANO
Carlsbad, California
creative people
Jose Serrano, Tracy Sabin
client
Costa Rican Properties

creative firm
2FRESH
Istanbul, Turkey
creative people
2FRESH
client
Anti Magazine

creative firm
TLC DESIGN
Churchville, Virginia
creative people
Trudy L. Cole
client
US Mint

creative firm
SERRANO
Carlsbad, California
creative people
Jose Serrano, Tracy Sabin
client
Costa Rican Properties

creative firm
TYP-A-LICIOUS
Columbia, Missouri
creative people
Deborah Huelsbergen
client
Deborah Huelsbergen
"Annie's Stars"

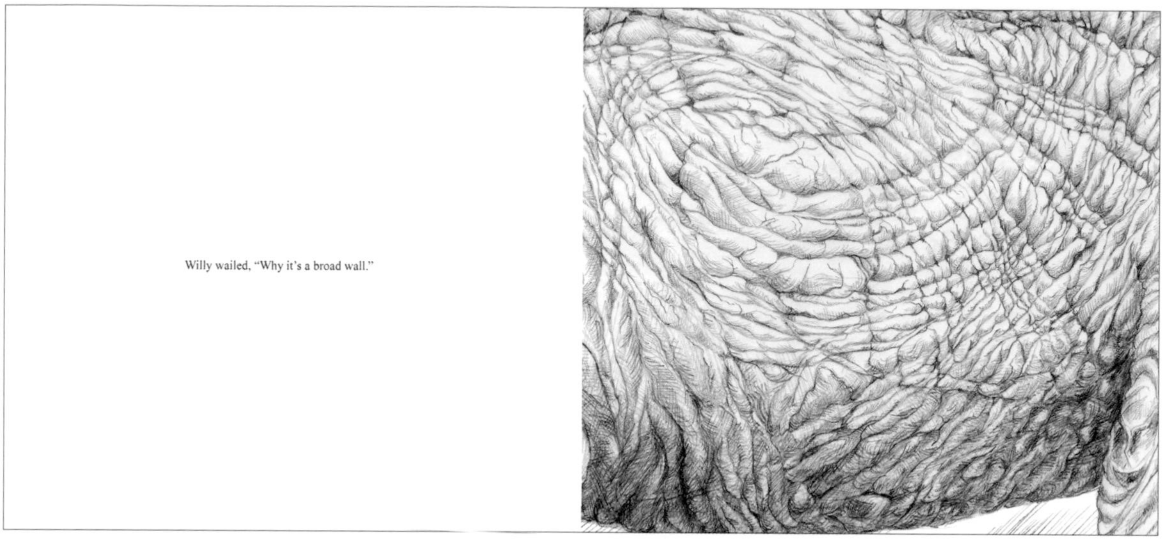
Willy wailed, "Why it's a broad wall."

creative firm
TLC DESIGN
Churchville, Virginia
creative people
Trudy L. Cole
client
Trudy L. Cole

creative firm
2FRESH
Istanbul, Turkey
creative people
2FRESH
client
Anti Magazine/Istanbul

creative firm
TYP-A-LICIOUS
Columbia, Missouri
creative people
Deborah Huelsbergen
client
Deborah Huelsbergen
"Annie's Stars"

creative firm
VELOCITY DESIGN WORKS
Winnipeg, Canada
creative people
Lasha Orzechowski, Eric Peters
client
Child Find Manitoba

creative firm
PARTNERS, INC.
Carlsbad, California
creative people
Steve Falen, Tracy Sabin
client
Advanced Imaging

creative firm
TYP-A-LICIOUS
Columbia, Missouri
creative people
Deborah Huelsbergen
client
Deborah Huelsbergen

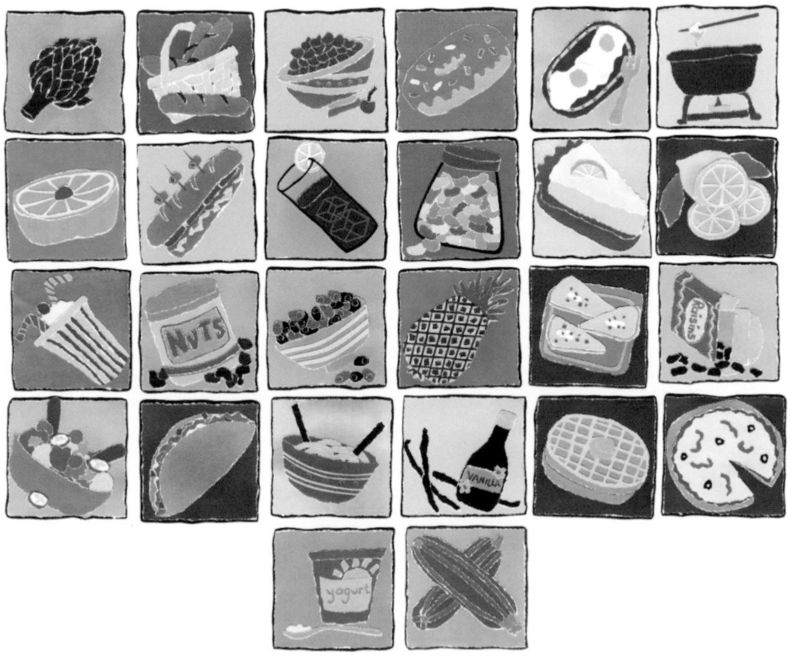

creative firm
TYP-A-LICIOUS
Columbia, Missouri
creative people
Deborah Huelsbergen
client
Global Kids

creative firm
TLC DESIGN
Churchville, Virginia
creative people
Trudy L. Cole
client
Trudy L. Cole

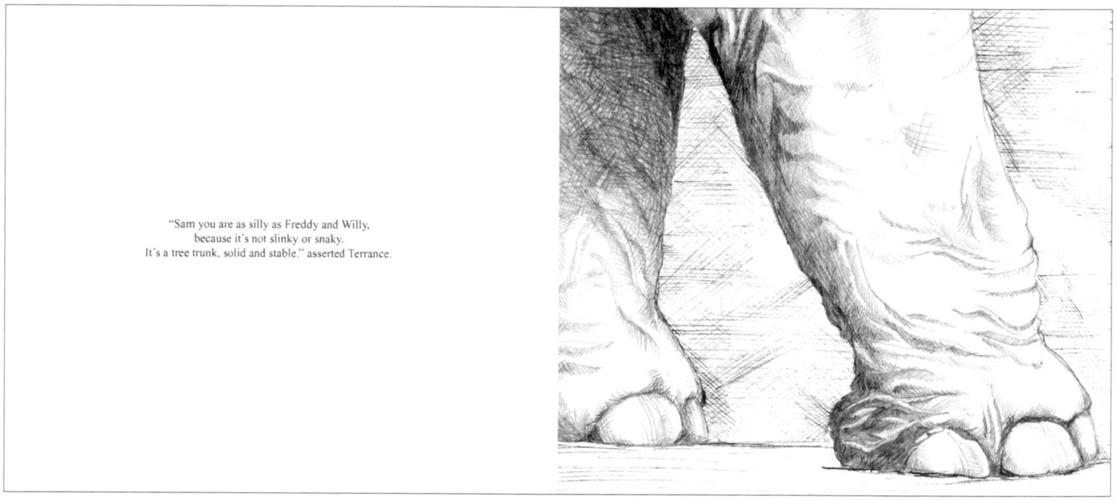
"Sam you are as silly as Freddy and Willy,
because it's not slinky or snaky.
It's a tree trunk, solid and stable." asserted Terrance.

creative firm
TRUEFACES CREATION SDN BHD
Subang Jaya, Malaysia
creative people
TrueFACES Creative Team
client
Star Publication (Malaysia) Bhd

Celebrate New York Cuisine
100 Fine Wines • 30 Great Wineries
10 Top Restaurants

creative firm
BUITENKANT DESIGN
Port Jefferson Station, New York
creative people
Vava Buitenkant
client
The New York Wine & Grape Foundation/HDI

creative firm
VELOCITY DESIGN WORKS
Winnipeg, Canada
creative people
Lasha Orzechowski, Eric Peters
client
Child Find Manitoba

creative firm
TLC DESIGN
Churchville, Virginia
creative people
Trudy L. Cole
client
Trudy L. Cole

searching for the piece of golden light.

creative firm
TYP-A-LICIOUS
Columbia, Missouri
creative people
Deborah Huelsbergen
client
Deborah Huelsbergen
"When I'm Out of the House"

creative firm
TWOINTANDEM LLC
Ozone Park, New York
creative people
Sanver Kanidinc, Elena Ruano Kanidinc
client
Twointandem

creative firm
NEVER BORING DESIGN ASSOCIATES, INC.
Modesto, California
creative people
Ethen Beavers
client
Prime Shine Express

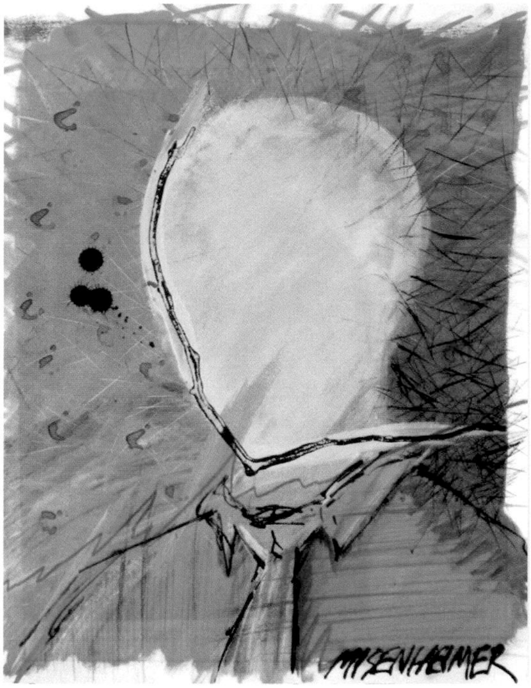
MISENHEIMER

creative firm
MISENHEIMER CREATIVE, INC.
Alpharetta, Georgia
creative people
Mark Misenheimer
client
SouthPark Update Magazine

creative firm
VELOCITY DESIGN WORKS
Winnipeg, Canada
creative people
Lasha Orzechowski, Eric Peters
client
Child Find Manitoba

SCHOOL

creative firm
TLC DESIGN
Churchville, Virginia
creative people
Trudy L. Cole
client
Trudy L. Cole

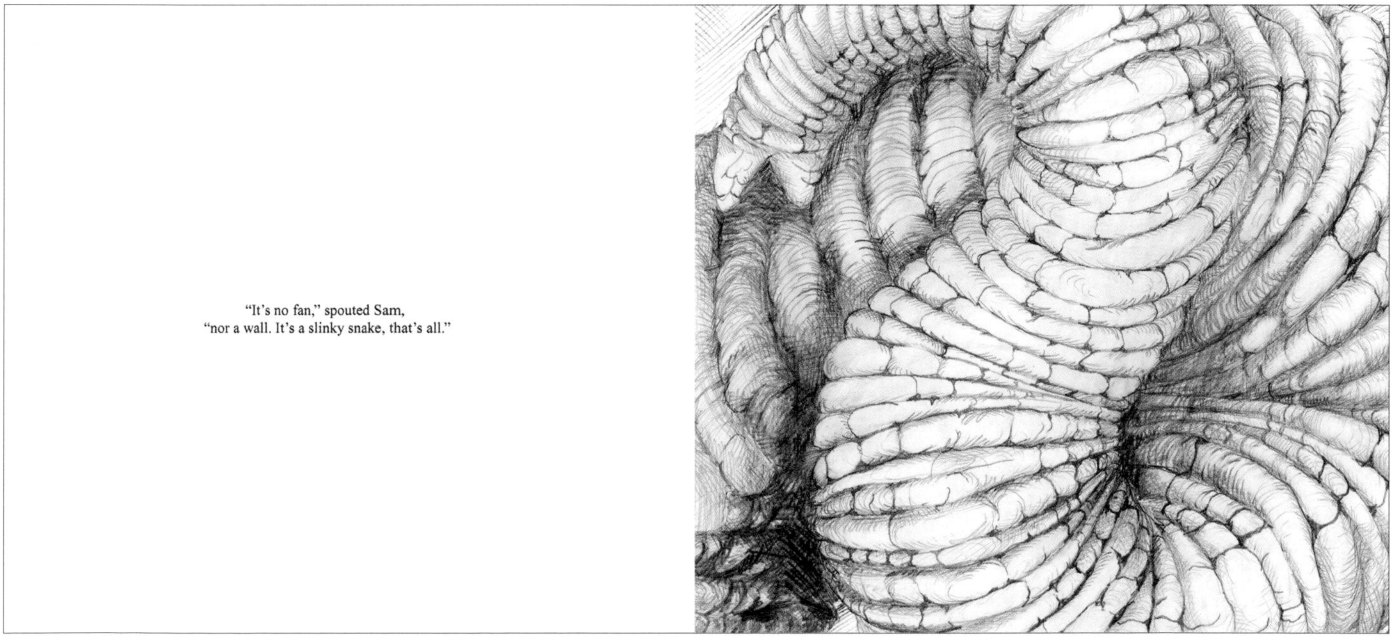
"It's no fan," spouted Sam,
"nor a wall. It's a slinky snake, that's all."

So they swam up,

creative firm
TLC DESIGN
Churchville, Virginia
creative people
Trudy L. Cole
client
Trudy L. Cole

creative firm
FUNK/LEVIS & ASSOCIATES
Eugene, Oregon
creative people
Lada Korol
client
Food for Lane County

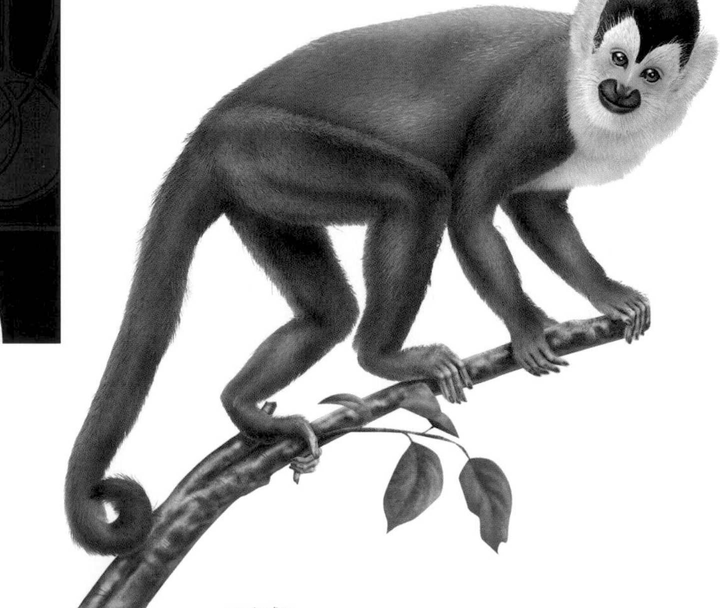

creative firm
SERRANO
Carlsbad, California
creative people
Jose Serrano, Tracy Sabin
client
Costa Rican Properties

creative firm
FRY HAMMOND BARR
Orlando, Florida
creative people
Tim Fisher, Sean Brunson
client
Contemporary Wood Concepts

creative firm
BETH SINGER DESIGN LLC
Arlington, Virginia
creative people
Sucha Snidvongs, Suheun Yu
client
Museum Word

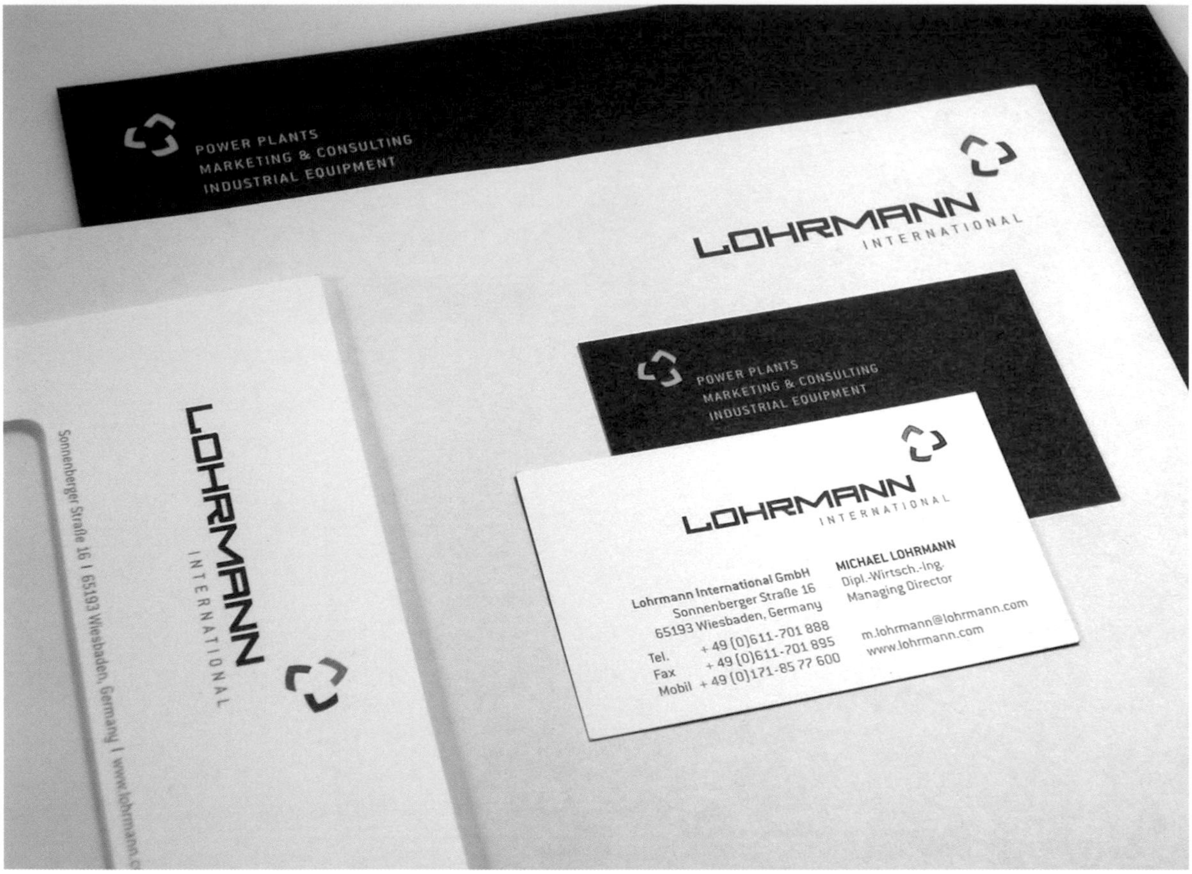

creative firm
Q
Wiesbaden, Germany
creative people
Marcel Kummerer
client
Lohrmann International

creative firm
NEVER BORING DESIGN ASSOCIATES, INC.
Modesto, California
creative people
Betty Gay
client
Apropos

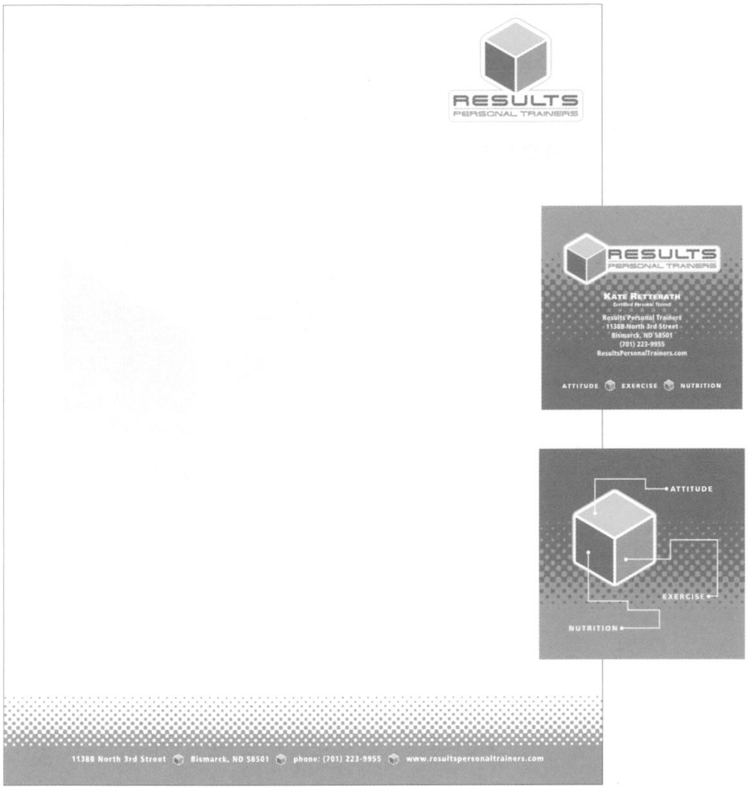

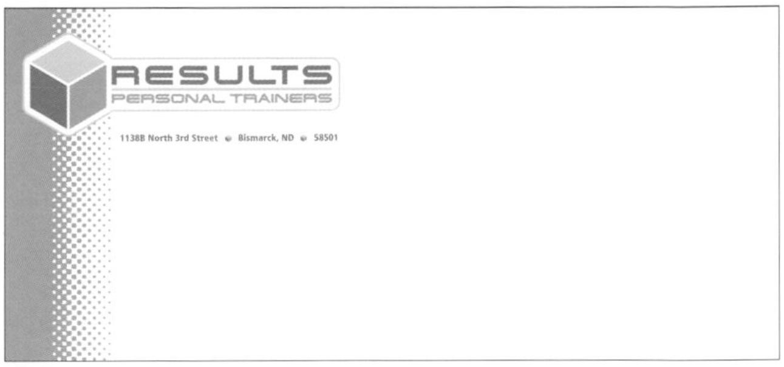

creative firm
MFDI
Selinsgrove, Pennsylvania
creative people
Mark Fertig
client
Results Personal Trainers

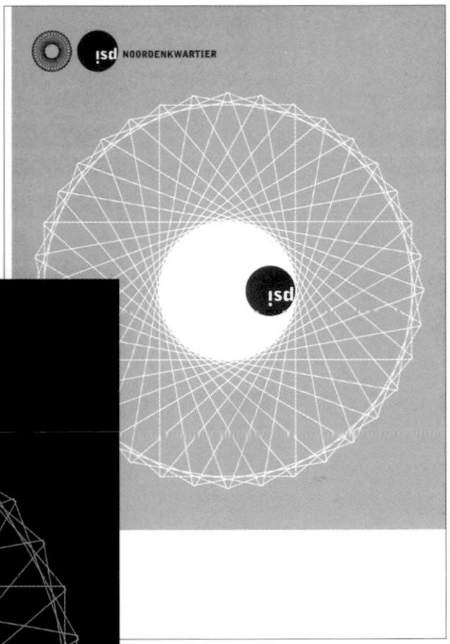

creative firm
ERWIN ZINGER GRAPHIC DESIGN
Groningen, The Netherlands
creative people
Erwin Zinger
client
ISD (Intergemeentelijke Sociale Dienst)

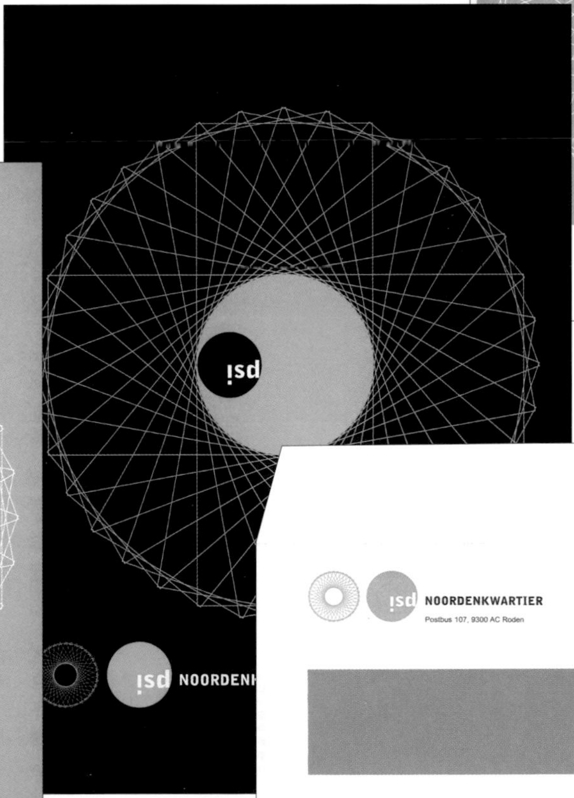

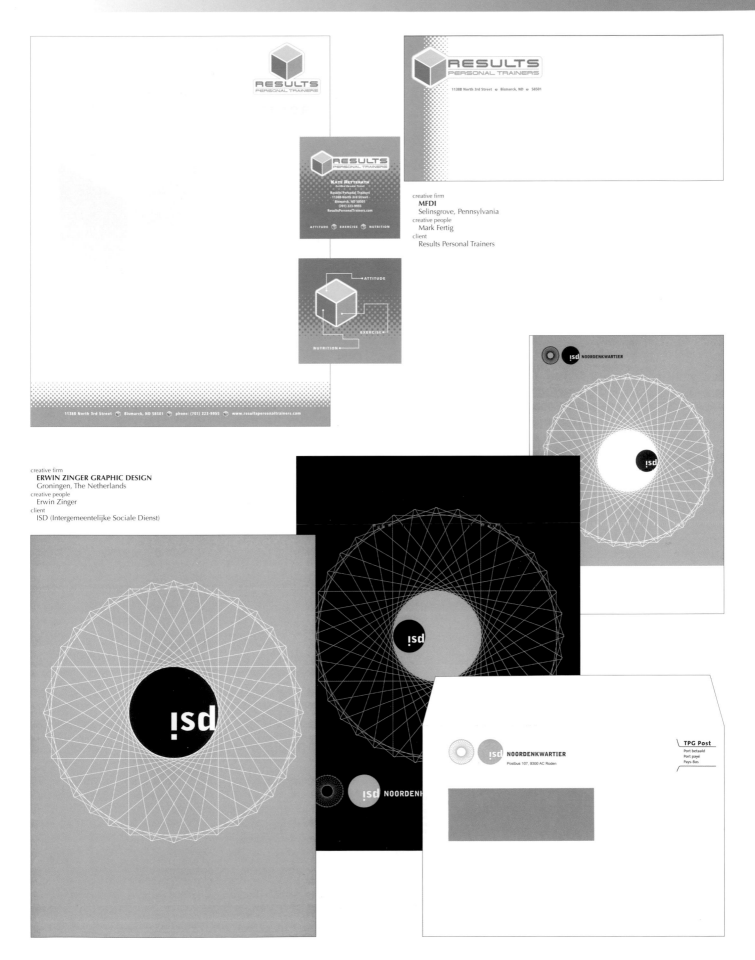

creative firm
ZERO GRAVITY DESIGN GROUP
Smithtown, New York
creative people
Zero Gravity Design Group
client
Attwood Equestrian Surfaces

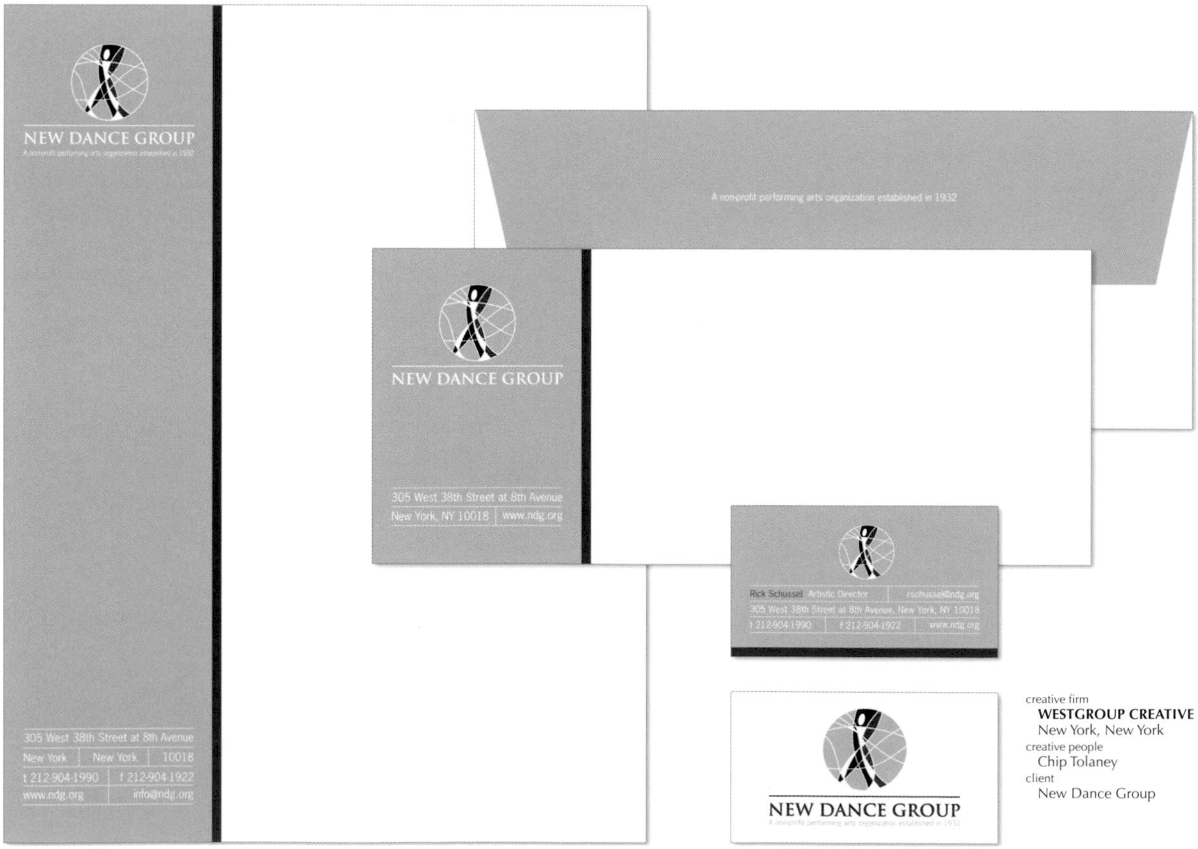

creative firm
WESTGROUP CREATIVE
New York, New York
creative people
Chip Tolaney
client
New Dance Group

creative firm
DESIGN SOURCE
Aptos, California
creative people
Cari Class, Stacey Boscoe
client
Design Source

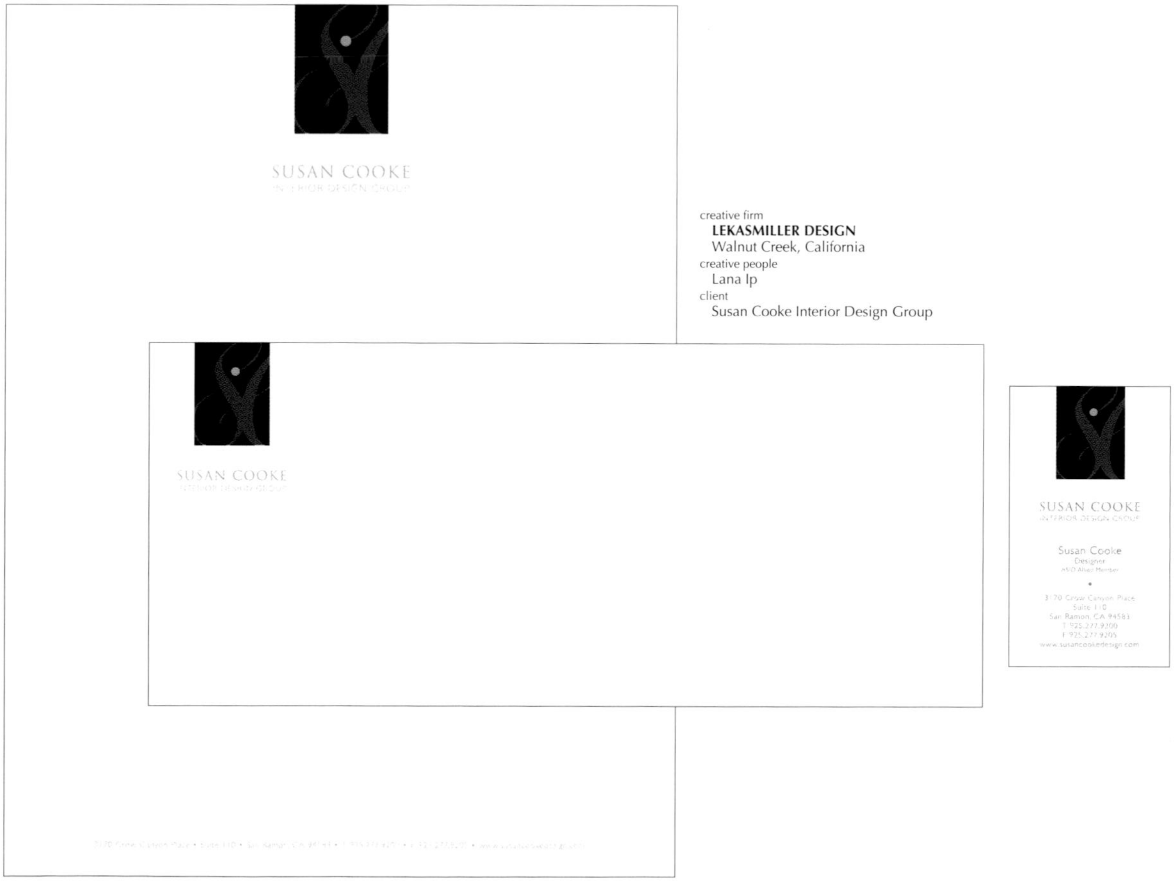

creative firm
LEKASMILLER DESIGN
Walnut Creek, California
creative people
Lana Ip
client
Susan Cooke Interior Design Group

creative firm
DARLING DESIGN GROUP
New York, New York
creative people
Courtney Darling, Amanda Sica
client
M&N Installation

creative firm
NEVER BORING DESIGN ASSOCIATES, INC.
Modesto, California
creative people
Betty Gay
client
Boyer

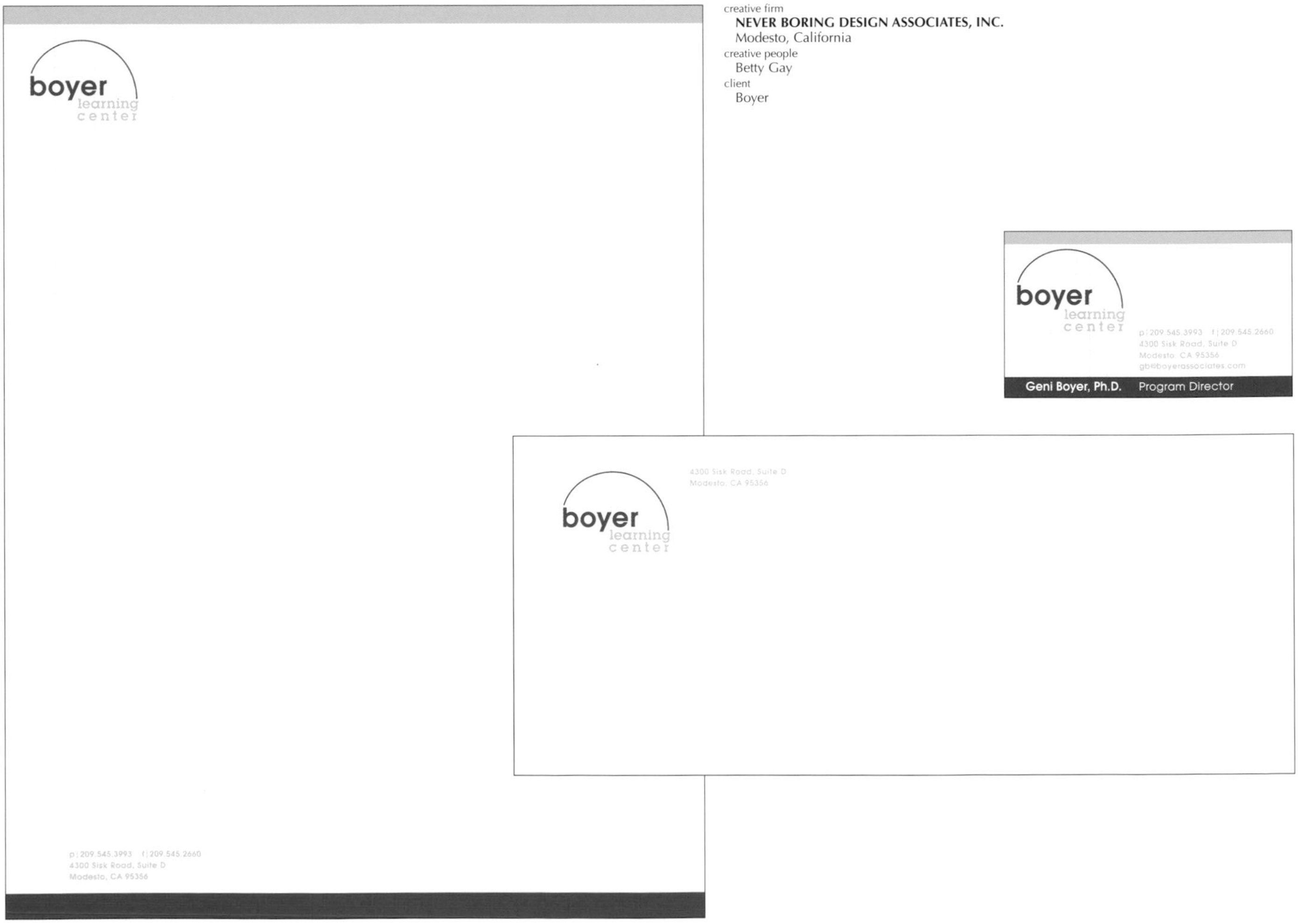

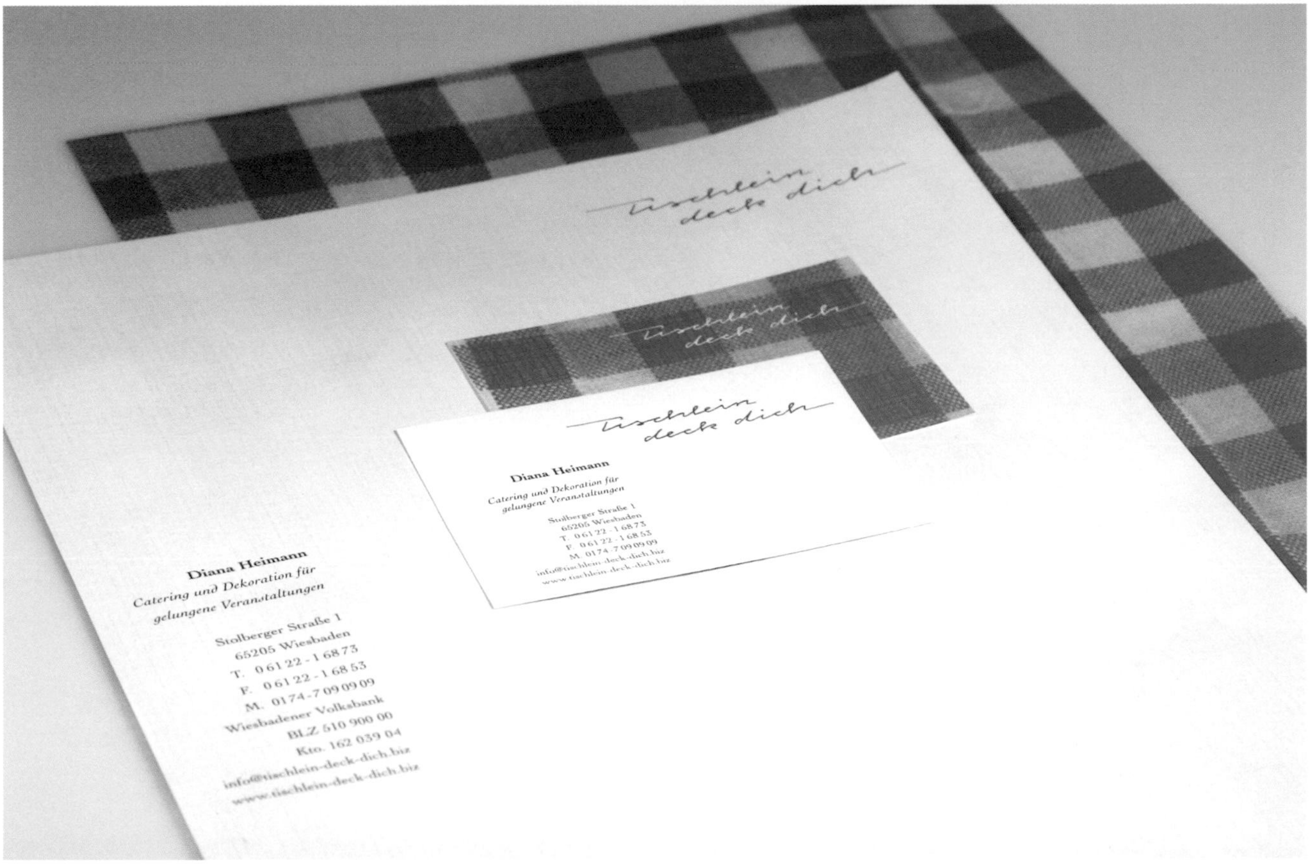

creative firm
Q
Wiesbaden, Germany
creative people
Laurenz Nielbock
client
Tischlein Deck Dich, Catering

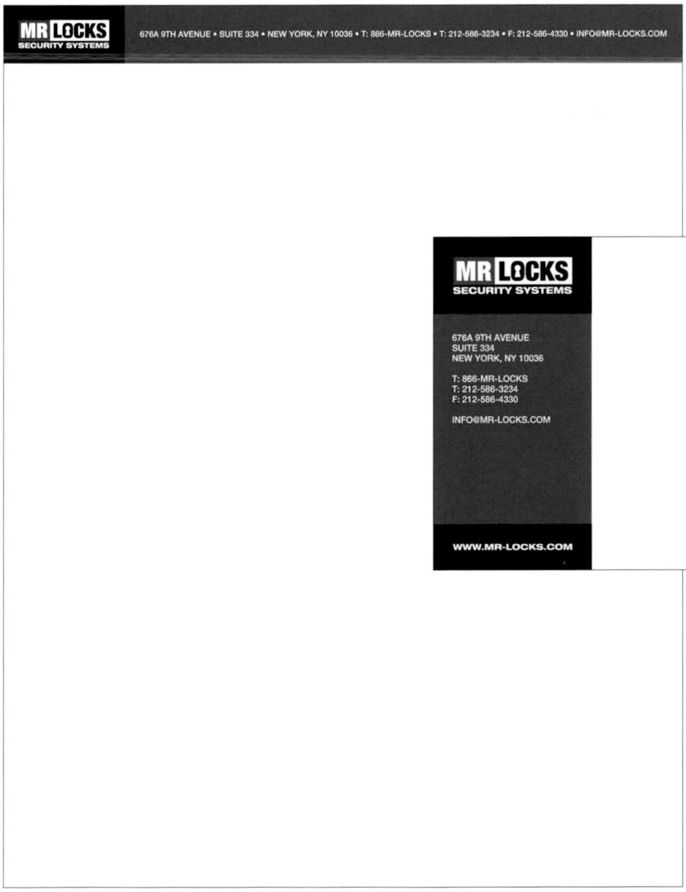

creative firm
GRAPHIC ADVANCE
Palisades Park, New Jersey
creative people
Aviad Stark
client
Mr Locks

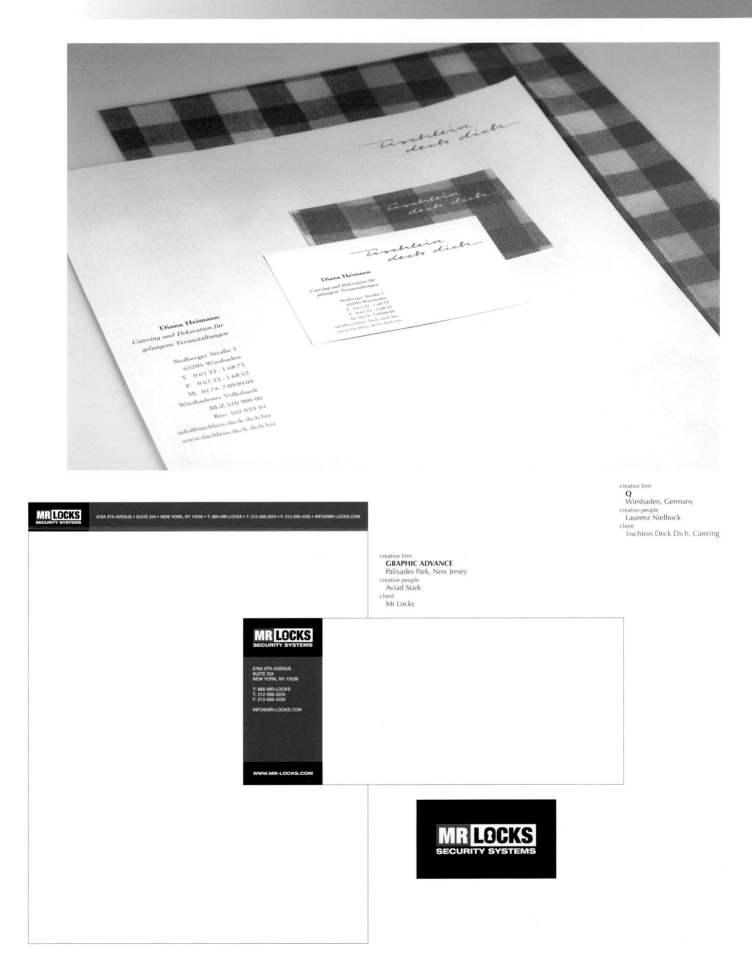

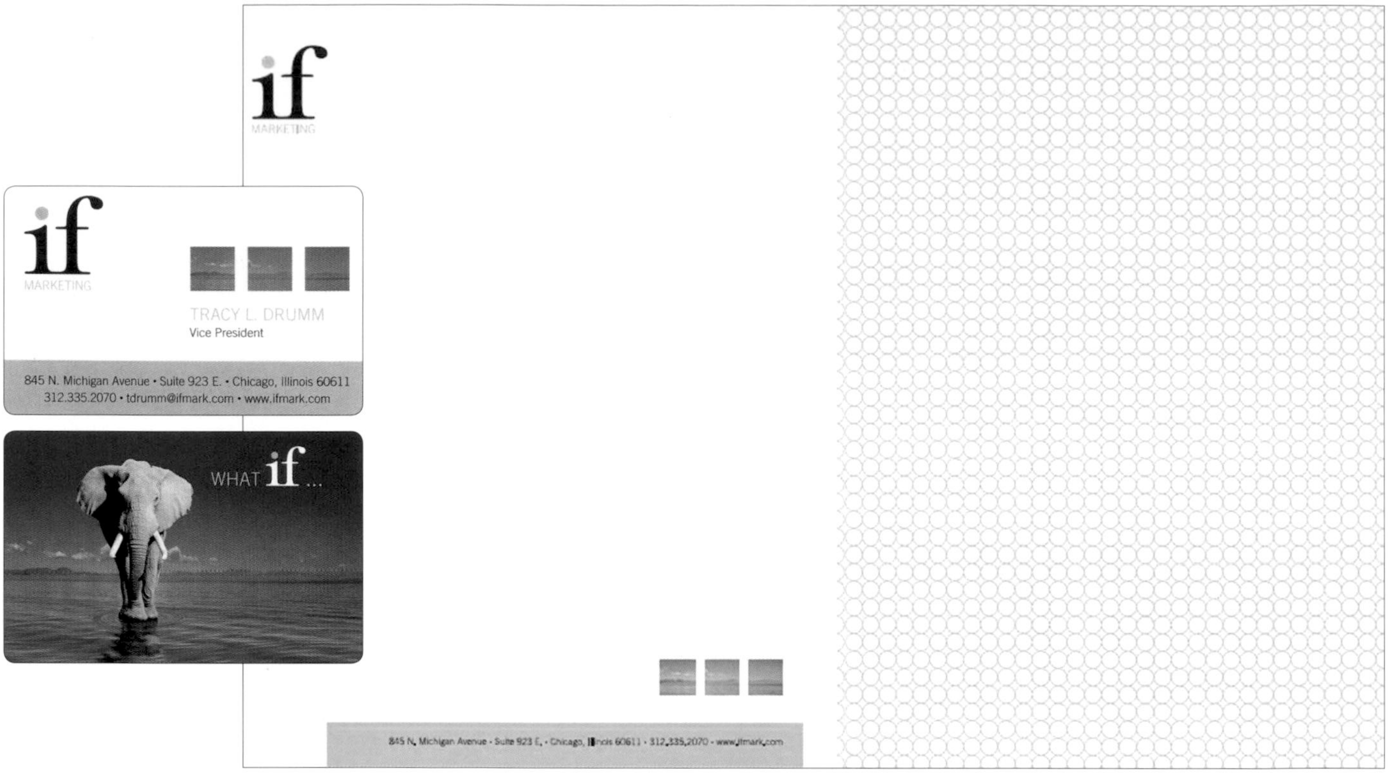

creative firm
IF MARKETING
Chicago, Illinois
creative people
Tracy Drumm
client
IF Marketing

creative firm
KROG
Ljubljana, Slovenia
creative people
Edi Berk
client
Posestvo Crni kos

DISTRIBUIDORA DE PRODUCTOS ALIMENTICIOS
DELICAT
Blvd. Lázaro Cárdenas No. 556-3
Tel. 01 352 5 26 50 20
C.P. 59300 La Piedad Michoacán
delicat@interlinea.com.mx
PRODUCTOS ALIMENTICIOS DE CALIDAD
LACTEOS • CARNES SELECTAS
DELICAT
Blvd. Lázaro Cárdenas No. 556-3
Tel. 01 352 5 26 50 20
C.P. 59300 La Piedad Michoacán
delicat@interlinea.com.mx
DISTRIBUIDORA DE PRODUCTOS ALIMENTICIOS
LACTEOS • CARNES SELECTAS
JOSÉ JESÚS OLVERA NOLASCO
DELICAT
DISTRIBUIDORA DE PRODUCTOS ALIMENTICIOS
LACTEOS • CARNES SELECTAS

creative firm
KENNETH DISEÑO
Uruapan, Mexico
creative people
Kenneth Treviño
client
Delicat Fine Foods

creative firm
BETH SINGER DESIGN LLC
Arlington, Virginia
creative people
Sucha Snidvongs
client
Jewish Social Services Agency (JSSA)

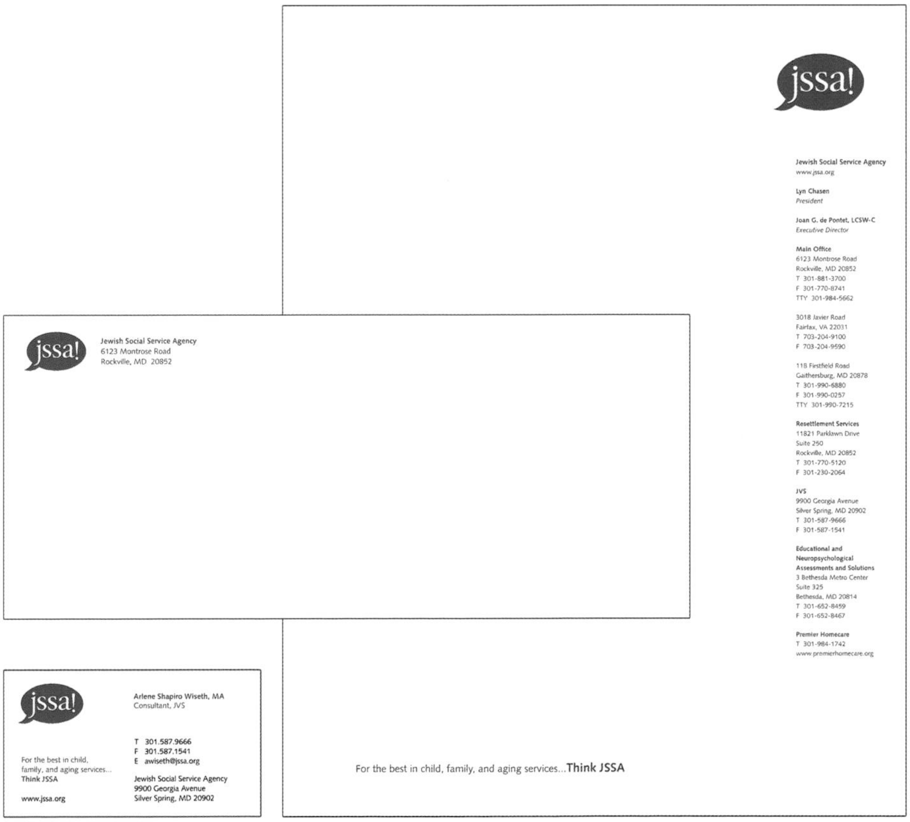
jssa!
Jewish Social Service Agency
www.jssa.org
Lyn Chasen
President
Joan G. de Pontet, LCSW-C
Executive Director
Main Office
6123 Montrose Road
Rockville, MD 20852
T 301-881-3700
F 301-770-8741
TTY 301-984-5662
3018 Javier Road
Fairfax, VA 22031
T 703-204-9100
F 703-204-9590
118 Firstfield Road
Gaithersburg, MD 20878
T 301-990-6880
F 301-990-0257
TTY 301-990-7215
Resettlement Services
11821 Parklawn Drive
Suite 250
Rockville, MD 20852
T 301-770-5120
F 301-230-2064
JVS
9900 Georgia Avenue
Silver Spring, MD 20902
T 301-587-9666
F 301-587-1541
Educational and Neuropsychological Assessments and Solutions
3 Bethesda Metro Center
Suite 325
Bethesda, MD 20814
T 301-652-8459
F 301-652-8467
Premier Homecare
T 301-984-1742
www.premierhomecare.org
For the best in child, family, and aging services...Think JSSA
jssa!
Jewish Social Service Agency
6123 Montrose Road
Rockville, MD 20852
jssa!
Arlene Shapiro Wiseth, MA
Consultant, JVS
T 301.587.9666
F 301.587.1541
E awiseth@jssa.org
Jewish Social Service Agency
9900 Georgia Avenue
Silver Spring, MD 20902
For the best in child, family, and aging services... Think JSSA
www.jssa.org

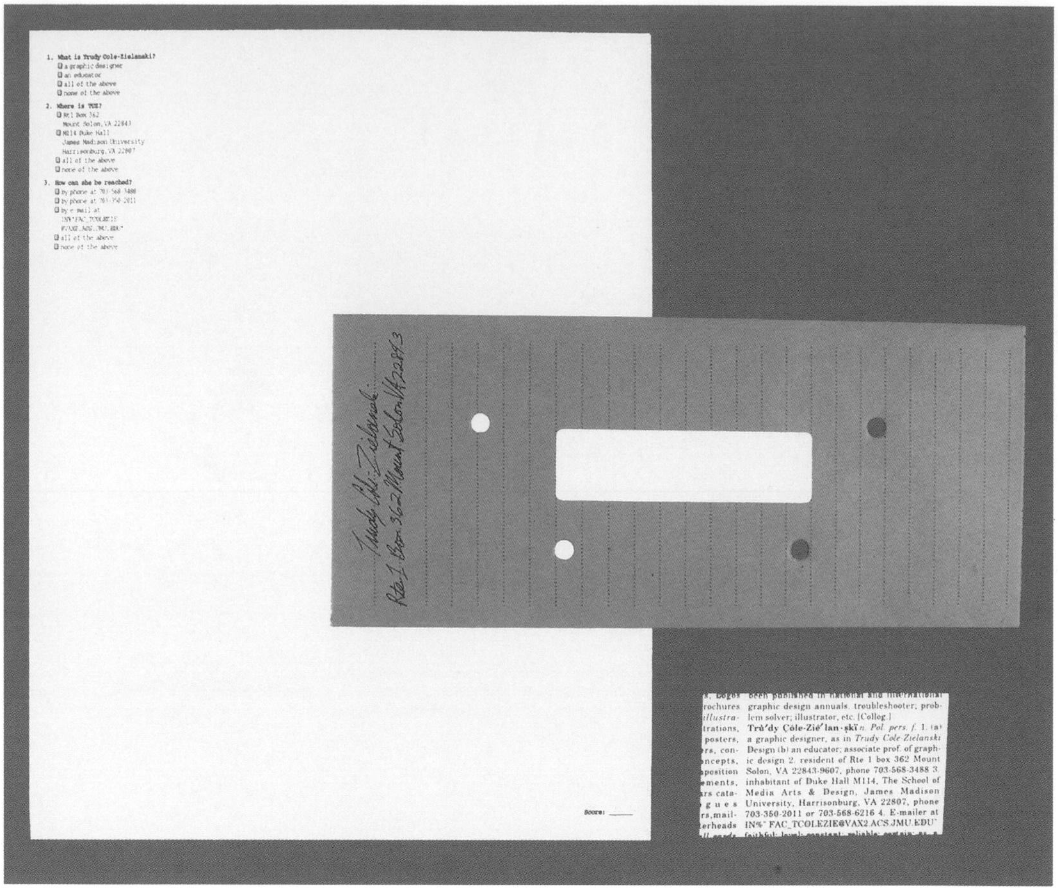

creative firm
TLC DESIGN
Churchville, Virginia
creative people
Trudy L. Cole
client
TLC Design

creative firm
LEKASMILLER DESIGN
Walnut Creek, California
creative people
Lana Ip
client
Boalt Hall School of Law, UC Berkeley

Perfectly unique gourmet cookies!
sweet impressions

sweet impressions

creative firm
VELOCITY DESIGN WORKS
Winnipeg, Canada
client
Sweet Impressions

creative firm
ROUGHSTOCK STUDIOS
San Francisco, California
creative people
Jessica Sand
client
Vista Clara Films

James Jandak Wood
Director
studio 415.331.1145
james@vistaclarafilms.com
CRUDE IMPACT
www.crudeimpact.com

creative firm
SIGHTLINE MARKETING
Washington, D.C.
creative people
Alison Seth
client
Orchestra Therapeutics

ORCHESTRA
THERAPEUTICS

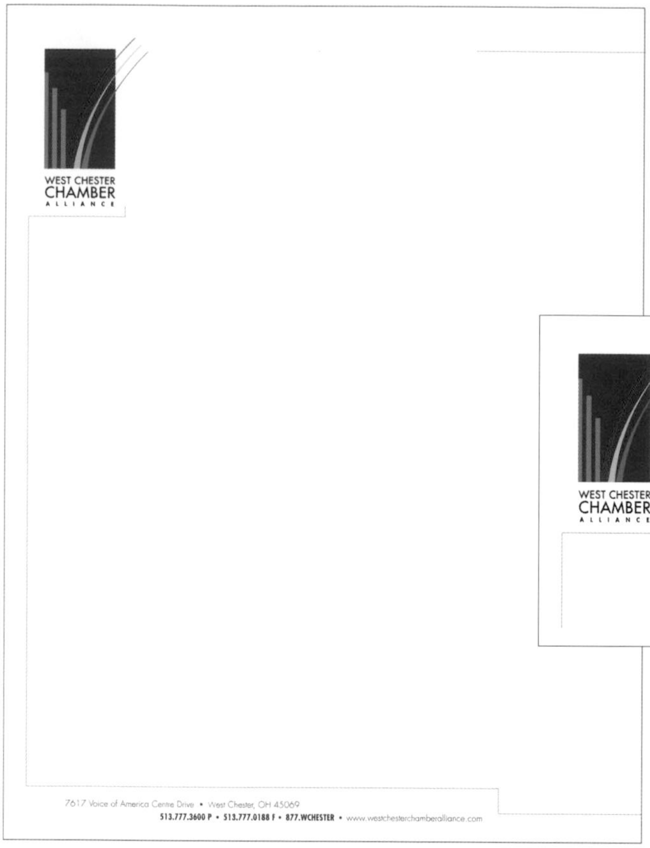

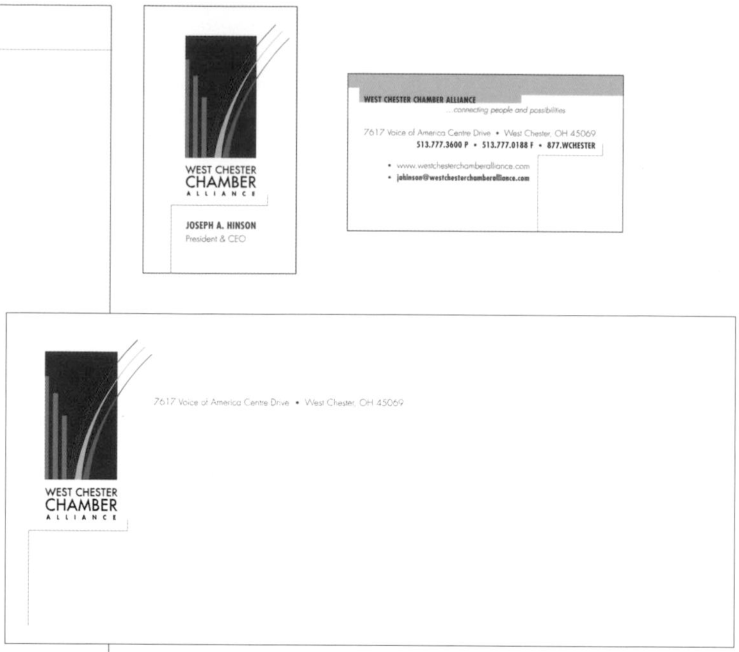

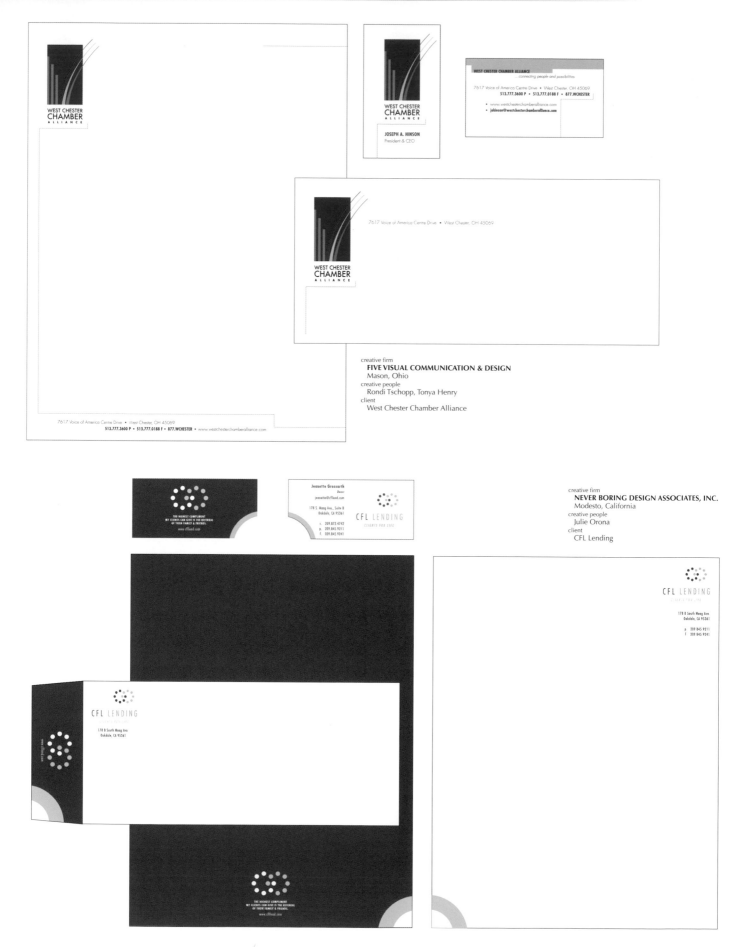

creative firm
FIVE VISUAL COMMUNICATION & DESIGN
Mason, Ohio
creative people
Rondi Tschopp, Tonya Henry
client
West Chester Chamber Alliance

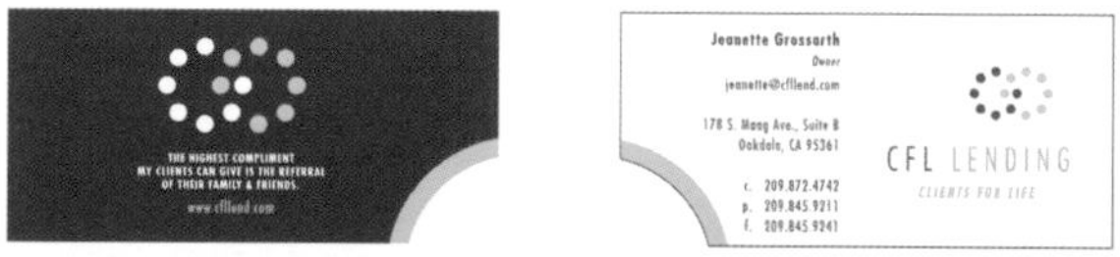

creative firm
NEVER BORING DESIGN ASSOCIATES, INC.
Modesto, California
creative people
Julie Orona
client
CFL Lending

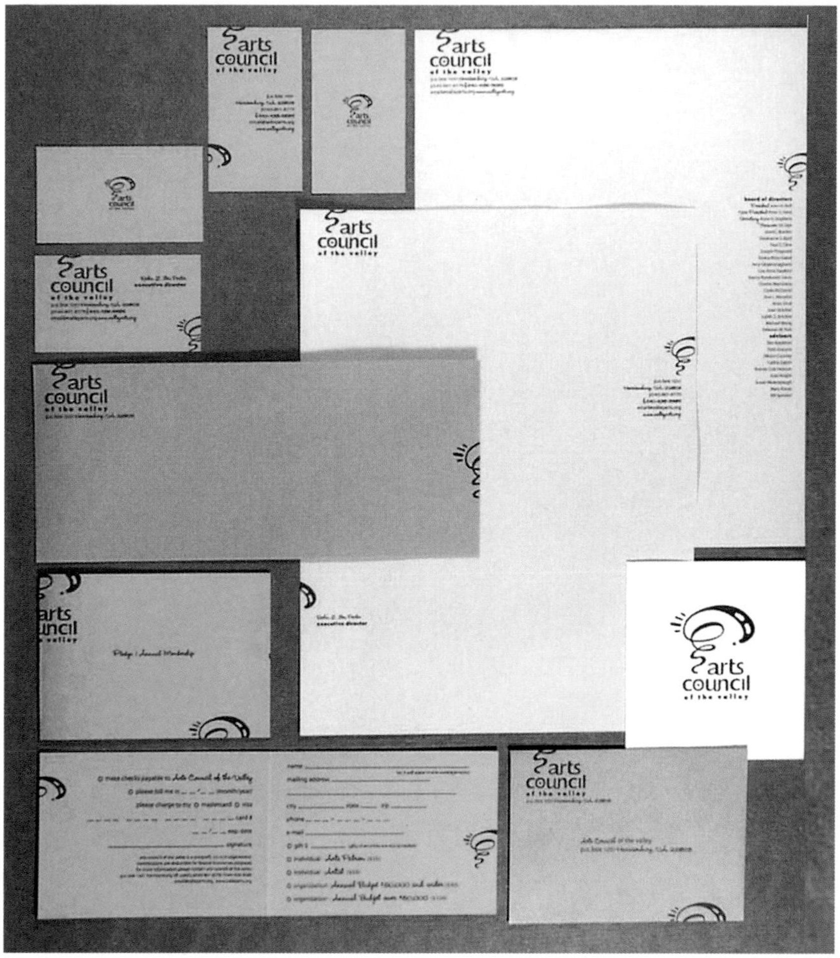

creative firm
TLC DESIGN
Churchville, Virginia
creative people
Trudy L. Cole
client
Arts Council of the Valley, Harrisonburg, VA

creative firm
SAYLES GRAPHIC DESIGN
Des Moines, Iowa
creative people
John Sayles
client
Des Moines Playhouse

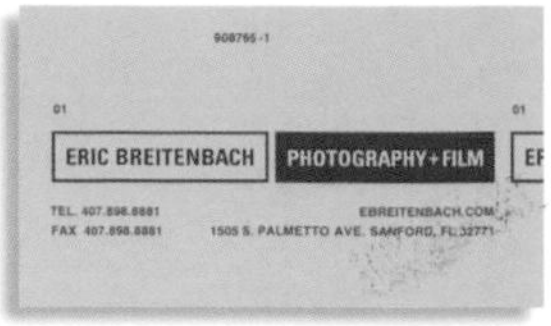

creative firm
FRY HAMMOND BARR
Orlando, Florida
creative people
Tim Fisher, Sean Brunson
client
Eric Breitenbach

creative firm
RIORDON DESIGN
Ontario, Canada
creative people
Dawn Charney, Ric Riordon, Steven Noble
client
Chelster Hall

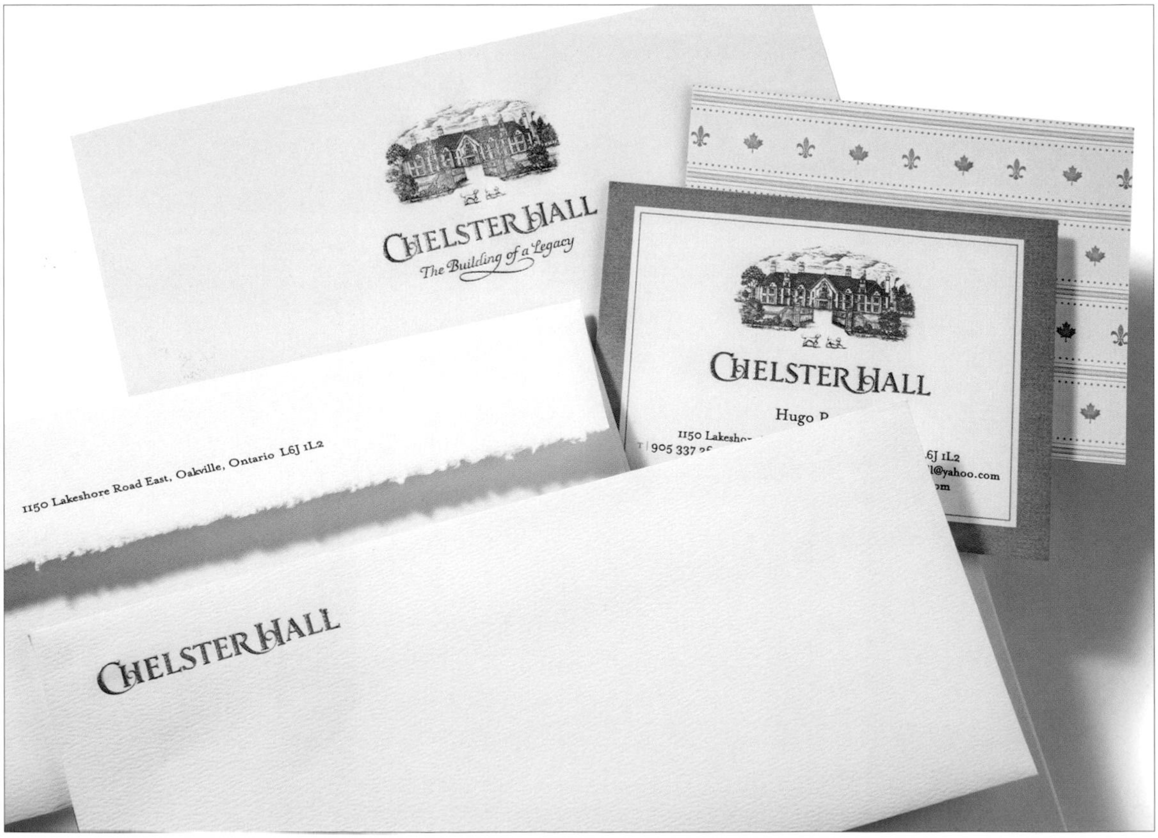

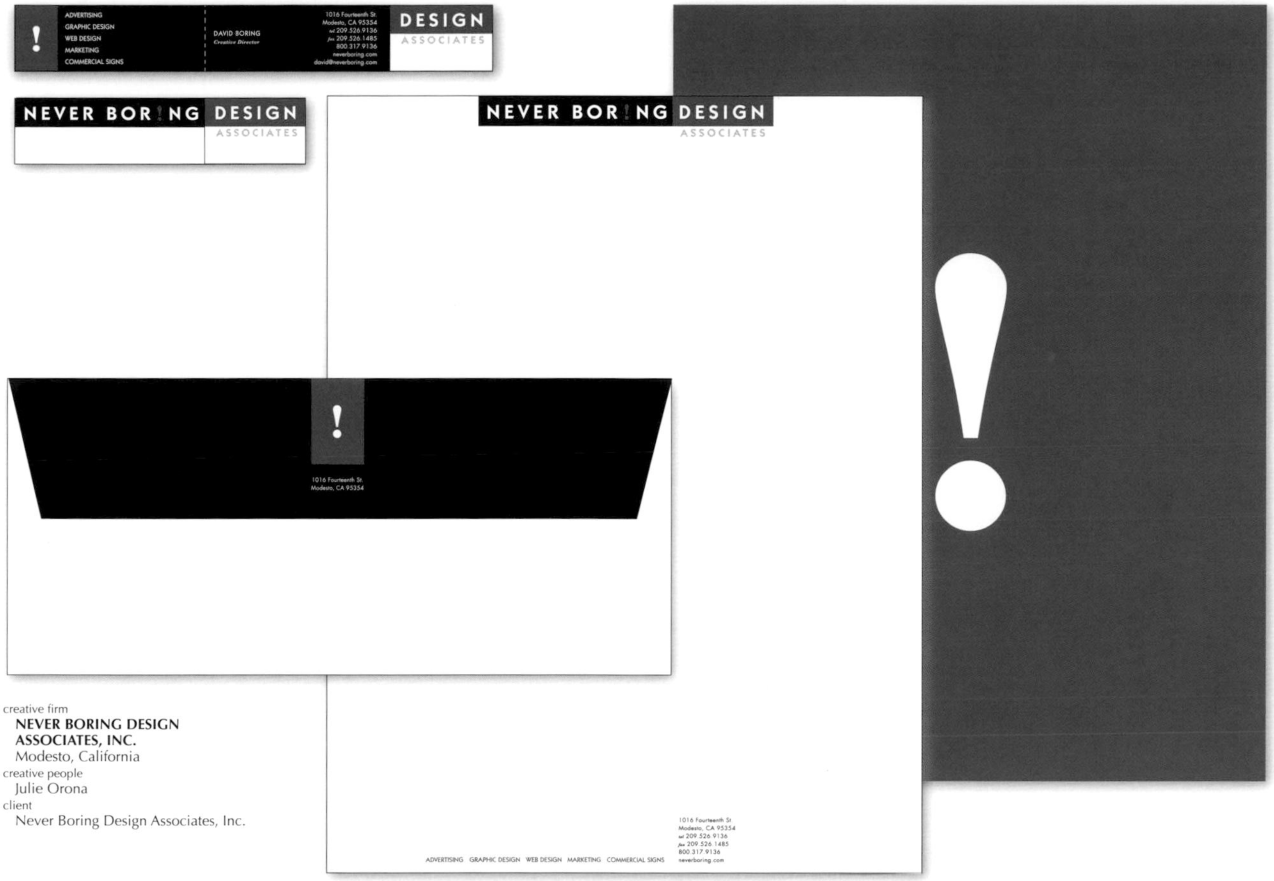

creative firm
NEVER BORING DESIGN ASSOCIATES, INC.
Modesto, California
creative people
Julie Orona
client
Never Boring Design Associates, Inc.

creative firm
HORNALL ANDERSON DESIGN
Seattle, Washington
creative people
Jack Anderson, Andrew Wicklund, Peter Anderson, Ensi Mofasser, Belinda Bowling, Kathleen Gibson
client
Majestic America Line

creative firm
KENNETH DISEÑO
Uruapan, Mexico
creative people
Kenneth Treviño, Minerva Galván
client
Paracho Guitar Manufacturers Assoc.

creative firm
ANGRYPORCUPINE*DESIGN
Park City, Utah
creative people
Cheryl Roder-Quill
client
Wurx Consulting, Inc.

creative firm
VELOCITY DESIGN WORKS
Winnipeg, Canada
creative people
Lasha Orzechowski
client
Revizon

creative firm
SAYLES GRAPHIC DESIGN
Des Moines, Iowa
creative people
John Sayles
client
Beaverdale Books

creative firm
JOHN SPOSATO DESIGN & ILLUSTRATION
Piermont, New York
creative people
John Sposato
client
Loretta Lenore Leiva

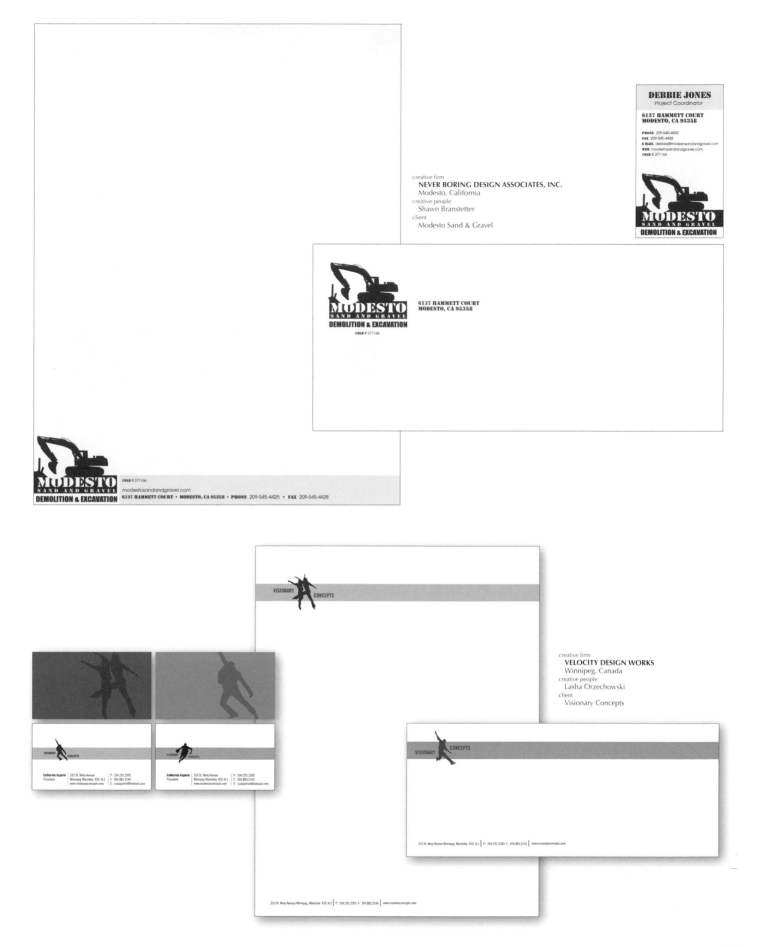

creative firm
NEVER BORING DESIGN ASSOCIATES, INC.
Modesto, California
creative people
Shawn Branstetter
client
Modesto Sand & Gravel

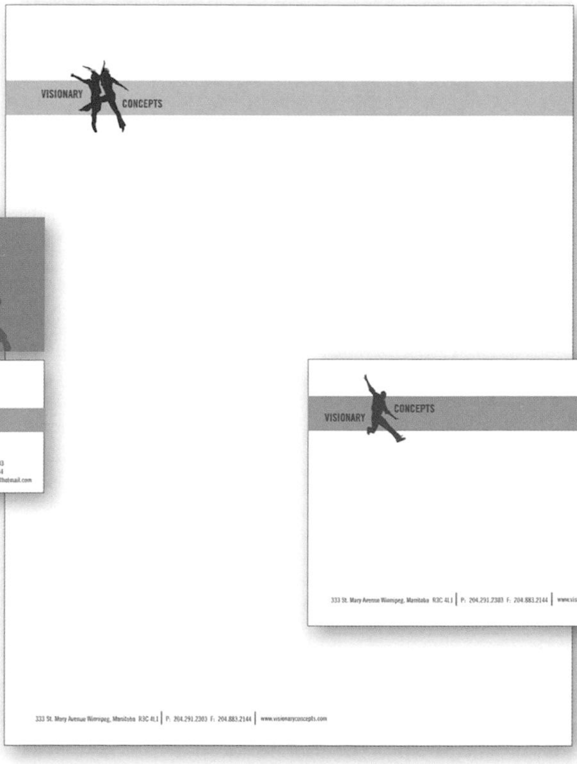

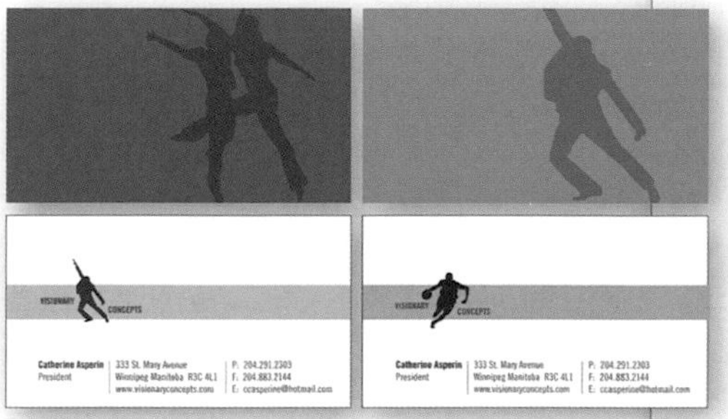

creative firm
VELOCITY DESIGN WORKS
Winnipeg, Canada
creative people
Lasha Orzechowski
client
Visionary Concepts

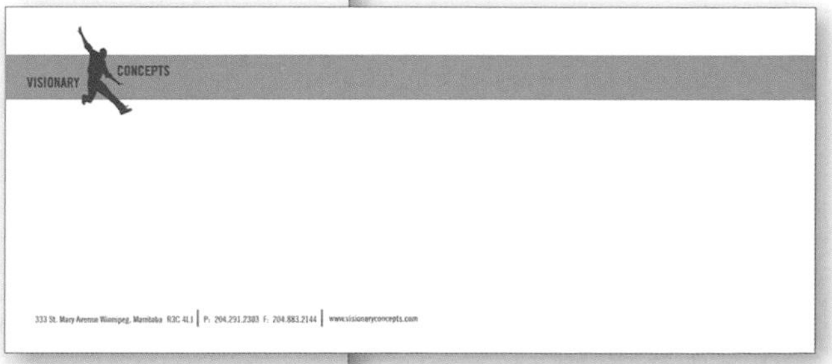

creative firm
EUPHORIANET
Monterrey, Mexico
creative people
Mabel Morales, Francisco de la Vega
client
Toma Products

creative firm
VELOCITY DESIGN WORKS
Winnipeg, Canada
creative people
Lasha Orzechowski, Dave Hardy
client
Carbon Interactive Software

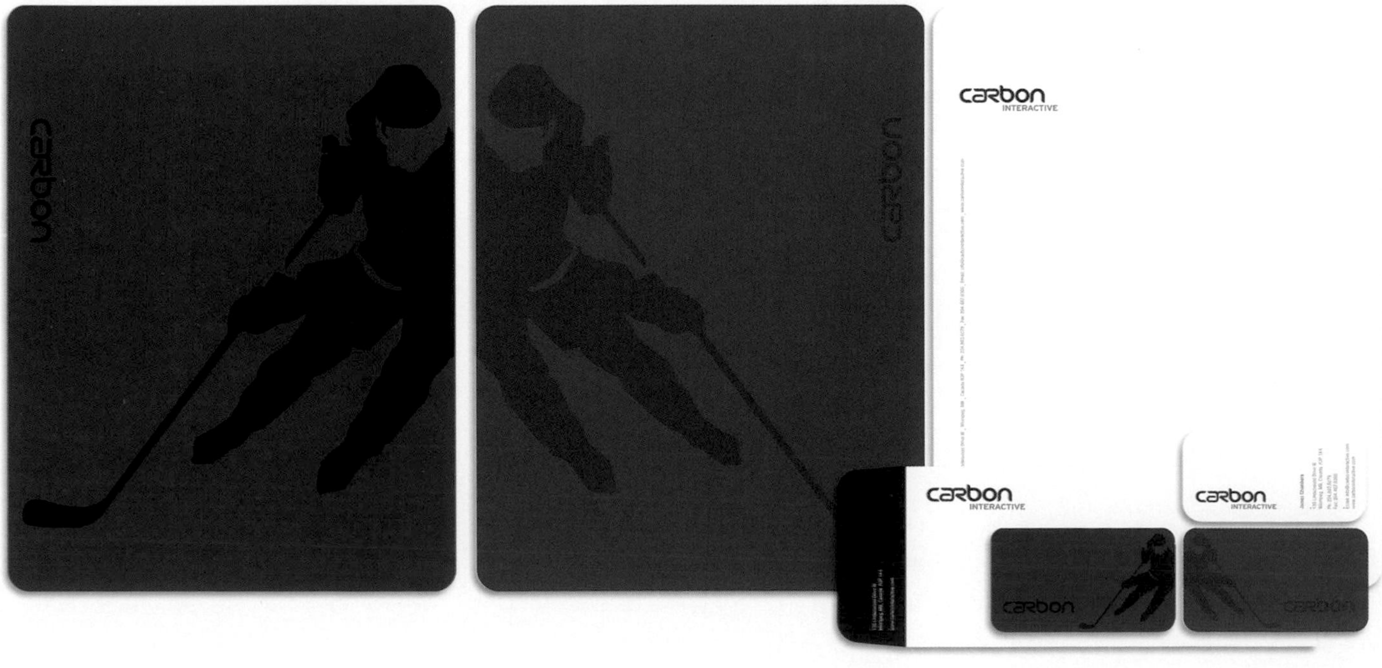

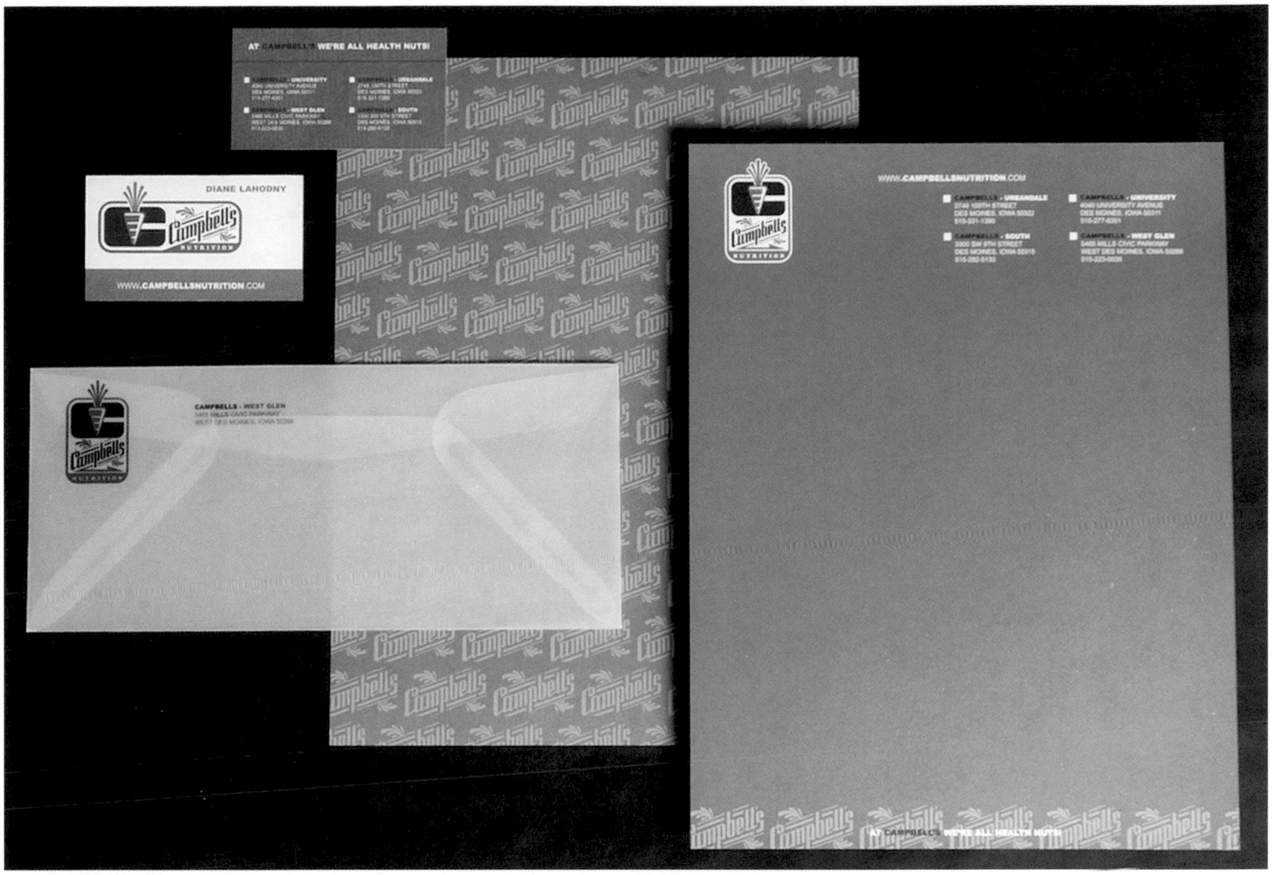

creative firm
SAYLES GRAPHIC DESIGN
Des Moines, Iowa
creative people
John Sayles
client
Campbell's Nutrition

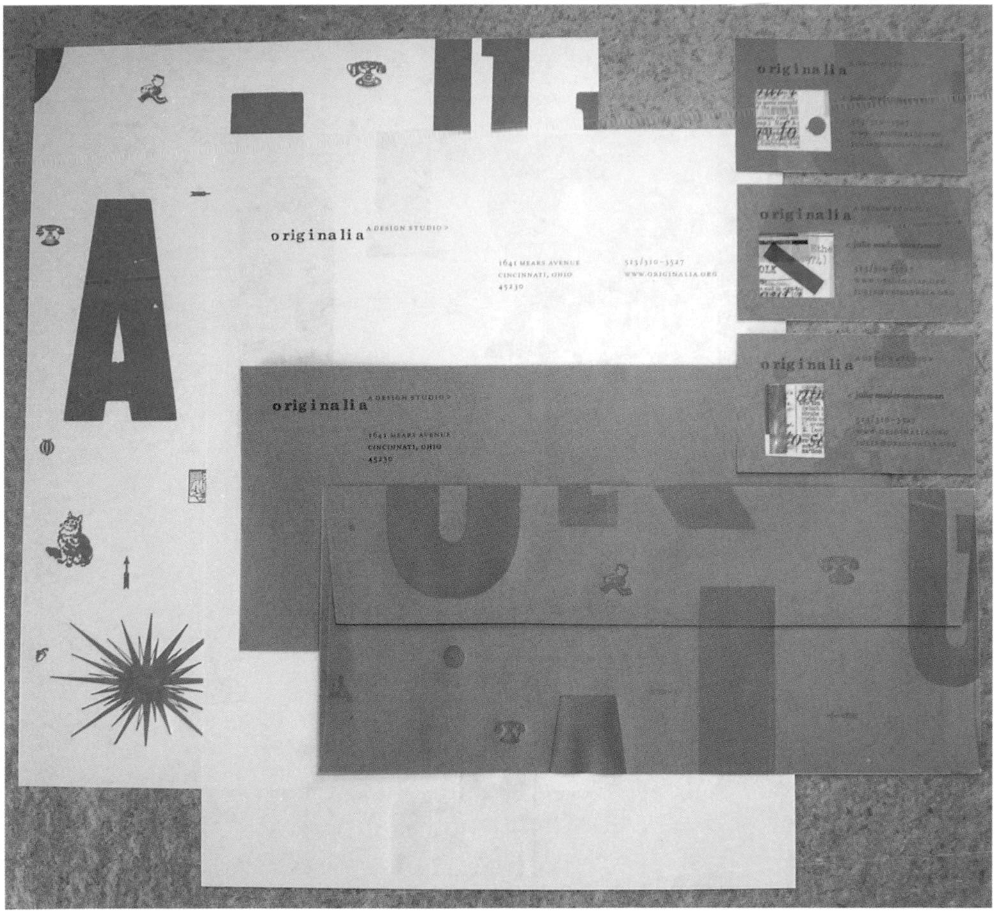

creative firm
ORIGINALIA > A DESIGN STUDIO
Cincinnati, Ohio
creative people
Julie Mader-Meersman
client
originalia > a design studio

PHOTOGRAPHY +
FILM
BEN VAN HOOK

creative firm
FRY HAMMOND BARR
Orlando, Florida
creative people
Tim Fisher, Sean Brunson
client
Ben Van Hook

EL PEDAL
BICICLETAS
venta · servicio · accesorios
DESDE 1956
Fco. Sarabia 63 / c.p. 60050 / Uruapan Michoacán México / Tel (452) 523 08 69 / elpedal@prodigy.com.mx
Alejandro García
GERENTE GENERAL

creative firm
KENNETH DISEÑO
Uruapan, Mexico
creative people
Kenneth Treviño
client
El Pedal Bike Shop

creative firm
TLC DESIGN
Churchville, Virginia
creative people
Trudy L. Cole
client
Valmontis Bed and Breakfast

creative firm
FRY HAMMOND BARR
Orlando, Florida
creative people
Tim Fisher, Sean Brunson
client
Deeb Studios

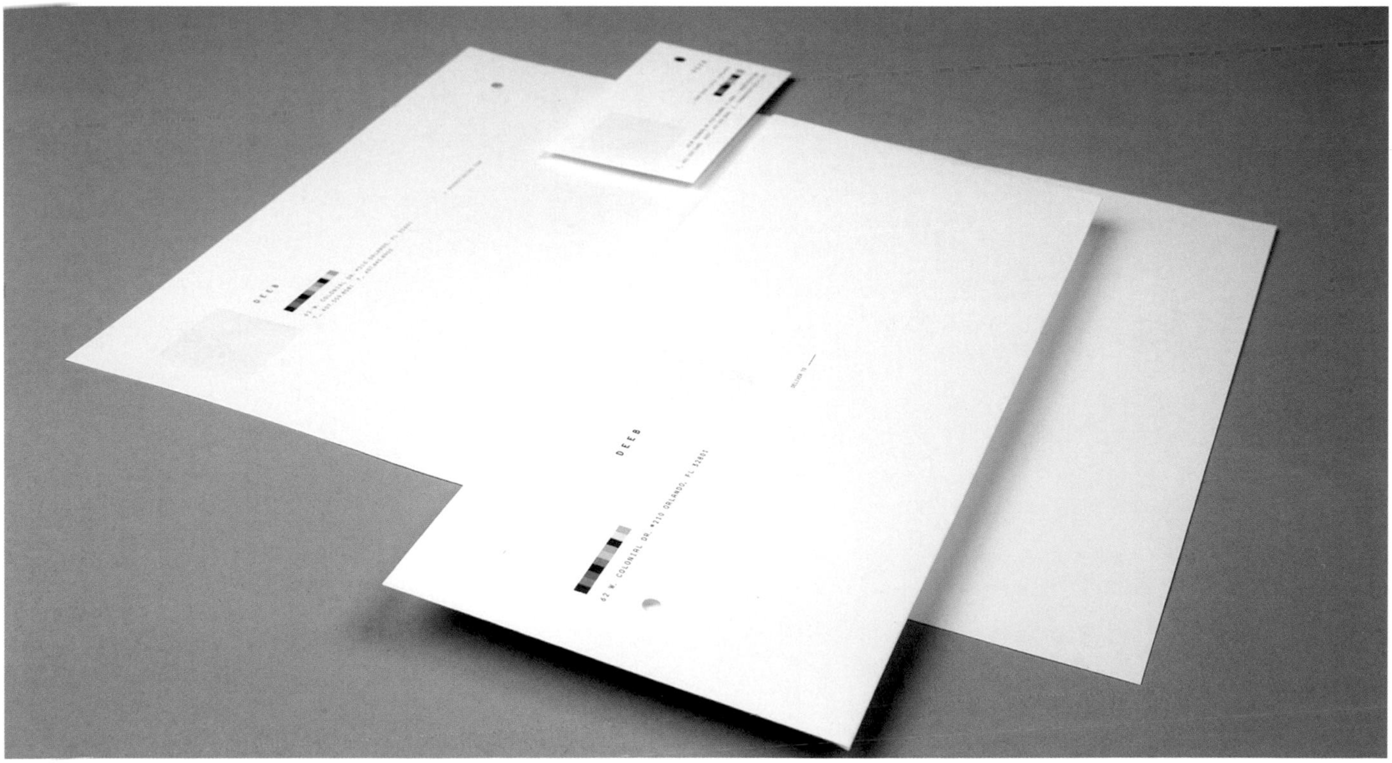

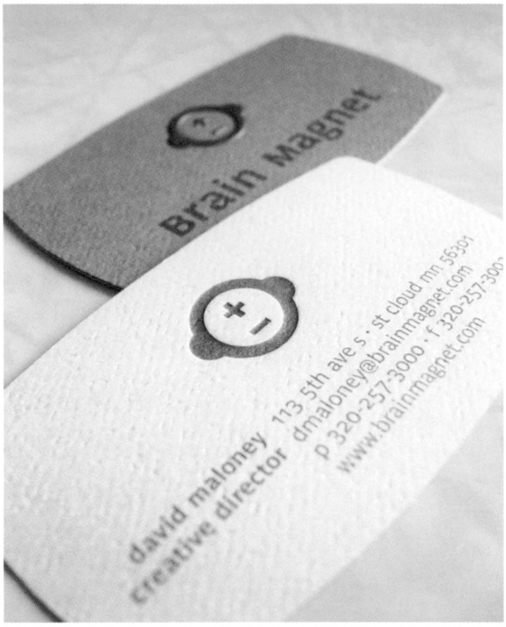

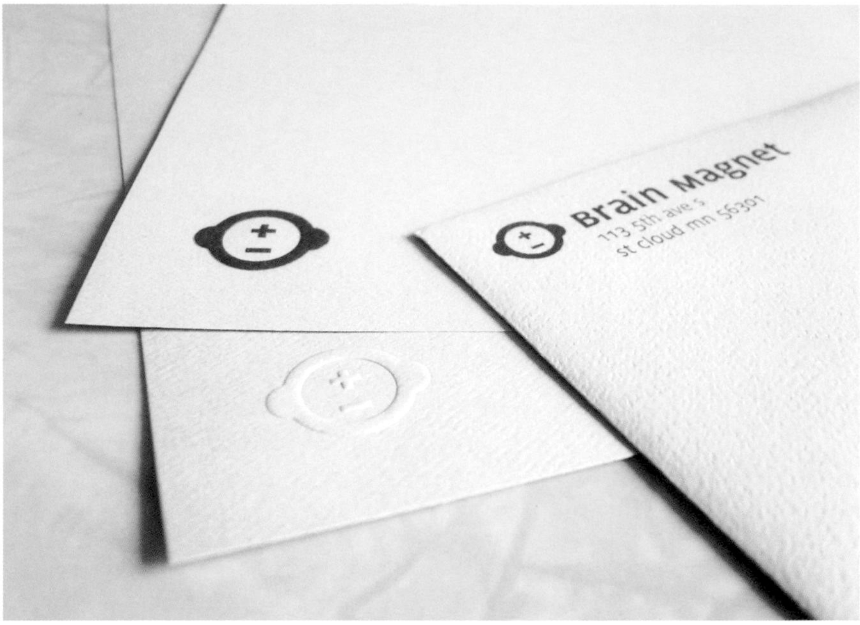

creative firm
BRAIN MAGNET
St. Louis Park, Minnesota
creative people
David Maloney
client
Brain Magnet

creative firm
VELOCITY DESIGN WORKS
Winnipeg, Canada
client
Midnight Ritual

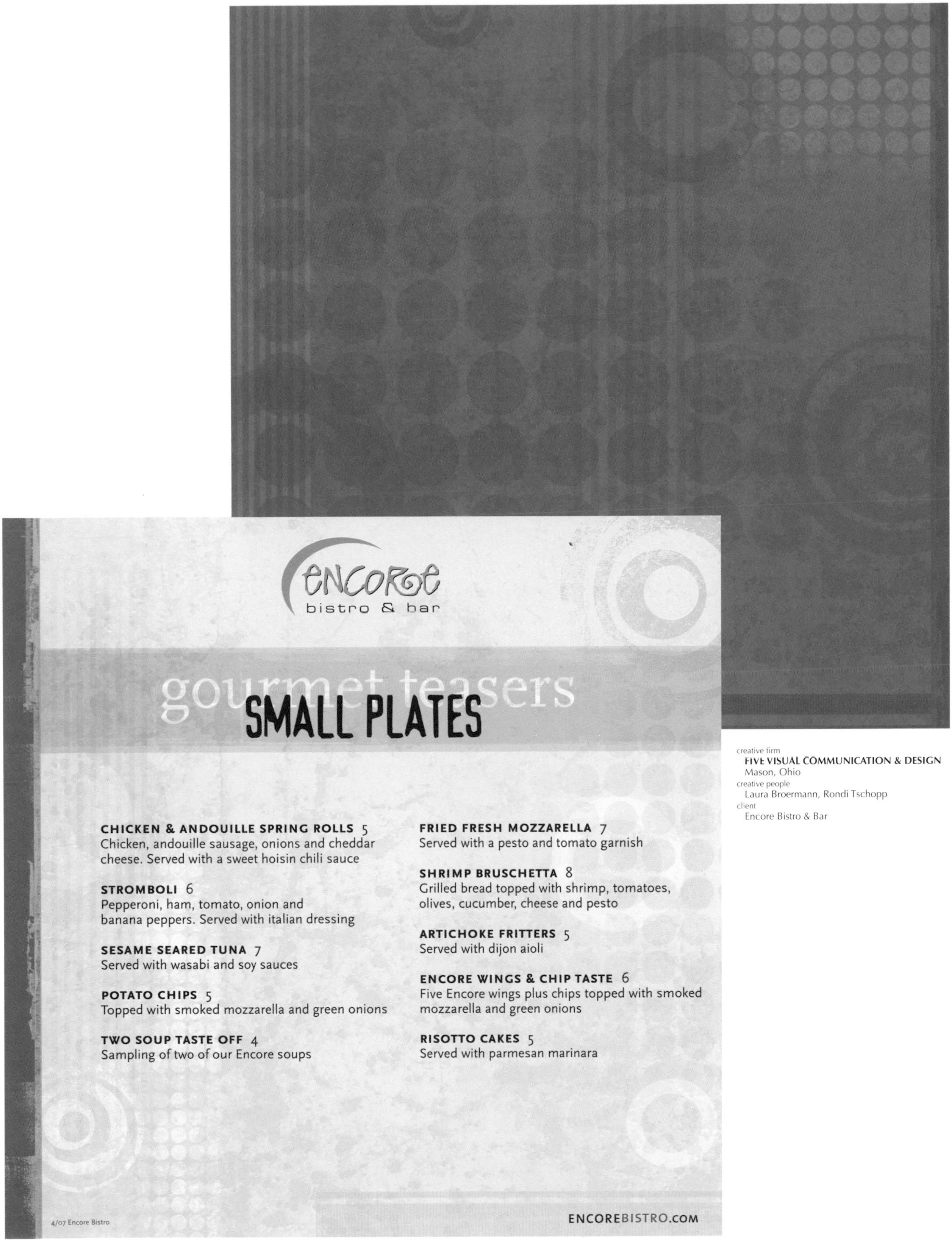

encore
bistro & bar

gourmet teasers

SMALL PLATES

CHICKEN & ANDOUILLE SPRING ROLLS 5
Chicken, andouille sausage, onions and cheddar cheese. Served with a sweet hoisin chili sauce

STROMBOLI 6
Pepperoni, ham, tomato, onion and banana peppers. Served with italian dressing

SESAME SEARED TUNA 7
Served with wasabi and soy sauces

POTATO CHIPS 5
Topped with smoked mozzarella and green onions

TWO SOUP TASTE OFF 4
Sampling of two of our Encore soups

FRIED FRESH MOZZARELLA 7
Served with a pesto and tomato garnish

SHRIMP BRUSCHETTA 8
Grilled bread topped with shrimp, tomatoes, olives, cucumber, cheese and pesto

ARTICHOKE FRITTERS 5
Served with dijon aioli

ENCORE WINGS & CHIP TASTE 6
Five Encore wings plus chips topped with smoked mozzarella and green onions

RISOTTO CAKES 5
Served with parmesan marinara

4/07 Encore Bistro

ENCOREBISTRO.COM

creative firm
FIVE VISUAL COMMUNICATION & DESIGN
Mason, Ohio
creative people
Laura Broermann, Rondi Tschopp
client
Encore Bistro & Bar

creative firm
GO GRAPHIC
Beirut, Lebanon
creative people
Maria Assi, Rasha Jeaid
client
InterContinental Phoenicia,
Wok Wok Restaurant

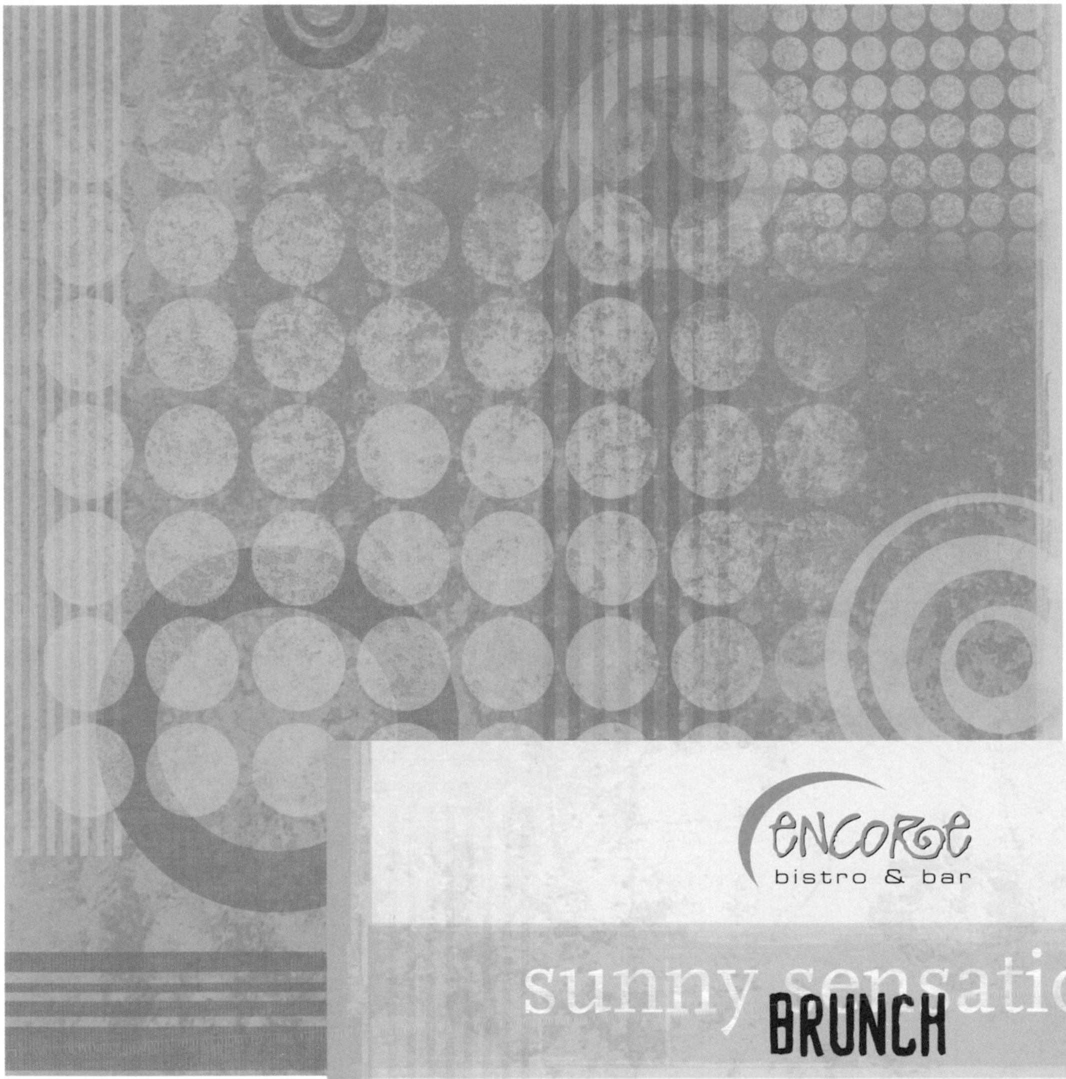

creative firm
FIVE VISUAL COMMUNICATION & DESIGN
Mason, Ohio
creative people
Laura Broermann, Rondi Tschopp
client
Encore Bistro & Bar

encore
bistro & bar
sunny sensations
BRUNCH
CRAB CAKE BENEDICT 12
Two lump crab cakes, pan-seared and topped with two poached eggs and red bell pepper hollandaise
BISCUITS & GRAVY 9
Three eggs scrambled served with buttermilk biscuits, country gravy and choice of applewood smoked bacon or sausage
STRAWBERRY FRENCH TOAST 8
French toast topped with fresh strawberries and honey pecan butter Served with maple syrup
BURRITO 9
Three eggs scrambled with andouille sausage and pepper jack cheese wrapped in a tortilla
OMELET 10
Chef's choice omelet with hash browns and choice of applewood smoked bacon or sausage
BELGIAN WAFFLE 8
Encore Belgian waffle with fresh seasonal berries, honey pecan butter and maple syrup
4/07 Encore Bistro
ENCOREBISTRO.COM

creative firm
GO GRAPHIC
Beirut, Lebanon
creative people
Maria Assi, Morava Zgheib
client
InterContinental Doha,
Pool Restaurant

creative firm
GO GRAPHIC
Beirut, Lebanon
creative people
Maria Assi, Mina Abdul Hussein
client
InterContinental Phoenicia,
Caffé Mondo Restaurant

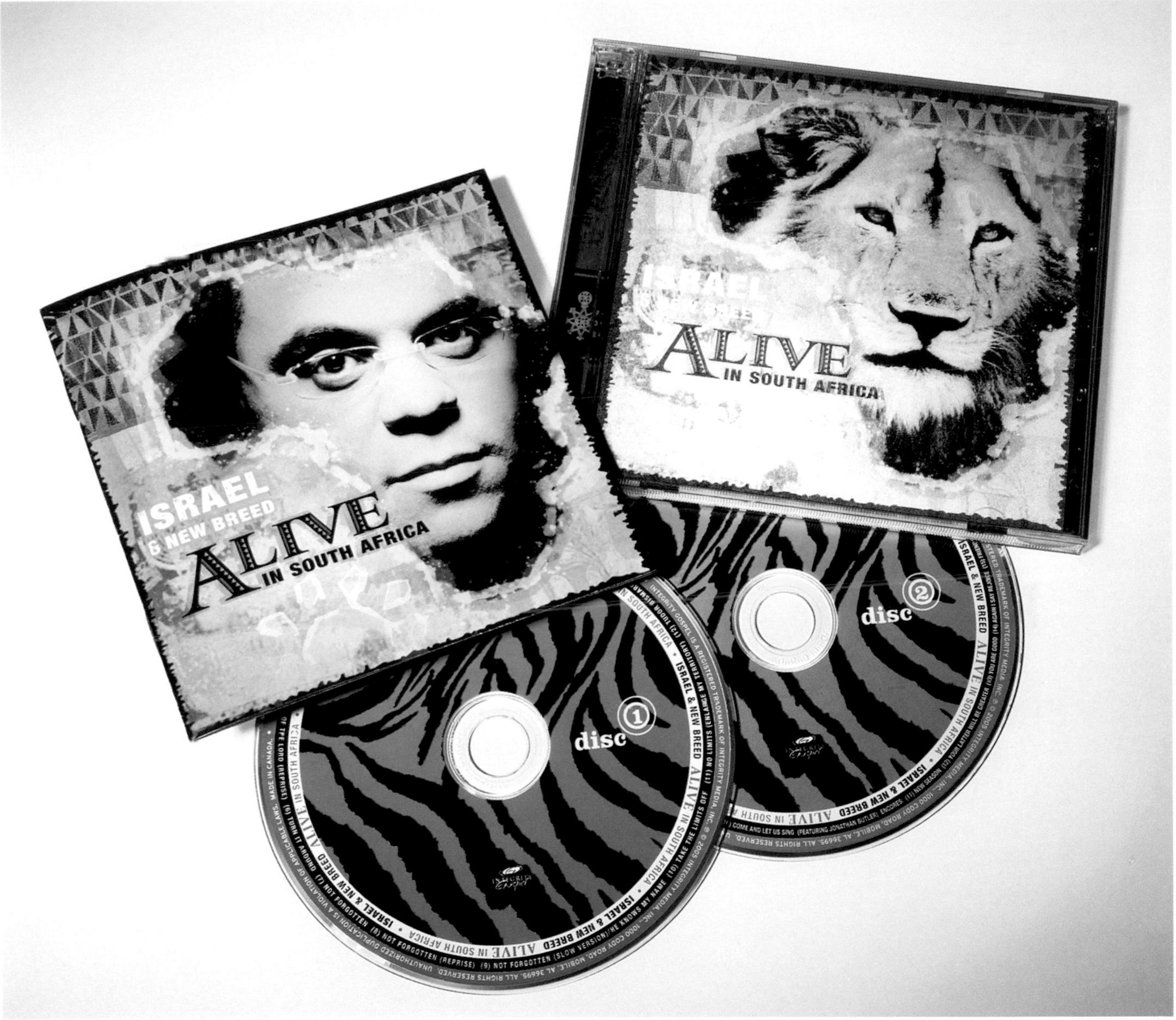

creative firm
RIORDON DESIGN
Ontario, Canada
creative people
Shirley Riordon
client
Integrity Music

creative firm
VELOCITY DESIGN WORKS
Winnipeg, Canada
creative people
Lasha Orzechowski
client
Quantus Software

creative firm
WESTGROUP CREATIVE
New York, New York
creative people
Chip Tolaney
client
Eric Wollman Trio

creative firm
HIGGINS DESIGN
Shoreline, Washington
creative people
Jane Higgins, Teri Dixon/Getty Images, Yoshiki Nakamura, Julie Beckman, Sophie Lippert
client
Raspbery Records/Paul Lippert

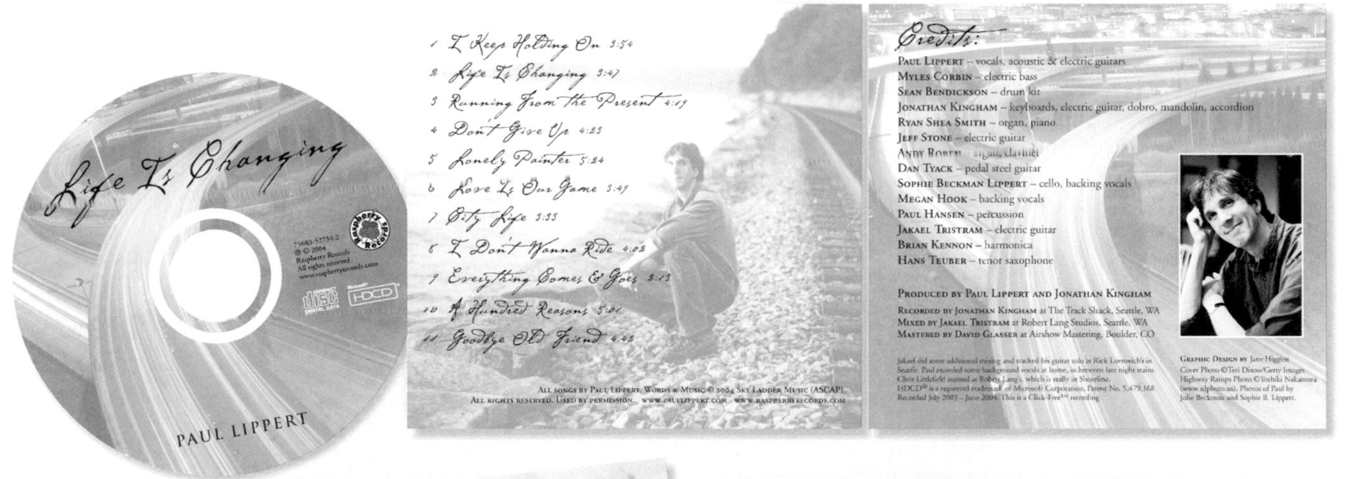

Sophie Berkal Sarbit
The Gypsy in My Soul

creative firm
VELOCITY DESIGN WORKS
Winnipeg, Canada
creative people
Lasha Orzechowski, Dave Hardy
client
Sophie Berkal Sarbit

1. Midnight Sun 4:18
2. Fascinating Rhythm 4:39
3. I've Got A Right To Sing The Blues 5:30
4. Whatever Lola Wants 4:35
5. Both Sides Now 4:51
6. Baltimore Oriole 4:31
7. The Gypsy In My Soul 5:21
8. Someone To Watch Over Me 6:01
9. Sunday 3:36
10. Skylark 4:51
11. Circle 3:54
12. The Man I Love 4:39
The Gypsy in My Soul

Célébration
MOZART The Braude Ensemble
ration
Braude Ensemble
olon et pianoforte, KV 296
Allegro vivace
Andante sostenuto
Rondo, Allegro

creative firm
WESTGROUP CREATIVE
New York, New York
creative people
Chip Tolaney
client
The Braude Ensemble

creative firm
RIORDON DESIGN
Ontario, Canada
creative people
Shirley Riordon
client
Integrity Music

creative firm
AYSE ÇELEM DESIGN
Istanbul, Turkey
creative people
Ayse Çelem, Sibel Esen
client
Ayhan Sicimoglu

creative firm
Q
Wiesbaden, Germany
creative people
Matthias Frey
client
CKP

creative firm
VELOCITY DESIGN WORKS
Winnipeg, Canada
client
Midnight Ritual

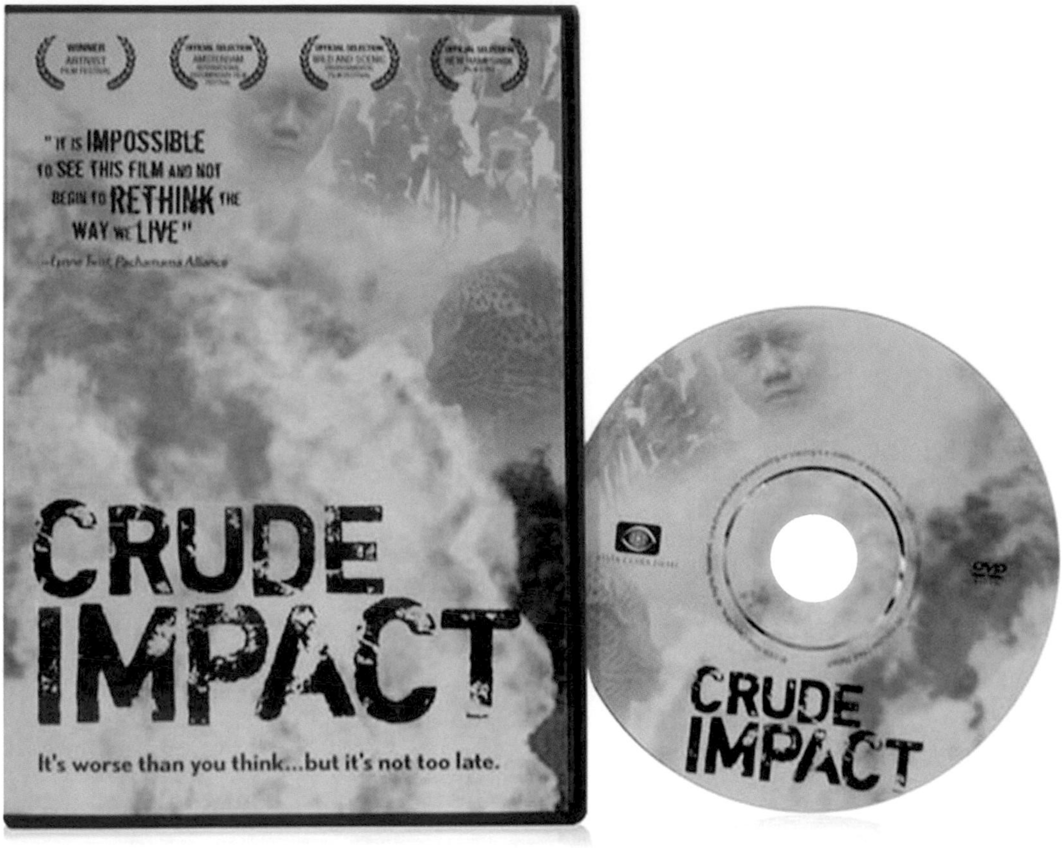

creative firm
ROUGHSTOCK STUDIOS
San Francisco, California
creative people
Jessica Sand
client
Vista Clara Films

creative firm
NEVER BORING DESIGN ASSOCIATES, INC.
Modesto, California
creative people
Shawna Bayers
client
David Paul Newell

creative firm
MIKE SALISBURY
Venice, California
creative people
Mike Salisbury
client
Triumph

creative firm
FUNK/LEVIS & ASSOCIATES
Eugene, Oregon
creative people
Chris Berner
client
Imagine Graphics

creative firm
FLOWDESIGN
Northville, Michigan
creative people
Dan Matauch, Dennis Nalezyty, Allison Tinsley
client
Oliver Winery

creative firm
30SIXTY ADVERTISING+DESIGN, INC.
Los Angeles, California
creative people
Henry Vizcarra, Pär Larsson, Mot Potives, Bruce Ventanilla, Tuyet Vong
client
Universal Studios Home Entertainment

creative firm
SMITH DESIGN
Glen Ridge, New Jersey
creative people
James C. Smith, Glenn Hagen
client
Unilever Foods North America

creative firm
HORNALL ANDERSON DESIGN
Seattle, Washington
creative people
Lisa Cerveny, Sonja Max, Belinda Bowling, Ensi Mofasser, Kathy Saito, Beth Grimm, Julie Jacobson
client
Tahitian Noni

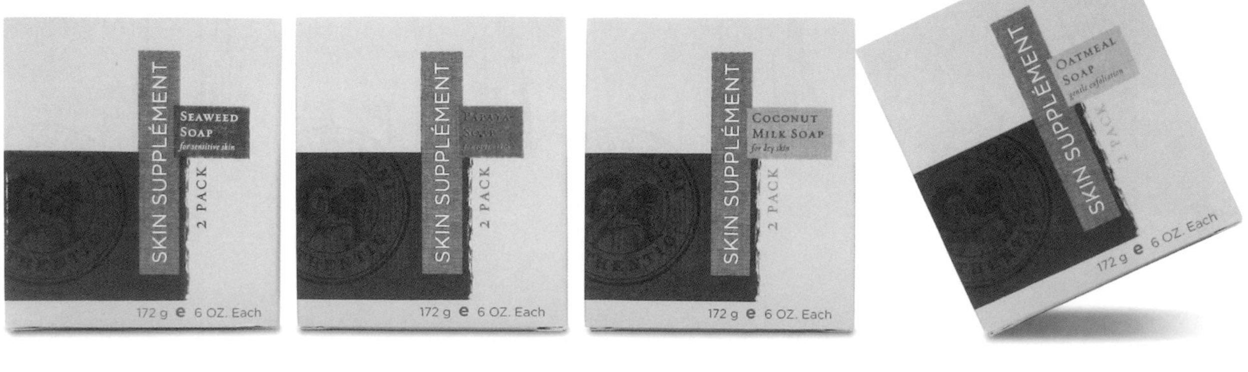

creative firm
CHUTE GERDEMAN RETAIL
Columbus, Ohio
creative people
Dennis Gerdeman, Brian Shafley, Wendy Johnson, Steve Pottschmidt, Bess Anderson, Steve Boreman, Susan Siewny, Jon Knodell
client
Mars Retail Group

creative firm
FLOWDESIGN
Northville, Michigan
creative people
Dan Matauch, Dennis Nalezyty
client
Hansen's

creative firm
JENN DAVID DESIGN
Irvine, California
creative people
Jenn David Connolly
client
La Tourangelle

creative firm
HORNALL ANDERSON DESIGN
Seattle, Washington
creative people
Jack Anderson, Kathy Saito, Sonja Max, Henry Yiu, Yuri Shvets
client
AMES International

creative firm
TOM FOWLER, INC.
Norwalk, Connecticut
creative people
Mary Ellen Butkus
client
Unilever Foods

creative firm
JENN DAVID DESIGN
Irvine, California
creative people
Jenn David Connolly
client
Mitsubishi International Corporation

creative firm
JENN DAVID DESIGN
Irvine, California
creative people
Jenn David Connolly
client
Agog Creative

creative firm
SABINGRAFIK, INC
Carlsbad, California
creative people
Tracy Sabin
client
Seafarer Baking Company

creative firm
ONE PICA, INC.
Boston, Massachusetts
creative people
Gregory Segall
client
American Innovative, LLC

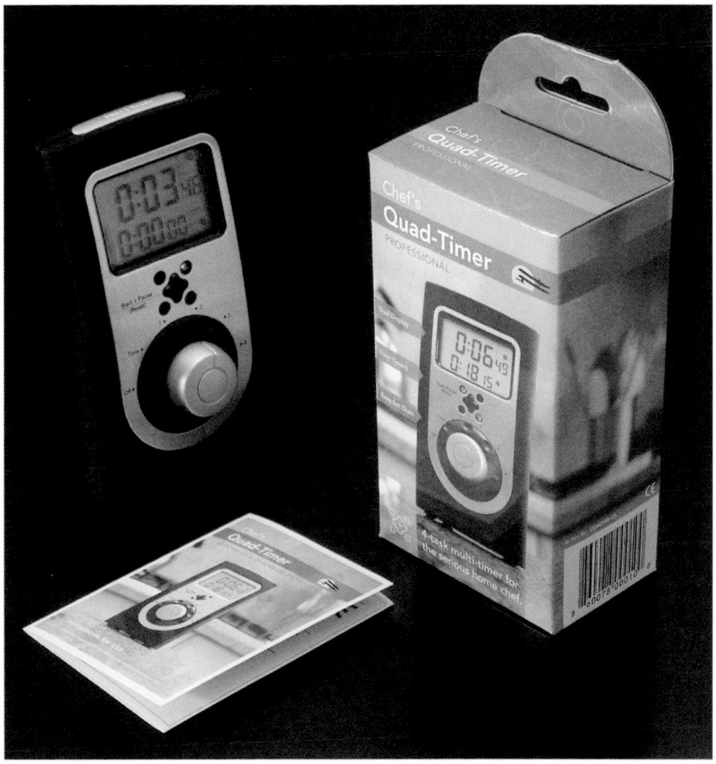

creative firm
HELENA SEO DESIGN
Sunnyvale, California
creative people
Helena Seo
client
Ineke, LLC

creative firm
CHUTE GERDEMAN RETAIL
Columbus, Ohio
creative people
Dennis Gerdeman, Brian Shafley, Wendy Johnson, Steve Pottschmidt, Bess Anderson, Steve Boreman, Susan Siewny, Jon Knodell
client
Mars Retail Group

creative firm
NANCY FRAME DESIGN
Durham, North Carolina
creative people
Sue Sneddon, Shallotte, North Carolina
Holly Dickens, Chicago, Illinois

creative firm
FLOWDESIGN
Northville, Michigan
creative people
Dan Matauch, Dennis Nalezyty
client
Hansen's

creative firm
KROG
Ljubljana, Slovenia
creative people
Edi Berk
client
Posestvo Crni kos

creative firm
ZEIST DESIGN LLC
Sausalito, California
creative people
Oscar V. Mulder, Richard Scheve
client
ACH Spice Islands Organic

creative firm
ZUNDA GROUP LLC
South Norwalk, Connecticut
creative people
Charles Zunda, Gary Esposito,
Lauren Millar, Matthew Okin
client
Unilever Home & Personal Care—USA

creative firm
HORNALL ANDERSON DESIGN
Seattle, Washington
creative people
Lisa Cerveny, Jana Nishi, Belinda Bowling, Leo Raymundo
client
Tahitian Noni

creative firm
DESIGN SOURCE
Aptos, California
creative people
Cari Class, Stacey Boscoe
client
La Filice Winery

creative firm
NANCY FRAME DESIGN
Durham, North Carolina
creative people
Getty Images

creative firm
FAI DESIGN GROUP
Irvington, New York
creative people
Allison Schwartz, Robert Scully
client
Bed Bath & Beyond

creative firm
FLOWDESIGN
Northville, Michigan
creative people
Dan Matauch, Dennis Nalezyty
client
Mountain Valley

creative firm
CHUTE GERDEMAN RETAIL
Columbus, Ohio
creative people
Elle Chute, Mindi Trank, Steve Pottschmidt, Bess Anderson, Jay Highland, Susan Siewny
client
New World Restaurant Group

creative firm
HORNALL ANDERSON DESIGN
Seattle, Washington
creative people
Jack Anderson, David Bates, Yuri Shvets
client
Kinetix Living

creative firm
30SIXTY ADVERTISING+DESIGN, INC.
Los Angeles, California
creative people
Henry Vizcarra, Pär Larsson, Bruce Ventanilla, Tuyet Vong
client
20th Century Fox Home Entertainment

creative firm
FLOWDESIGN
Northville, Michigan
creative people
Dan Matauch, Dennis Nalezyty
client
The Limu Company

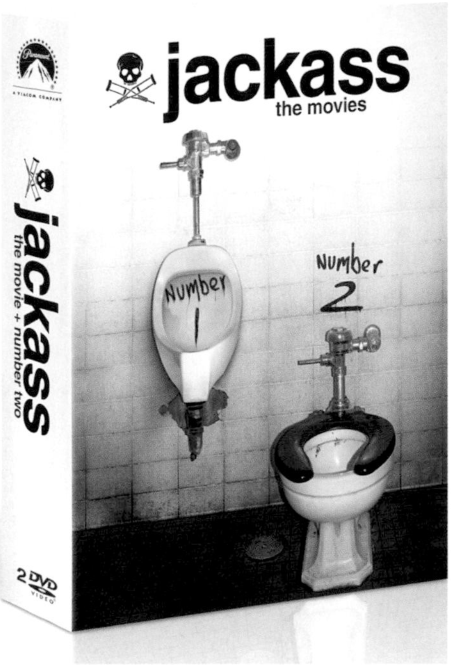

creative firm
30SIXTY ADVERTISING+DESIGN, INC.
Los Angeles, California
creative people
Henry Vizcarra, David Fuscellaro,
Marisa Ghiglieri, Charlie Le,
Eric Perez, Ernesto Portillo
client
Paramount Home Entertainment Global

creative firm
ZEIST DESIGN LLC
Sausalito, California
creative people
Oscar V. Mulder,
Richard Scheve
client
ACH Spice Islands Grinder

creative firm
TOM FOWLER, INC.
Norwalk, Connecticut
creative people
Mary Ellen Butkus
client
Acme United Corporation

creative firm
NANCY FRAME DESIGN
Durham, North Carolina
creative people
Becky Heavner,
Denver, Colorado

creative firm
KENNETH DISEÑO
Uruapan, Mexico
creative people
Kenneth Treviño
client
Tequila Tierra Caliente,
Industrial Mulsa

creative firm
ZUNDA GROUP LLC
South Norwalk, Connecticut
creative people
Charles Zunda, Gary Esposito,
Amy Dresner-Yules
client
The Dannon Company, Inc.

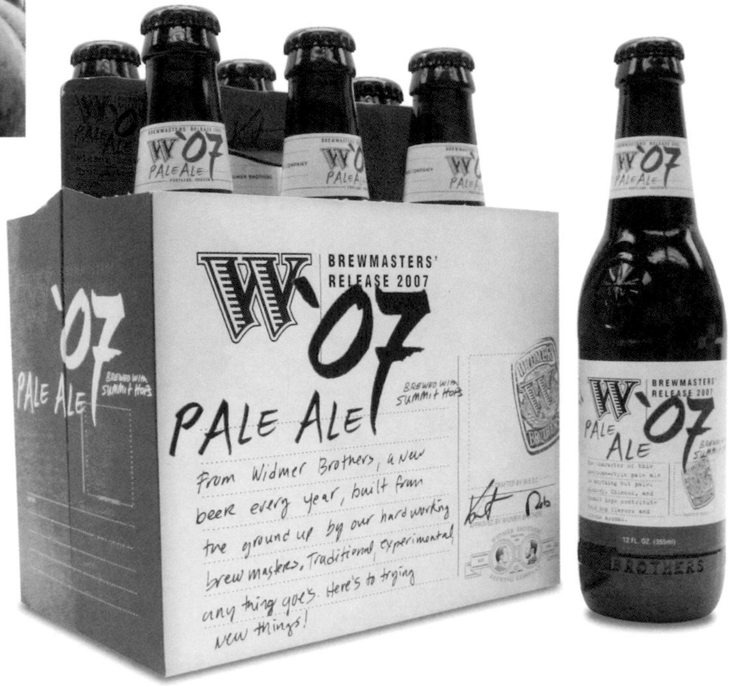

creative firm
HORNALL ANDERSON DESIGN
Seattle, Washington
creative people
Larry Anderson, Bruce Stigler,
Jay Hilburn, Vu Nguyen
client
Widmer Brothers Brewery

creative firm
KENNETH DISEÑO
Uruapan, Mexico
creative people
Kenneth Treviño
client
Soluna Wines

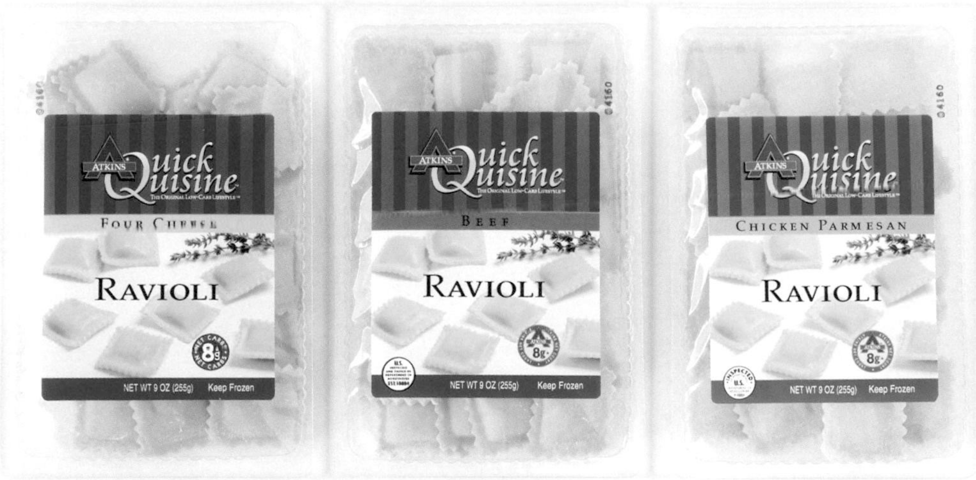

creative firm
NANCY FRAME DESIGN
Durham, North Carolina
creative people
Stewart Waller, Waller Digital,
Durham, North Carolina

creative firm
HORNALL ANDERSON DESIGN
Seattle, Washington
creative people
Lisa Cerveny, Sonja Max, Belinda Bowling,
Ensi Mofasser, Kathy Saito, Beth Grimm,
Julie Jacobson
client
Tahitian Noni

creative firm
SMITH DESIGN
Glen Ridge, New Jersey
creative people
James C. Smith, Glenn Hagen, Carol Konkowski, Angel Souto
client
The Topps Company Inc.

creative firm
SAYLES GRAPHIC DESIGN
Des Moines, Iowa
creative people
John Sayles
client
MaDIKwe

creative firm
JENN DAVID DESIGN
Irvine, California
creative people
Jenn David Connolly
client
Agog Creative

creative firm
MONDERER DESIGN
Cambridge, Massachusetts
creative people
Stuart McCoy, Stewart Monderer
client
Connected Software

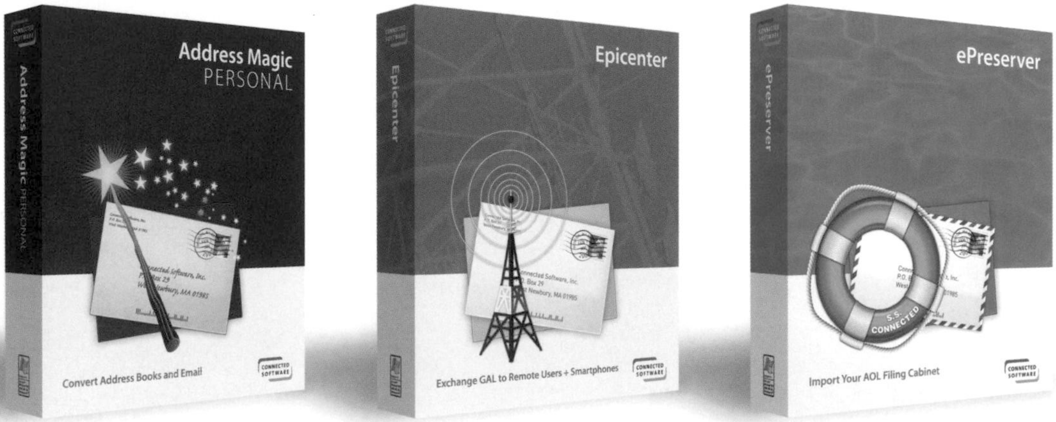

creative firm
FLOWDESIGN
Northville, Michigan
creative people
Dan Matauch, Dennis Nalezyty, Allison Tinsley
client
Honest Tea

creative firm
KROG
Ljubljana, Slovenia
creative people
Edi Berk
client
Slow Food Table

creative firm
HORNALL ANDERSON DESIGN
Seattle, Washington
creative people
Jack Anderson, David Bates, Beth Grimm, Kathleen Gibson, Jacob Carter
client
Wrigley's

creative firm
CHUTE GERDEMAN RETAIL
Columbus, Ohio
creative people
Elle Chute, Mindi Trank, Steve Pottschmidt, Bess Anderson, Jay Highland, Susan Siewny
client
New World Restaurant Group

creative firm
HORNALL ANDERSON DESIGN
Seattle, Washington
creative people
Lisa Cerveny, Mary Hermes, Julia LaPine, Jana Nishi, Belinda Bowling, Lauren DiRusso, Elmer dela Cruz
client
O.C. Tanner

creative firm
EVENSON DESIGN GROUP
Culver City, California
creative people
Dallas Duncan
client
CO-OP Financial Services

creative firm
KENNETH DISEÑO
Uruapan, Mexico
creative people
Kenneth Treviño
client
Tequila Solazul, Industrial Mulsa

creative firm
HORNALL ANDERSON DESIGN
Seattle, Washington
creative people
Lisa Cerveny, Mary Hermes, Holly Craven, Belinda Bowling, Mary Chin Hutchison, Tiffany Place
client
Benjamin Moore

creative firm
FLOWDESIGN
Northville, Michigan
creative people
Dan Matauch, Dennis Nalezyty, Allison Tinsley
client
Punati Chemical Co.

creative firm
HORNALL ANDERSON DESIGN
Seattle, Washington
creative people
Lisa Cerveny, Sonja Max, Belinda Bowling, Ensi Mofasser, Kathy Saito, Beth Grimm, Julie Jacobson
client
Tahitian Noni

creative firm
EUPHORIANET
Monterrey, Mexico
creative people
Mabel Morales, Beba Mier
client
Toma Products

creative firm
HORNALL ANDERSON DESIGN
Seattle, Washington
creative people
Jack Anderson, Bruce Stigler, Don Stayner, Vu Nguyen, Beth Grimm, Andrew Well, Jana Nishi
client
Redhook Brewery

creative firm
NANCY FRAME DESIGN
Durham, North Carolina
creative people
Nancy Frame

creative firm
EVENSON DESIGN GROUP
Culver City, California
creative people
Mark Sojka, Weina Dinata
client
Oscapes

creative firm
DESIGN SOURCE
Aptos, California
creative people
Cari Class, Heather Dunnigan, Annette Webb
client
Whole Grain Natural Bread Co.

creative firm
FAI DESIGN GROUP
Irvington, New York
creative people
Robert Scully, Derek Hunter, Uriel Rivera
client
Linens N Things

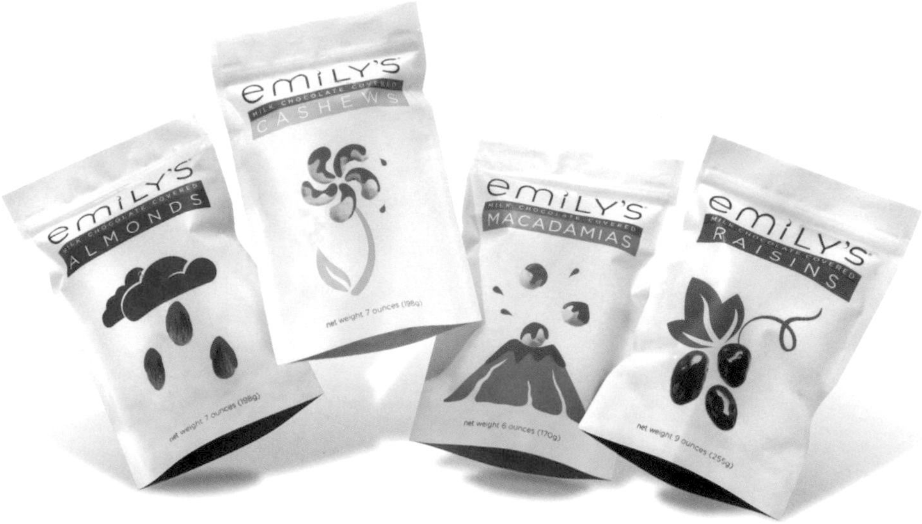

creative firm
HORNALL ANDERSON DESIGN
Seattle, Washington
creative people
Jack Anderson, Kathy Saito, Sonja Max, Henry Yiu, Yuri Shvets
client
AMES International

creative firm
KROG
Ljubljana, Slovenia
creative people
Edi Berk
client
Festival Ljubljana

creative firm
CHUTE GERDEMAN RETAIL
Columbus, Ohio
creative people
Dennis Gerdeman, Brian Shafley, Wendy Johnson, Steve Pottschmidt, Bess Anderson, Steve Boreman, Susan Siewny, Jon Knodell
client
Mars Retail Group

creative firm
HORNALL ANDERSON DESIGN
Seattle, Washington
creative people
Mark Popich, Ethan Keller, Andrew Well, Jon Graeff, Rachel Lancaster
client
T-Mobile

T-Mobile
sidekick 3
D·WADE

creative firm
JENN DAVID DESIGN
Irvine, California
creative people
Jenn David Connolly
client
Magito Wines

Magito
Magito
Magito

creative firm
ZEIST DESIGN LLC
Sausalito, California
creative people
Oscar V. Mulder, Richard Scheve
client
DNP Midsummer Exotics

PREMIUM QUALITY
MIDSUMMER EXOTICS™
Mushrooms
OYSTER
All Natural

creative firm
OCTAVO DESIGNS
Frederick, Maryland
creative people
Sue Hough
client
Frederick Cellars

creative firm
ZEIST DESIGN LLC
Sausalito, California
creative people
Oscar V. Mulder, Richard Scheve
client
Torani Pure Flavor

creative firm
TOM FOWLER, INC.
Norwalk, Connecticut
creative people
Mary Ellen Butkus, Phillip Doherty, Brien O'Reilly
client
Honeywell Consumer Group

creative firm
CHUTE GERDEMAN RETAIL
Columbus, Ohio
creative people
Dennis Gerdeman, Brian Shafley, Wendy Johnson, Steve Pottschmidt, Bess Anderson, Steve Boreman, Susan Siewny, Jon Knodell
client
Mars Retail Group

creative firm
FLOWDESIGN
Northville, Michigan
creative people
Dan Matauch, Dennis Nalezyty
client
Aqua Deco

creative firm
CHUTE GERDEMAN RETAIL
Columbus, Ohio
creative people
Elle Chute, Mindi Trank, Steve Pottschmidt, Bess Anderson, Jay Highland, Susan Siewny
client
New World Restaurant Group

creative firm
FAI DESIGN GROUP
Irvington, New York
creative people
Robert Scully, Steve Cox
client
Linens N Things

creative firm
NANCY FRAME DESIGN
Durham, North Carolina
creative people
David Watts, Durham, North Carolina

creative firm
HORNALL ANDERSON DESIGN
Seattle, Washington
creative people
Jack Anderson, Andrew Wicklund, David Bates, Elmer dela Cruz, Jacob Carter, Peter Anderson, Chris Freed, Laura Jakobsen
client
Microsoft Corporation

creative firm
ZUNDA GROUP LLC
South Norwalk, Connecticut
creative people
Charles Zunda, Gary Esposito, Daniel Price, Lorraine Casscles
client
Colgate-Palmolive Company

creative firm
KROG
Ljubljana, Slovenia
creative people
Edi Berk
client
Pravna fakulteta, Ljubljana

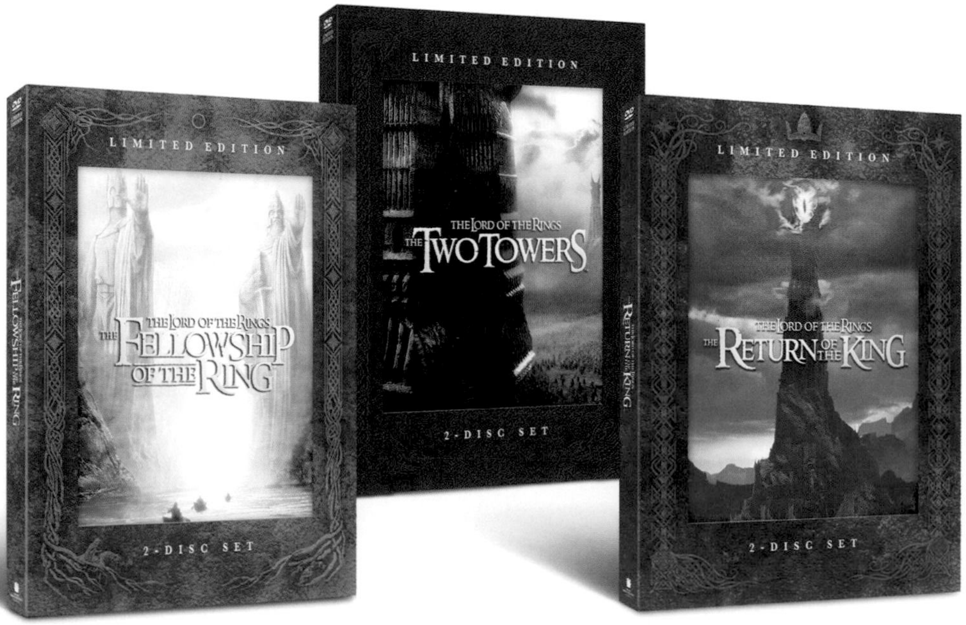

creative firm
30SIXTY ADVERTISING+DESIGN, INC.
Los Angeles, California
creative people
Henry Vizcarra, Pär Larsson, Mot Potives, Eric Perez, Tuyet Vong
client
New Line Home Entertainment

creative firm
FLOWDESIGN
Northville, Michigan
creative people
Dan Matauch, Dennis Nalezyty
client
Frank's Red Hot

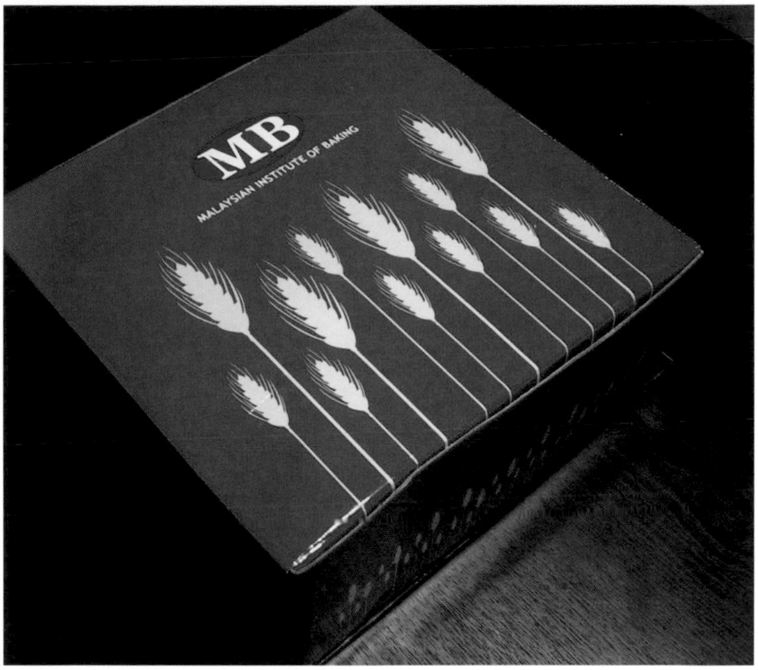

creative firm
TRUEFACES CREATION SDN BHD
Selangor, Malaysia
creative people
TrueFACES Creative Team
client
MIB—Malaysian Institute of Baking

creative firm
CHUTE GERDEMAN RETAIL
Columbus, Ohio
creative people
Dennis Gerdeman, Brian Shafley, Wendy Johnson, Steve Pottschmidt, Bess Anderson, Steve Boreman, Susan Siewny, Jon Knodell
client
Mars Retail Group

creative firm
EUPHORIANET
Monterrey, Mexico
creative people
Mabel Morales, Beba Mier, Carmen Rodríguez
client
Toma Products

creative firm
EVENSON DESIGN GROUP
Culver City, California
creative people
Mark Sojka
client
Luna Roasters Gourmet Coffee & Tea

creative firm
AYSE ÇELEM DESIGN
Istanbul, Turkey
creative people
Ayse Çelem
client
Divino Wine

creative firm
HORNALL ANDERSON DESIGN
Seattle, Washington
creative people
Jack Anderson, Larry Anderson, Jay Hilburn, Bruce Stigler, Elmer dela Cruz, Daymon Bruck, Hayden Schoen
client
Widmer Brothers Brewery

creative firm
ZEIST DESIGN LLC
Sausalito, California
creative people
Oscar V. Mulder, Richard Scheve
client
ACH Tones Pure Vanilla Extract

This bike has a story
TRIUMPH

creative firm
MIKE SALISBURY
Venice, California
creative people
Mike Salisbury
client
Triumph

creative firm
TOM FOWLER, INC.
Norwalk, Connecticut
creative people
Elizabeth P. Ball
client
The Norwalk Emergency Shelter

creative firm
SOMMESE DESIGN
Port Matilda, Pennsylvania
creative people
Lanny Sommese, Ryan Russel
client
The Quanto Project

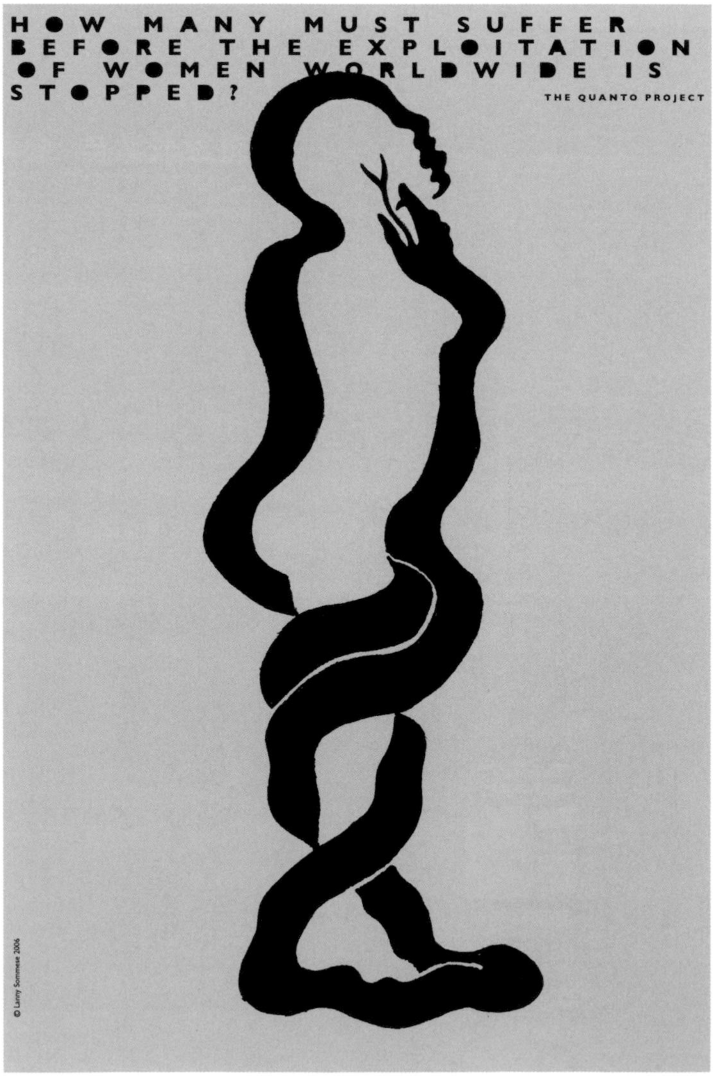

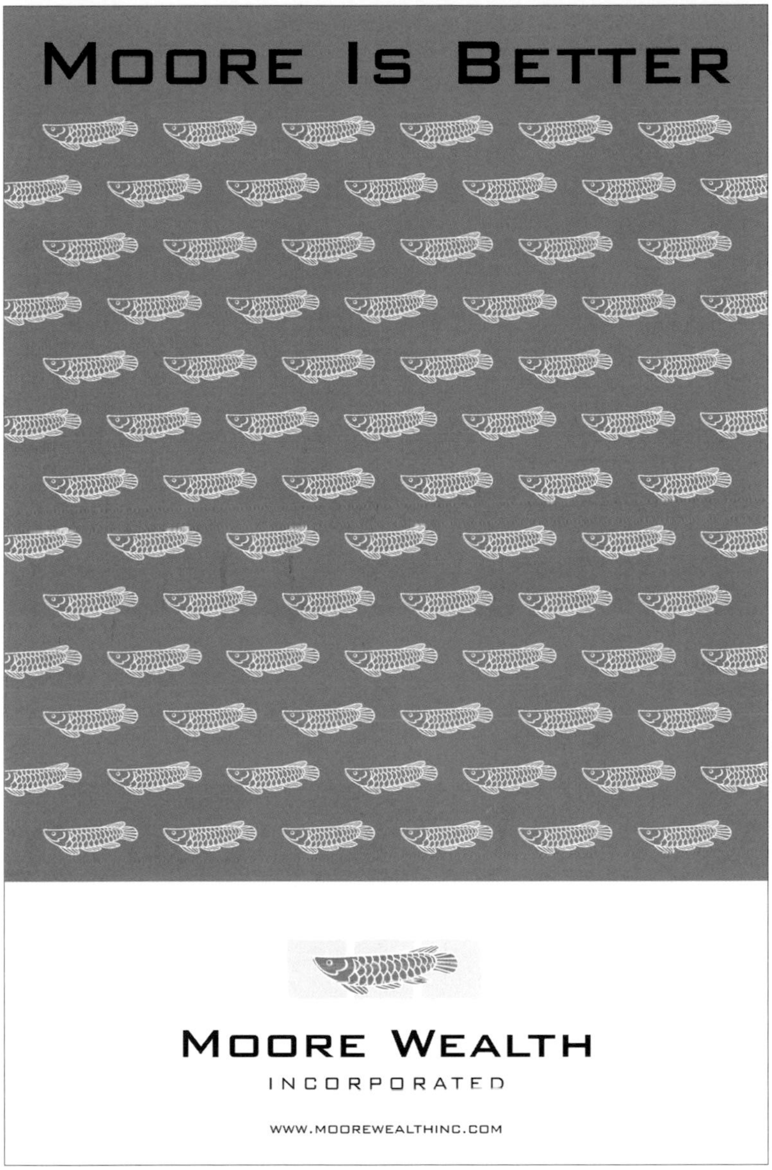

creative firm
OCTAVO DESIGNS
Frederick, Maryland
creative people
Sue Hough
client
Moore Wealth Incorporated

creative firm
TLC DESIGN
Churchville, Virginia
creative people
Trudy L. Cole
client
TLC Design

creative firm
STUDIO D
Indianapolis, Indiana
creative people
Holly Decker
client
St. John Lutheran School

creative firm
FRY HAMMOND BARR
Orlando, Florida
creative people
Tim Fisher, Sean Brunson, Lara Mann
client
Central Florida YMCA

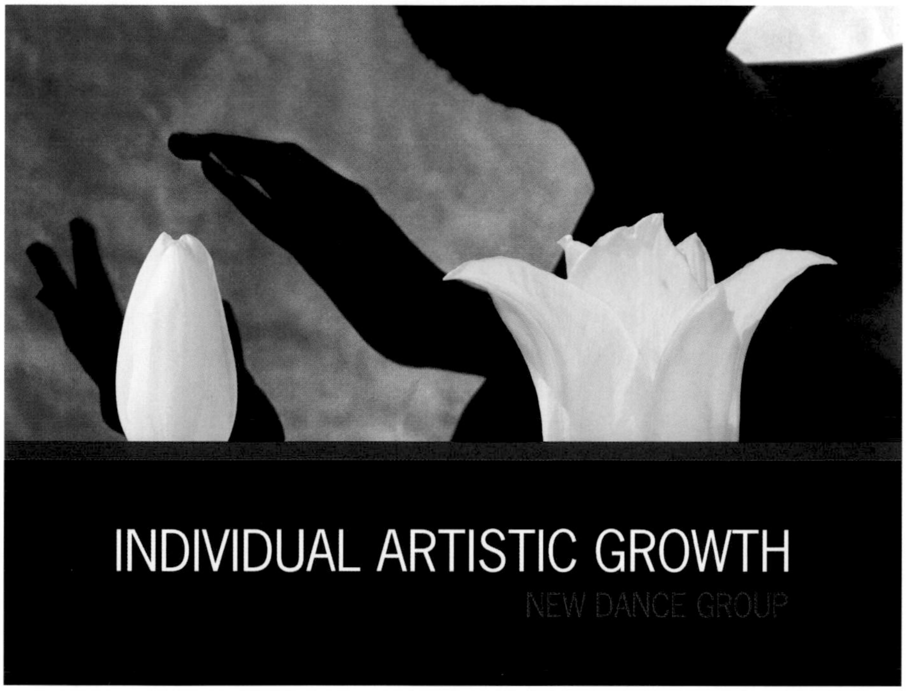

creative firm
WESTGROUP CREATIVE
New York, New York
creative people
Chip Tolaney
client
New Dance Group

creative firm
FIVE VISUAL COMMUNICATION & DESIGN
Mason, Ohio
creative people
Laura Broermann, Rondi Tschopp
client
West Chester Parks & Recreation

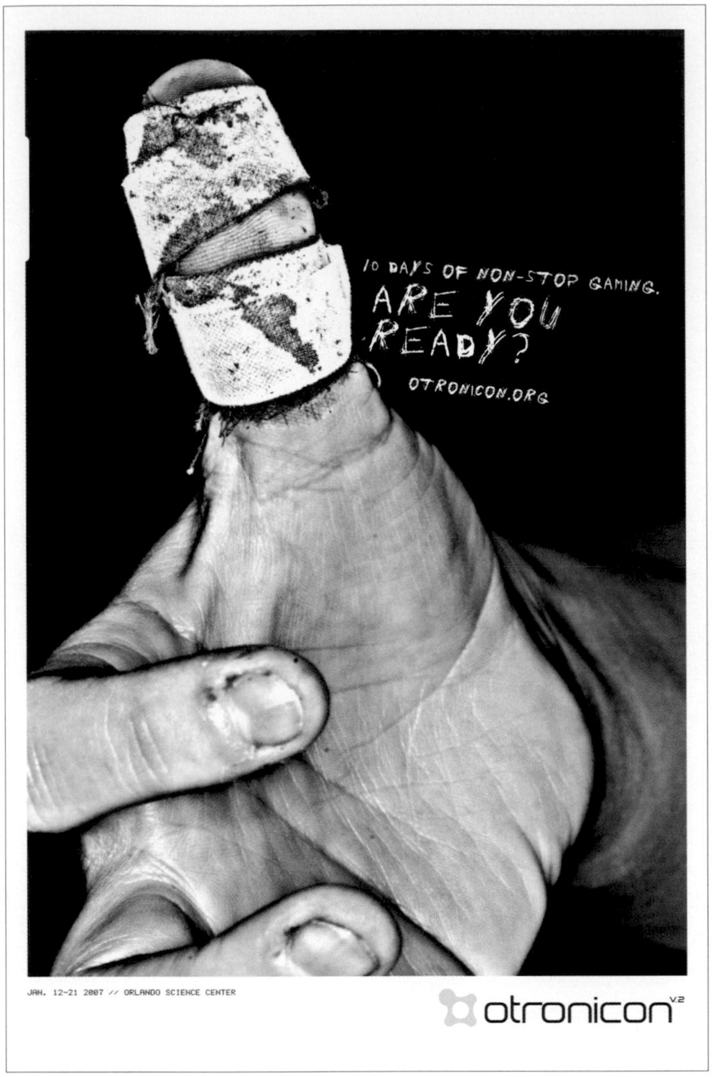
10 DAYS OF NON-STOP GAMING.
ARE YOU READY?
OTRONICON.ORG
JAN. 12-21 2007 // ORLANDO SCIENCE CENTER
otronicon v.2

creative firm
FRY HAMMOND BARR
Orlando, Florida
creative people
Tim Fisher, Sean Brunson, Sandra Lawton
client
Orlando Science Center

creative firm
GUNNAR SWANSON DESIGN OFFICE
Greenville, North Carolina
creative people
Gunnar Swanson, Craig Malmrose, Lisa Beth Robinson, Matt Egan, Michael Ehlbeck, Tyler Philips, Courtney Barr
client
East Carolina University School of Art & Design

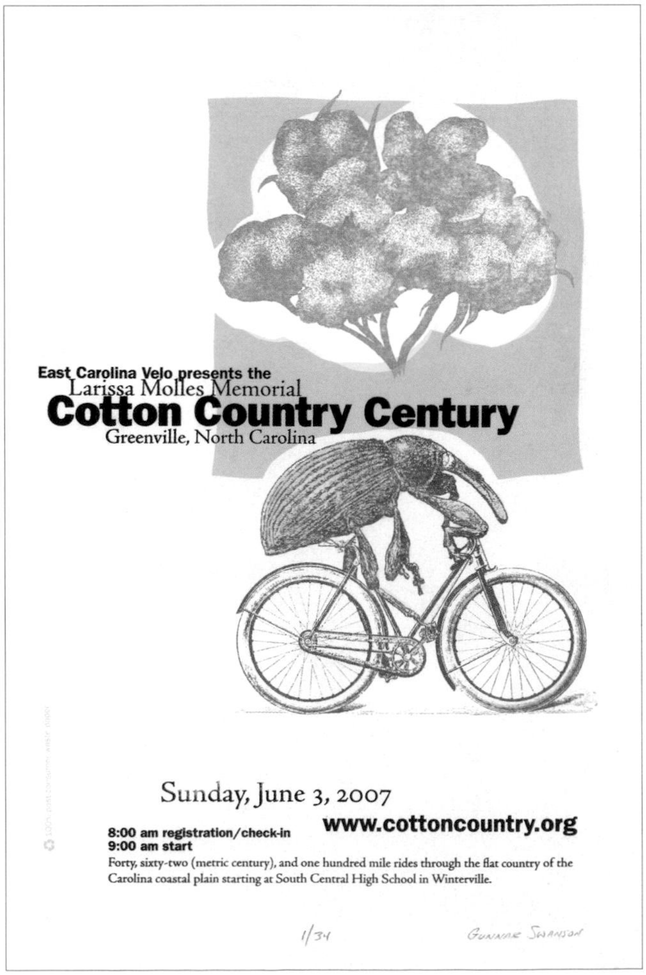
East Carolina Velo presents the
Larissa Molles Memorial
Cotton Country Century
Greenville, North Carolina
Sunday, June 3, 2007
8:00 am registration/check-in
9:00 am start
www.cottoncountry.org
Forty, sixty-two (metric century), and one hundred mile rides through the flat country of the Carolina coastal plain starting at South Central High School in Winterville.
1/34
Gunnar Swanson

INDIVIDUAL ARTISTIC GROWTH
NEW DANCE GROUP

creative firm
TLC DESIGN
Churchville, Virginia
creative people
Trudy L. Cole
client
TLC Design

creative firm
WESTGROUP CREATIVE
New York, New York
creative people
Chip Tolaney
client
New Dance Group

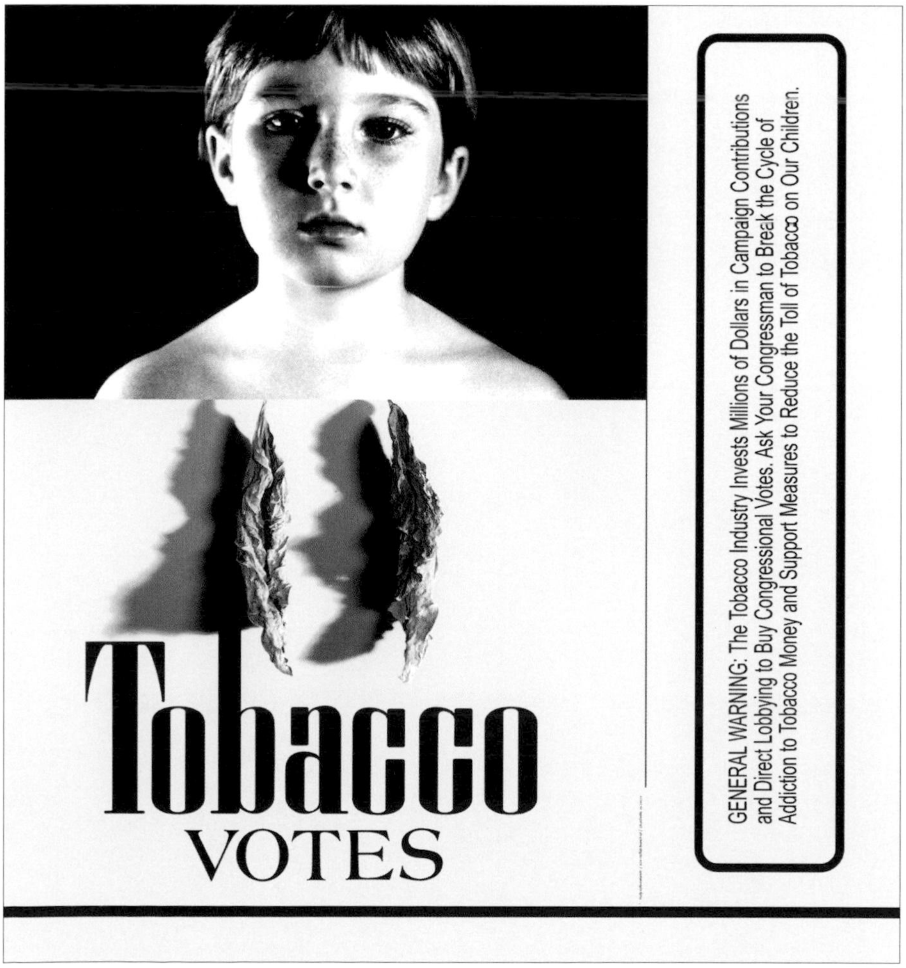
Tobacco
VOTES
GENERAL WARNING: The Tobacco Industry Invests Millions of Dollars in Campaign Contributions and Direct Lobbying to Buy Congressional Votes. Ask Your Congressman to Break the Cycle of Addiction to Tobacco Money and Support Measures to Reduce the Toll of Tobacco on Our Children.

creative firm
TLC DESIGN
Churchville, Virginia
creative people
Trudy L. Cole
client
Bob Driver, Steve Parks, Neal Knicely

creative firm
WESTGROUP CREATIVE
New York, New York
creative people
Chip Tolaney
client
New Dance Group

creative firm
DAVIS DESIGN PARTNERS
Holland, Ohio
creative people
Matt Davis, Karen Davis
client
Purdue Theatre, Purdue University

creative firm
MAMORDESIGN
Tehran, Iran
creative people
Maliheh Ghajargar
client
pluralistic

creative firm
FRY HAMMOND BARR
Orlando, Florida
creative people
Tim Fisher, Sean Brunson, John Logan
client
Habitat For Humanity

creative firm
MAMORDESIGN
Tehran, Iran
creative people
Maliheh Ghajargar
client
H. Panahi

creative firm
TLC DESIGN
Churchville, Virginia
creative people
Trudy L. Cole
client
TLC Design

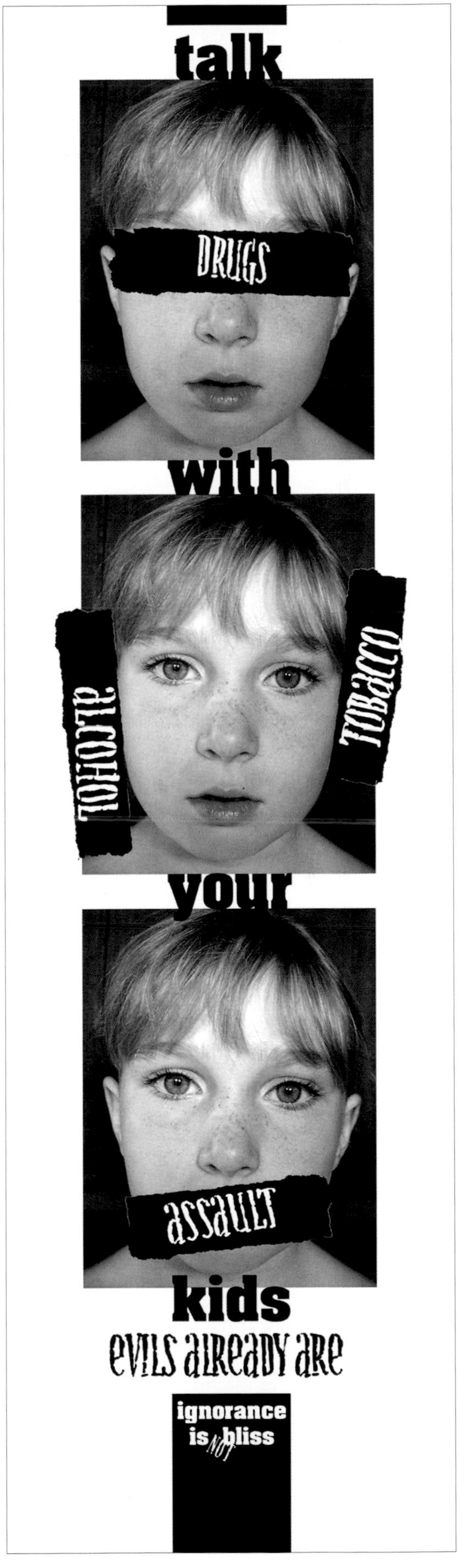

creative firm
DAVIS DESIGN PARTNERS
Holland, Ohio
creative people
Matt Davis, Karen Davis
client
Purdue Theatre, Purdue University

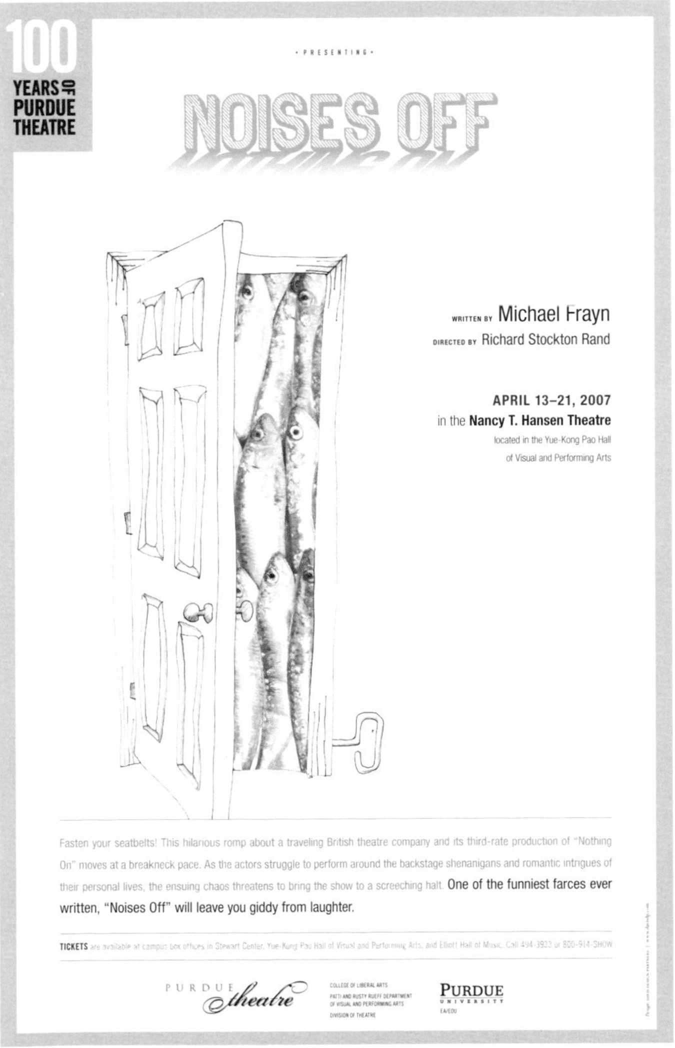

creative firm
MAMORDESIGN
Tehran, Iran
creative people
Maliheh Ghajargar
client
Ceftizox-Chemidarou pharma

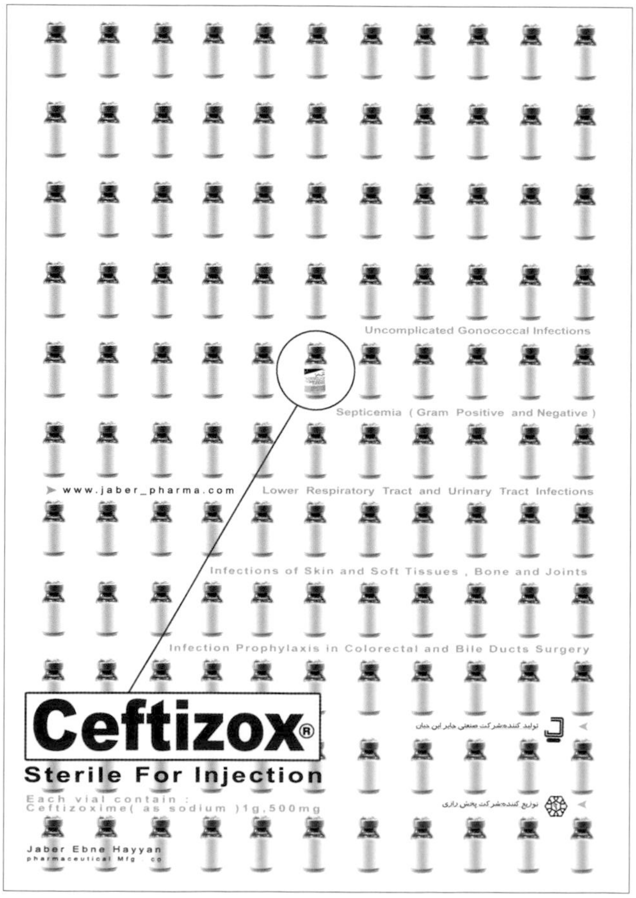

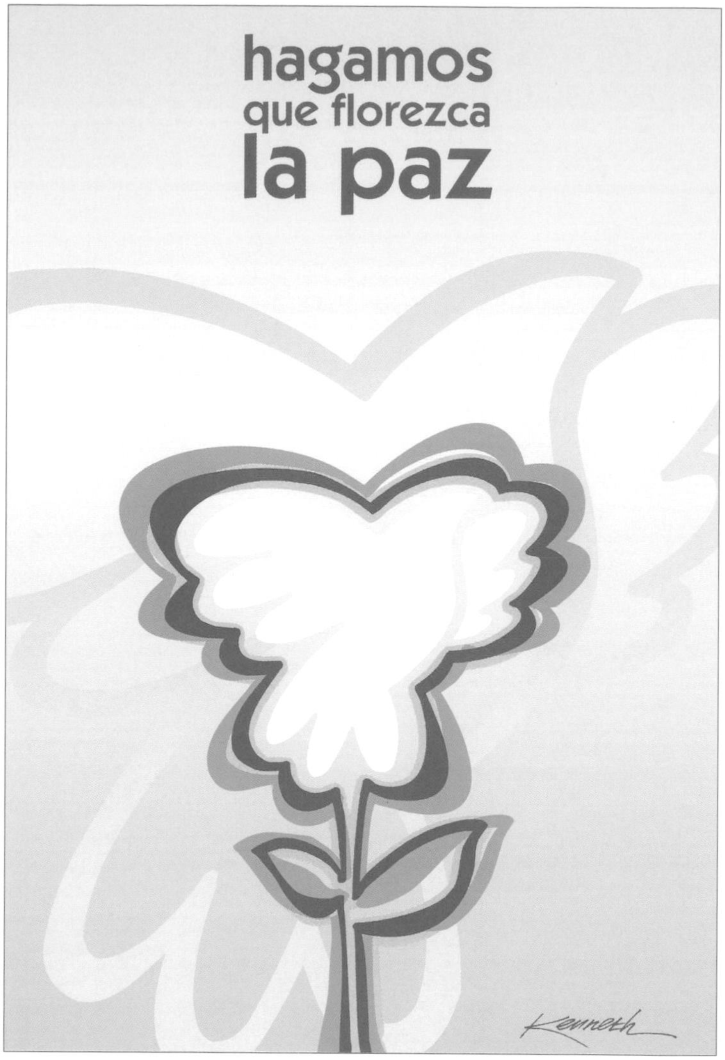

creative firm
KENNETH DISEÑO
Uruapan, Mexico
creative people
Kenneth Treviño
client
City of Uruapan Municipal Government

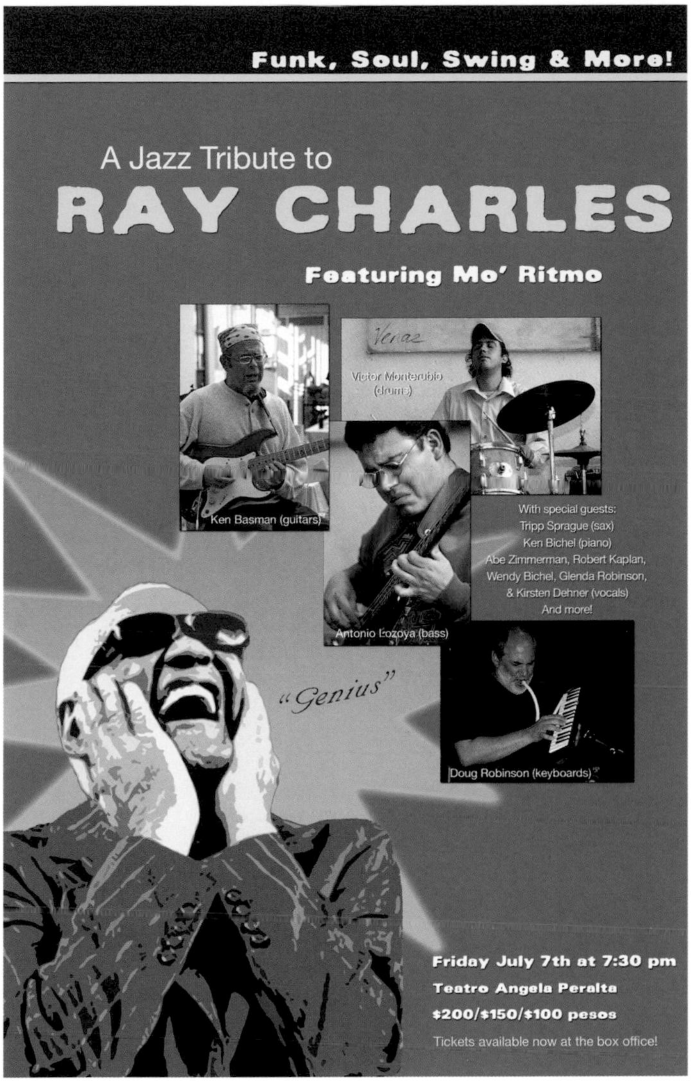

creative firm
THE IMAGINATION COMPANY
Bethel, Vermont
creative people
Kristen Smith
client
Mo Ritmo

creative firm
TLC DESIGN
Churchville, Virginia
creative people
Trudy L. Cole
client
TLC Design

creative firm
SOMMESE DESIGN
Port Matilda, Pennsylvania
creative people
Lanny Sommese, Jason Dietrick
client
Central Pennsylvania Festival of the Arts

creative firm
TLC DESIGN
Churchville, Virginia
creative people
Trudy L. Cole
client
Harrisonburg/Rockingham Daycare

creative firm
DEB NEUFELL DESIGN
Waltham, Massachusetts
creative people
Deb Neufell
client
Condemned Productions

creative firm
SAYLES GRAPHIC DESIGN
Des Moines, Iowa
creative people
John Sayles
client
Cedar Rapids Advertising Federation

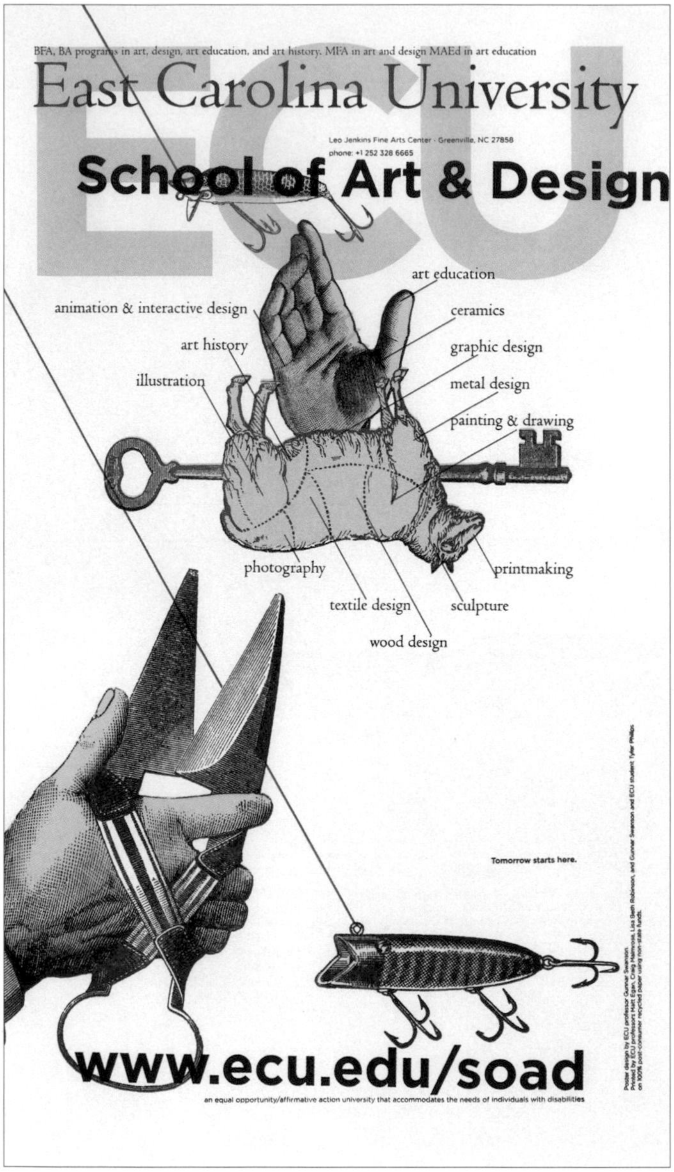

creative firm
GUNNAR SWANSON DESIGN OFFICE
Greenville, North Carolina
creative people
Gunnar Swanson, Ed McKim, Chris Schwing, Kate LaMere, Craig Malmrose
client
EC Velo

creative firm
TOM FOWLER, INC.
Norwalk, Connecticut
creative people
Thomas G. Fowler
client
Willi's Wine Bar

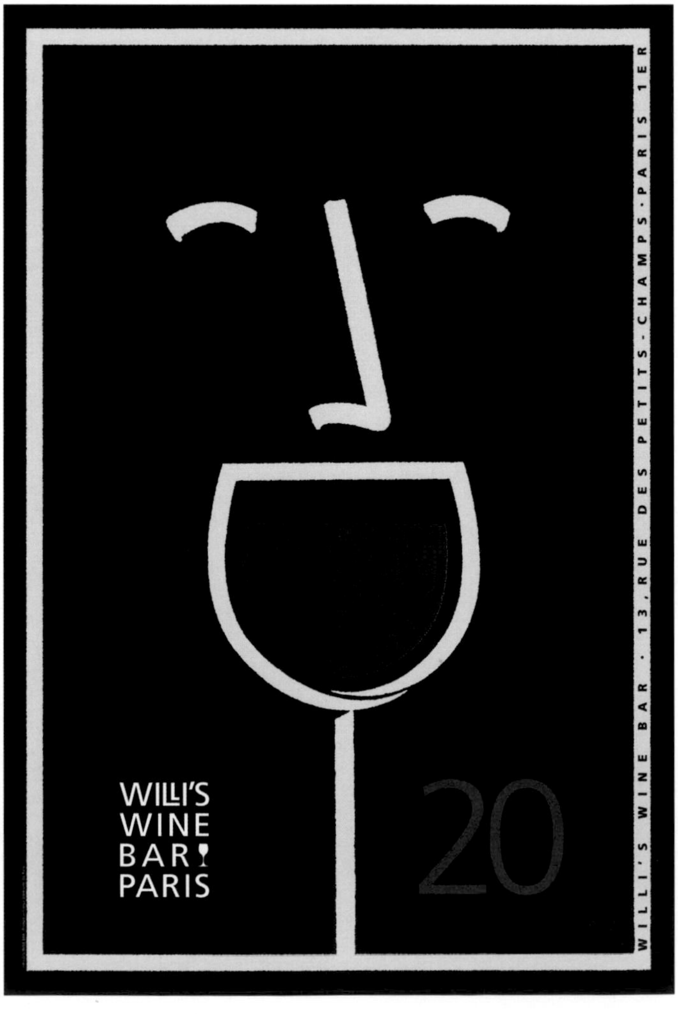

creative firm
FRY HAMMOND BARR
Orlando, Florida
creative people
Tim Fisher, Sean Brunson, Sandra Lawton
client
Orlando Science Center

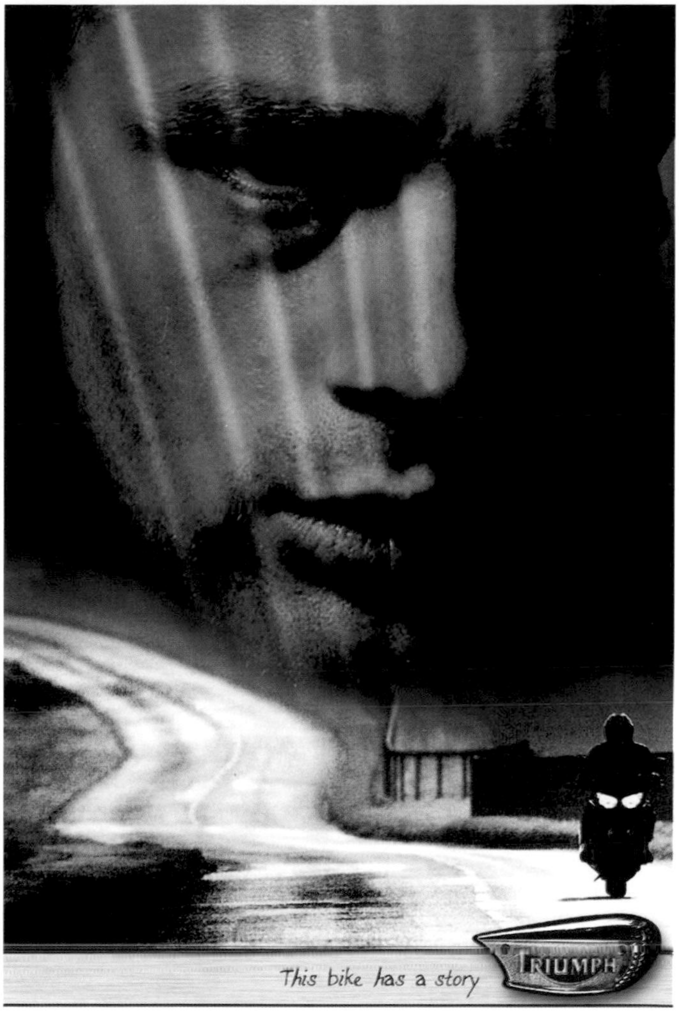

creative firm
MIKE SALISBURY
Venice, California
creative people
Mike Salisbury
client
Triumph

creative firm
TLC DESIGN
Churchville, Virginia
creative people
Trudy L. Cole
client
James Madison University

creative firm
OCTAVO DESIGNS
Frederick, Maryland
creative people
Mark Burrier
client
Soft Images Salon

creative firm
FRY HAMMOND BARR
Orlando, Florida
creative people
Tim Fisher, Sean Brunson, Lara Mann
client
Florida Film Festival

creative firm
FUNK/LEVIS & ASSOCIATES
Eugene, Oregon
creative people
Lada Korol, Jack Liu
client
Lane Community College

creative firm
SAYLES GRAPHIC DESIGN
Des Moines, Iowa
creative people
John Sayles
client
The Fargo North Dakota Advertising Federation

creative firm
FRY HAMMOND BARR
Orlando, Florida
creative people
Tim Fisher, Sean Brunson
client
Mac Papers

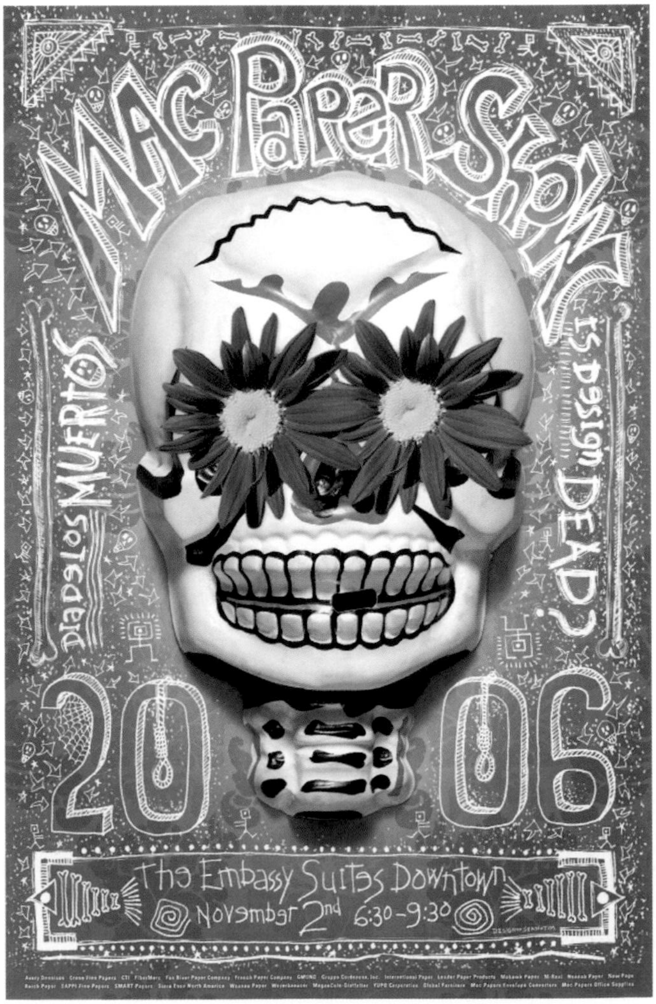

creative firm
BERRY DESIGN, INC.
Alpharetta, Georgia
creative people
Bob Berry, Chip Waller
client
Popeyes Louisiana Kitchen

creative firm
TLC DESIGN
Churchville, Virginia
creative people
Trudy L. Cole
client
TLC Design

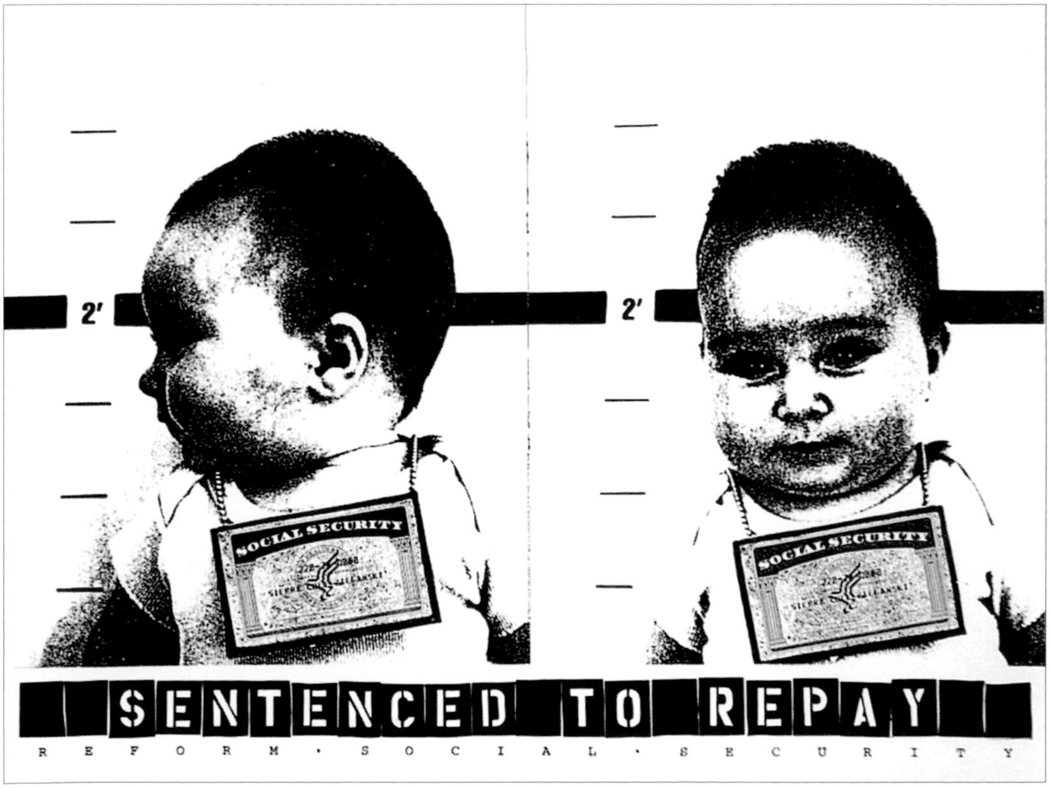

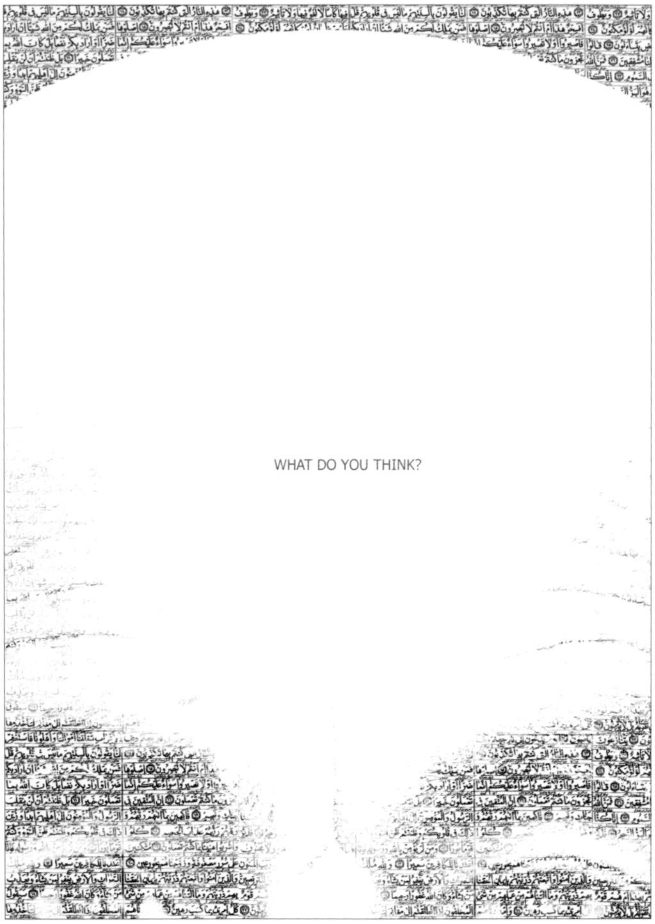

creative firm
MAMORDESIGN
Tehran, Iran
creative people
Maliheh Ghajargar
client
What do you ...

creative firm
FRY HAMMOND BARR
Orlando, Florida
creative people
Tim Fisher, Sean Brunson, Lara Mann
client
Florida Film Festival

creative firm
TLC DESIGN
Churchville, Virginia
creative people
Trudy L. Cole
client
JMU School of Theatre and Dance

creative firm
FRY HAMMOND BARR
Orlando, Florida
creative people
Tim Fisher, Ray Kilinski, Tom Kane
client
ABC

creative firm
TLC DESIGN
Churchville, Virginia
creative people
Trudy L. Cole
client
JMU School of Theatre and Dance

creative firm
MAMORDESIGN
Tehran, Iran
creative people
Maliheh Ghajargar
client
Ballon Festival

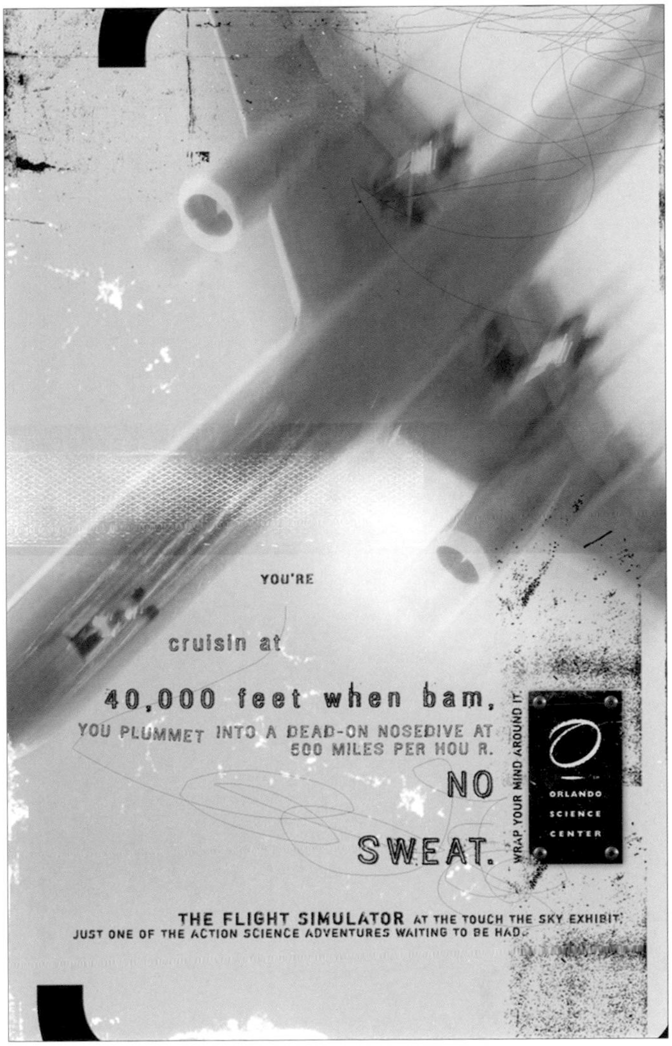

creative firm
FRY HAMMOND BARR
Orlando, Florida
creative people
Tim Fisher, Sean Brunson, Sandra Lawton
client
Orlando Science Center

creative firm
DAVIS DESIGN PARTNERS
Holland, Ohio
creative people
Matt Davis, Karen Davis
client
Purdue Theatre, Purdue University

creative firm
BERRY DESIGN, INC.
Alpharetta, Georgia
creative people
Bob Berry, Chip Waller
client
Popeyes Louisiana Kitchen

creative firm
FIDLER & STUCKER DESIGN
Grand Rapids, Ohio
creative people
Amy Fidler, Jennifer Stucker
client
Bowling Green State University

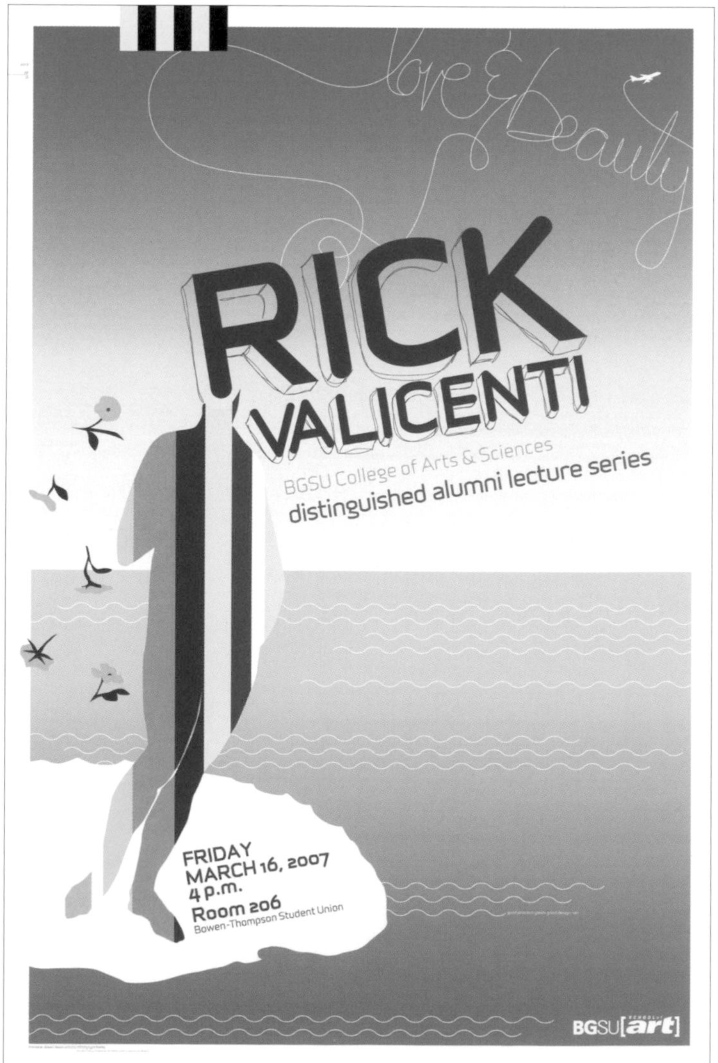

YAMAHA
YZF R1 STREET BIKE
$11,299
RideNow
WITH OVER 30 DEALERSHIPS NATIONWIDE, WE HAVE WHAT YOU'RE LOOKING FOR.
www.ridenow.com

creative firm
FRY HAMMOND BARR
Orlando, Florida
creative people
Tim Fisher, Sean Brunson, John Logan
client
Ride Now

creative firm
MAMORDESIGN
Tehran, Iran
creative people
Maliheh Ghajargar
client
Vigor Watch

V
VIGOR
JAPAN QUARTZ

creative firm
TLC DESIGN
Churchville, Virginia
creative people
Trudy L. Cole
client
United Way of Harrisonburg
and Rockingham County

creative firm
BOELTS DESIGN
Tucson, Arizona
creative people
Jackson Boelts
client
Boelts Design

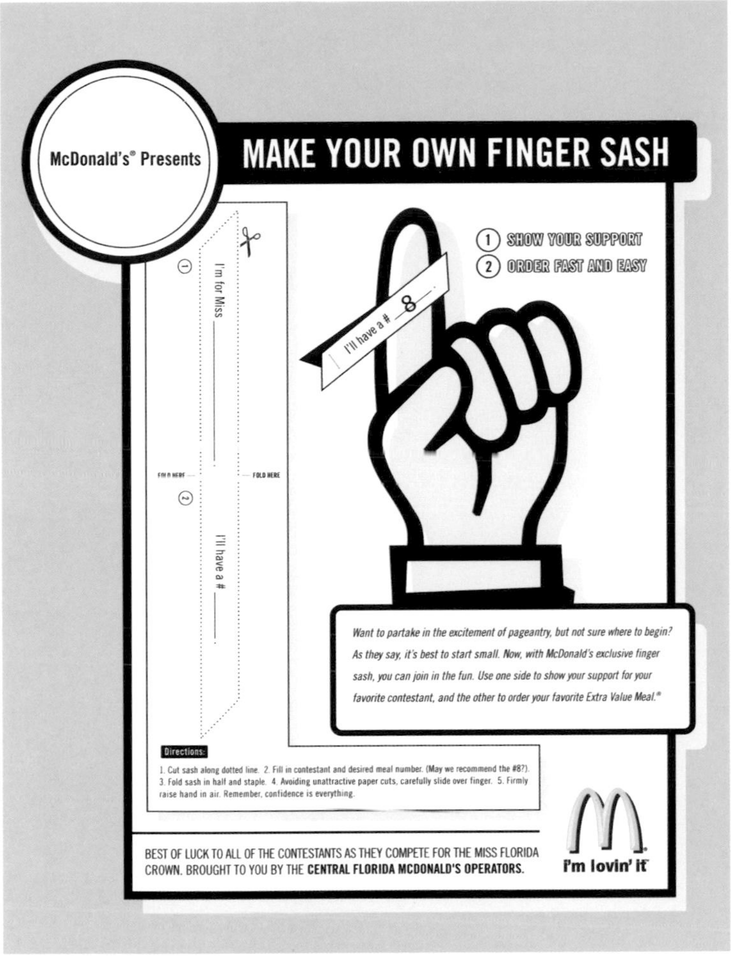

creative firm
FRY HAMMOND BARR
Orlando, Florida
creative people
Tim Fisher, Sean Brunson, Lara Mann
client
McDonald's

creative firm
MFDI
Selinsgrove, Pennsylvania
creative people
Mark Fertig
client
Susquehanna University, Michael Smith

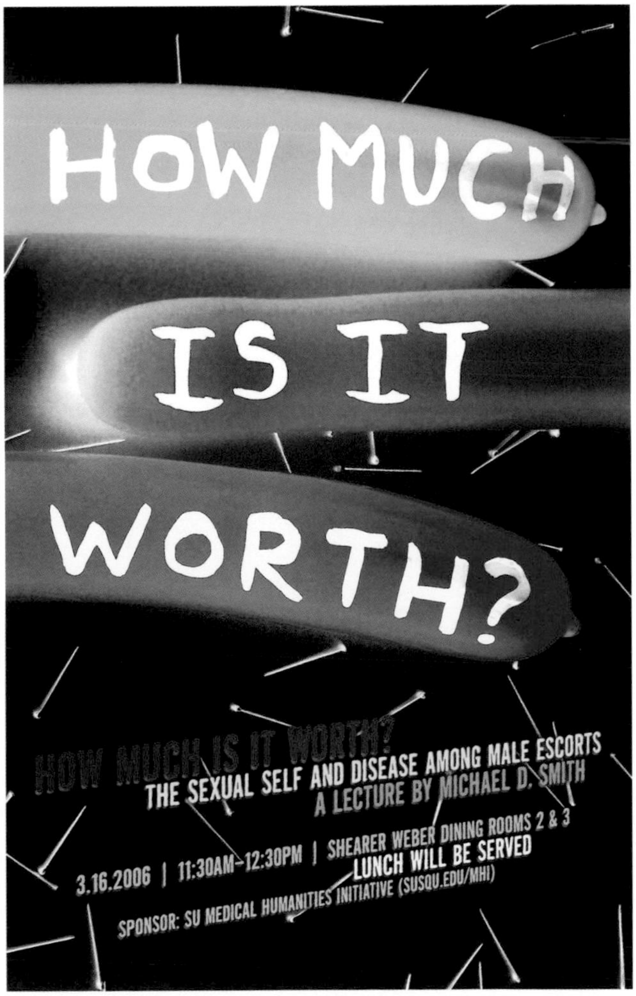

WHO WAS POWEL CROSLEY JR.?
E. A. HOWLAND
Inventor and entrepreneur Powel Crosley Jr. was born September 18, 1886 in Cincinnati.
He studied engineering and law at the University of Cincinnati, but never completed either degree.
Crosley was obsessed with the way things worked, but his passion was automobiles. He built his fortune with a mail order business selling automobile parts as well as other gadgets he invented.
Because Crosley invested in his own company instead of the stock market, he was not hurt by the great stock market crash of 1929. He had diversified into major appliances, particularly refrigerators that, like his radios, he could price below his competitors. During the Depression he was able to keep his plants running and workers employed. His strong cash position allowed his company to ride through relatively unscathed. In fact, he was able to expand.
Crosley died on March 28, 1961 at the age of 74. Crosley appliances—and radios—are still manufactured today and sold through a nationwide network of independent distributors.

creative firm
FIVE VISUAL COMMUNICATION & DESIGN
Mason, Ohio
creative people
Laura Broermann, Rondi Tschopp
client
Mercy Health Partners of Southwest Ohio

creative firm
ATOMIC DESIGN
Crowley, Texas
creative people
Lewis Glaser
client
TCU School of Classical & Contemporary Dance

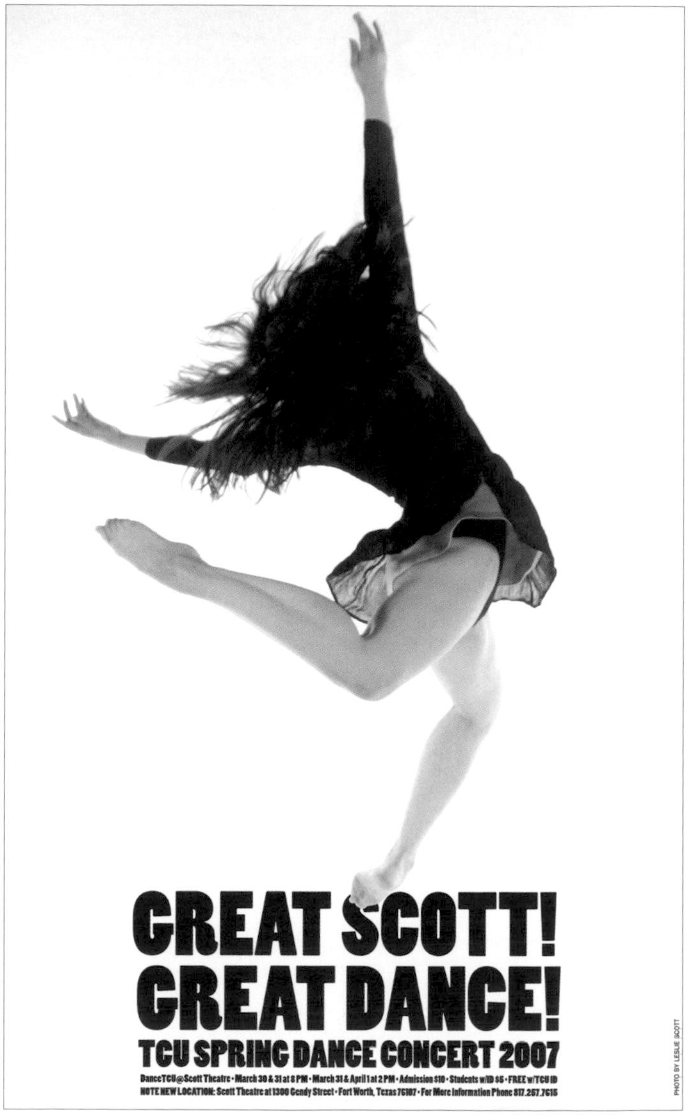
GREAT SCOTT!
GREAT DANCE!
TCU SPRING DANCE CONCERT 2007
DanceTCU@Scott Theatre • March 30 & 31 at 8 PM • March 31 & April 1 at 2 PM • Admission $10 • Students w/ID $5 • FREE w/TCU ID
NOTE NEW LOCATION: Scott Theatre at 1300 Gendy Street • Fort Worth, Texas 76107 • For More Information Phone 817.257.7615
PHOTO BY LESLIE SCOTT

creative firm
TLC DESIGN
Churchville, Virginia
creative people
Trudy L. Cole
client
JMU Theatre and Dance

creative firm
DAVIS DESIGN PARTNERS
Holland, Ohio
creative people
Matt Davis, Karen Davis
client
Purdue Theatre, Purdue University

creative firm
MFDI
Selinsgrove, Pennsylvania
creative people
Mark Fertig
client
Susquehanna University Department of Music

creative firm
FRY HAMMOND BARR
Orlando, Florida
creative people
Tim Fisher, Sean Brunson, Sandra Lawton
client
Orlando Science Center

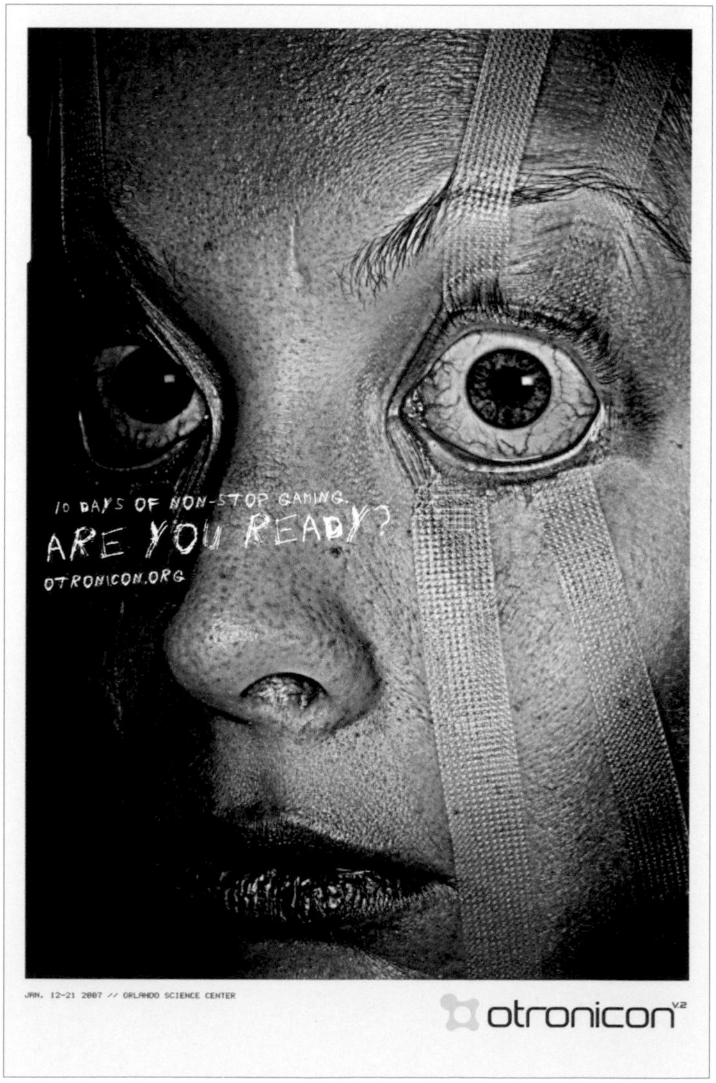

creative firm
MAMORDESIGN
Tehran, Iran
creative people
Maliheh Ghajargar
client
Blue Room

creative firm
AYSE ÇELEM DESIGN
Istanbul, Turkey
creative people
Ayse Çelem
client
GMK (Turkish Society of Graphic Designers)

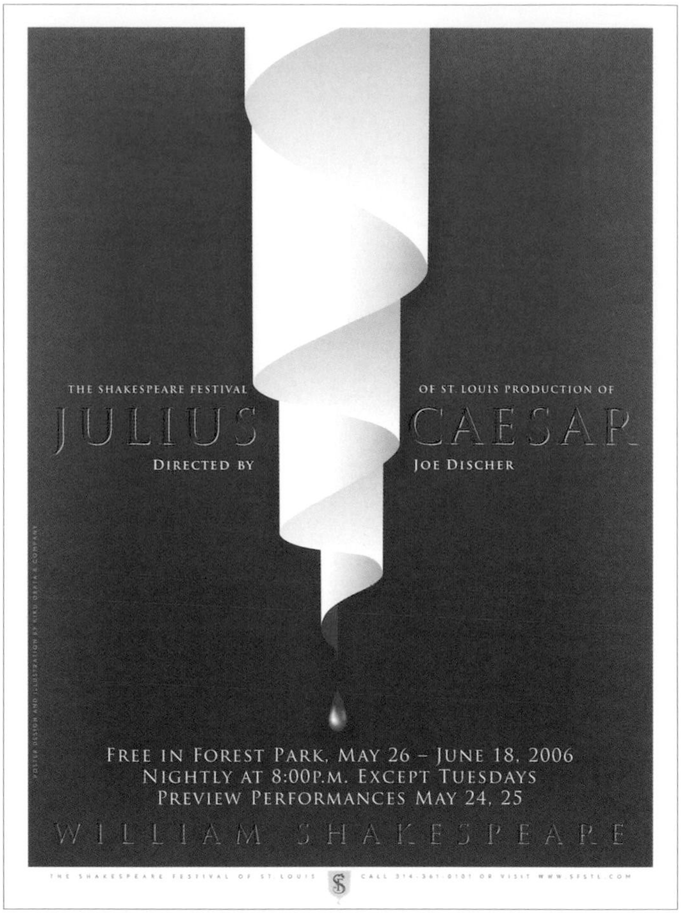

creative firm
KIKU OBATA & COMPANY
St. Louis, Missouri
creative people
Rich Nelson
client
Shakespeare Festival of St. Louis

creative firm
FRY HAMMOND BARR
Orlando, Florida
creative people
Tim Fisher, Sean Brunson, Tom Kane
client
Hard Rock Café

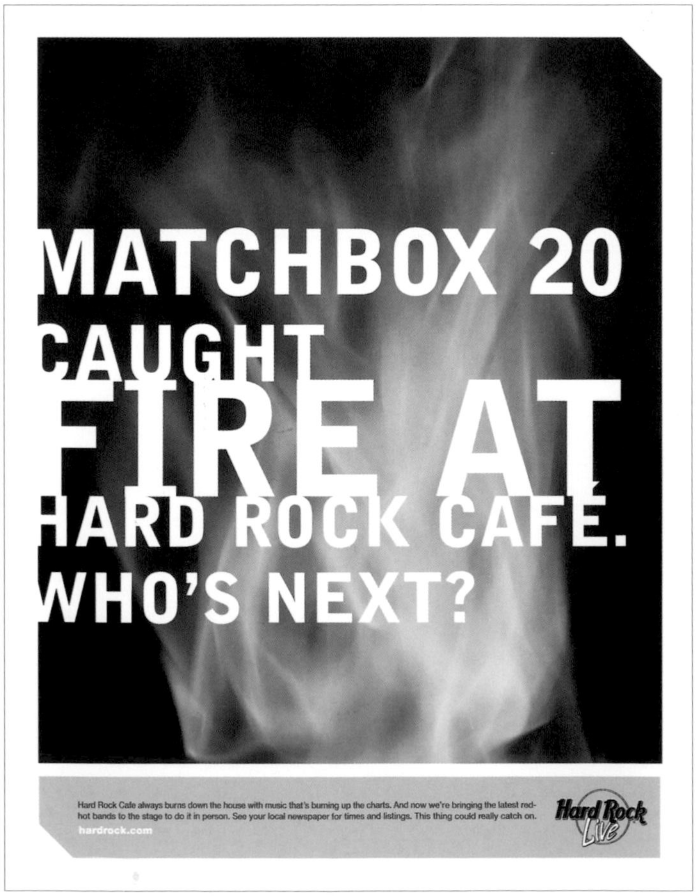

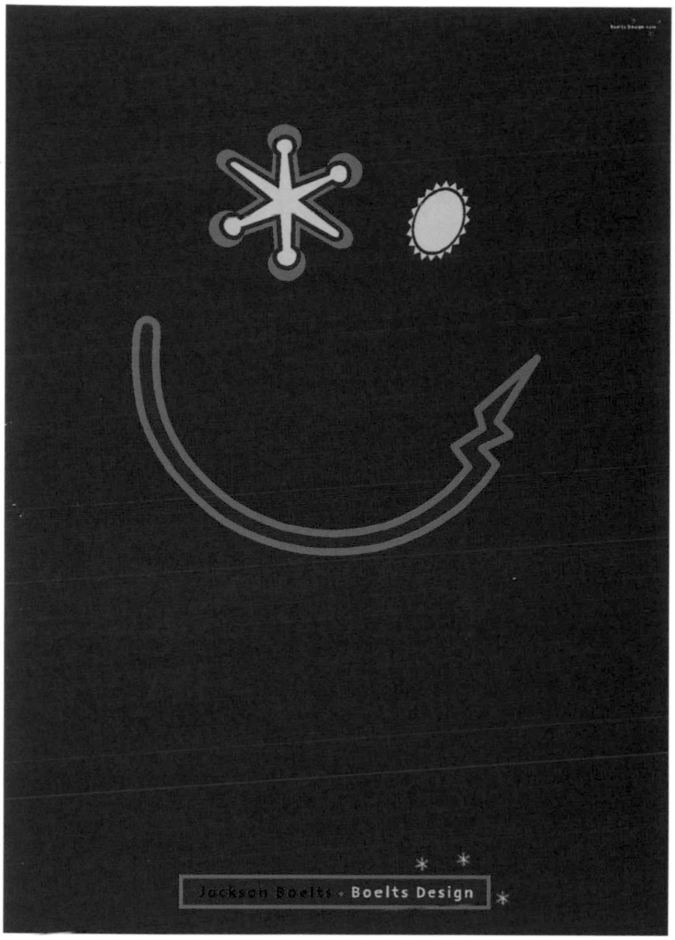

creative firm
BOELTS DESIGN
Tucson, Arizona
creative people
Jackson Boelts
client
Boelts Design

creative firm
DEB NEUFELL DESIGN
Waltham, Massachusetts
creative people
Deb Neufell
client
Sweet Revenge

creative firm
WESTGROUP CREATIVE
New York, New York
creative people
Chip Tolaney
client
New Dance Group

creative firm
FIDLER & STUCKER DESIGN
Grand Rapids, Ohio
creative people
Amy Fidler, Jennifer Stucker
client
Bowling Green State University

creative firm
MAMORDESIGN
Tehran, Iran
creative people
Maliheh Ghajargar
client
H. Panahi

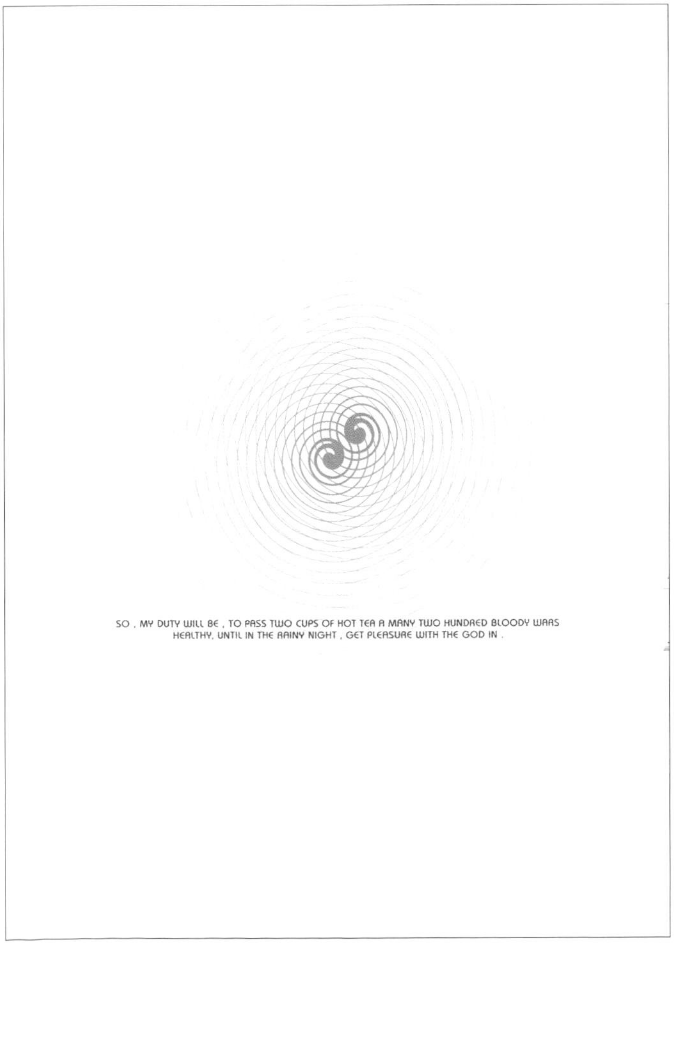
SO , MY DUTY WILL BE , TO PASS TWO CUPS OF HOT TEA A MANY TWO HUNDRED BLOODY WARS
HEALTHY, UNTIL IN THE RAINY NIGHT , GET PLEASURE WITH THE GOD IN .

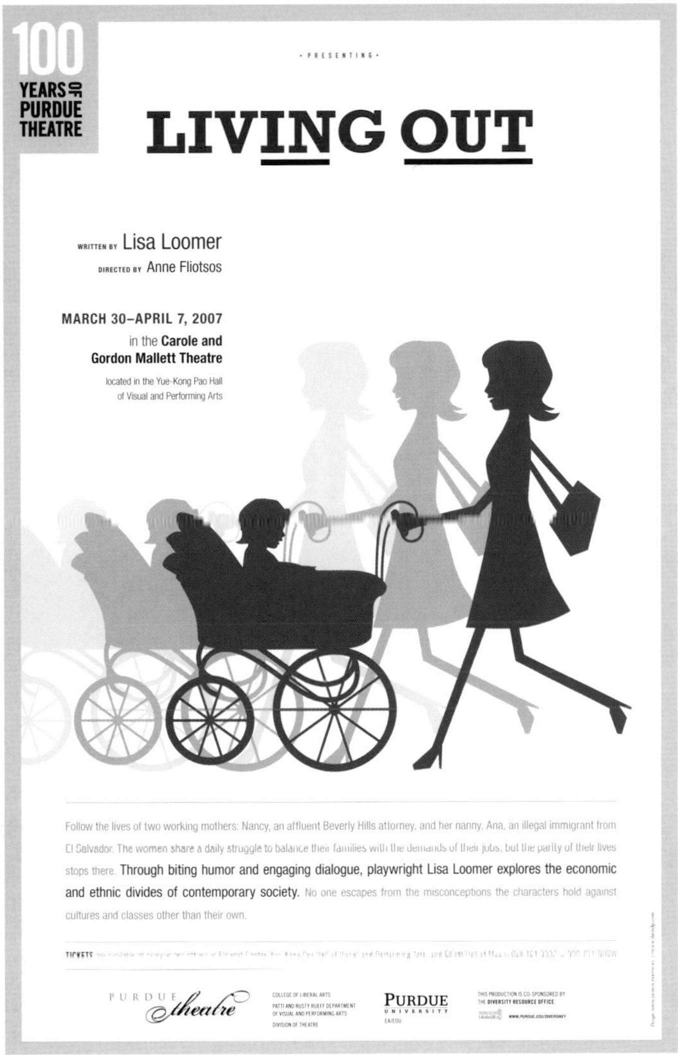

creative firm
DAVIS DESIGN PARTNERS
Holland, Ohio
creative people
Matt Davis, Karen Davis
client
Purdue Theatre, Purdue University

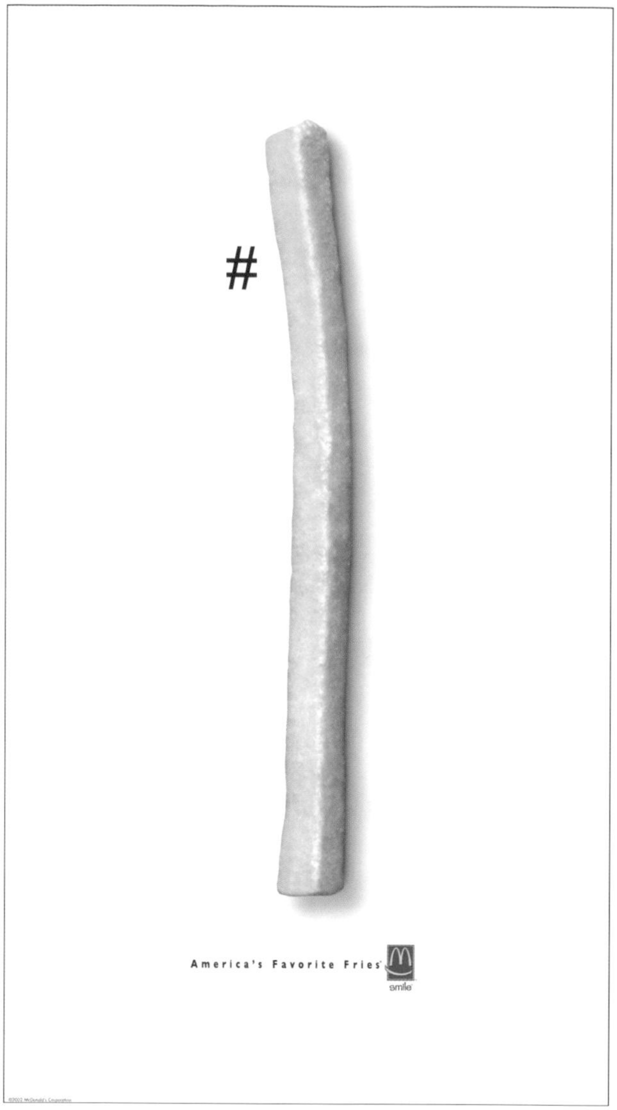

creative firm
FRY HAMMOND BARR
Orlando, Florida
creative people
Tim Fisher, Ray Kilinski
client
McDonald's

creative firm
MFDI
Selinsgrove, Pennsylvania
creative people
Mark Fertig
client
Susquehanna University,
Robert Stephens

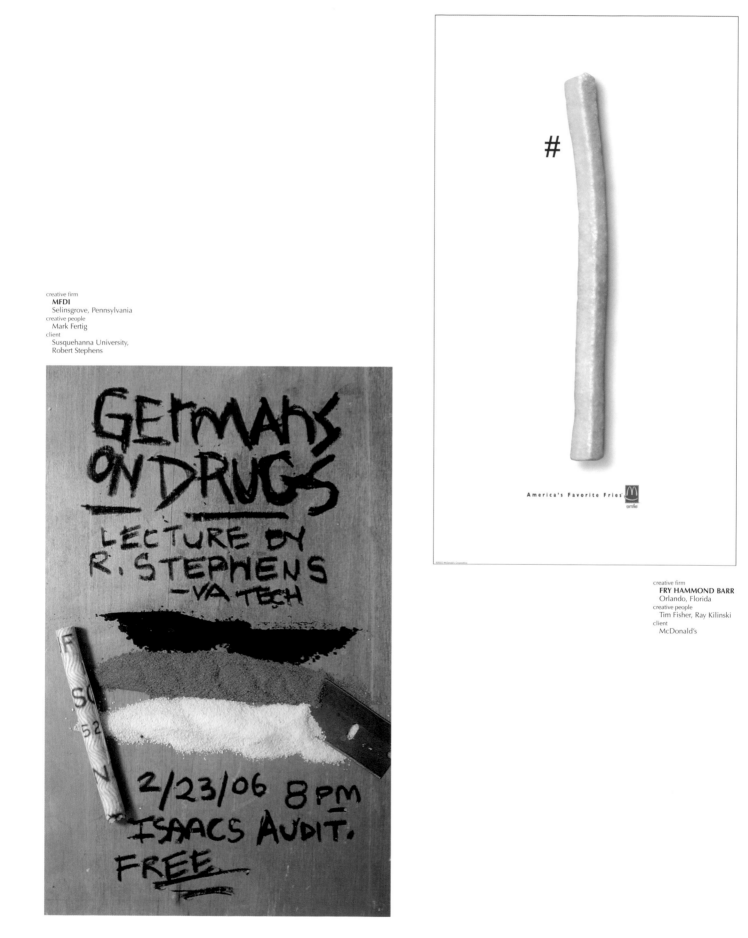

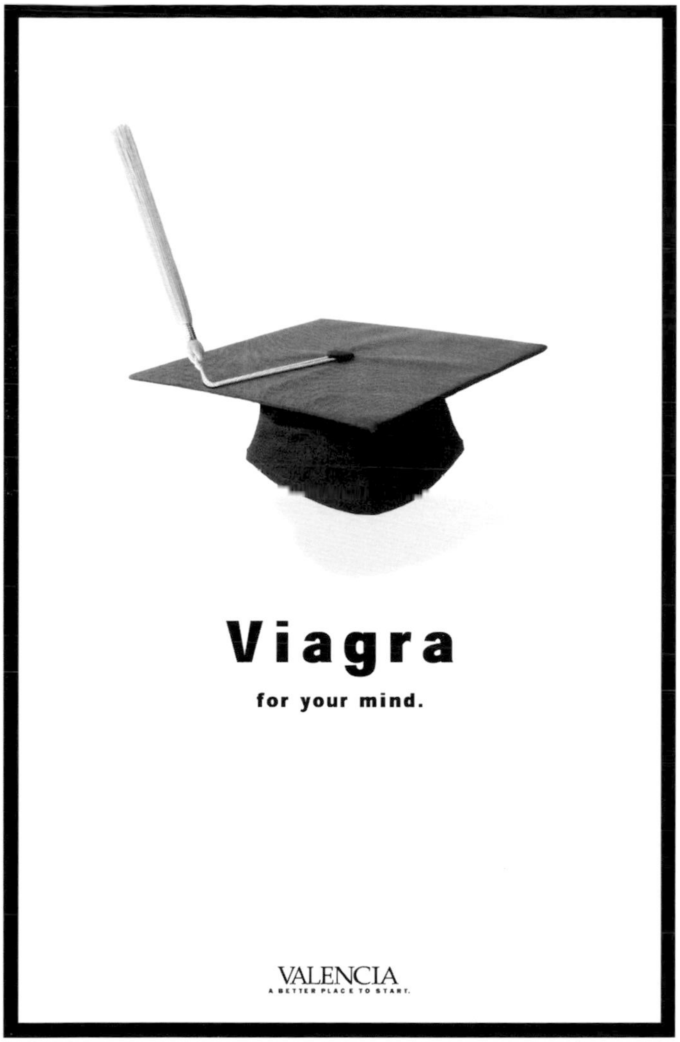

creative firm
FRY HAMMOND BARR
Orlando, Florida
creative people
Tim Fisher, Sean Brunson, John Logan
client
Valencia Community College

creative firm
FIVE VISUAL COMMUNICATION & DESIGN
Mason, Ohio
creative people
Laura Broermann, Rondi Tschopp
client
Mercy Health Partners of Southwest Ohio

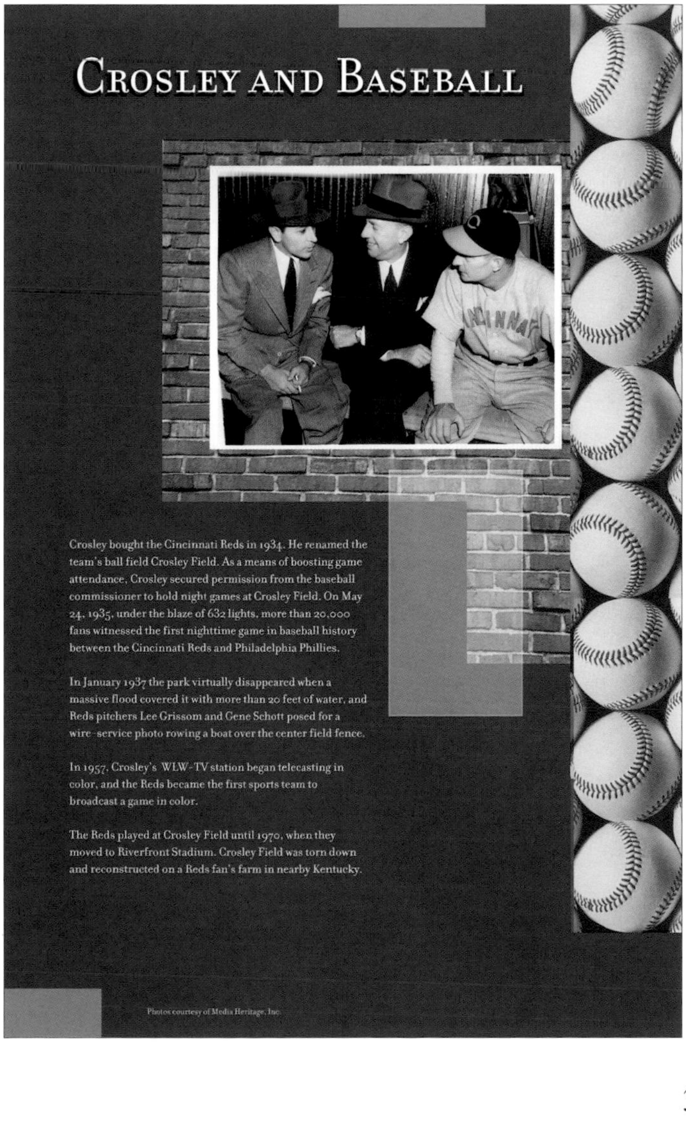

creative firm
NOLEN & ASSOCIATES
Atlanta, Georgia
creative people
Ed Young
client
Orange Business Services

creative firm
TOM FOWLER, INC.
Norwalk, Connecticut
creative people
Elizabeth P. Ball
client
Tom Fowler, Inc.

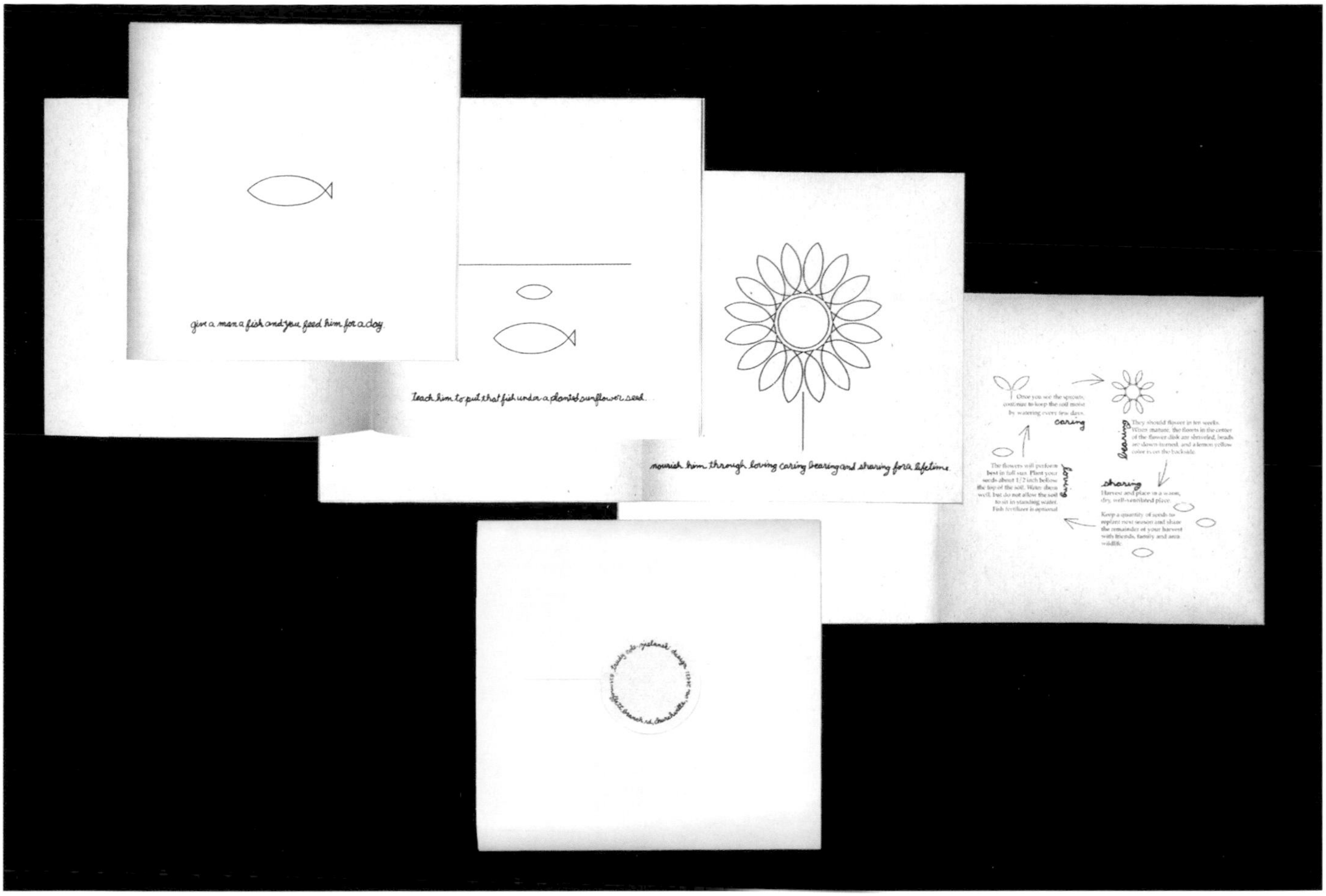

creative firm
TLC DESIGN
Churchville, Virginia
creative people
Trudy L. Cole
client
TLC Design

creative firm
GO GRAPHIC
Beirut, Lebanon
creative people
Maria Assi, Yasmina Baz
client
InterContinental Le Vendôme

VELOCITY DESIGNWORKS
VELOCITY DESIGNWORKS

creative firm
VELOCITY DESIGN WORKS
Winnipeg, Canada
client
Velocity Design Works

creative firm
GO GRAPHIC
Beirut, Lebanon
creative people
Maria Assi
client
Go Graphic

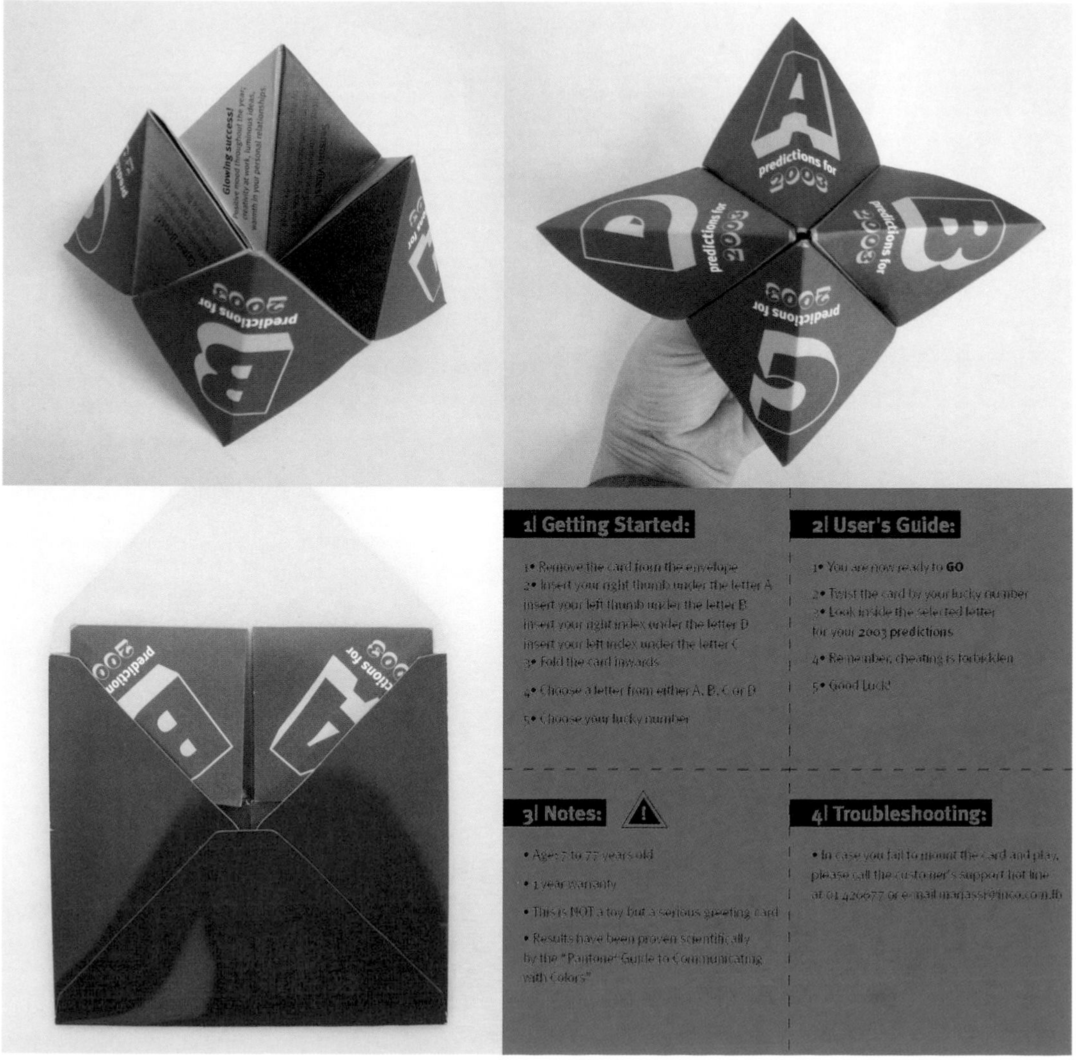
predictions for 2003
1| Getting Started:
1• Remove the card from the envelope
2• Insert your right thumb under the letter A
insert your left thumb under the letter B
insert your right index under the letter D
insert your left index under the letter C
3• Fold the card inwards
4• Choose a letter from either A, B, C or D
5• Choose your lucky number
2| User's Guide:
1• You are now ready to GO
2• Twist the card by your lucky number
3• Look inside the selected letter
for your 2003 predictions
4• Remember, cheating is forbidden
5• Good Luck!
3| Notes:
• Age: 7 to 77 years old
• 1 year warranty
• This is NOT a toy but a serious greeting card
• Results have been proven scientifically
by the "Pantone" Guide to Communicating
with Colors"
4| Troubleshooting:
• In case you fail to mount the card and play,
please call the customer's support hot line

creative firm
VELOCITY DESIGN WORKS
Winnipeg, Canada
client
Edward Carriere Salon

creative firm
DOIT ADVERTISING
Mumbai, India
creative people
Nilesh Parab
client
Goldshield Healthcare Pvt. Ltd.

creative firm
SAYLES GRAPHIC DESIGN
Des Moines, Iowa
creative people
John Sayles
client
Iowa State Fair 2003

creative firm
VELOCITY DESIGN WORKS
Winnipeg, Canada
client
Midnight Ritual

creative firm
PINNACLE GRAPHICS
Addison, Texas
client
Bulls Eye Racing Team

Helvetica Bold

TRAJAN

Garamond

New York

creative firm
AYSE ÇELEM DESIGN
Istanbul, Turkey
creative people
Ayse Çelem
client
Ayse Çelem Design

creative firm
AYSE ÇELEM DESIGN
Istanbul, Turkey
creative people
Ayse Çelem
client
Ayse Çelem Design

creative firm
STEPHEN LONGO DESIGN ASSOCIATES
West Orange, New Jersey
creative people
Stephen Longo
client
Ekko Restaurant

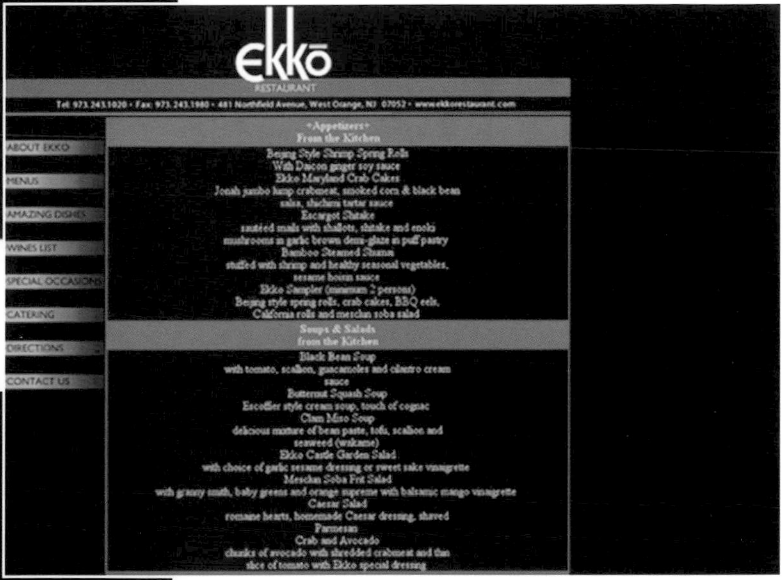

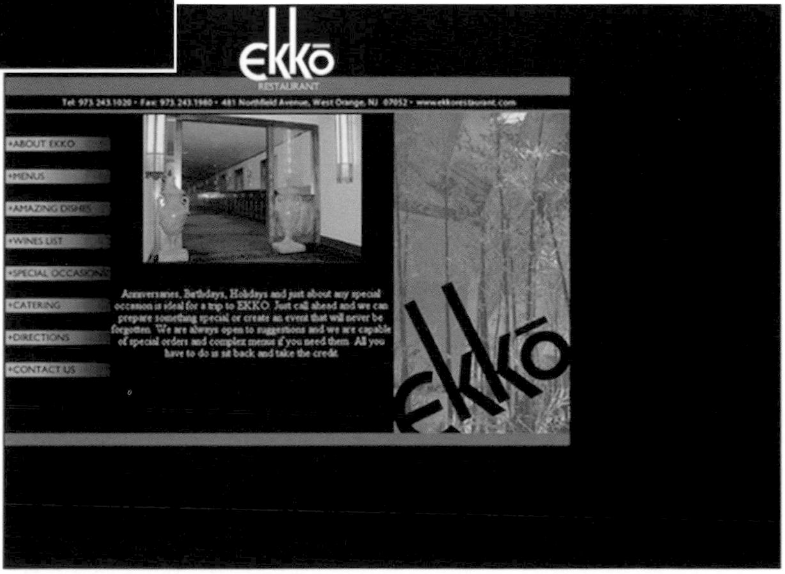

creative firm
ZERO GRAVITY DESIGN GROUP
Smithtown, New York
creative people
Zero Gravity Design Group
client
Wölffer Estate Stables
wolfferestatestables.com

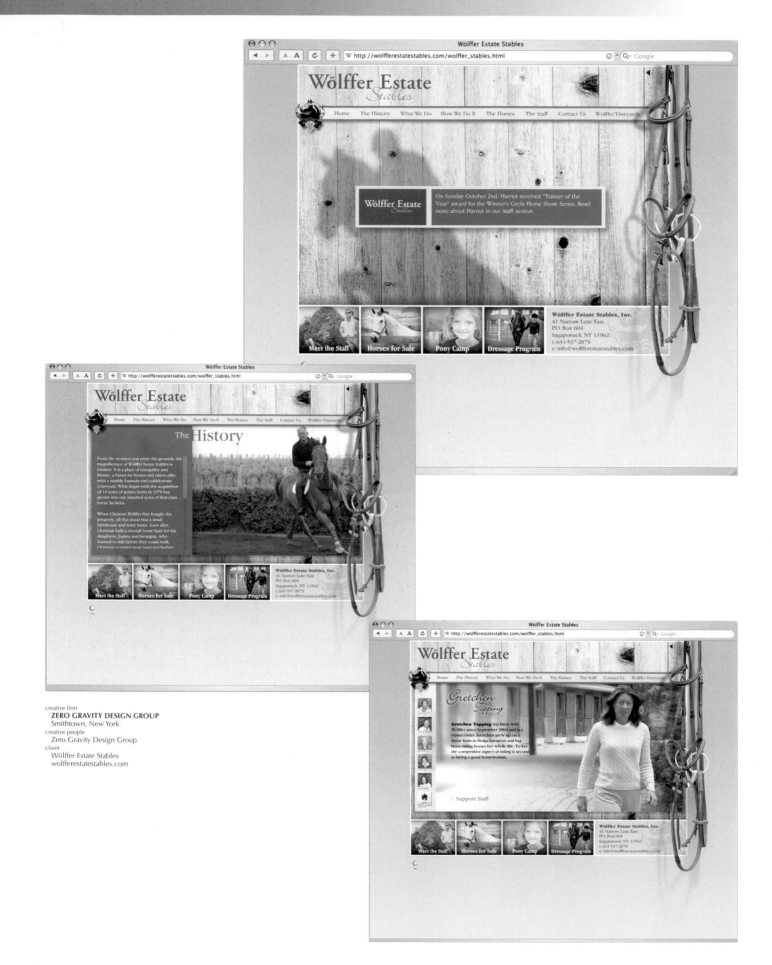

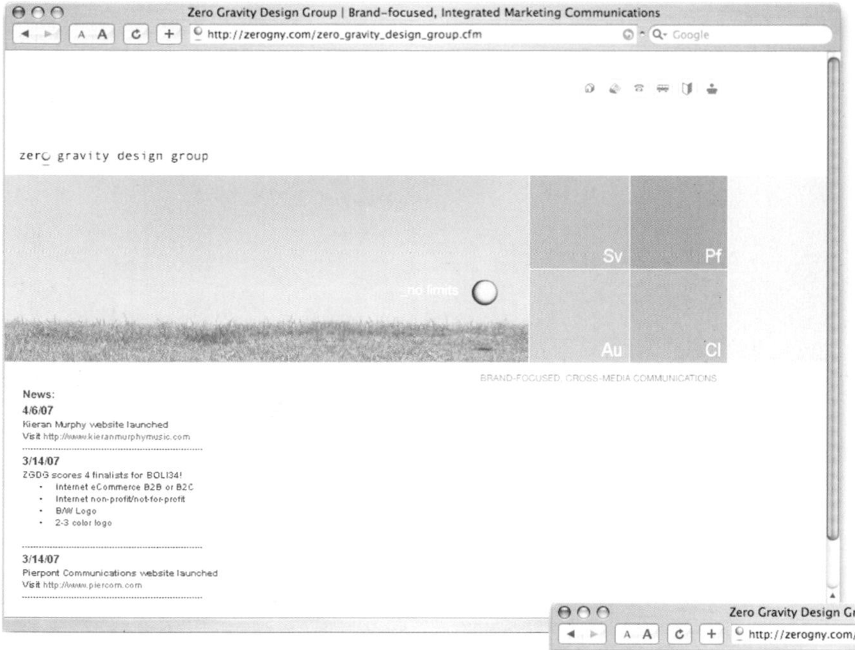

creative firm
ZERO GRAVITY DESIGN GROUP
Smithtown, New York
creative people
Zero Gravity Design Group
client
Zero Gravity Design Group
zerogny.com

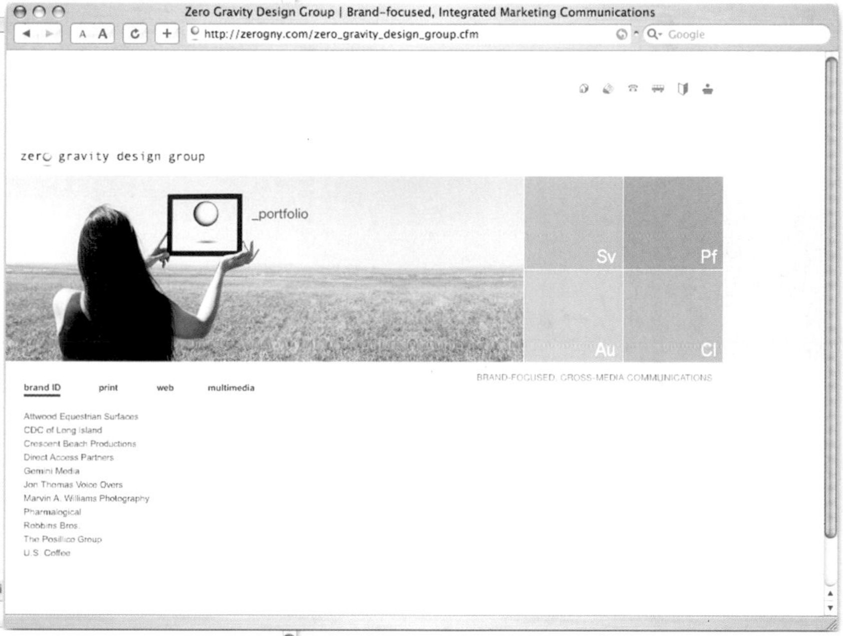

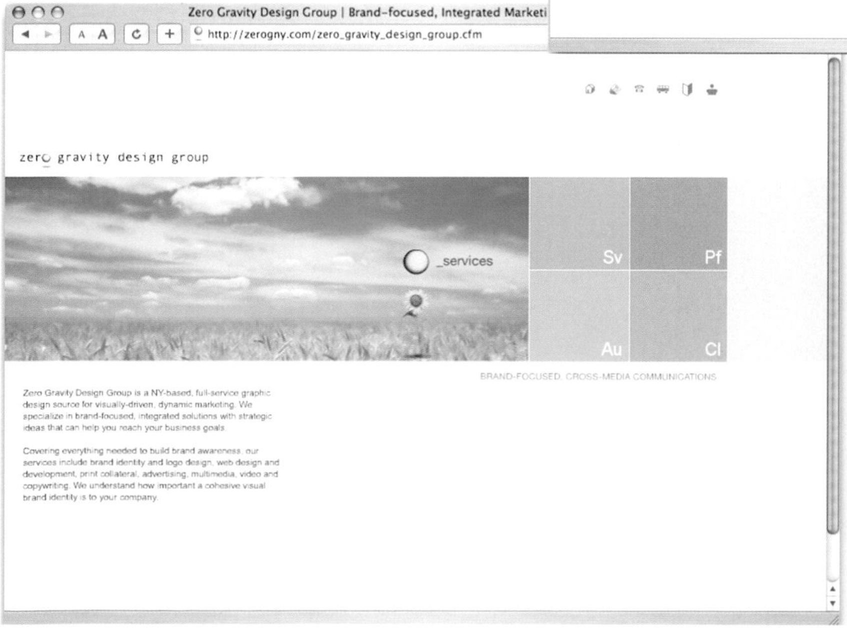

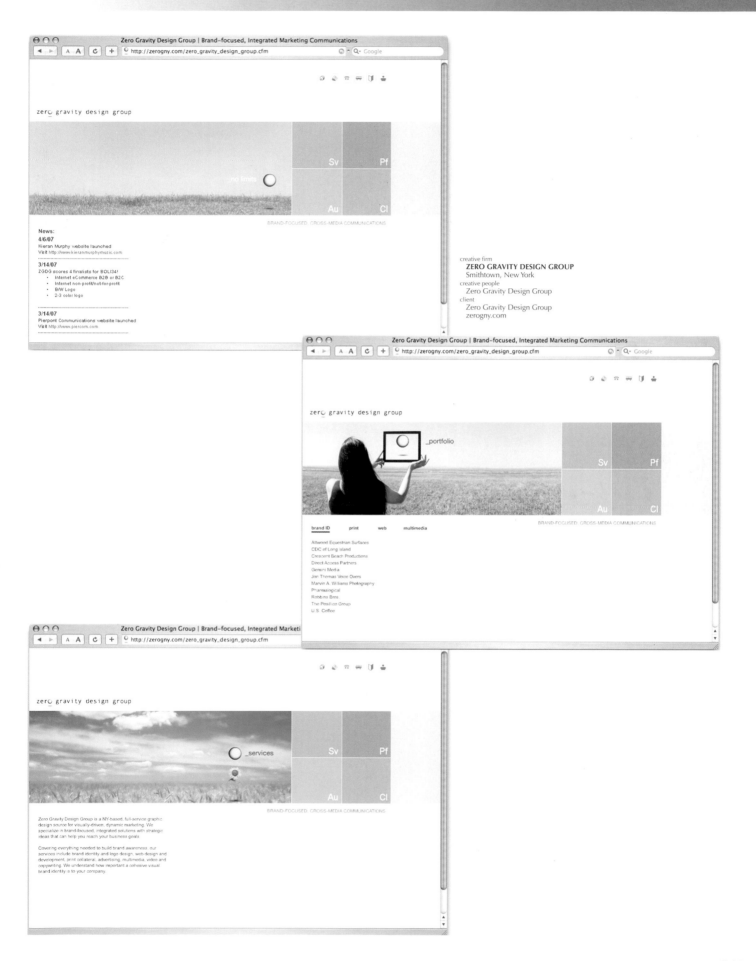

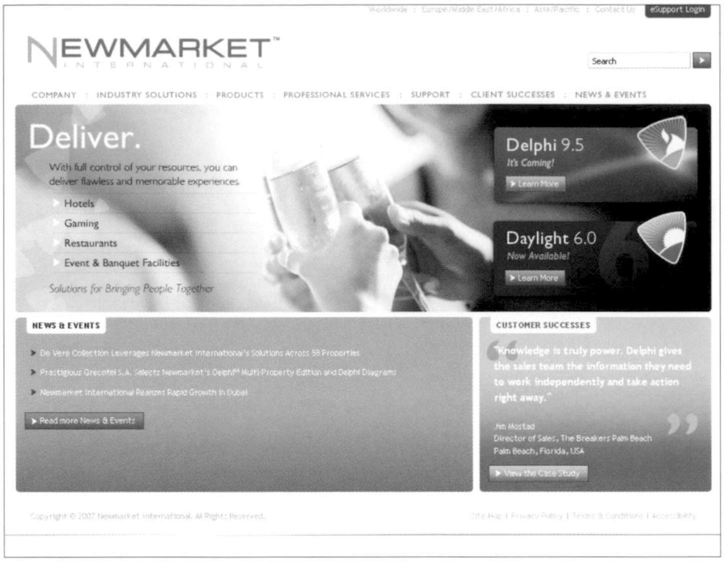

creative firm
ONE PICA, INC.
Boston, Massachusetts
creative people
Darren Bourque, Jim O'Neill, Gregory Segall
client
Newmarket International, Inc.

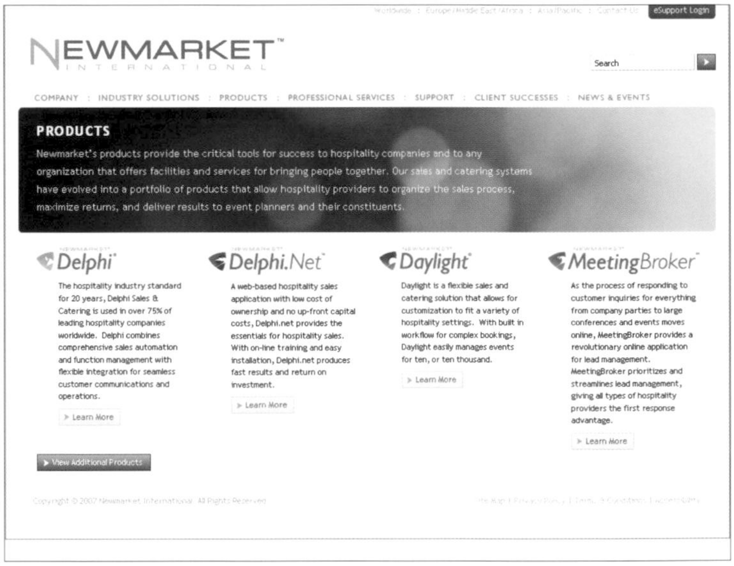

creative firm
GRAPHIC ADVANCE
Palisades Park, New Jersey
creative people
Aviad Stark
client
Frye Boots (The JIMLAR Corporation)

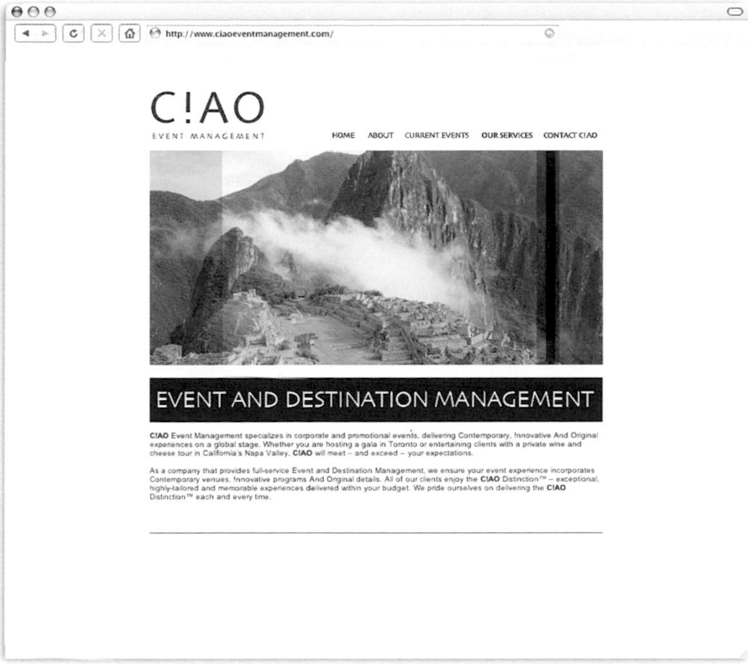

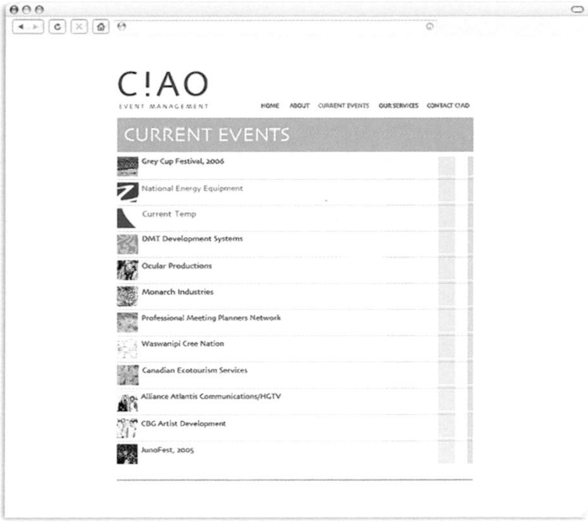

creative firm
VELOCITY DESIGN WORKS
Winnipeg, Canada
client
C!AO Event Management

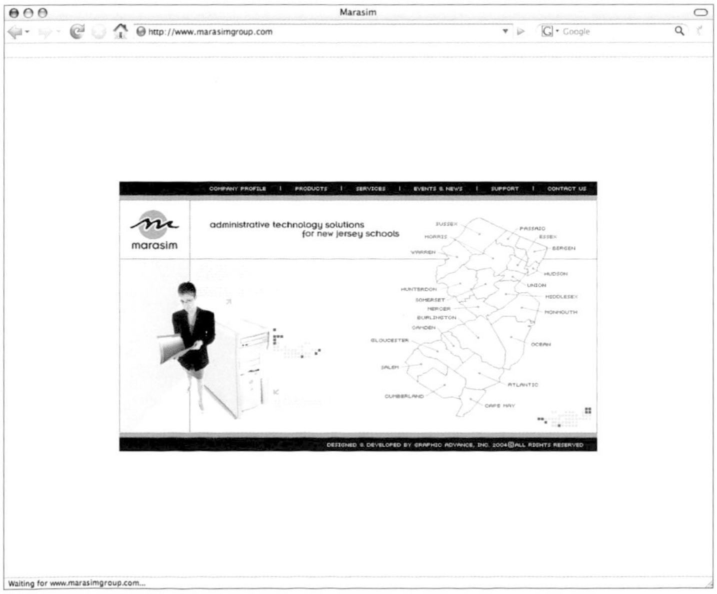

creative firm
GRAPHIC ADVANCE
Palisades Park, New Jersey
creative people
Aviad Stark
client
The Marasim Group

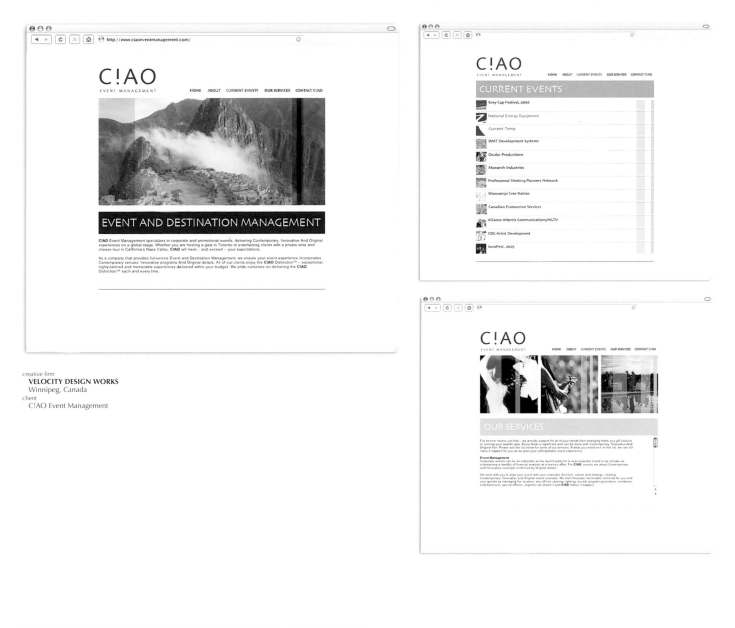

creative firm
DARLING DESIGN GROUP
New York, New York
creative people
Courtney Darling
client
New York AcuHealth

creative firm
OCTAVO DESIGNS
Frederick, Maryland
creative people
Mark Burrier, Sue Hough
client
CineGraphic Studios

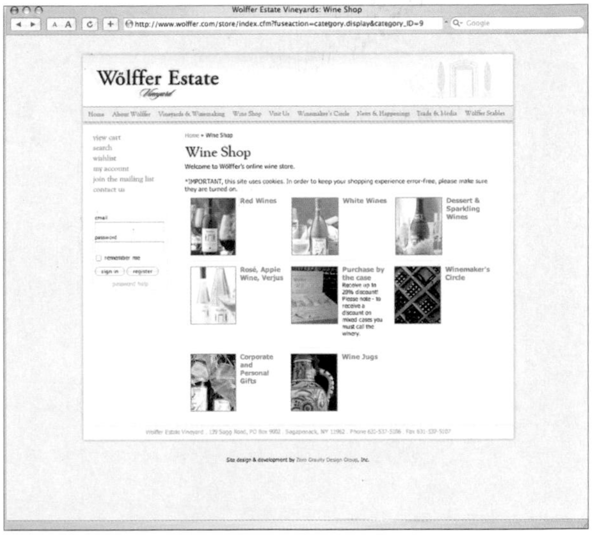

creative firm
ZERO GRAVITY DESIGN GROUP
Smithtown, New York
creative people
Zero Gravity Design Group
client
Wölffer Estate Vineyard
wolffervineyards.com

creative firm
DAVIS DESIGN PARTNERS
Holland, Ohio
creative people
Matt Davis, Karen Davis
client
Mattingly Corporation

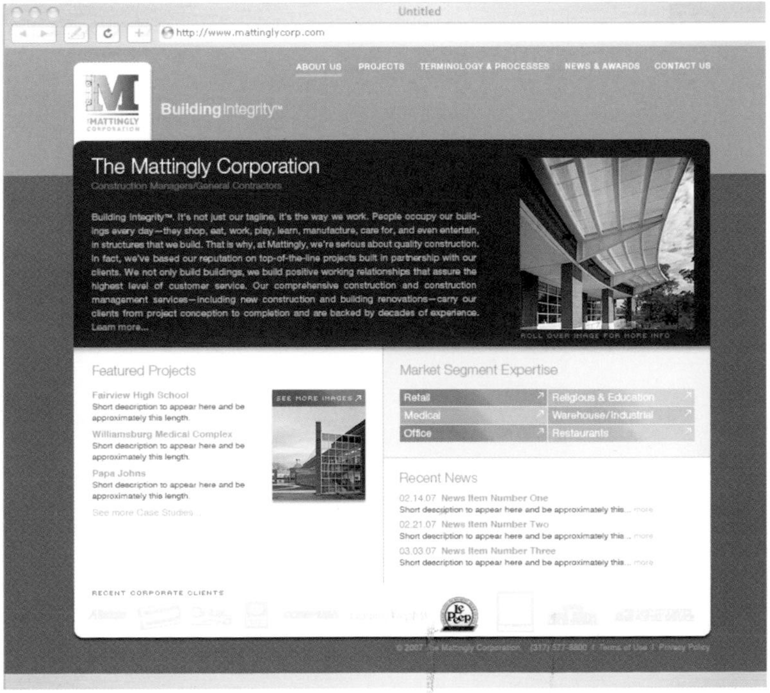

creative firm
DAVIS DESIGN PARTNERS
Holland, Ohio
creative people
Matt Davis, Karen Davis
client
Optiform

creative firm
OCTAVO DESIGNS
Frederick, Maryland
creative people
Mark Burrier, Sue Hough
client
BeSt Foto LLC

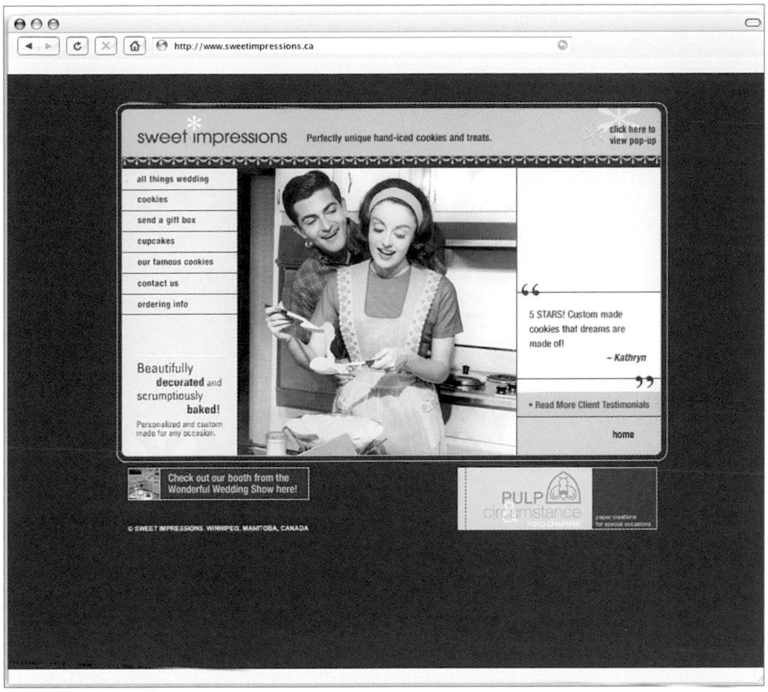

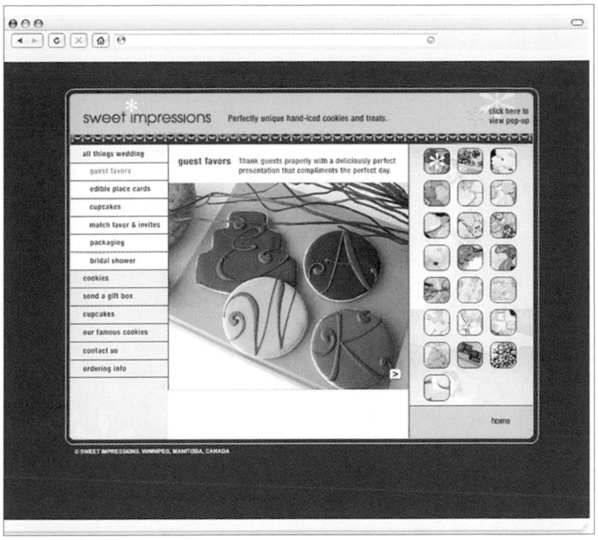

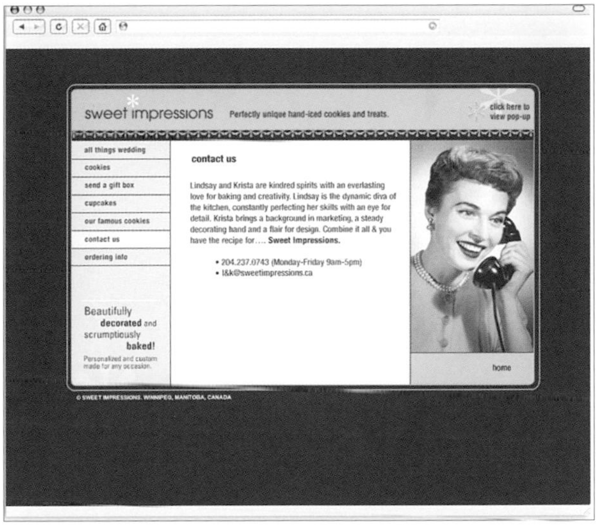

creative firm
VELOCITY DESIGN WORKS
Winnipeg, Canada
client
Sweet Impressions

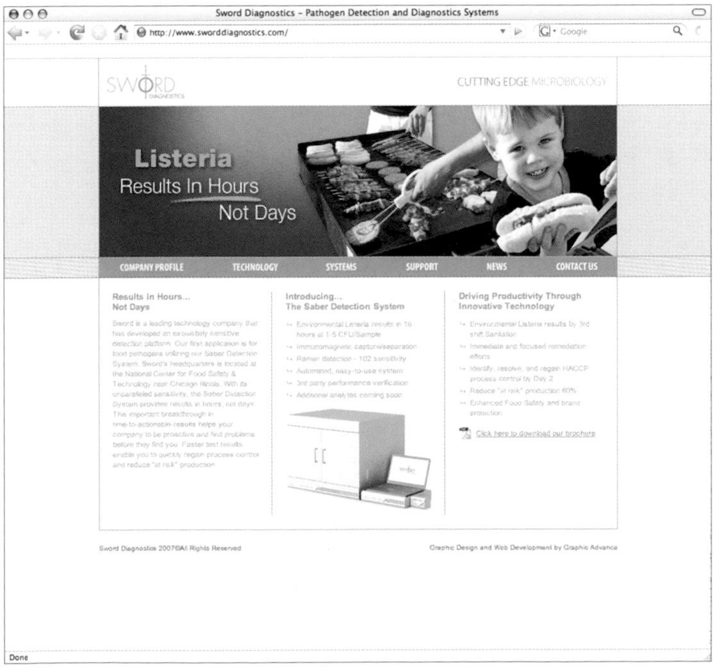

creative firm
GRAPHIC ADVANCE
Palisades Park, New Jersey
creative people
Aviad Stark
client
Sword Diagnostics

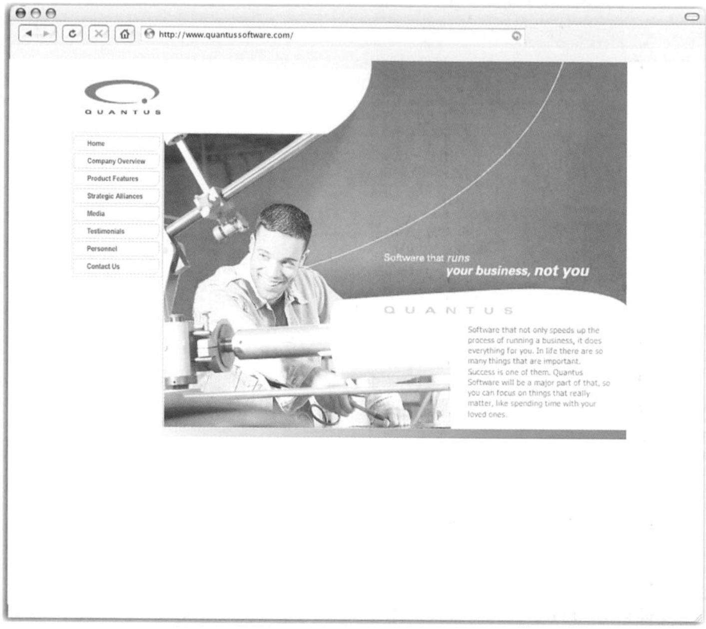

creative firm
VELOCITY DESIGN WORKS
Winnipeg, Canada
creative people
Lasha Orzechowski
client
Quantus Software

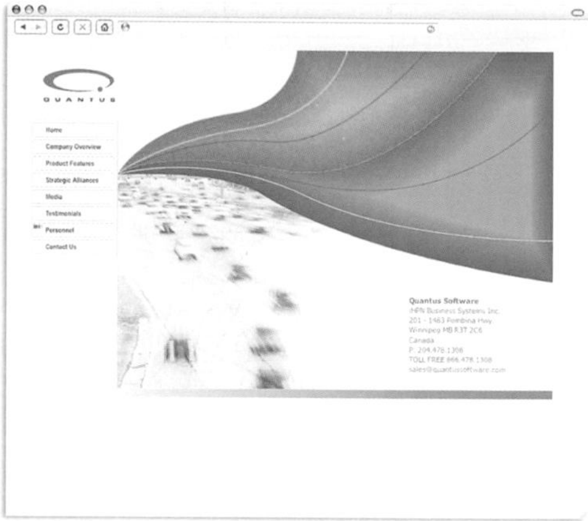

creative firm
HORNALL ANDERSON DESIGN
Seattle, Washington
creative people
Erica Goldsmith, Hans Krebs, Joe King, Curt Collinsworth, Adrien Lo, Michele Godfrey, Corey Paganucci, Dana Kruse, Mike Francis
client
International Trucking

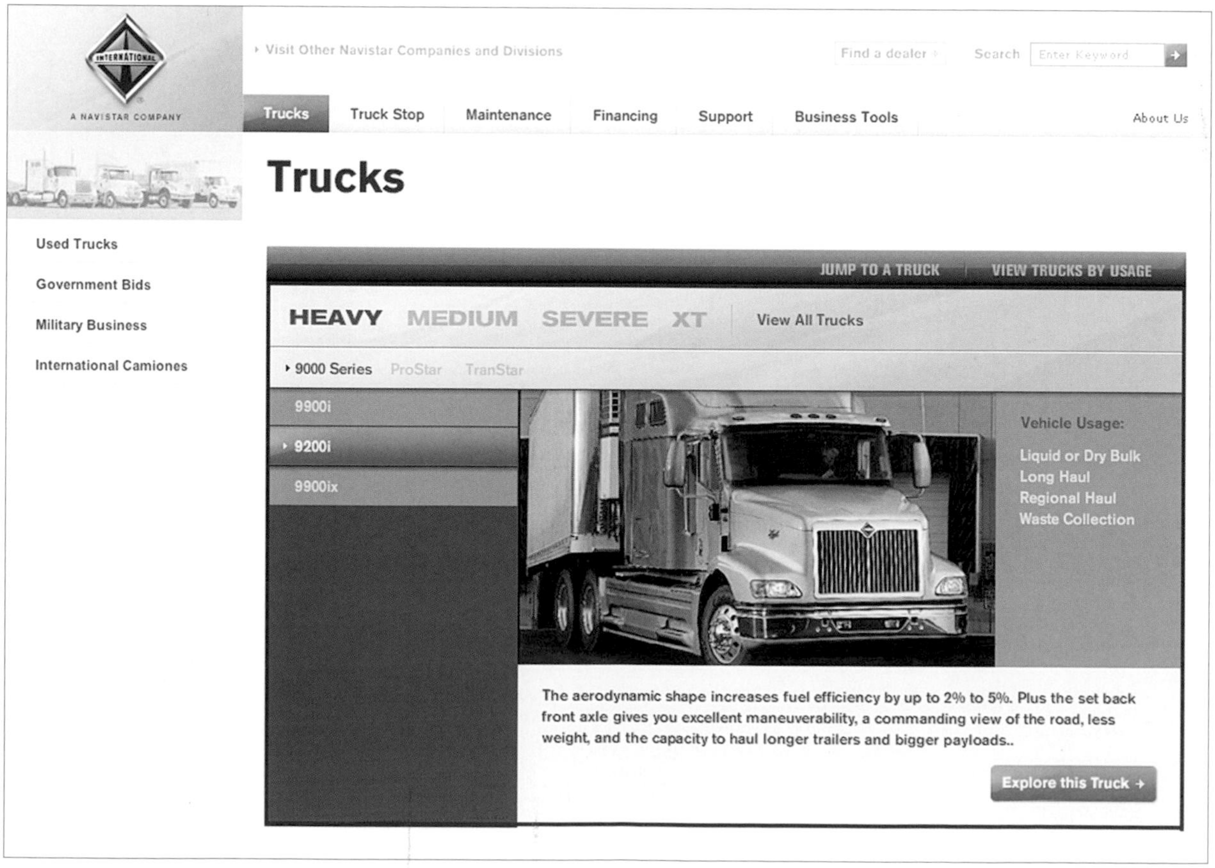

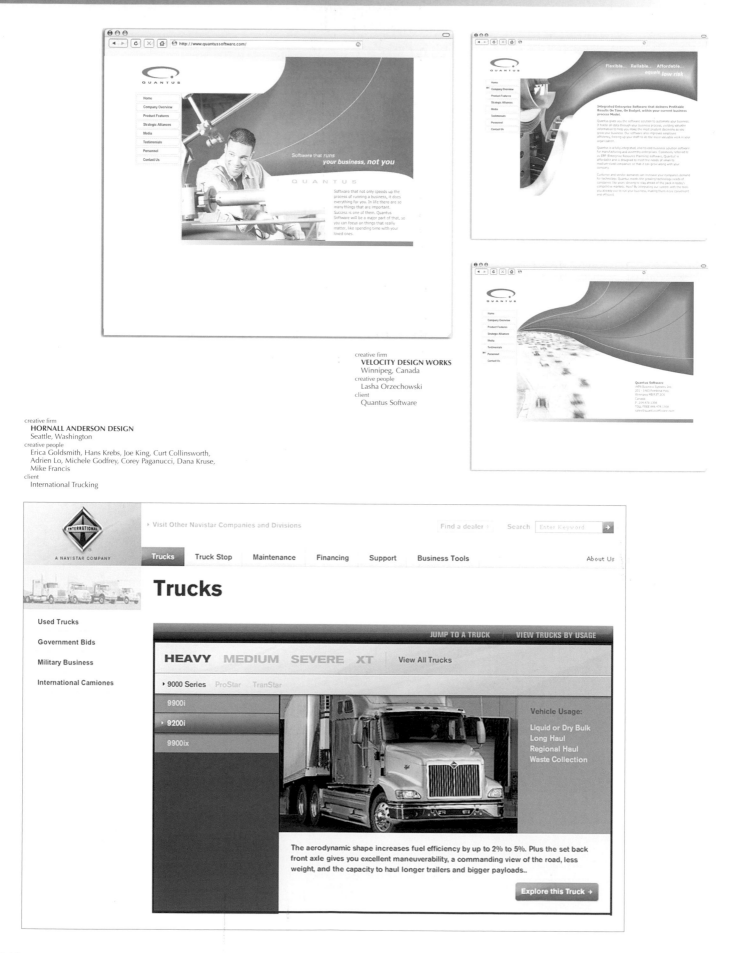

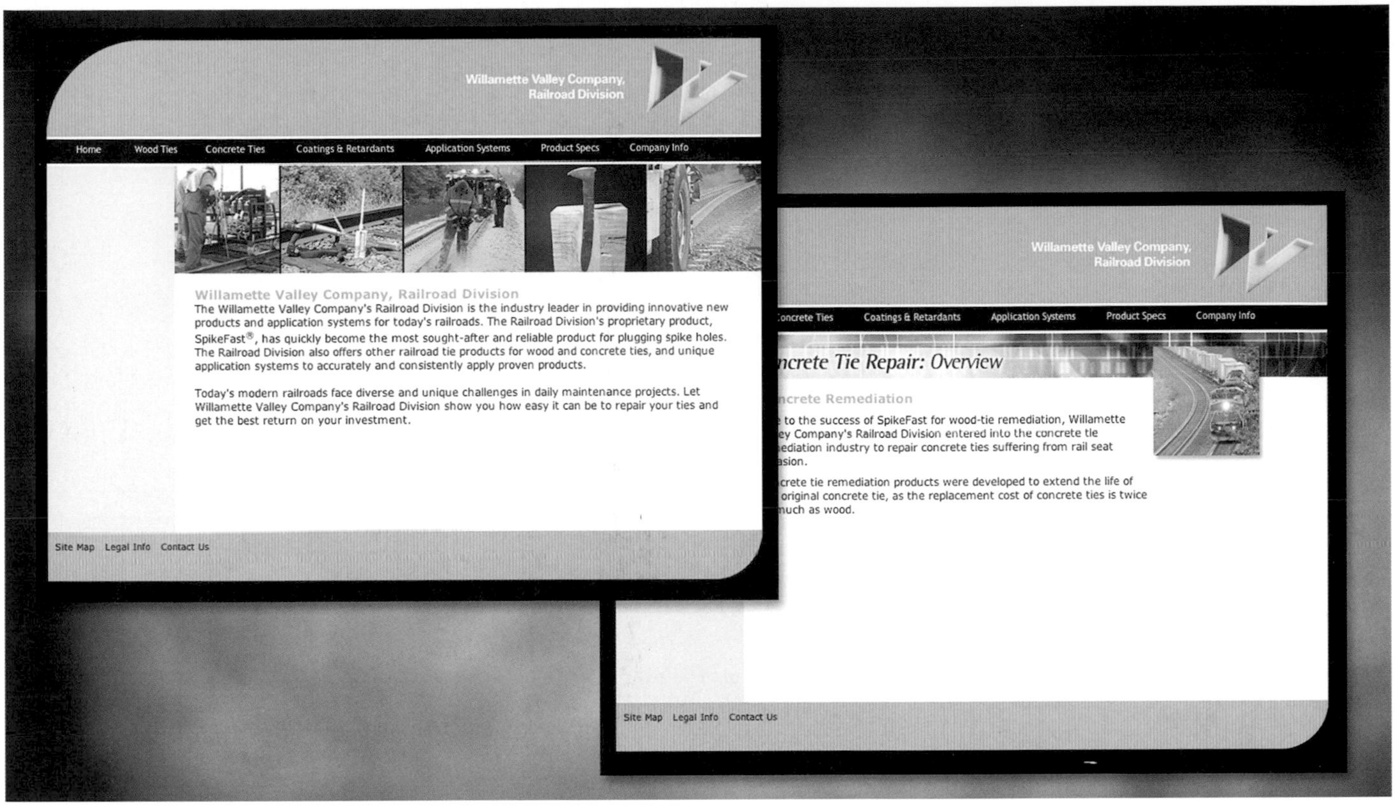

creative firm
FUNK/LEVIS & ASSOCIATES
Eugene, Oregon
creative people
Jason Anderson
client
Willamette Valley Company—Railroad Division (Spikefast)

creative firm
021 COMUNICACIONES
Mexico City, Mexico
creative people
Edson Gutiérrez, Ramón Sandoval
client
HUMMER

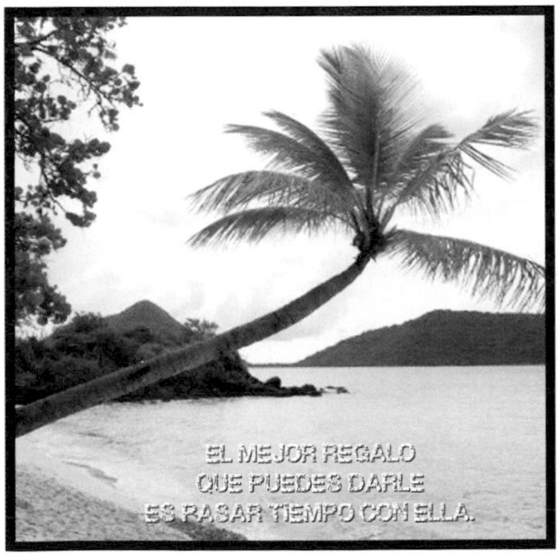

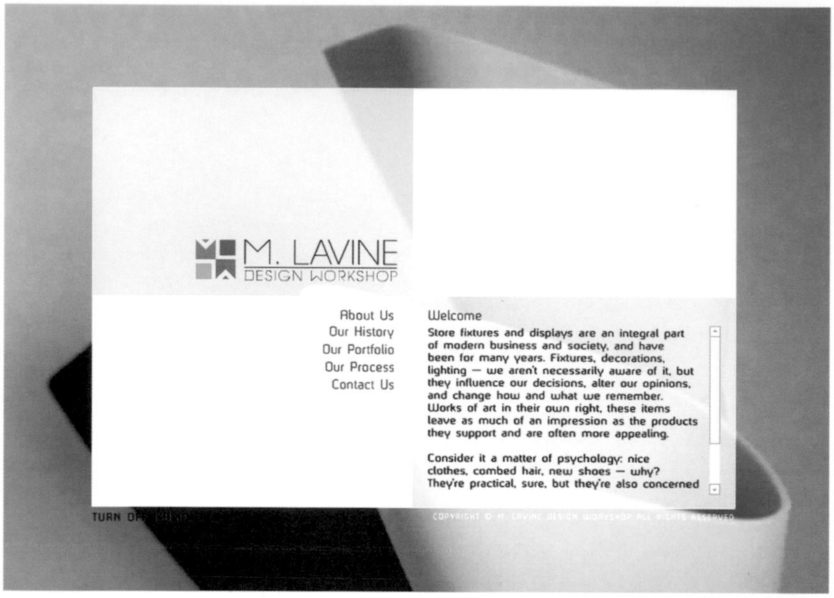

creative firm
BRAIN MAGNET
St. Louis Park, Minnesota
creative people
David Maloney, Josh Gagner
client
M. Lavine Design Workshop

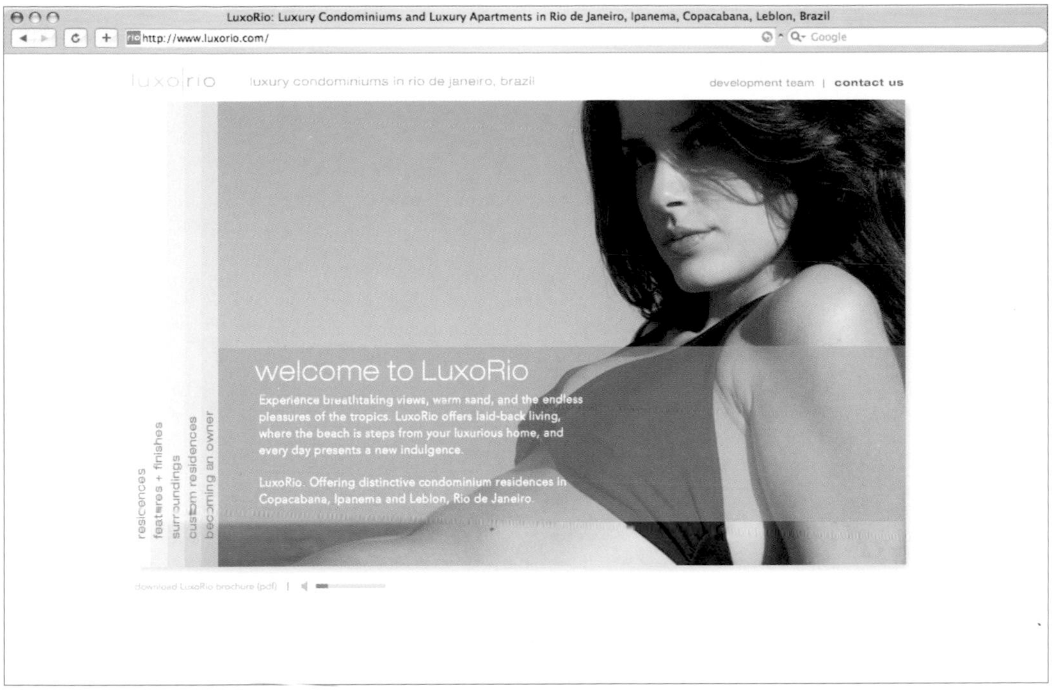

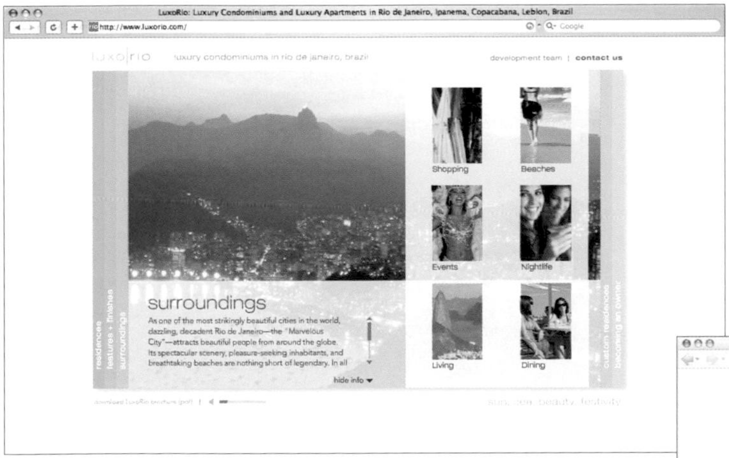

creative firm
DARLING DESIGN GROUP
New York, New York
creative people
Courtney Darling, Sarah Skapik,
Jonathan Schnapp, Cindy L'Esperance
client
LuxoRio

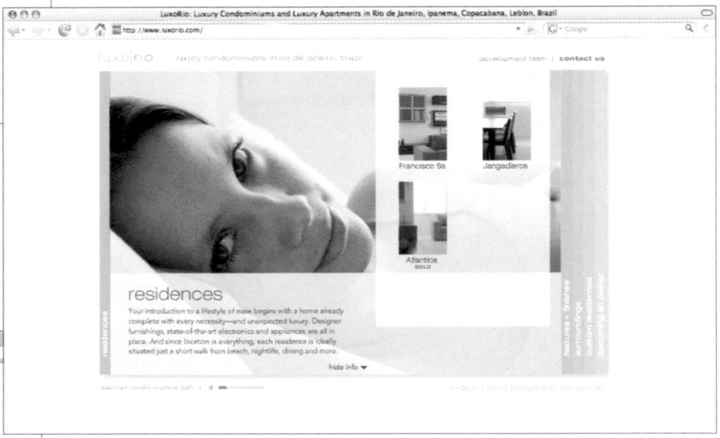

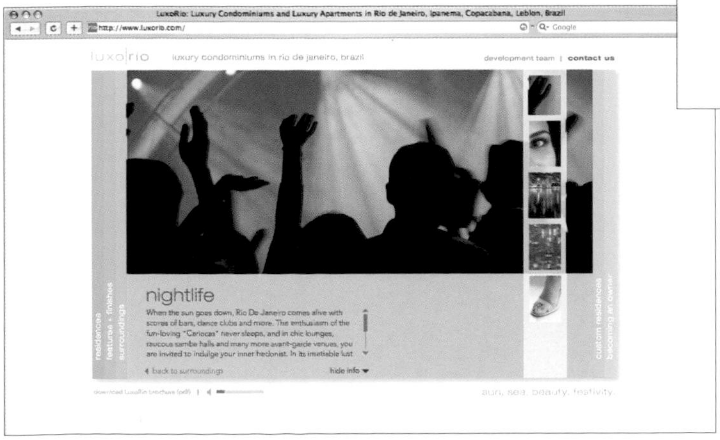

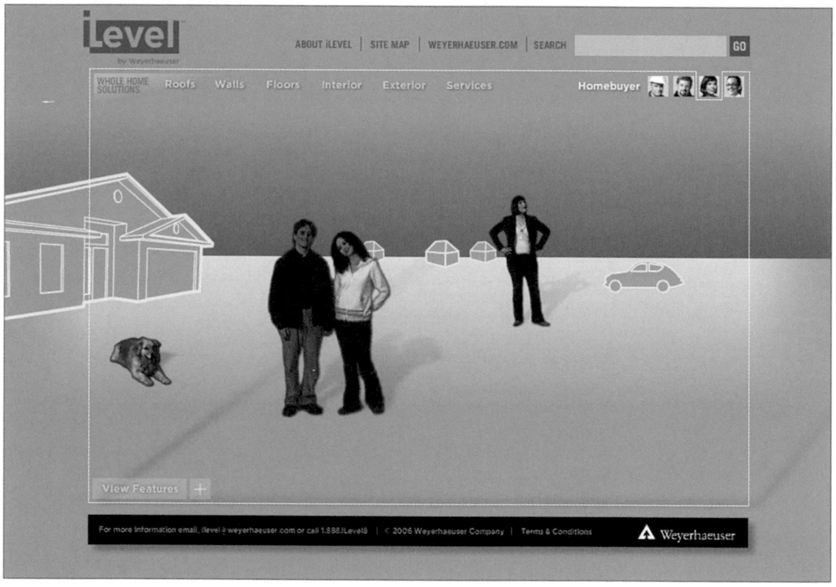

creative firm
HORNALL ANDERSON DESIGN
Seattle, Washington
creative people
Nathan Young, Jason Hickner, Adrien Lo, Curt Collinsworth, Erica Goldsmith, Dina Robinson, James Tee
client
Weyerhaeuser Corporation

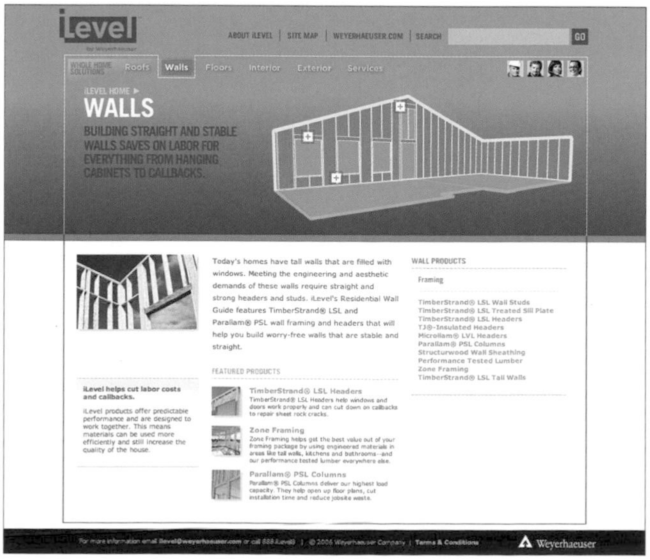

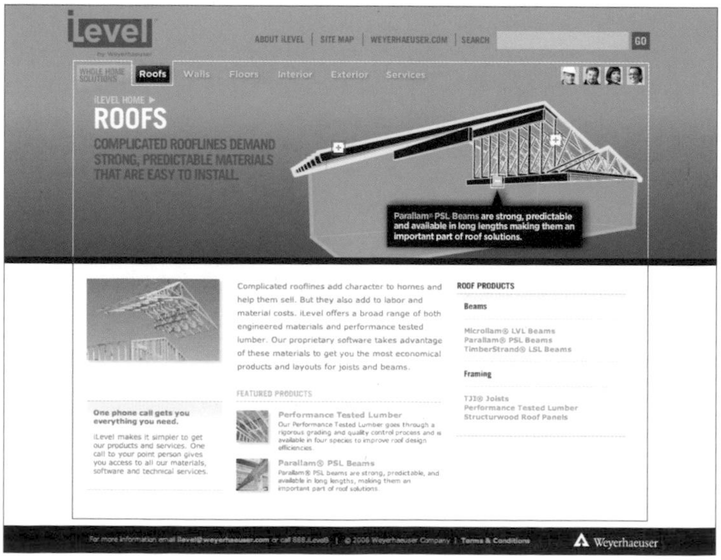

creative firm
PINNACLE GRAPHICS
Addison, Texas
creative people
Russ Aman, JR Runyon
client
Gold Buckle Network

creative firm
OCTAVO DESIGNS
Frederick, Maryland
creative people
Mark Burrier
client
The Perfect Truffle

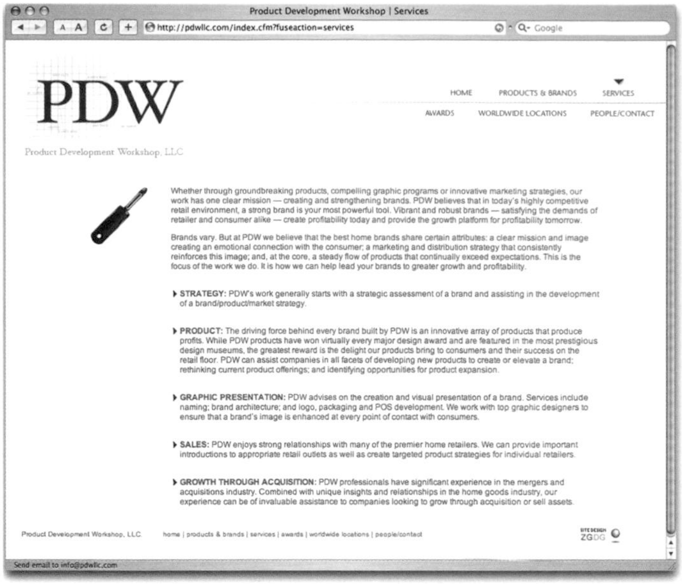

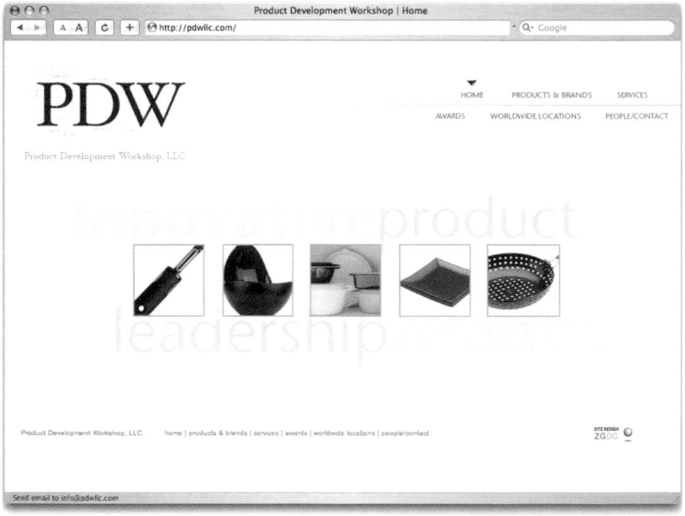

creative firm
ZERO GRAVITY DESIGN GROUP
Smithtown, New York
creative people
Zero Gravity Design Group
client
Product Development Workshop
pdwllc.com

creative firm
OCTAVO DESIGNS
Frederick, Maryland
creative people
Mark Burrier, Sue Hough
client
Octavo Designs

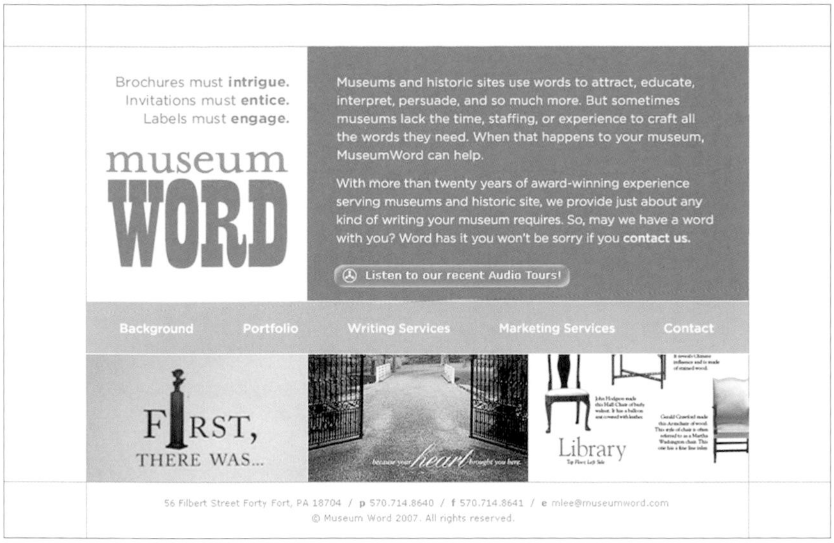

creative firm
BETH SINGER DESIGN LLC
Arlington, Virginia
creative people
Suheun Yu
client
Museum Word

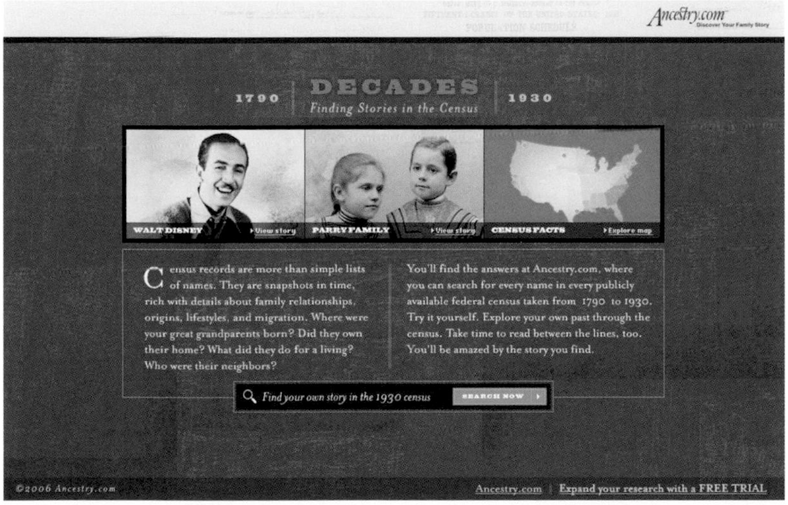

creative firm
HORNALL ANDERSON DESIGN
Seattle, Washington
creative people
Erica Goldsmith, Hans Krebs, Joe King, Jason Hickner, Adrien Lo
client
MyFamily

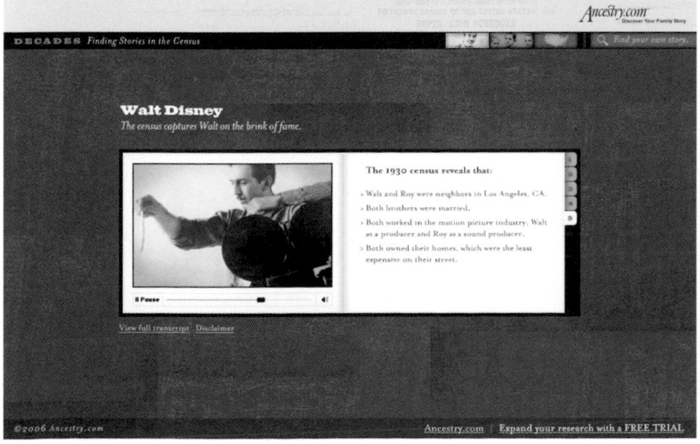

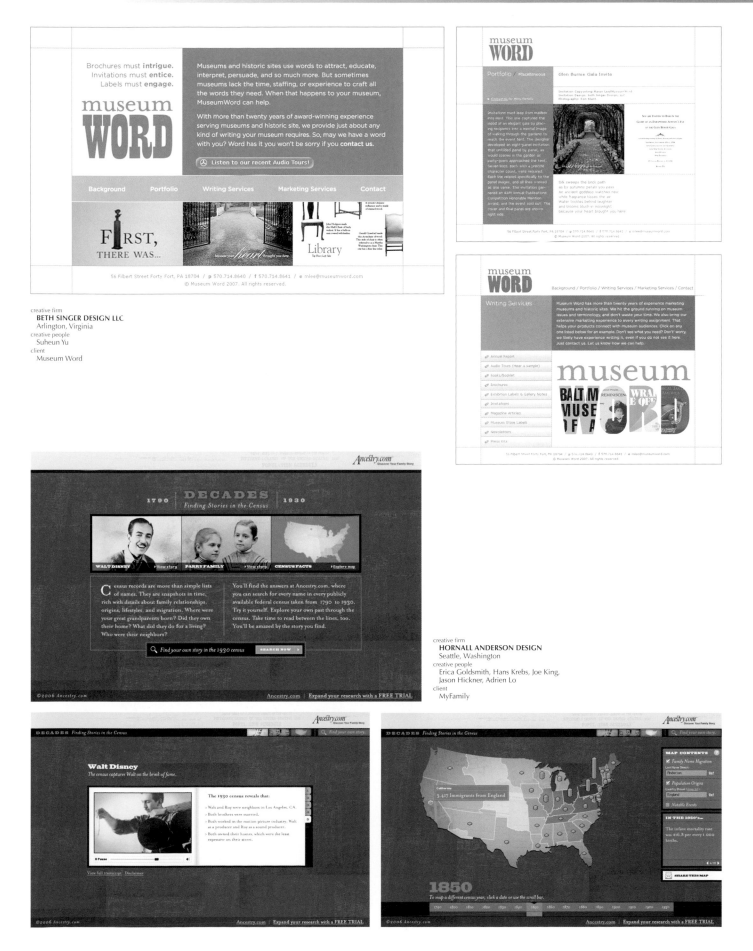

creative firm
ZERO GRAVITY DESIGN GROUP
Smithtown, New York
creative people
Zero Gravity Design Group
client
Kieran Murphy
kieranmurphymusic.com

creative firm
AYSE ÇELEM DESIGN
Istanbul, Turkey
creative people
Ayse Çelem, Cengiz Zorlu
client
Attila Durak Photography

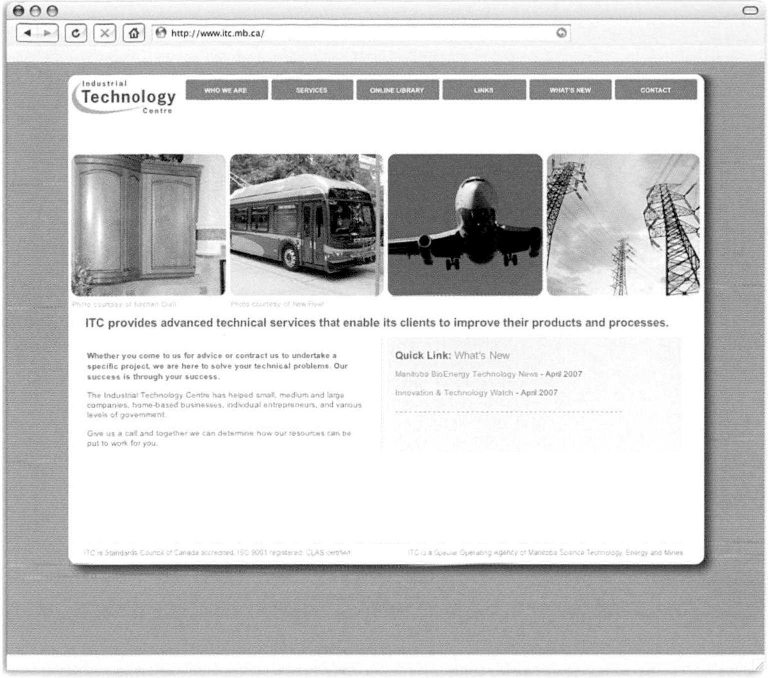

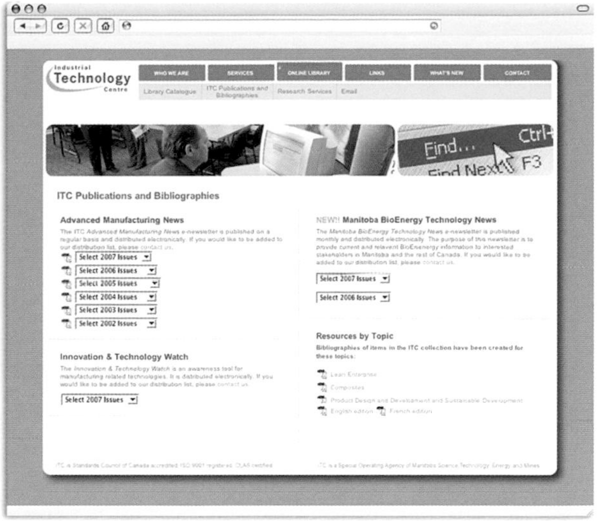

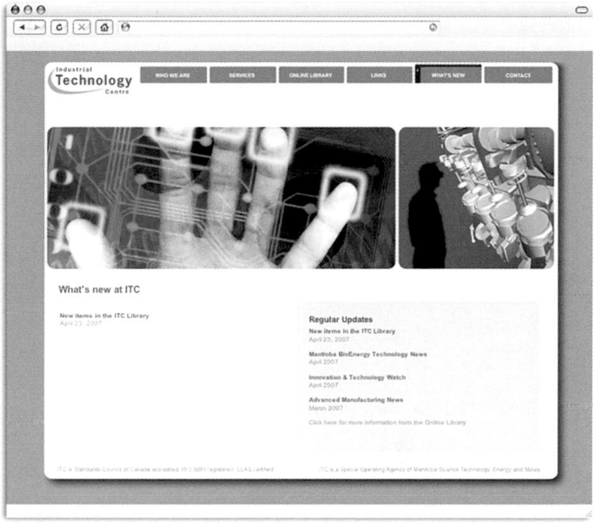

creative firm
VELOCITY DESIGN WORKS
Winnipeg, Canada
creative people
Lasha Orzechowski, Dave Hardy
client
Industrial Technology Centre (ITC)

creative firm
GRAPHIC ADVANCE
Palisades Park, New Jersey
creative people
Aviad Stark
client
Vision Sciences

VOLK
Center for Cosmetic & Plastic Surgery
DR. VOLK
PROCEDURES
PATIENTS
SKIN CARE
CONTACT
TRICEP EXTENSIONS, EVERY OTHER DAY
VOLK, ONCE.
PILATES, 3 TIMES A WEEK
"As a board certified plastic surgeon, I understand the importance of education and experience. It's an essential part of a patient's decision in placing their trust in us. Equally important is our culture of care, so everything at Volk Center For has been designed around delivering an exceptional patient-centered experience."
Dr. Volk
Member
AMERICAN SOCIETY OF PLASTIC SURGEONS
WELCOME TO THE VOLK CENTER
The search for eternal youth has been enduring since ancient times. After all, it's natural to want a face and body that reflect your youthful spirit and nature never deals anyone a perfect hand. Fortunately, exciting advancements in medical science, cosmetic and reconstructive surgical techniques can correct many imperfections.
Both men and women of all ages and from all walks of life benefit from surgery to improve their appearance. Some seek correction of a lifelong deformity. Some wish to subtly improve their overall appearance, while others want to enhance or rejuvenate their features for greater confidence and self-esteem.
The Volk Center for Cosmetic and Plastic Surgery offers the experience, state-of-the-art technology and caring professionals to turn your dreams into reality.
IS CLINICAL

creative firm
CRAMERSWEENEY
Mount Laurel, New Jersey
creative people
Dave Girgenti, Susan Hammell
client
The Volk Center

creative firm
DAVIS DESIGN PARTNERS
Holland, Ohio
creative people
Matt Davis, Karen Davis
client
St. Vincent Health (SVH)

Untitled
St.Vincent HEALTH
LOG IN
Employment Center
About St.Vincent Health
FOR HEALTHCARE PROFESSIONALS:
Nurses
Associates
Physicians
Education
SEARCH
GO
Our Locations
Our Services
For Patients & Visitors
Find A Physician
the spirit of caring
close to home
St.Vincent Health is dedicated to the mission of improving the lives and health status of residents of Indiana by providing holistic and high quality health care services. Our 16 hospitals and 3,000 physicians serving 45 counties bring the spirit of caring close to home.
FIND A LOCATION NEAR YOU »
SVH HEADLINES
HEALTH NEWS
MR-Guided Breast Biopsies Offered
Presbyterian Hospital Named Accredited Chest Pain Center
New Chief Nursing Officer
ST.VINCENT HEALTH INTRODUCES
Women's Health
Information for every woman
VISIT THIS EXCITING NEW AREA ›
Discover our great
Classes & Programs
SEARCH HERE!
Send Us A Message | Site Map
Copyright © 2003–2004 St.Vincent Health
Copyright Policy | Web Site Privacy Policy | Terms of Service

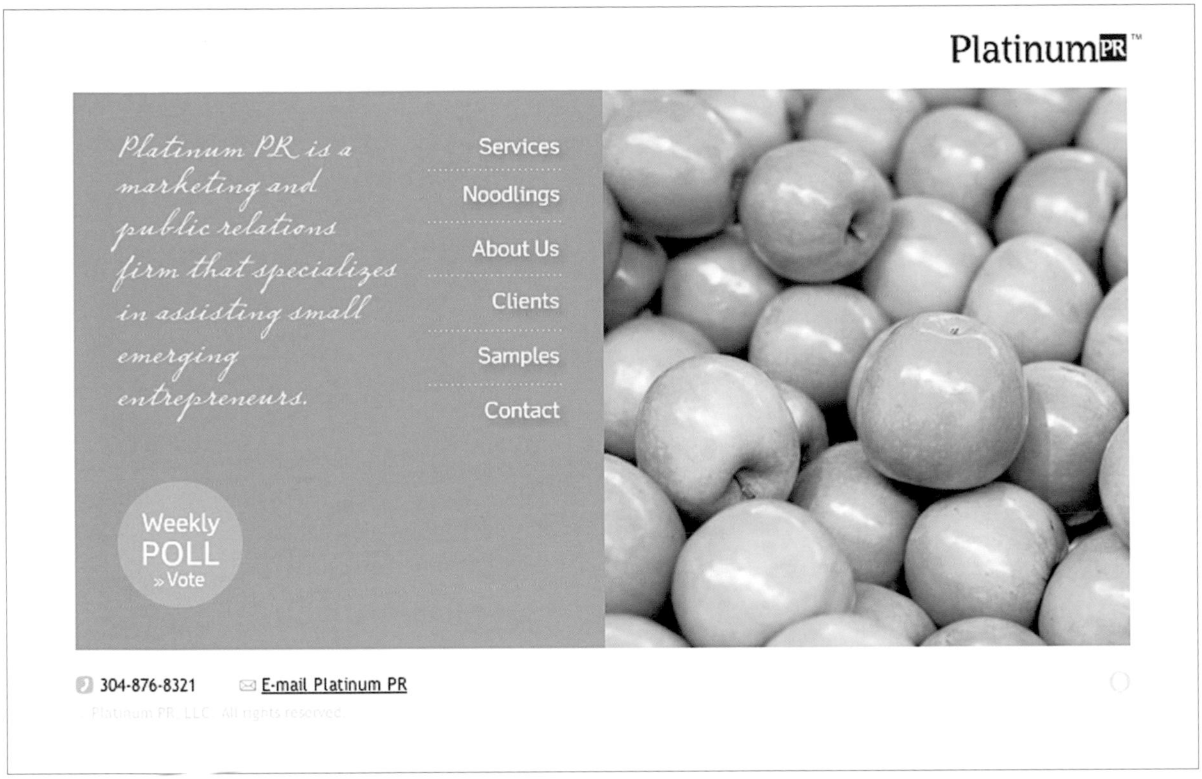
PlatinumPR™
Platinum PR is a marketing and public relations firm that specializes in assisting small emerging entrepreneurs.
Services
Noodlings
About Us
Clients
Samples
Contact
Weekly POLL »Vote
304-876-8321
E-mail Platinum PR

creative firm
OCTAVO DESIGNS
Frederick, Maryland
creative people
Mark Burrier, Sue Hough
client
Platinum PR

creative firm
ART270, INC.
Jenkintown, Pennsylvania
creative people
Kenric Strohm, Mike Mayton
client
Rockefeller Philanthropy Advisors

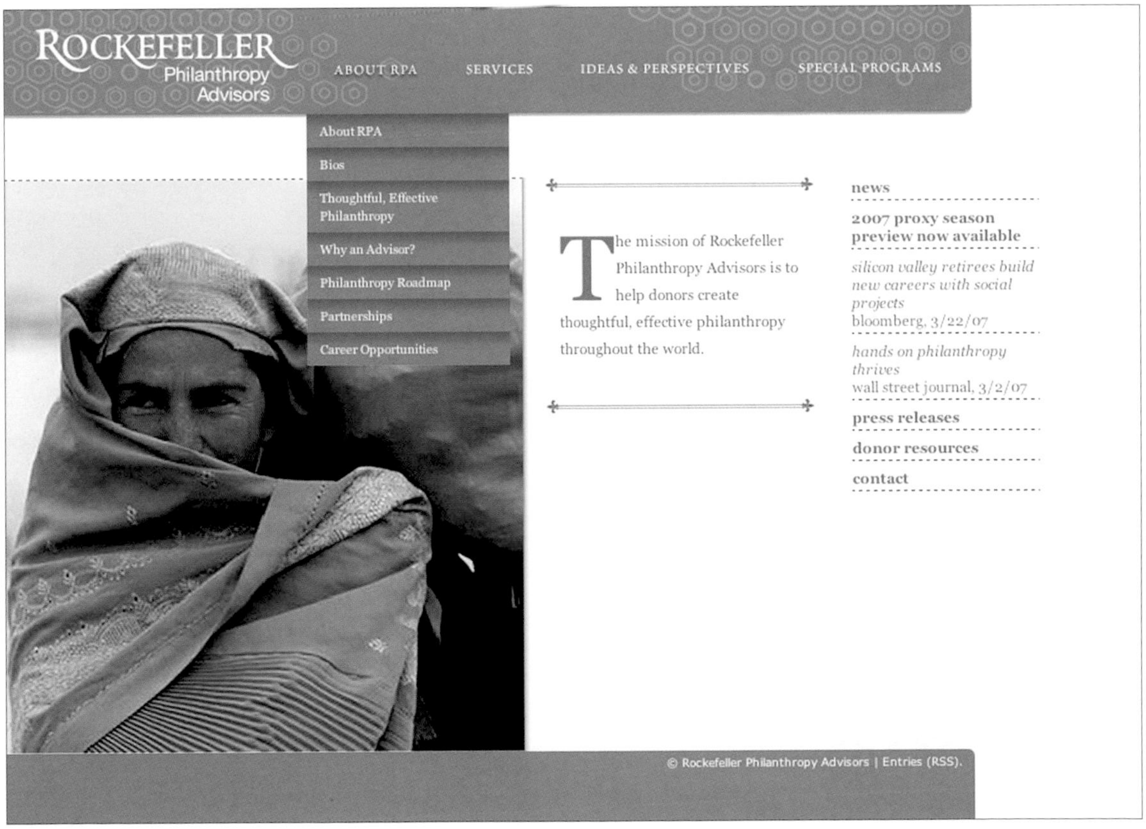
Rockefeller Philanthropy Advisors
ABOUT RPA
SERVICES
IDEAS & PERSPECTIVES
SPECIAL PROGRAMS
About RPA
Bios
Thoughtful, Effective Philanthropy
Why an Advisor?
Philanthropy Roadmap
Partnerships
Career Opportunities
The mission of Rockefeller Philanthropy Advisors is to help donors create thoughtful, effective philanthropy throughout the world.
news
2007 proxy season preview now available
silicon valley retirees build new careers with social projects
bloomberg, 3/22/07
hands on philanthropy thrives
wall street journal, 3/2/07
press releases
donor resources
contact
© Rockefeller Philanthropy Advisors | Entries (RSS).

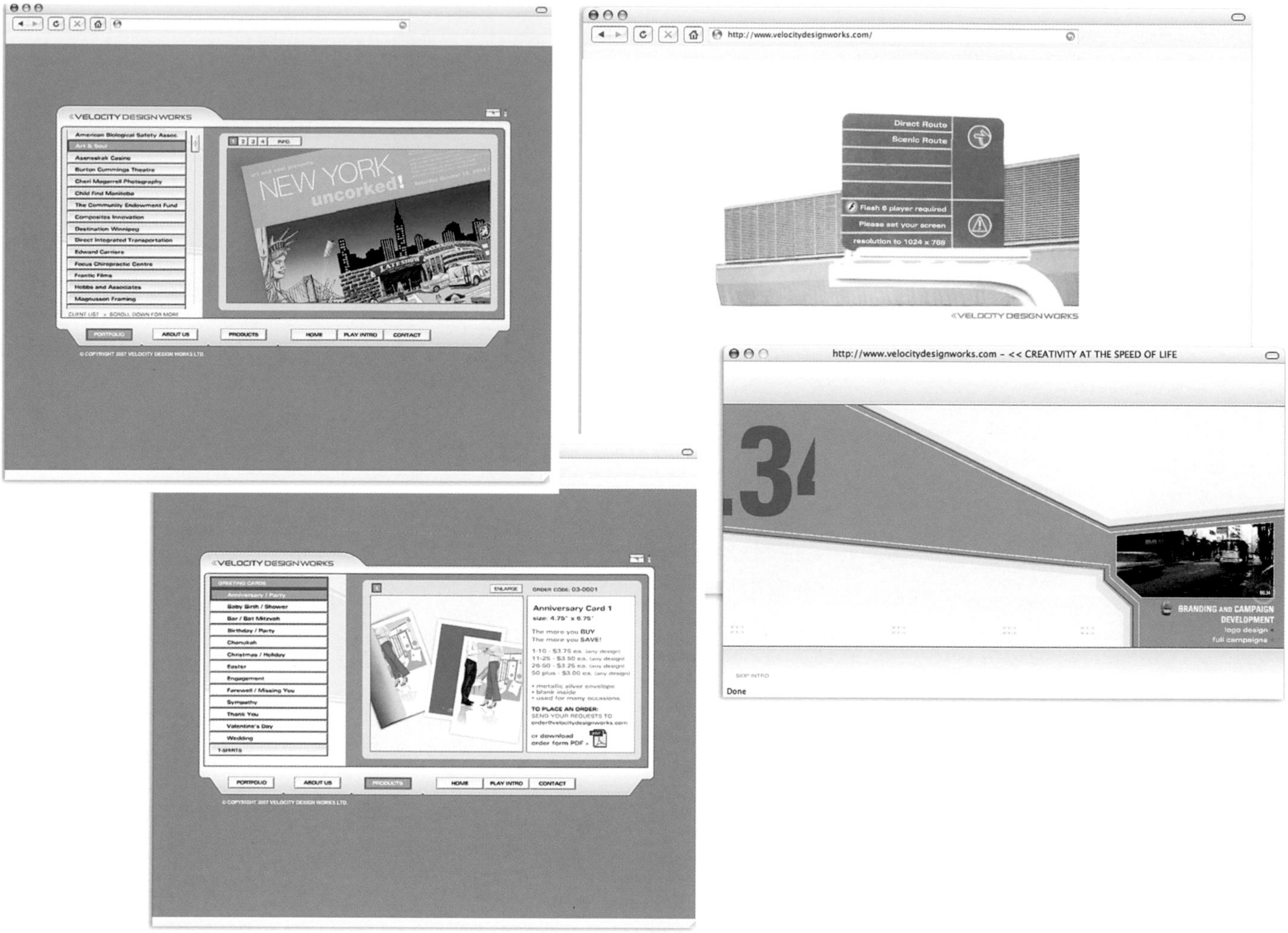

creative firm
VELOCITY DESIGN WORKS
Winnipeg, Canada
client
Velocity Design Works

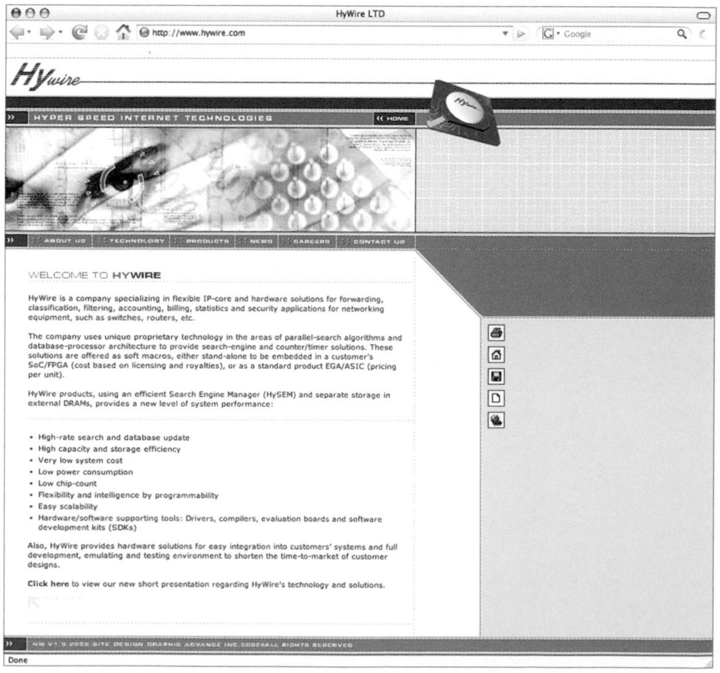

creative firm
GRAPHIC ADVANCE
Palisades Park, New Jersey
creative people
Aviad Stark
client
Hy Wire LTD

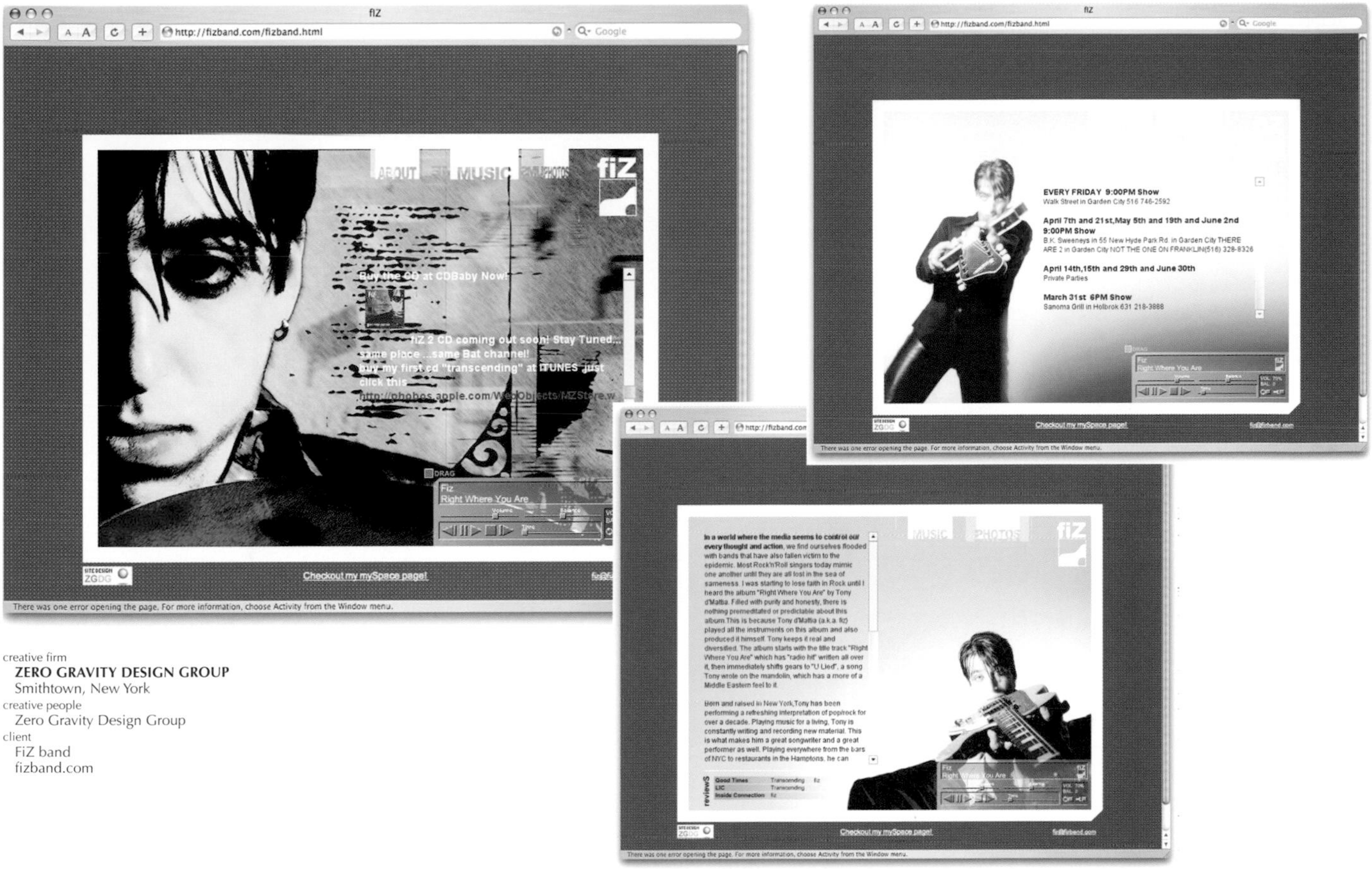

creative firm
ZERO GRAVITY DESIGN GROUP
Smithtown, New York
creative people
Zero Gravity Design Group
client
FiZ band
fizband.com

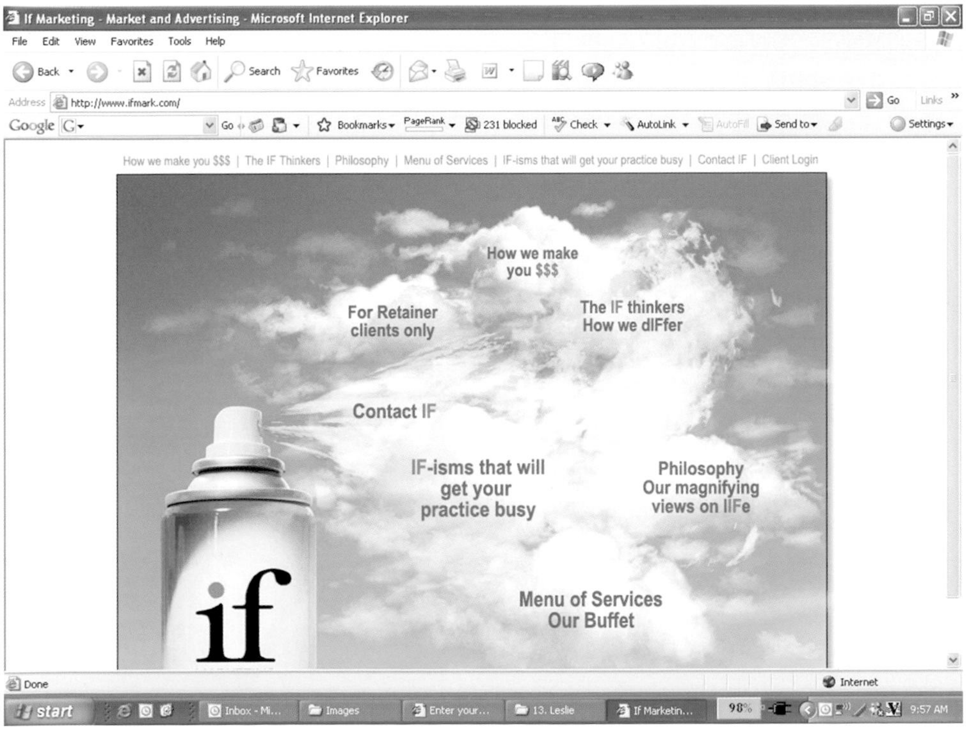

creative firm
IF MARKETING
Chicago, Illinois
creative people
Tracy Drumm
client
IF Marketing

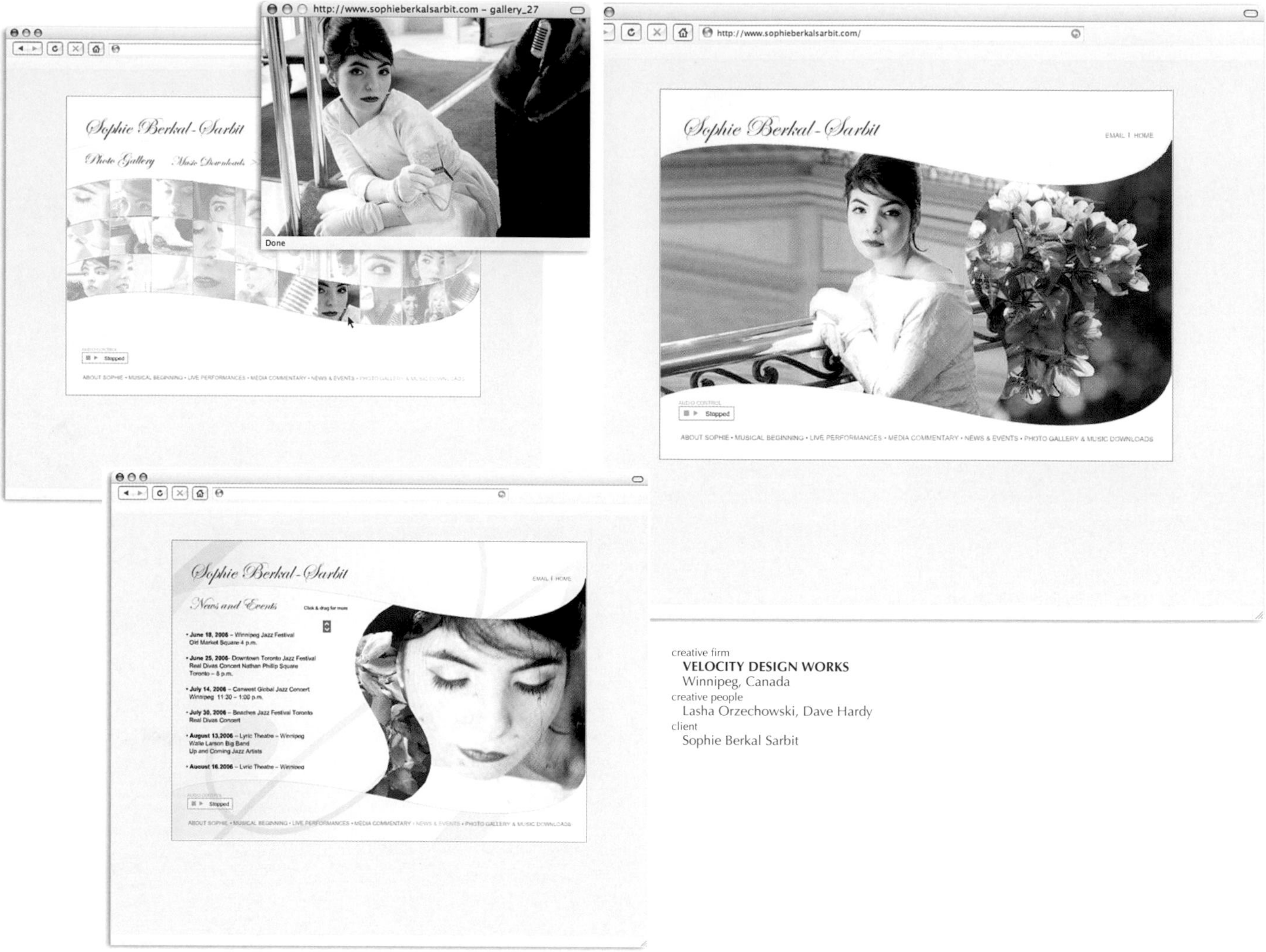

creative firm
VELOCITY DESIGN WORKS
Winnipeg, Canada
creative people
Lasha Orzechowski, Dave Hardy
client
Sophie Berkal Sarbit

creative firm
GRAPHIC ADVANCE
Palisades Park, New Jersey
creative people
Aviad Stark
client
Weckerle Cosmetics

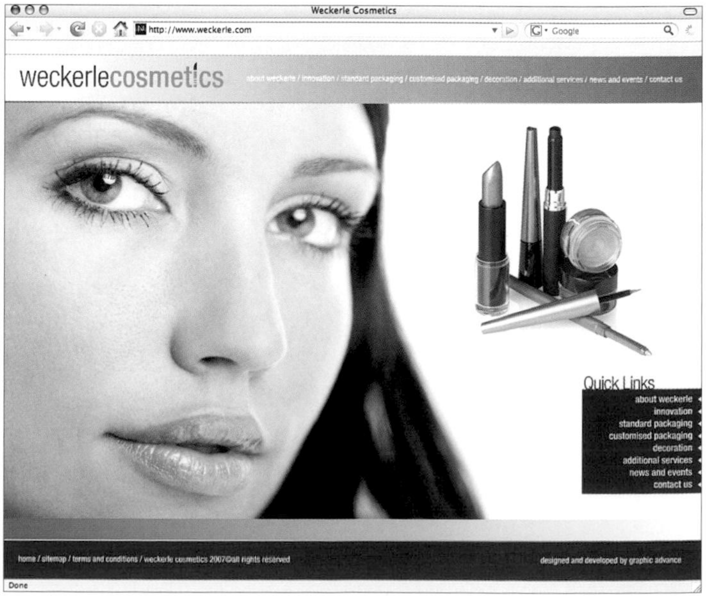

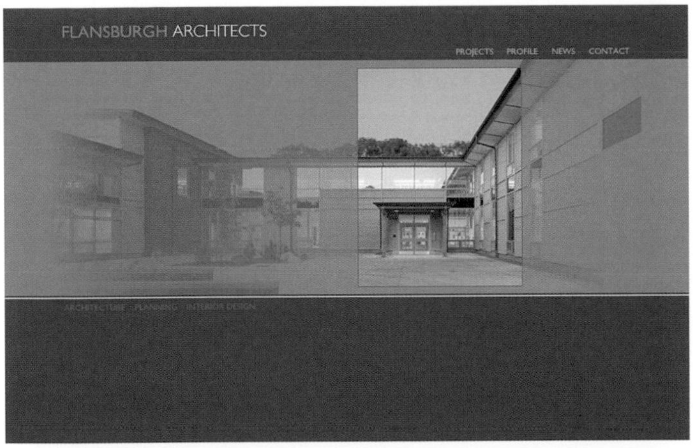

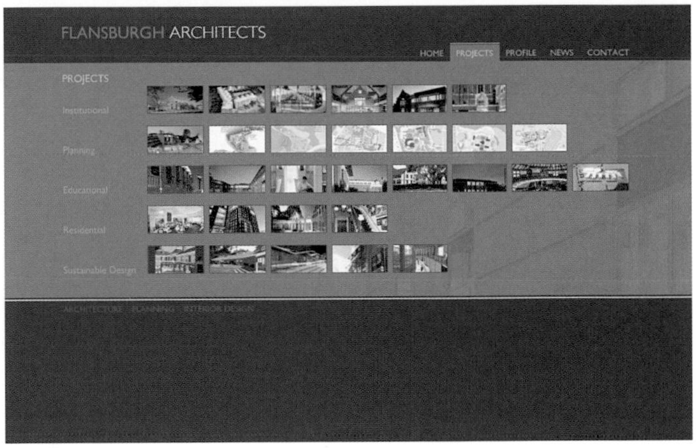

creative firm
ONE PICA, INC.
Boston, Massachusetts
creative people
Darren Bourque, Gregory Segall
client
Flansburgh Architects, Inc.

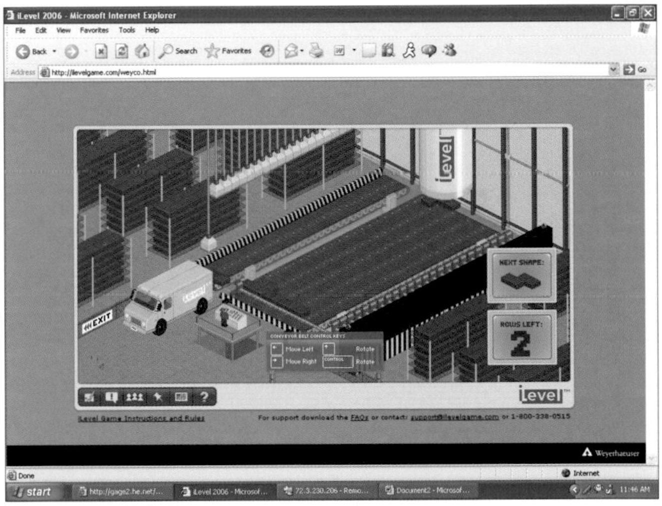

creative firm
HORNALL ANDERSON DESIGN
Seattle, Washington
creative people
Jamie Monberg, Chris Monberg, Nathan Young, Joe King, Jason Hickner, Adrien Lo
client
Weyerhaeuser Corporation

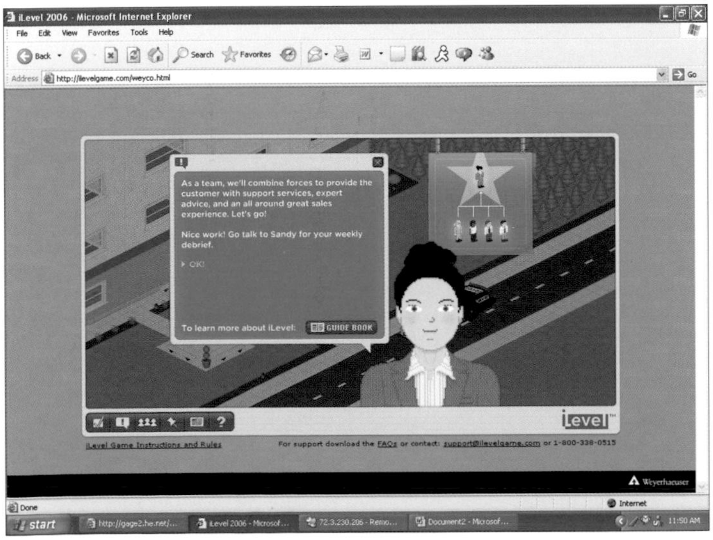

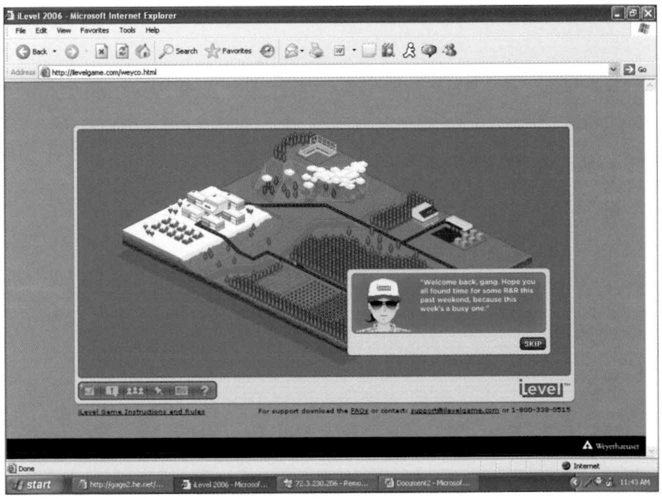

creative firm
BETH SINGER DESIGN LLC
Arlington, Virginia
creative people
Sucha Snidvongs
client
Museum of the Shenandoah Valley

creative firm
DEB NEUFELL DESIGN
Waltham, Massachusetts
creative people
Deb Neufell
client
Warner Brothers Studios

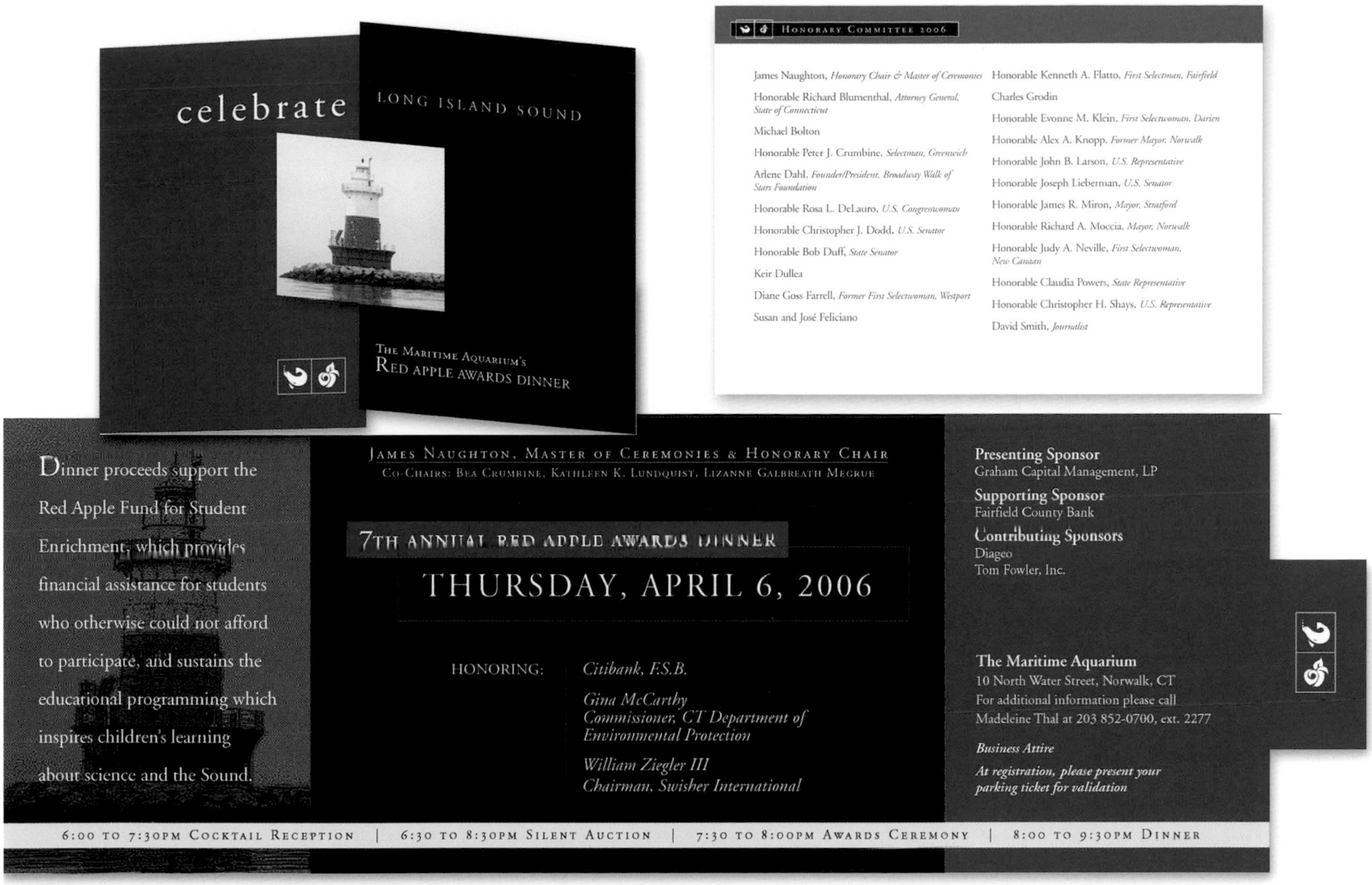
celebrate
LONG ISLAND SOUND
THE MARITIME AQUARIUM'S
RED APPLE AWARDS DINNER
HONORARY COMMITTEE 2006
James Naughton, Honorary Chair & Master of Ceremonies
Honorable Richard Blumenthal, Attorney General, State of Connecticut
Michael Bolton
Honorable Peter J. Crumbine, Selectman, Greenwich
Arlene Dahl, Founder/President, Broadway Walk of Stars Foundation
Honorable Rosa L. DeLauro, U.S. Congresswoman
Honorable Christopher J. Dodd, U.S. Senator
Honorable Bob Duff, State Senator
Keir Dullea
Diane Goss Farrell, Former First Selectwoman, Westport
Susan and José Feliciano
Honorable Kenneth A. Flatto, First Selectman, Fairfield
Charles Grodin
Honorable Evonne M. Klein, First Selectwoman, Darien
Honorable Alex A. Knopp, Former Mayor, Norwalk
Honorable John B. Larson, U.S. Representative
Honorable Joseph Lieberman, U.S. Senator
Honorable James R. Miron, Mayor, Stratford
Honorable Richard A. Moccia, Mayor, Norwalk
Honorable Judy A. Neville, First Selectwoman, New Canaan
Honorable Claudia Powers, State Representative
Honorable Christopher H. Shays, U.S. Representative
David Smith, Journalist
Dinner proceeds support the Red Apple Fund for Student Enrichment, which provides financial assistance for students who otherwise could not afford to participate, and sustains the educational programming which inspires children's learning about science and the Sound.
JAMES NAUGHTON, MASTER OF CEREMONIES & HONORARY CHAIR
CO-CHAIRS: BEA CRUMBINE, KATHLEEN K. LUNDQUIST, LIZANNE GALBREATH MEGRUE
7TH ANNUAL RED APPLE AWARDS DINNER
THURSDAY, APRIL 6, 2006
HONORING:
Citibank, F.S.B.
Gina McCarthy
Commissioner, CT Department of Environmental Protection
William Ziegler III
Chairman, Swisher International
Presenting Sponsor
Graham Capital Management, LP
Supporting Sponsor
Fairfield County Bank
Contributing Sponsors
Diageo
Tom Fowler, Inc.
The Maritime Aquarium
10 North Water Street, Norwalk, CT
For additional information please call
Madeleine Thal at 203 852-0700, ext. 2277
Business Attire
At registration, please present your parking ticket for validation
6:00 TO 7:30PM COCKTAIL RECEPTION | 6:30 TO 8:30PM SILENT AUCTION | 7:30 TO 8:00PM AWARDS CEREMONY | 8:00 TO 9:30PM DINNER

creative firm
TOM FOWLER, INC.
Norwalk, Connecticut
creative people
Brien O'Reilly
client
Maritime Aquarium at Norwalk

O.C. TANNER
O.C. TANNER

creative firm
HORNALL ANDERSON DESIGN
Seattle, Washington
creative people
Julia LaPine, Lisa Cerveny, Jana Nishi, Lauren DiRusso, Hayden Schoen, Mary Hermes, Holly Craven, Bruce Branson-Meyer, Nory Emori
client
O.C. Tanner

creative firm
HORNALL ANDERSON DESIGN
Seattle, Washington
creative people
John Anicker, Andrew Wicklund, Leo Raymundo, Yuri Shvets
client
Schnitzer Northwest

creative firm
STAN GELLMAN GRAPHIC DESIGN, INC.
St. Louis, Missouri
creative people
Britni Eggers
client
Henneman Engineering

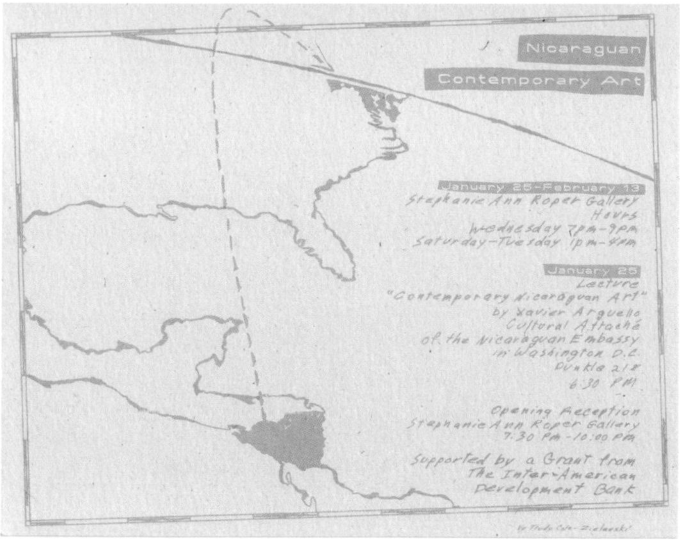

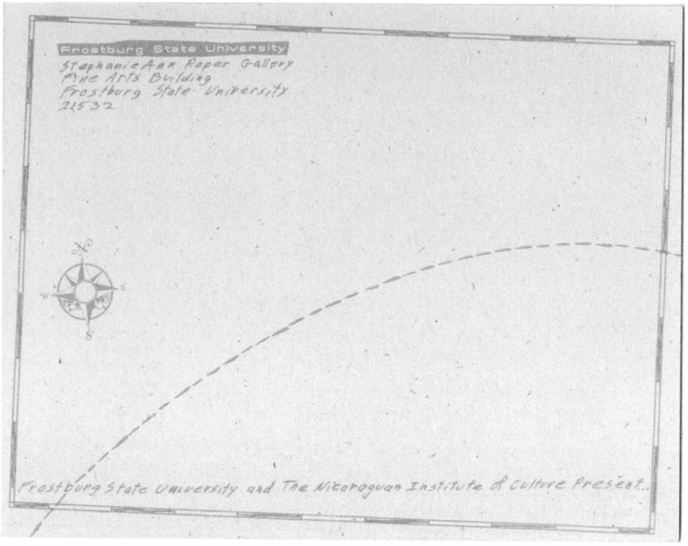

creative firm
TLC DESIGN
Churchville, Virginia
creative people
Trudy L. Cole
client
Frostburg State University

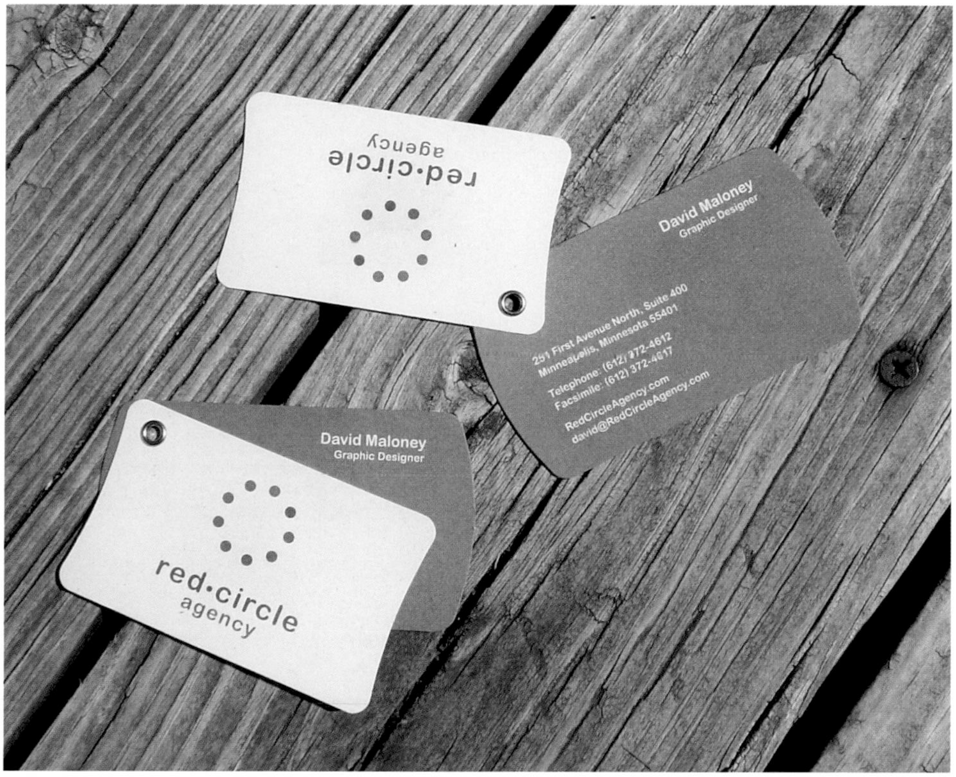

creative firm
RED CIRCLE AGENCY
St. Louis Park, Minnesota
creative people
David Maloney
client
Suquamish Clearwater Casino Resort

creative firm
UNIVERSITY OF CINCINNATI FOUNDATION
Cincinnati, Ohio
creative people
Melissa Lutz
client
Yard 2 Yard Lawncare Service

creative firm
DEB NEUFELL DESIGN
Waltham, Massachusetts
creative people
Deb Neufell
client
Warner Brothers Studios

creative firm
ROMAN DESIGN
Golden, Colorado
creative people
Lisa Romanowski
client
Kaleidico, LLC

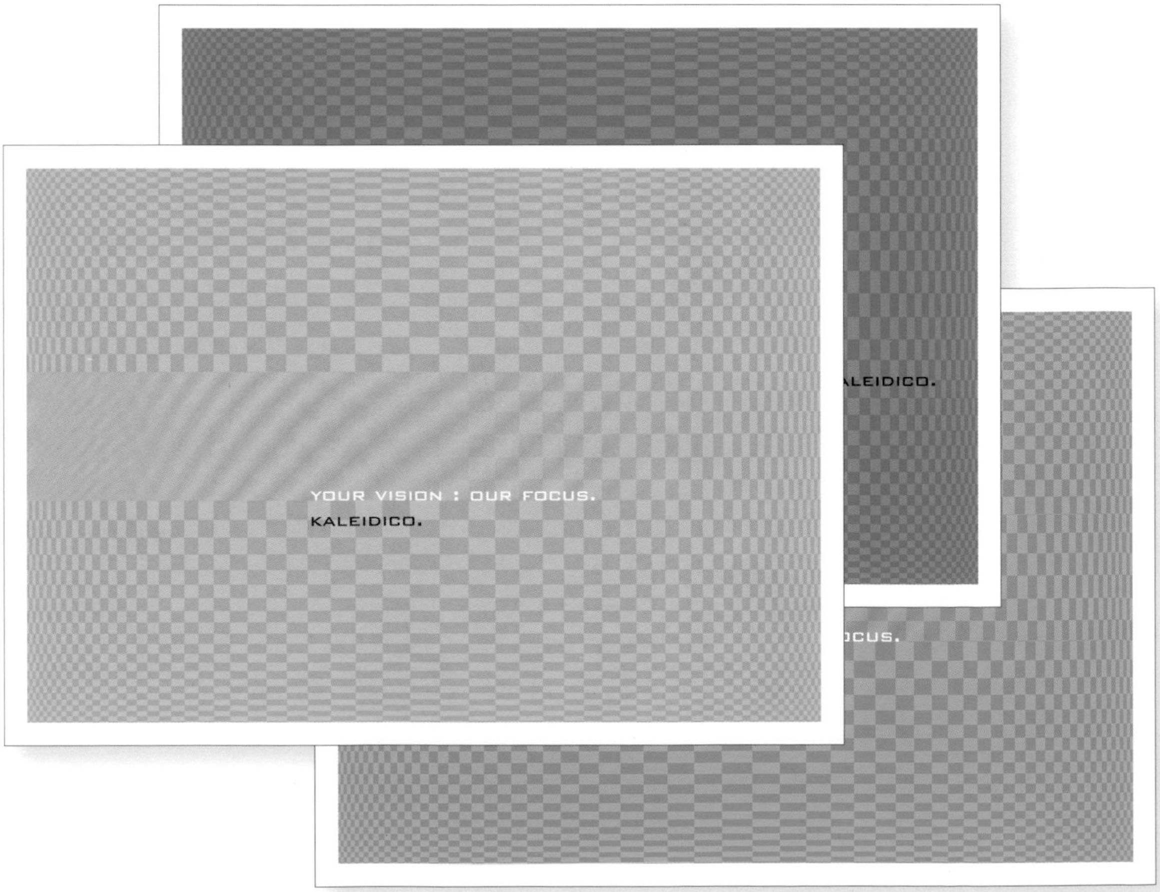

creative firm
UNIVERSITY OF CINCINNATI FOUNDATION
Cincinnati, Ohio
creative people
Melissa Lutz
client
College of Engineering

creative firm
TLC DESIGN
Churchville, Virginia
creative people
Trudy L. Cole
client
John and Trudy Zielanski

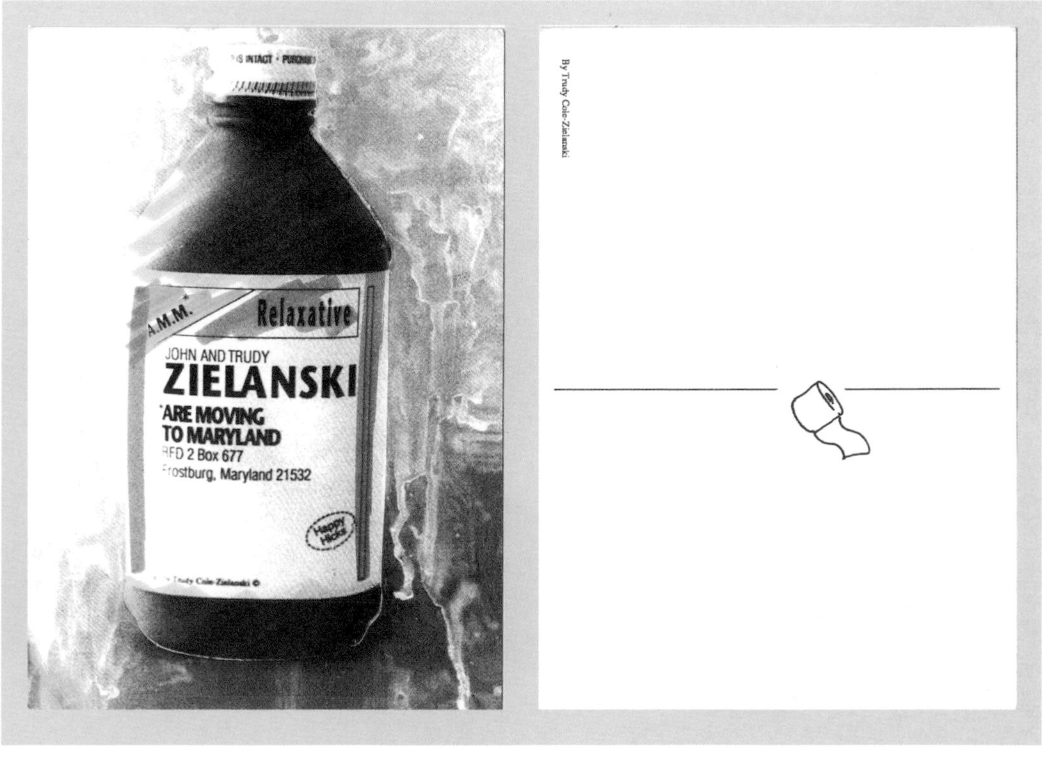

creative firm
UNIVERSITY OF CINCINNATI FOUNDATION
Cincinnati, Ohio
creative people
Melissa Lutz
client
University of Cincinnati Foundation

creative firm
HORNALL ANDERSON DESIGN
Seattle, Washington
creative people
Mark Popich, Peter Anderson, Yuri Shvets, Mignonne Mysiak, Michael Brugman
client
OnRequest Images

creative firm
TLC DESIGN
Churchville, Virginia
creative people
Trudy L. Cole
client
John and Trudy Zielanski

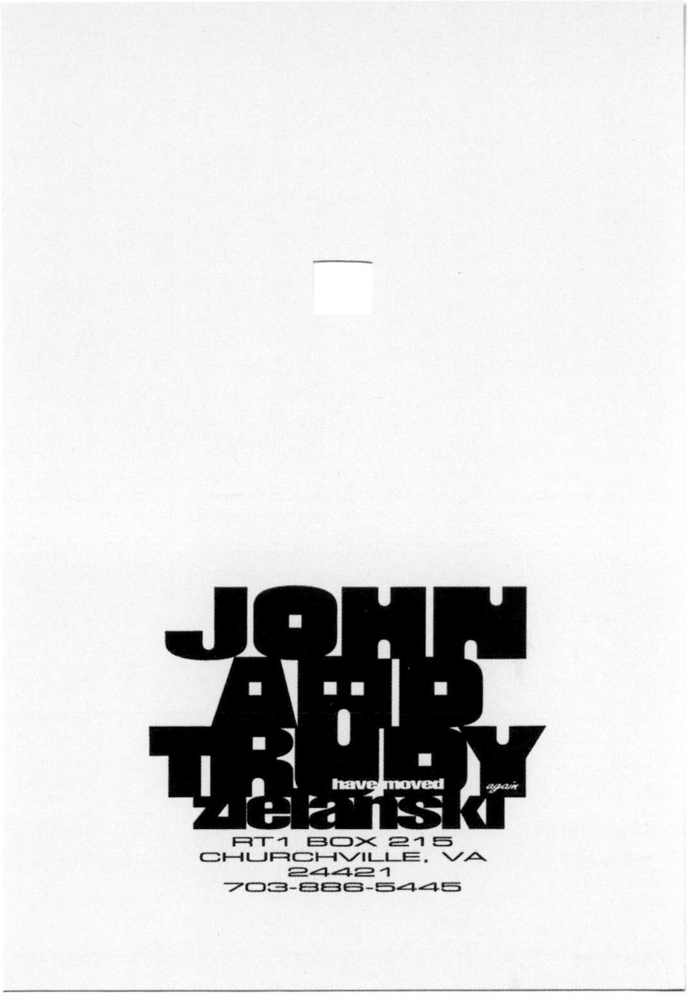

creative firm
GRAPHICAT LIMITED
Hong Kong, China
creative people
Colin Tillyer
client
GR Asia Motorsport

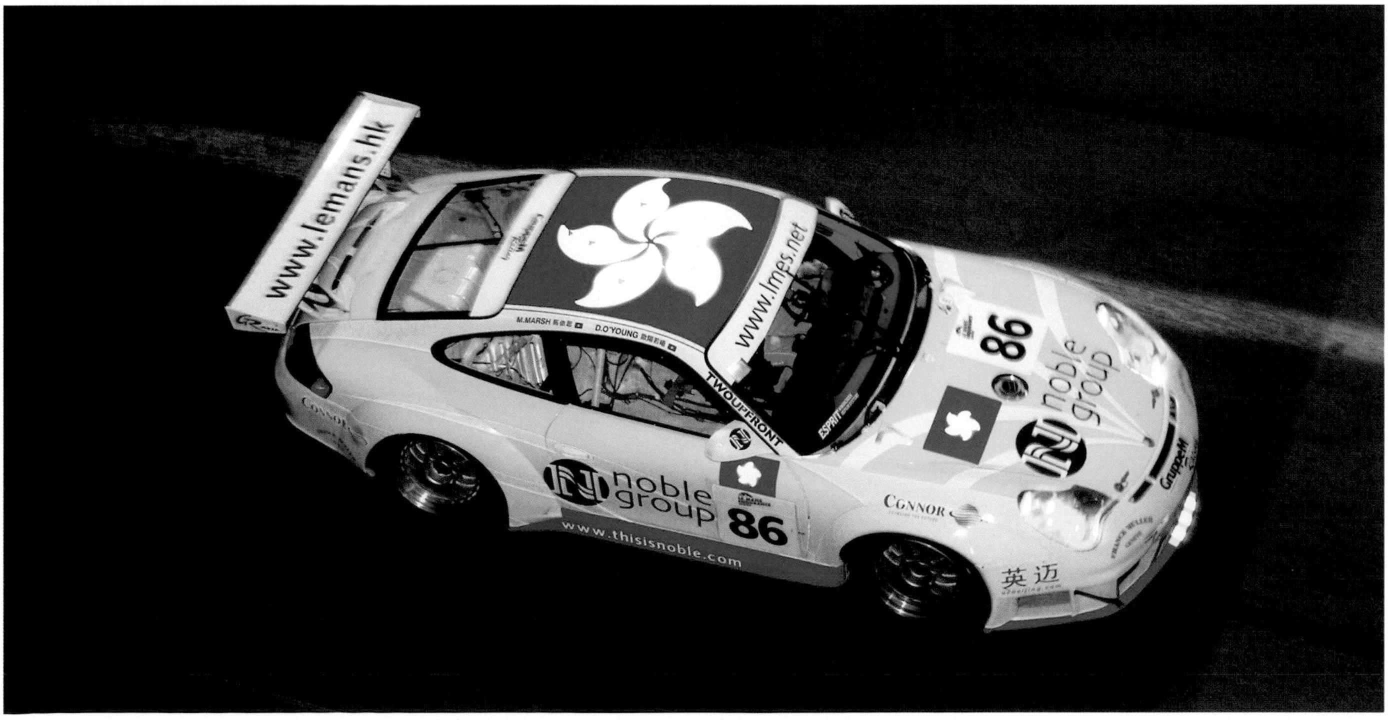

creative firm
HORNALL ANDERSON DESIGN
Seattle, Washington
creative people
Jack Anderson, James Tee, Andrew Wicklund, Elmer dela Cruz, Holly Craven, Jay Hilburn, Hayden Schoen, Belinda Bowling, Yuri Shvets, Michael Connors, Larry Anderson, Chris Freed, Erin McFarlan
client
Weyerhaeuser Corporation

creative firm
30SIXTY ADVERTISING+DESIGN, INC.
Los Angeles, California
creative people
Henry Vizcarra, Pär Larsson, Yujin Ono, Eric Perez, Mot Potives, Bruce Ventanilla, Tuyet Vong
client
Paramount Home Entertainment Global

creative firm
RIORDON DESIGN
Ontario, Canada
creative people
Dawn Charney, Ric Riordon, Steven Noble
client
Chelster Hall

hint
DRINK WATER. NOT SUGAR™

creative firm
DARLING DESIGN GROUP
New York, New York
creative people
Courtney Darling, Sarah Skapik
client
Hint Water

creative firm
OCTAVO DESIGNS
Frederick, Maryland
creative people
Mark Burrier, Sue Hough
client
Frederick County Office of Economic Development

Field of Dreams
... If we build it, they will come.
4TH ANNUAL
BUS TOUR
The Frederick County Office of Economic Development invites you to "go the distance" and do business in Frederick County.
FREDERICK COUNTY, MARYLAND
OFFICE OF
ECONOMIC
DEVELOPMENT

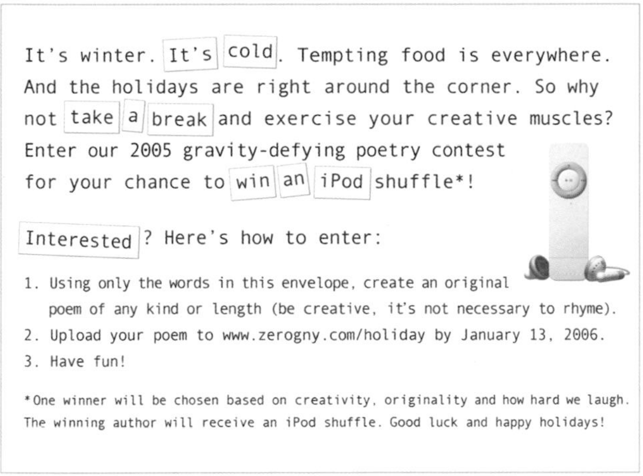
It's winter. It's cold. Tempting food is everywhere. And the holidays are right around the corner. So why not take a break and exercise your creative muscles? Enter our 2005 gravity-defying poetry contest for your chance to win an iPod shuffle*!
Interested? Here's how to enter:
1. Using only the words in this envelope, create an original poem of any kind or length (be creative, it's not necessary to rhyme).
2. Upload your poem to www.zerogny.com/holiday by January 13, 2006.
3. Have fun!
*One winner will be chosen based on creativity, originality and how hard we laugh. The winning author will receive an iPod shuffle. Good luck and happy holidays!

celebrate the holidays with
zero gravity design group ' s
2005 gravity - defying
holiday poetry contest
win an iPod !

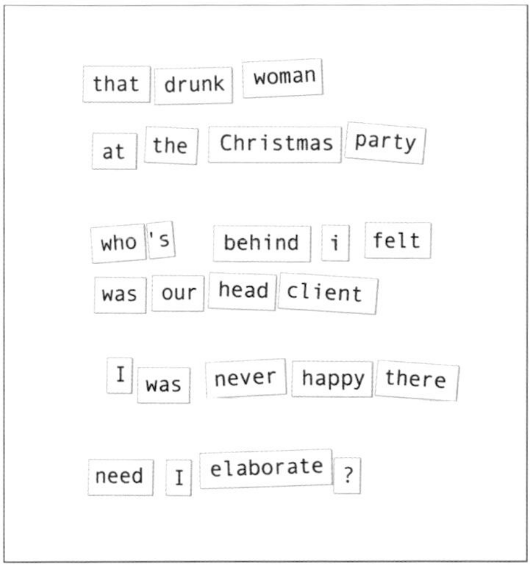
that drunk woman
at the Christmas party
who 's behind i felt
was our head client
I was never happy there
need I elaborate ?

Thank you for making our first year a success!
Happy Holidays from
zero gravity design group

creative firm
ZERO GRAVITY DESIGN GROUP
Smithtown, New York
creative people
Zero Gravity Design Group
client
Zero Gravity Design Group

JOY
JOY

JOY

creative firm
FRANKE+FIORELLA
Minneapolis, Minnesota
creative people
Craig Franke, Leslie McDougall
client
Franke+Fiorella

creative firm
WESTGROUP CREATIVE
New York, New York
creative people
Chip Tolaney, John Holloman, Marvin Berk
client
Elliegraphics, LLC

creative firm
ANNE LEHMAN DESIGN
Cranberry Township, Pennsylvania
creative people
Anne Lehman
client
In-Vision Studio

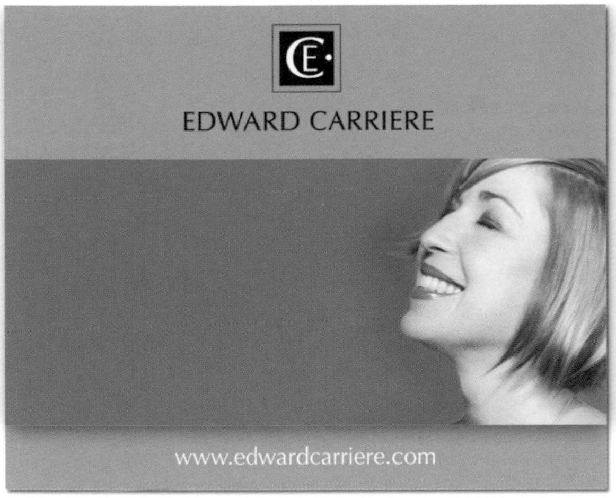

creative firm
VELOCITY DESIGN WORKS
Winnipeg, Canada
client
Edward Carriere Salon

creative firm
TLC DESIGN
Churchville, Virginia
creative people
Trudy L. Cole
client
TLC Design

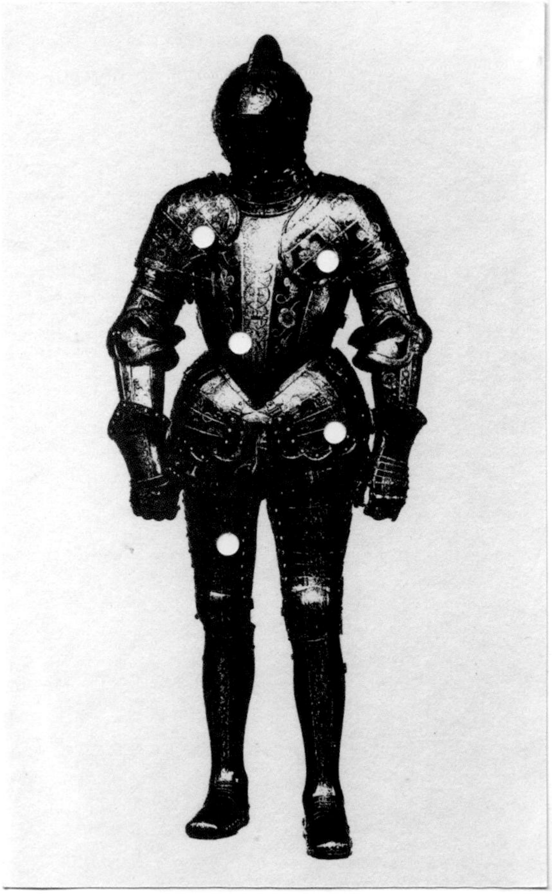

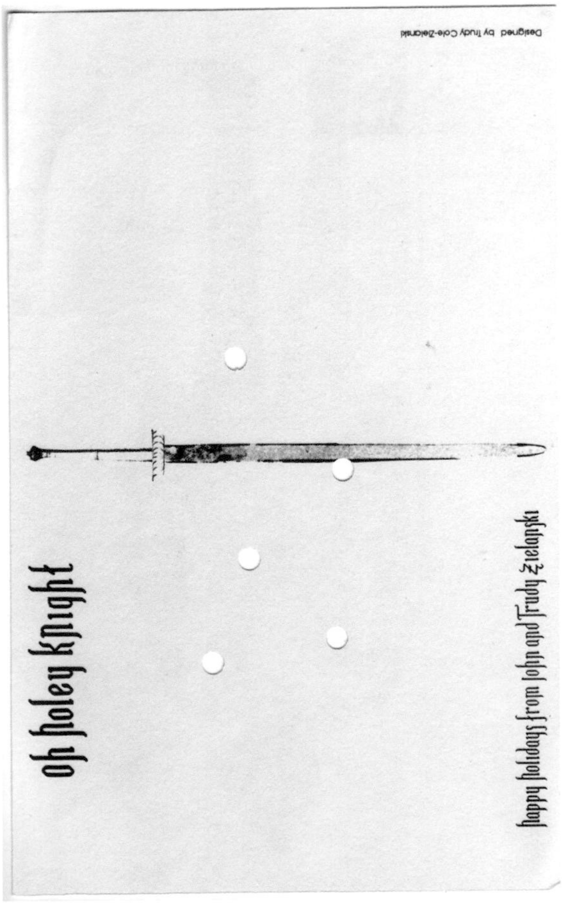

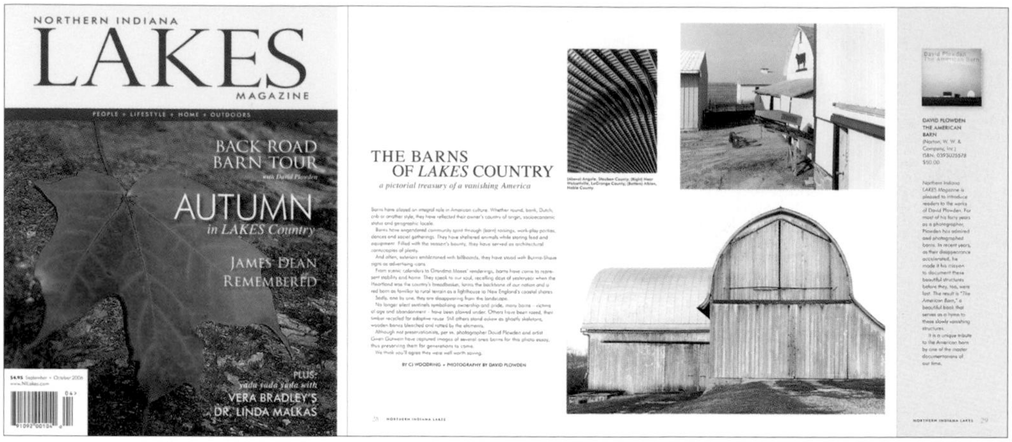

creative firm
STUDIO D
Indianapolis, Indiana
creative people
Holly Decker,
Allen Brenneman + David Plowden
client
Northern Indiana Lakes Magazine

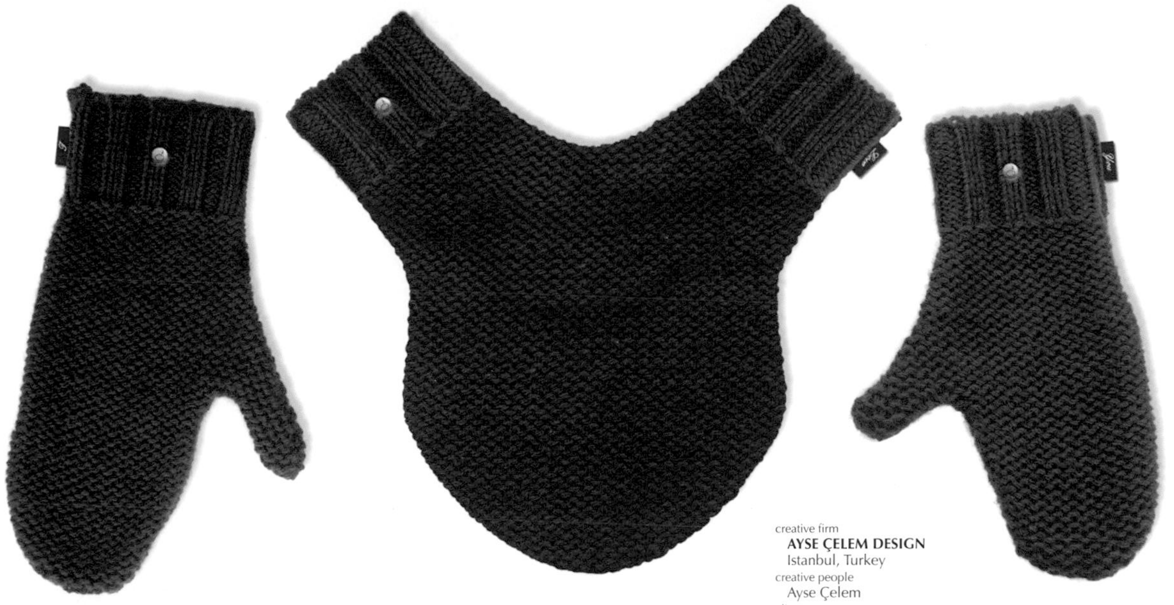

creative firm
AYSE ÇELEM DESIGN
Istanbul, Turkey
creative people
Ayse Çelem
client
Ayse Çelem Design

Olivetto
Aceite de Oliva
Extra Virgen
Olivetto
Olio Extra Vergine di Oliva
Aceite de Oliva Extra Virgen
Primera Prensada en Frío
De Nuestra Cosecha
Olivarera
Italo-Mexicana S.A. de C.V.

creative firm
EUPHORIANET
Monterrey, Mexico
creative people
Mabel Morales, Beba Mier
client
Olivarera

INDEX